EMPIRE, DEVELOPMENT & COLONIALISM

EMPIRE, DEVELOPMENT & COLONIALISM

The Past in the Present

Edited by

MARK DUFFIELD
Professor of Development Politics, Department of Politics, University of Bristol

VERNON HEWITT
Senior Lecturer, Department of Politics, University of Bristol

JAMES CURREY

James Currey
an imprint of
Boydell & Brewer Ltd
PO Box 9
Woodbridge
Suffolk
IP12 3DF
www.boydell.co.uk
and of
Boydell & Brewer Inc.
668 Mt Hope Avenue
Rochester
NY 14620 USA
www. boydellandbrewer.com

First published 2009

1 2 3 4 5 13 12 11 10 09

British Library Cataloguing in Publication Data
Empire, development & colonialism : the past in the present.
1. Colonies—Administration—History—Congresses.
2. Humanitarian intervention—Decision making—Congresses.
3. International relations—History—Congresses.
I. Duffield, Mark. II. Hewitt, Vernon.
327.1'01–dc22

ISBN 978-1-84701-011-7 (James Currey hardback)

Typeset in 10/11 pt Photina
by Avocet Typeset, Chilton, Aylesbury, Bucks
Printed and bound in Great Britain by
CPI Antony Rowe, Chippenham and Eastbourne

Contents

Acknowledgements

The authors would like to thank Matt Merefield for his help in organising the seminars and workshop on which this book is based. A debt is also owed to the Institute of Advanced Studies (IAS) at the University of Bristol for providing a venue and financial assistance. Finally, mention must be made of Jean Pretlove at Bristol's Department of Politics. Jean's administrative support and good humour kept the whole project together.

Notes on Contributors

Henrik Chetan Aspengren is a Ph.D candidate in the Department of Politics and International Studies, School of Oriental and African Studies, London.

April R. Biccum is a lecturer in Politics and International Relations at Lancaster University. Her forthcoming book *Global Citizenship and the Legacy of Empire: Marketing Development* brings post-colonial theory to bear on development studies.

Mark Duffield is Professor of Development Politics at the University of Bristol. During the 1980s, he was Oxfam's Country Representative for Sudan. His most recent books are *Development, Security and Unending War: Governing the World of Peoples* (2007) and *Global Governance and the New Wars: The Merging of Development and Security* (2001).

Vernon Hewitt is a Senior Lecturer in the Department of Politics at the University of Bristol. He writes on South Asian politics with a broad interest in international development and colonialism. His most recent book is *Political Mobilisation and Democratisation in India: States of Emergency?* (2008).

Douglas H. Johnson is an independent scholar on the Sudan and author of *The Root Causes of Sudan's Civil Wars* (2003). He served on the Abyei Boundaries Commission in 2005, and has been an advisor to the Government of South Sudan on the North-South boundary.

Paul Kelemen teaches at the University of Manchester on development and colonial history. He has published articles mainly on Palestine and East Africa.

Uma Kothari is Reader at the Institute for Development Policy and Management, University of Manchester. Her research interests include histories and theories of development, colonial and postcolonial analyses of development and transnational migration.

Matthew Merefield is a research assistant for the Immigration Advisory Service, and Honorary Research Fellow at the Centre on Race, Ethnicity and Migration at City University. His current research examines the post-return situation of failed asylum seekers.

Suthaharan Nadarajah is a doctoral candidate in the Department of Politics and International Studies, School of Oriental and African Studies, London. His research examines international intervention and liberal peace in the global South.

Patricia Noxolo is a lecturer in human geography at Loughborough University. Her work stands at the intersection between postcolonial development and cultural geography, and deals specifically with the inter-relations between Caribbean literature, slavery and contemporary inequality.

Richard Sheldon teaches social and economic history at the University of Bristol. He was a contributor to Adrian Randall and Andrew Charlesworth (eds) *Markets, Market Culture and Popular Protest* (1996). Current research includes the comparative history of famine economics and policy, and the history of social and economic rights.

Lisa Smirl is a doctoral candidate at the Centre for International Studies, University of Cambridge. Her thesis examines the material and spatial effects of the international community in post-crisis reconstruction. Her areas of specialisation include conflict prevention, crisis management, peacebuilding and the harmonisation of aid.

David Williams is a Senior Lecturer in International Politics in the Department of International Politics at City University. He is the author of The World Bank and Social Transformation in International Politics, published in 2008 by Routledge.

Tom Young is a Senior Lecturer in the Department of Politics and International Studies at the School of Oriental and African Studies, London. His research interests include the international and domestic politics of Southern Africa.

Introduction

MARK DUFFIELD
& VERNON HEWITT

This collection of essays resulted, in the main, from a workshop held at the University of Bristol, in September 2007, entitled 'Development and Colonialism: The Past in the Present'. It was instigated by the Department of Politics' international development research group, and sought to explore interests in the similarities, and differences, between contemporary debates on socio-economic development, humanitarian intervention and aid, and the historical artefacts of European empire. It consciously sought to include historians and students of politics, and encouraged a broad eclecticism in terms of methodology and approach. Some of the papers presented here were given to a seminar series, which paralleled the workshop, having been generously funded by the Institute for Advanced Studies.

Comparing and contrasting differing historical periods with an apparently 'unproblematic present' is fraught with obvious risks. This is particularly true of comparisons involving colonialism and imperialism. The terms themselves are contested and difficult to contextualise, and historical periodisation is premised on the subjective interests of the student of politics and not necessarily the rigour of the historian. This difference in professional temperament was a noticeable feature of the workshop itself. Historians are far more cautious about embarking on macro-temporal comparisons, being concerned with specific, often singular, events reasoned within a narrow context. For them the apparent relevance of Empire to contemporary world politics is frequently rendered polemical, facile or tautologous, and is usually premised on a mistaken verisimilitude. The British may well have used the term 'mad Mullah' with reference to Somaliland, and articulated the need for British intervention by demonising Islamic clerics and defending 'civilisation' in ways that are strikingly familiar to a contemporary Western audience, but it does not follow that the causes or results of intervention there, or in Somalia, or Afghanistan, or Iraq, are the same or have the same consequence. Other striking comparisons come to light in the following chapters. Many commentators have noted the similarities between NGO activities and nineteenth-century missionaries, and have sought to compare a generation of young Western 'volunteers' with the background and interests of their predecessors. Does this reveal anything about the emergence, impact or consequence of contemporary activism and NGO behaviour? Their links to the international order, the Western state, or their own social background? Or are these parallels merely of interest?

Finally, is it more than a question of irony that, for the undertaking of Operation *Restore Hope*, the US used information on Somalia compiled at the time of its British administration? Or, as Douglas Johnson discusses, that attempts to demarcate the Southern Sudan follow precedents laid down by the so-called Southern policy of the British? Or that, in its planning for the reconstruction of the Iraqi state, the US State Department utilises concepts and policies that would have been profoundly familiar to the British, active in much the same area after World War I, and driven (apparently) by much the same designs? More centrally, to what extent is current developmental aid and practice, involving social, cultural and economic 'conditionalities', premised on the same liberal project made manifest by nineteenth-century imperial and colonial strategies? If not, how and in what ways are they different?

The basic premise of the workshop, and the main contribution made by this book, is to articulate the belief that these comparisons are not just anecdotal but analytically revealing. From the language of moral necessity and conviction, the design of specific aid packages, through to the devised forms of intervention and governmentality, and finally to the lifestyle, design and location of NGO encampments, the authors seek to account for the numerous, often striking parallels between contemporary issues of international security, humanitarian aid and international developmental assistance and the logic and form of Empire. Some are more sceptical than others, and some are more inclined to stress the risk of 'misrepresenting' the past and reducing the complex aetiologies of Empire to fit current positions or postures. Others note the dangers of distorting the present, and simplifying the ways that contemporary uses of Empire fit with ideas of sovereign states, multinational flows of capital and the forces of globalisation. Warnings against forced comparisons are well taken. Even at the height of the European empires, attempts to reduce their form and logic to economic necessity (if not the stark needs of capital) underplayed the role of political, cultural and liberal processes in compelling and justifying external intervention. They also, as often as not, downplayed their contemporary debates over the need for Imperial withdrawal and isolationism, as articulated in the 1840s, and then briefly in the post-1880 period. Yet others note that critics of Empire were ever buried within the Imperial project itself, often contesting not the ends but the means, to achieve the objectives of the civilising mission, both at 'home' and 'abroad' – spatial nodes that Empire proved capable of transgressing and redefining.

Strong parallels exist between the arguments of the 1840s ('what is Empire for?') and current debates about the need for 'Western' or humanitarian intervention, the need for a social turn, and concern as to where the limits of liberty lie in a world order premised on anxieties over migration, terrorism, economic competition and social upheaval. Does intervention solve these or cause these? A majority of the contributors here conclude that an analytical understanding of these parallels raises serious, if not controversial, questions about the causes and the consequences that follow from current humanitarian and liberal interventionism, and that, in many startling ways, such interventionism represents the continuation of governance articulated and explored by European empires. While specific changes to the international system and the capacities of international organisations since World War II may have reconfigured some of these techniques, they remain embedded in the same assumptions and work towards very much the same outcomes. Intriguingly, such a close fit between the long nineteenth century and the relatively 'short' twentieth century condemns the emancipatory language of twenty-first-century development (such as empowerment, democracy and 'improvement') by stressing the controlling and coercive architecture of imperialism. In the language of post-development, such intervention creates the context in which it is justified and sustained. It is the problem posing as the solution.

However, by the same token, the close fit also reveals a more progressive light on aspects of European imperialism – which often strove to engineer a social turn premised on universal notions of citizenship and genuine commitment to improvement, despite pre-occupations of race, cultural hierarchy and security. The contradictions within the liberal project live on.

The Book

Several of the chapters in this book set out explicitly to compare and contrast nineteenth-century techniques of imperial and colonial governmentality with techniques and technologies of humanitarian intervention and development. Around the general conviction that colonialism is a direct relative of contemporary debates on development, others explore specific facets of the relationship within liberalism between freedom and security, universalism and 'exceptionalism' either through the works of specific liberal thinkers, such J.S. Mill, events such as slave revolts and forms of native administration, or contemporary theoretical turns inspired by post-structural and postcolonial studies.

Aspengren's chapter on early twentieth-century Bombay examines in detail how colonial forms of governance shifted from minimalist, repressive control towards one that engaged with a vocabulary of social reform. Looking at issues such as housing for the working class, sanitation and education, Aspergren argues that colonial reform and social progress were intimately related to British ideas of Empire, and explores how the 'turn to the social' within liberalism saw no immediate contradictions between 'human progress' and restrictions on the political participation of Indians within the Raj. As with many contributors to this volume, Aspengren notes the universalism implicit within the ideas of social improvement, and in calls for extending the role of the state to provide relief from the vagaries of industrialised urban society. In seeking to establish the 'minimum opportunity for the development of human personality', British colonial policies both mirrored, and indeed, anticipated the social turn within the metropolis. Liberalism's reformist and progressive agenda was not limited to Britain, but was 'compelled' through social activism to extend itself throughout the Empire, and indeed to wherever British power prevailed. Yet, the contradictions between empowerment and constraint, social improvement and representation, often provoked a return to coercive government, especially when the colonial authorities could not sustain the distinction between 'devising and enacting' social legislation and direct political participation. By the mid-1920s the social turn within the liberal conception of Empire was returning to a more repressive view of social order, but significantly the contradictions – and the dynamics they sustained – continued towards de-colonisation, resurfacing at critical moments in the Raj's slow dissolution.

Johnson's chapter, focusing on the relationship between 'ethnic' territories and national development in the Sudan, looks at the continuities between British colonial practices in the Sudan under the Condominium, subsequent attempts to map ethnic boundaries onto territories within a sovereign state, and the current tenuous Comprehensive Peace Agreement (CPA) in Sudan which, while allowing the non-Muslim South to hold a referendum by 2011, does not prevent the 'national state' redefining the Southern border in ways to exclude it from valuable resources – notably minerals and oil. Johnson argues that such a process is made possible by the legacies of separate, native administration that sought to shield the South from

Northern interests but actually lent itself to excluding the South from national development strategies. The apparent boundary, never as clearly defined or as 'obvious' as colonial practice implied, was politicised through British mediation over land rights and usage between competing tribal groups that changed ideas of provincial space by creating alliances between British administrators and local elites and subsequent nationalist parties after independence. Colonial expediency preserved a separate boundary that could nonetheless be manipulated at will. There is thus, for Johnson, an immediate parallel between Britain's 'southern policy', the isolation of the South after independence, and the failure of nationalist development and the civil war. Yet ironically, the CPA seeks to reinstate such a boundary as part of the solution to the conflict.

David Williams and Tom Young, along with Vernon Hewitt and Paul Kelemen, all present comparisons between aspects of contemporary development theory and practice and specific imperial socio-economic and political policy. Williams and Young set out a compelling case for a 'longue duree' on the liberal project, mapping ideas of social progress articulated by late nineteenth-century empires onto the ideologies of international development encountered after World War II, despite the formal end of Empire and the emergence of international institutions such as the United Nations, the World Bank and the International Monetary Fund. These apparent differences mask enormous continuities. Here the language of the civilising mission is reconfigured into contemporary ideas on managing and imposing development and social change, 'at a distance' through conditionality and the role and intervention of outside agencies, professional bodies and non-state actors. The logic of social change here is derived from colonialism, which is in turn derived from the language of nineteenth-century paternalistic liberalism and the associated ideas of human progress. The British empire, like the contemporary 'development business', was global, contained a number of non-state actors as 'experts' and 'advocates', and was in itself de-centred, highly pluralistic and heterodox.

While, for Williams and Young, a progressive commitment towards social engineering was combined and in tension, with more conservative strategies of preservation (such as indirect rule), Hewitt argues that the inter-war crisis within the British Empire over finance and security led to a distinct move towards accepting the inevitability of social change in the colonies (through urbanisation, trade and migration) and a commitment to accommodate it, both as a way of shoring up British power and, as Williams and Young argue, articulating and defending the 'moral purpose' of having an Empire at all. The parallels between the British use of the term ''good government', its expansive trajectory away from issues of 'shoe-string' financial solvency towards creating institutions for local (and ultimately) national government, and the World Bank's use of the term from 1997 onwards, are striking, despite the obvious change to the international context (both institutional and normative) marked by the end of Empire.

Key turns in the language of Empire, away from 'native authorities' and indirect rule towards concepts of good government, local development boards and an enhanced role for the state in education mark a distinct transformation in the ways that liberalism sought to reconcile the responsibilities of trusteeship in Africa with economic decline in the metropolis and growing international criticism of colonial policy. Kelemen, like Hewitt, stresses the importance of Fabian and socialist ideas that saw the 'disintegrating effects of capitalism' compel the reinvention of social and collectivist solutions, within Britain, and through the works of radical liberals and Labour Party officials, throughout the colonial Empire. Kelemen reveals how left-wing and radical critiques on Empire were premised not on whether the Empire should be abandoned, but on how it should be governed, and how it could achieve its goals. Radical thinkers from within government, and increasingly within international organisations like the League of Nations, missionaries and, importantly, international research bodies (like the Rowntree Trust and the Rhodes Foundation), funded critical research that pointed out the failure of successive British governments to defend Africans from the erosion of their 'traditional life' and prepare them for the modern world.

Such critiques provided the context in which the inter-war debates on Empire focused on peasant economies, the tensions between peasants, settlers and traders, the role of the state, and the relationship between capitalism, democracy and colonial reform. The influences of Lord Hailey, Arthur Creech Jones and Margery Perham all worked within a tactical acceptance that the moral purpose of Empire was in 'modernising' and 'transforming' society towards a universal way of life. Failure to see the project through would undermine the security of the Empire, impoverish the peasants and generate regional (and global) instability. The imbrications between security, humanitarianism and order are again strikingly contemporary. What these closely related chapters reveal is not just the broad genealogy between the social turn within liberal Empire, ideas on 'colonial' development, and current interests on civil society, social capital and intervention in so-called developing (or 'peripheral' societies). They also reveal an almost identical sequencing of types of different governmentality within the periods themselves., from control 'at a distance', models of 'self-reliance' for what were deemed self-producing populations, and finally annexation and direct administration.

With specific reference to Africa, Williams and Young note that social transformation 'at a distance' defined imperial strategy prior to the formal acquisition of territory from the 1880s onwards, and then again during the 1980s under Structural Adjustment Programmes (SAPs). Under the influence of market-based 'solutions' that, through international conditionality, disciplined state behaviour without physical coercion, Western agencies had no need for a formal presence. Yet as SAPs became subject to domestic and international controversy, the shift towards more overt interventionist strategies began, involving a variety of actors and agencies. This trend towards enhanced humanitarian intervention was accelerated in the wake of 9/11, just as, arguably enhanced concerns over European security sparked the shift towards formal annexation in the late nineteenth century. Just as Aspengren illustrated how the shift away from the 'social' back to the 'coercive' was a function of the wider anxieties within liberalism about order, several contributors to this volume reveal the extent to which shifts in the nature of governmentality – direct or 'at a distance' – are a function of the same concerns and fears playing out in the liberal imagination. Yet there is an additional irony here, noted by Keleman and many contributors in the context of contemporary development debates: so pervasive is the liberal project that it engulfs and often compromises criticisms and alternatives. Indeed, they become, if not well guarded, manifestations of the project itself.

Sheldon's chapter presents a series of parallels between British colonial thinking on India and contemporary international development theories and strategies of intervention. Focusing on poverty and famine, Sheldon shows how the apparent natural 'propensity' for India to suffer from famine justified the very colonial presence that caused it. Looking at the emergence of colonial development theory in the context of orientalist and, initially, mercantilist ideas on European land and power, Sheldon underscores the links with classical political economy, the debates and contradictions within liberalism over regulating markets and free trade, as well as revealing the extraordinary involvement between many key economic thinkers and British policy in India. Were the poor to be exposed to the vagaries of the market for their own good, or were they helpless in the face of British modernity because they lacked the necessary rationality to respond to market forces? Could they be provided with this rationality, or merely abandoned to their own devices? Would British intervention in the form of famine codes be adequate, or would it cause widespread distortions in economic activity? Sheldon notes how these debates echoed contemporary debates within neo-liberalism over the role between free markets and provisions for the poor, liberal and authoritarian government, and have obvious links with much so-called post-development thinking that sees 'developmental' intervention as the cause of contemporary poverty and not as a process capable of eliminating it.

Duffield's chapter explores the parallels that can be drawn between the current discourse on fragile states and earlier colonial debates on native administration and the concept of indirect rule. Noting the recent shift within the language of intervention from 'failed' states to fragile states, Duffield argues that fragile-state discourse, like native administration, is based upon the principle of tailoring the mechanisms of government to suit existing social conditions. Whereas native administration was concerned with devolving administrative tasks according to the cultural development of the tribe, reconstructing fragile states requires a simplification of the tools of economic management. In both cases, the devolved responsibilities function as evolutionary stepping-stones; as the tribe or fragile-state incumbents master one task, more demanding responsibilities can be added. In both cases, the devolution of tasks operates as a developmental mechanism encouraging the institutional maturity and eventual self-government of the tribe or fragile state. At the same time, they are both securitised. Native administration attempted to mobilise the rural population against the forces of urban nationalism. Fragile states, on the other hand, are important sites within the West's external sovereign frontier and the struggle against political instability and global terrorism.

Merefield sets up a series of theoretical perspectives through which to study a moment of crisis within the Victorian liberal empire, namely, the Morant Bay Rebellion of 1865. He explores the tensions within liberalism as it sought to incorporate emancipated slaves into the liberal world of security, individual liberty and social mobility, and how utilitarian and liberal ideas of government perceived and debated the issues, especially the conduct of the Governor, Edward Eyre. Utilising concepts such as 'surplus population', and Foucault's theories on governmentality and biopolitics, Merefield offers a critique of liberal strategies that promoted the abolition of slavery as progress, order and human development within the confines of a racial view that saw African society as backward and incapable of rational acts. The stress here is again on a series of contradictions, between the rational and violent body, between the small ex-slave free holding population, removed from the direct coercion of the plantation system, and plantation elites that needed cheap surplus labour to sustain the economic benefits of Empire for the metropolitan economy.

Drawing again on J. S. Mill, Merefield is interested in looking at the limits to freedom within a liberal ideology that sees the tutelage of more progressive social systems and bodies over less developed ones as justifying, during crisis and emergency, coercive action to compel (and defend) a liberal way of life. Moreover, these crises are endemic to the project itself and not, as the liberal imagination presents them, sporadic and exceptional. In conclusion, Merefield draws parallels with contemporary debates over immigration policy, international development strategies and the conduct of foreign policy, especially with reference to international development and intervention. While overt racial hierarchies (between irrational Africans and rational Europeans) have been eroded, they have been replaced by hierarchies of different 'zones' or types of states that experience these same contradictions. There is an obvious point here between Duffield's discussion on fragile states as an 'indefinite' holding ground for 'different' societies not yet able to prove their right to be included 'within the frontier', and Merefield's portrayal of the emancipated body of the slave.

Time and time again, in different contexts and made with differing degrees of emphasis, contributors to this book point to the basic flaw – running throughout the liberal project – as constituting the assertion, and then denial, of universal emancipation. This is a basic preoccupation of many post-structural and postmodern accounts of colonialism, humanitarian intervention, and development. Agencies and structures associated with extending liberty frequently (inevitably?) define it within the context of security and the fear of the other, or support illiberal outcomes. In his chapter entitled '"Conflict-Sensitive" Aid and Making Liberal Peace', Nadarajah also considers the paradoxical outcomes that result from well-meaning interventions into civil wars and areas of instability. With reference to Sri Lanka, and in particular the post-2002 ceasefire period, Nadarajah looks at how the laudable attempts by West-led donor states to shape their involvement in conflictual situations, involving so-called 'conflict-sensitivity' codes of practice, end up following a logic that drives the source of conflict itself. Associating current donor activity with the wider literature on the 'liberal peace', and the claimed links between poverty and conflict, Nadarajah argues that donors bring their own subjective views of the causes of the conflict to the fore, seek to facilitate the local outcomes they favour, and ultimately support state-based sovereignty as the preferred solution. In doing so, donors disregard the contribution that the modern state, or the specific configuration of the state itself, makes to the genesis and continuation of conflict. Nadarajah echoes Ayesha Jalal's keen observation that the causes of conflict in so-called third world or 'peripheral' states are not so much ethnicity and violent social pluralism, but the logic of the Westphalian state itself, imposed by a global liberal project and now supported by voluntary advocates of the liberal peace. International aid and development is thus a key tool of governmentality in the periphery, despite the argument that it is serving to bring about or sustain the conflicts used to justify its presence.

Patricia Noxolo's chapter looks at the ways in which NGOs have become increasingly involved in networks that define and practise humanitarian aid and development as an aspect of securitisation, working alongside states and other international structures, to effectively 'contain' displaced people in spatially defined territories exterior to the metropolis. How are these trends to be critiqued, and how best to comprehend the view of NGOs themselves? Like Merefield, Noxolo utilises Foucault's ideas on governmentality, especially his emphasis on the importance of historicising discourses through time, but in a very novel way associates them with the works of Wilson Harris, a literary critic and writer concerned with the emancipation of slavery and the unique hybridity of Caribbean culture. Noxolo is concerned to show how the politics of emancipation sought to deny the agency of former slaves by seeking to represent (and control) them, and reflected emergent racial anxieties and fears of 'real' liberty in seeking to control their bodies. There are striking parallels between Noxolo's and Merefield's chapters. Methodologically, Noxolo defends such an apparently free association across time and space on the grounds that it casts light on the rise and function of NGOs, but more radically on the contemporary re-shaping of the notions of 'universal' freedom and how it is to be achieved. Like Merefield, Noxolo is interested in the limits to liberty within the liberal project itself, and like Duffield, these limits are reached at the sovereign frontier in zones of 'fragile' states where communities are in need of guidance and control.

Comparison between Empire and development across a whole range of actors and agencies and narratives points consistently to convergence around a similar political agenda, or indeed, in Biccum's chapter, the wholesale continuity of history, despite recent and sustained attempts to posit a 'rupture' with the past and reconfigure current strategies of power and development as 'new', let alone successful. Lisa Smirl offers an intriguing comparison between colonial life and the spatial geography of the 'colonial' administrator, and the role and experiences of NGO workers deployed in current disaster relief and humanitarian intervention. Making extensive use of the current 'spatial turn' within the social sciences, Smirl takes issue with 'the perceived ethical neutrality of post-disaster intervention' and points out the similarities between such intervention and the spatial and material practices of colonialism. She concentrates on the construction and reorganisation of space within the humanitarian imaginary. In particular, and touching on issues raised by other writers, she focuses on the mobility of NGO workers from Northern global networks within the disaster area, their separation from the 'native' quarters, and the containment of the indigenous population itself. Architectural designs reflect status and power between NGO workers and their organisations, and between the local inhabitants and the volunteers. Again, the implications of such comparisons, between, in this case, specifically Anglo-Indian colonial experiences and humanitarian intervention, are to emphasise the limited or bounded nature of such international intervention and, through this, the proliferation of identities and images of the 'other' – people outside the compounds and hotels, people who are empowered but also victimised.

Uma Kothari utilises a similar methodology to Smirl, focusing on the spatiality of colonial and postcolonial power and discourse. Comparing the performative and discursive imaginary of former British colonial service officers alongside the contemporary developmental 'professional', Kothari explores the continuities – and discontinuities – between colonial practice and developmental interventions. This leads her to the conclusion that, despite decolonisation, such interventions represent not so much an epochal break with Empire, but a reconfiguration of many of the same ideas, in the same spaces, reinforced by many of the same rituals with the same peoples. Kothari looks at the social class behind colonial recruitment and the contemporary international voluntary community, but she is keen to explore how memories, images and experiences are interpreted through what she refers to as 'culturally located' knowledge, especially defined by the 'production, acquisition, subordination and settlement of space' (Kothari, citing Said). The productions and performances of colonial civil servants in 'distant' and 'exotic' spaces constructed not just such a cultural territory that needed to be governed, but a 'homeland' – an ex-pat nationalism – which constituted Britishness.

In contrast to NGOs and international experts, this underlying dynamic between 'foreign' space and nationalism is underplayed, although not necessarily absent. Loyalties to the institutions themselves (the World Bank, the UK Department for International Development or smaller organisations) – or to a globalising 'West' – are less compelling and more generally weaker. Moreover, Kothari notes that voluntary organisations need not so much a 'country expert' as a generalist administrator, and that the short-term intensity of most aid interventions detracts from a strong sense of 'belonging' or 'knowing' the country, a prominent feature of so many ex-pat tropes. Nonetheless, commonalities remain – a shared 'cultural knowledge' that draws on colonial images of *nobless oblige* and adventure, and a shared class basis of a middle professional class 'bored' with materiality. Like Smirl, Kothari notes the enclavic nature of spatial practices associated with development projects and humanitarian intervention, and the colonial compound and the bungalow. She concludes that many of the cultural experiences associated with the performance and practice of the voluntary aid worker have 'travelled over colonial space' and have been merely re-worked in the postcolonial period, 'belying epochal historical periodisations that conjure up a clear disjuncture between colonial and development eras' .

The image of a historical disjuncture or rupture lies at the heart of April Biccum's chapter, which eschews a specific comparison between Imperialism and development, and explicitly sets out to theorise Empire as a form of politics, central to the nineteenth century, but also of continued relevance to the politics of developmental practice in the early twenty-first century. Biccum thus sets out to theorise 'historical continuity' rather than the discontinuities represented by decolonisation, the emergence of an international system of sovereign states, and the concept of universal rights. Colonial history and Empire become not so much marginal to an understanding of contemporary politics and development, as central. Their apparent marginality is the product of an attempt, through a shift in vocabulary, to represent 'contemporary' humanitarian intervention, poverty reduction, the use of civil society as something 'new', something qualitatively different from the imperial past. This representation of 'contemporaneity' is, however, in crisis within academic disciplines such as International Relations and Development Studies. How to reclaim Empire in such a way that if critiques current development thinking (the 'failed state', 'poverty-as-degeneracy') without re-narrating Empire as the solution to the crisis itself? In surveying the contributions that post-structural and postcolonial studies can make in resolving this crisis, Biccum also notes that there are other theorists, notably neo-liberal conservatives such as Niall Ferguson, Samuel Huntington and Adam Roberts, who are narrating their own historical continuities with Empire and the liberal project. For Biccum, not only 'is development not distinct from Empire, it bears significant threads of continuity which are masked by a complex shift in vocabulary and the persistent narration of historical rupture'.

Specifying Liberal Colonialism

So how and in what ways can the continuities and discontinuities debated here be summed up? Is there a collective vision or theory within these chapters that convincingly links liberal interventionism through Empire with contemporary forms of humanitarian aid and development? Colonialism and development do not, at first sight, sit together easily or lend themselves to comparison. For many, they are antithetical. Colonialism, for example, usually suggests violent annexation, racial dictatorship and gross exploitation (Patel and McMichael 2004; Sylvester 2004). These markers of excess are precisely what development, with its emphasis on voluntarism, empowerment and betterment, measures itself against and uses to establish its claim to difference and authenticity. The colonial project, however, was broader than its founding violence and maintenance through martial law. While often overlooked, and more evident in the British and Dutch empires than elsewhere (Furnivall 1948; Arendt [1951]; Mehta 1999), it also had an educative or liberal face. Indeed, in terms of colonialism's overall maintenance and most cogent forms of public defence, it was inseparable from essentially liberal, indeed, developmental forms of justification. From this perspective, colonialism involved a 'dual mandate' in which the rational development of a colony's economy and natural resources was synonymous with the social and political progress of its people (Lugard [1922]). If a colonial past is recognisable within a developmental present, and *vice versa*, what is being compared is this specifically liberal form of colonial governance.

As a design of power, liberalism is notoriously difficult to isolate and pin down (Jahn 2007). It usually reveals itself in the form of a response to the problems it encounters. It is as if, without such difficulties, liberalism would have no real existence. Liberalism constantly dissolves, for example, into problems of poverty, ignorance and social breakdown. These conditions, however, are not, strictly speaking, external to it. Liberalism itself has chosen them, given them meaning and called them forth. Did colonised or Third World peoples, for example, know they were 'backward' or 'underdeveloped' until they were told so by those offering help and solutions? Rather than backwardness or underdevelopment being a separate, pre-existing condition, it is constitutive of liberalism itself. Attempting to excavate a liberal colonialism from the rubble of decolonisation is important for several reasons. While the racial and hegemonic aspects of colonialism are now routinely rejected, its liberal *alter ego* lives on unchallenged and continues to uncritically shape our experience of the world. Colonialism and development are different but, at the same time, they both share a liberal problematic of security. Since the dawn of modernity, rather than states and armies, liberalism's object of security has been individuals, groups and people – indeed, life itself (Dean 1999; Abulafia 2008). It is concerned with the uncertainty, unpredictability and mobility that are synonymous with, and inseparable from, the urge to live.

Isolating a liberal colonialism should not be confused with attempts to rehabilitate the colonial project (for example, Ferguson 2003). Without question, the bedrock of colonialism was a racially defined right to govern through the endless decisionism of emergency rule (Hussain 2003). Liberal colonialism is understood as inseparable from, and existing in a formative relationship with, a racialised state of exception. It lives in the shadow of rule through emergency and the exercise of arbitrary personal power. While often criticising its violence and short-sightedness (Seeley [1883]; Hobson [1902]; Morel 1920), liberal colonialism was dependent upon the expansionary logic of emergency to establish its own conditions of existence. Consequently, it does not provide a critique of imperial conquest. On the contrary, accepting that capacities and abilities are unequally shared, for liberal colonialism this is an inevitable, if unfortunate, outcome. However, given its concern for the human condition of the conquered race, and its interest in fostering change, liberal colonialism both qualified and limited the imperial state of exception while simultaneously justifying it. Through its empathy with the difficulties faced by the incomplete-life encountered, and the power this knowledge conferred, liberal colonialism claimed to govern more humanely and voluntaristicly, and thus more effectively, than its militarised and exterminatory alternative (Cromer 1913; Morel 1920; Lugard [1922] 1965; MacMichael 1923).

Development as a Regulatory Technology of Security

Liberal colonialism and development are similar yet different. They share a liberal problematic of security that takes life at its referent object. At the same time, however, the former was 'internal' to the colonial state, while the latter, in its present configuration, is internationalised and acts 'externally' on populations living within states originating from the colonial encounter. Regarding the shared problematic of security, if liberal colonialism needed the exceptional circumstances of conquest to establish its conditions of existence, since decolonisation development has maintained a formative relationship with emergency in the form of what is now called the 'security-development nexus' (Buur, et al. 2007). In both cases, states of emergency or insecurity call forth remedial forms of external tutelage and trusteeship.

Having life as its objective, for liberalism this unease has historically been associated with the unintended and unpredictable social consequences of the never-ending change, ceaseless disruption and pervasive violence otherwise known as economic progress; in particular, the tendency of progress to undermine existing customs and skills, to fragment established bonds of kin and community, and thus foster social anomie (Cowen and Shenton 1996). While economic progress and liberalism are inseparable, unless remedial action is taken, such unintended consequences can produce surplus populations lacking the skills and capacity for a proper existence; even worse, they can create dangerous, unpredictable and degenerate forms of human existence.

Given the threat of social anomie, as a technology of security development has typically involved measures to reconstitute authentic social and communal bonds. Usually, this has taken the form of either direct attempts to *preserve* 'tradition', for example, forms of colonial indirect rule, or, alternatively, to *modernise* it while retaining and building on its essential communal elements. This includes colonial community development, rural cooperatives and, not least, contemporary forms of sustainable development. However, since these different inflections are both based upon the construct of tradition, they are not mutually exclusive; each has the other inscribed within it. In both cases, moreover, the reconfirmation of community is ultimately for reasons of security. Concerned about the erosion of tribal authority in Kenya at the beginning of the twentieth century, for example, Sir Percy Girouard warned that the numerically small colonial administration,

> ...shall be obliged to deal with a rabble, with thousands of persons in a savage and semi-savage state, all acting on their own impulses, and making themselves a danger to society generally. (quoted by MacMichael 1923: 2)

In colonial Sudan this danger was used, among other things, to urge the shift from direct to indirect rule or Native Administration as a means of preserving and asserting communal values. Not only would the devolution of administrative duties restore an eroded tribal integrity, it also offered the possibility of a rural bulwark against the spread of urban nationalism by 'sterilising and localising the political germs which must spread from the lower Nile to Khartoum' (Maffey 1927: 2). Three decades later, with the onset of decolonisation, Harold Wilson, who would become the leader of the Labour Party and Britain's Prime Minister, was concerned at how the misguided colonial economic policies of the past had exacerbated the problem of poverty, hunger and social malaise in the emerging Third World. This, rather than any belief in the efficiency of the Communism creed,

> ...explains the success of the Kremlin in the backward areas of the world. The twentieth century has stood Marxism on its head: its successes have been not among the urban proletariat to whom Marx appealed, but among landless peasants and starving families in under-industrialised areas. (Wilson 1953: 14)

As a way of countering the threat of Communism, Wilson not only advocated more international aid from liberal countries, he went on to found the campaigning non-governmental organisation War on Want (Luetchford and Burns 2003). Moving forward a further half-century, Gordon Brown, Britain's current Prime Minister, in reflecting on the continuing problem of world poverty claims that development is not only right in itself,

> ...it is a political imperative – central to our long-term national security and peace – to tackle the poverty that leads to civil wars, failed states and safe havens for terrorists. (Christian Aid 2004)

While these colonial, Cold War and post-Cold War examples come from very different times and political contexts, they are connected by a similar strategisation or design of power. Whether the threat is tribal anomie, nationalism, communism or terrorism, it is related to the risks and consequences of poverty, backwardness and social breakdown. If development embodies a relation of security, it is not a condition of physical security or safety. Development actors, for example, seldom cordon off villages, patrol the streets and screen all those entering and leaving an area. While it can complement such policing activities, development as security is more regulatory in nature. If the object of liberalism is life, that of liberal development is life that, due to poverty, ignorance or gender, is experienced as somehow incomplete (Mehta 1999). Due to inability, incapacity or an absence, it is unable to live a full and secure life. Through educative and remedial measures, development aims to guide this incomplete life to a more independent, fuller and more secure mode of existence.

Development as security is well illustrated in the liberal tendency to link poverty with political instability. While this is an old relationship, a current reworking goes something like this: insofar as it is able to reduce poverty, development can also lessen the risk of social breakdown and conflict (Collier et al. 2003). In altering the balance of power between social groups through favouring those elements that support community and peace, development becomes a means of conflict resolution (Anderson 1996). In reducing alienation and frustration, it is also able to choke off the flow of potential recruits to terrorist networks (DAC 2003). As a regulatory technology of security, development typically exerts a moral or educative trusteeship over its deficient object (Cowen and Shenton 1996). Through introducing new forms of social organisation, methods of working or communal enterprise, in short, by changing the social environment, development seeks to engender betterment by changing behaviour and attitudes. Even if the aim of this trusteeship is one of empowerment, or partnership, or 'putting the last first' (Chambers 1983), it is still, nonetheless, a relation of external tutelage (Cooke and Kothari 2001). If there is a connection between development and liberal colonialism, it exists in relation to power, in particular, to a paternalistic and educative design of power that underpins relations of trusteeship.

The Significance of the Post-Cold War Period

Following a short period of independence, by the 1980s the economic management of many former colonies was increasingly becoming an international responsibility. Similar to Egypt's relation to Britain a century earlier, the accumulation of unsustainable debt resulting from state-led efforts to modernise society provided an entrée for growing World Bank, IMF and donor governments' influence regarding overall development policy. Until this period, helped by superpower rivalry, many developing countries had been able to define their own terms of engagement with the leading liberal states and their representatives (Harrison 2004). Beginning with structural adjustment and the opening of what were to become client economies to the world market, the power to set social and economic agendas moved significantly. With the ending of the Cold War, however, not only have the institutions of external financial management continued to deepen, more direct forms of trusteeship have also emerged. In particular, there has been a major shift regarding the willingness of liberal states to intervene openly within zones of crisis and political breakdown.

Following the collapse of the former Yugoslavia in 1991–2, much of the justification for this new interventionism was the widespread perception that the world was on the brink of a new emergency. With the disappearance of communist discipline, an epidemic of previously contained ethnic tensions and internal wars was seen as threatening the stability and future prosperity of liberal states (van Creveld 1991; Boutros-Ghali (1995); Freedman 1993). In response to these 'new wars' (Kaldor 1999), the number of UN peacekeeping operations, for example, increased from four in 1990 to fifteen in 2002 (HSC 2005: 251). An accompanying step-change has occurred in relation to the level of international support for peacekeeping, the number of negotiated settlements, and the growth of post-conflict peace operations. Moreover, compared with the Cold War, peace interventions today are not only more numerous, they are larger and more ambitious; from monitoring ceasefires the UN has graduated to nation-building. The upsurge in this liberal interventionism, however, goes beyond the UN and participating militaries. It also involves the active participation of such bodies as the World Bank, donor governments, regional organisations and literally hundreds of thousands of international and national NGOs that 'have both complemented the UN activities and played independent prevention and peacebuilding roles of their own' (*ibid.*: 152). While admittedly applying them unevenly, the international community has actively encouraged the proliferation of sanctions regimes; the questioning of the culture of impunity; the growth of international tribunals and states prosecuting war criminals; a stronger emphasis on reconciliation; and not least, in some circumstances a willingness to use force in the name of international stability. On their own, these various departures and initiatives have limited impact. When taken together, however, they combine to suggest an important and enduring, if selective and contingent, reworking of North-South relations.

While the upswing of liberal interventionism has been a defining feature of the post-Cold War period, what is less in evidence is an appreciation of the spatial aspects of this interventionism (Barnett 2005), in other words, the growing physical, institutional and architectural footprint that interventionism is creating and leaving within zones of crisis. The enduring lesson of the past decade is that it is relatively easy for effective states to end wars or change regimes within ineffective ones; far more difficult is winning the peace among the people (Smith 2006). While the number of open and ongoing civil wars may have declined as a result of liberal interventionism (HSC 2005), they have been replaced by a growing spatial presence of international actors and their local counterparts in the territories concerned. It is what Michael Ignatieff (2003), somewhat apologetically, has called 'Empire Lite'. In terms of its basic empirical and sociological dimensions, this physical and architectural presence remains little explored. Like liberalism generally, it camouflages itself against the backdrop of emergency and the problems of poverty and breakdown it has elected to solve.

Its spatiality, however, is embodied at several levels. There are the expanding numbers and widening mandates of donor bodies, military establishments, UN missions, aid agencies, international NGOs, security outfits and consultants, together with their associated local NGOs, counterparts and allied community-based organisations. This institutional presence, however, is increasingly contained within the international 'gated communities' of UN and NGO compounds separated by security personnel from the communities they are there to serve and interconnected by exclusive forms of transport. From this perspective, post-Cold War liberal interventionism is increasingly looking like a process of pacification and international occupation. It represents an important change in the nature of political space within the liberalism's external frontier. In particular, it marks the advent of what could be called 'post-interventionary society' as an enduring political relationship.

Compared with the constraints and diplomatic niceties of the Cold War period, post-interventionary society offers new opportunities to govern. During the Cold War, the political architecture of the international system combined respect for territorial integrity with sovereign competence or non-interference in domestic affairs. The 'humanitarian wars' of the early post-Cold War period (Roberts 1993) have significantly altered this architecture. According to how well life is deemed to be supported or valued, the international system has been reordered into effective and ineffective states. While respect for the territorial integrity of ineffective states remains, sovereignty over life within them has become internationalised, negotiable and contingent (Elden 2005). Contingent sovereignty is a shifting zone or frontier that brings together national and international actors and is shaped by the interactions, exchanges and antagonisms that interconnect them (Harrison 2004). It defines a contested post-interventionary political terrain, including the privileged existence of an aid industry having both a special relationship with the host government and, at the same time, defining links toits home organisations. Unprecedented since the colonial period, within the contested limits of contingent sovereignty, through NGOs and other implementing partners, donor governments find themselves once again working directly at the level of community and population. This forms a new, yet strangely familiar, responsibility to govern (ICISS 2001).

Since the end of the Cold War, liberal interventionism has gone through two main phases. The early 1990s was a time of expansionary humanitarian intervention. In the last decade this has shifted to a more consolidatory concern with state and societal reconstruction. Within the emerging political space of post-interventionary society, effective liberal states once more find themselves with a responsibility to govern. It is in relation to this responsibility that one can rediscover the problematic of an earlier liberal colonialism. This is not a linear relationship; the contexts and relations are very different. There is little or no direct continuity between the past and the present. The connection is more in terms of resonances and echoes, unresolved antagonisms and, especially, recurrent designs of power and urges to govern. Rather than colonialism constituting some form of heritage or memory, it is more the case that the will to power that shaped it lives on through new institutions and actors. It continues to discover the world anew, and actively to shape our experiences and expectations. With an eye to history and an awareness of our present predicament, the chapters in this book seek in different ways to disturb and unsettle this narrative.

Bibliography

Abulafia, D. (2008) *The Discovery of Mankind: Atlantic Encounters in the Age of Columbus*. New Haven, CT and London: Yale University Press.

Anderson, M. (1996) *Do No Harm: Supporting Local Capacities for Peace Through Aid*. Cambridge, MA: Local Capacities for Peace Project, The Collaborative for Development Action, Inc.

Arendt, H. (1994 [1951) *The Origins of Totalitarianism*. New York: Harcourt.

Barnett, M. (2005) 'Humanitarianism Transformed'. *Perspectives on Politics* 3(3): 723–40.

Boutros-Ghali, B. (1995) 'An Agenda For Peace: Preventive Diplomacy, Peacemaking and Peace-Keeping (17 June 1992)'. In Boutros-Ghali, B. (ed.) *An Agenda for Peace: 1995*. New York: United Nations, pp. 39–72.

Buur, L., Jensen, S., and Stepputat, F. (eds) (2007) *The Security-Development Nexus: Expressions of Sovereignty and Securitization in Southern Africa*. Uppsala: Nordic Africa Institute.

Chambers, R. (1983) *Rural Development: Putting the Last First*. Basildon: Longman.

Christian Aid (2004) *The Politics of Aid. Aid in the New Cold War*. London: Christian Aid.

CHS (2003) *Human Security Now*. New York: Commission on Human Security, New York.

Collier, P., Elliot, L., Hegre, H., Hoeffler, A., Reynal-Querol, M., and Sambanis, N. (2003) *Breaking the Conflict Trap: Civil War and Development Policy*. Washington, DC and Oxford: World Bank and Oxford University Press.

Cooke, B. And Kothari, U. (2001) *Participation: The New Tyranny?* London: Zed Books.

Cowen, M.P. And Shenton, R.W. (1996) *Doctrines of Development*. London and New York: Routledge.

Cromer, Earl of (1913) 'The Government of Subject Races'. In *Political and Literary Essays: 1908–1913*. London: Macmillan and Co., pp. 1–56.

DAC (2003) *A Development Co-operation Lens on Terrorism Prevention: Key Entry Points for Action*. Paris: OECD Development Assistance Committee (DAC).

Dean, M. (1999) *Governmentality: Power and Rule in Modern Society*. London: Sage.

Elden, S. (2005) 'Territorial Integrity and the War on Terror'. *Environment and Planning A* 37: 2083–104.

Ferguson, N. (2003) *Empire: How Britain Made the Modern World*. London: Allen Lane.

Freedmann, L. (1993) 'Humanitarian War, the New United Nations and Peacekeeping'. *International Affairs* 69(3): 425–27.

Furnivall, J.S. (1948) *Colonial Policy and Practice: A Comparative Study of Burma and Netherlands India*. Cambridge: Cambridge University Press.

Harrison, G. (2004) *The World Bank and Africa: The Construction of Governance States*. London: Routledge.

Hobson, J.A. ([1902] 1938) *Imperialism: A Study*. London: George Allen and Unwin Ltd.

HSC (2005) *The Human Security Report 2005: War and Peace in the 21st Century*. Vancouver: Human Security Centre, University of British Colombia.

Hussain, N. (2003) *The Jurisprudence of Emergency: Colonialism and the Rule of Law*. Ann Arbor, MI: University of Michigan.

ICISS (2001) *The Responsibility to Protect: Report of the International Commission on Intervention and State Sovereignty*. Ottawa: International Development Research Centre.

Ignatieff, M. (2003) *Empire Lite: Nation-Building in Bosnia, Kosovo and Afghanistan*. London: Vintage.

Jahn, B. (2007) 'The Tragedy of Liberal Diplomacy: Democratization, Intervention, Statebuilding (Part I)'. *Journal of Intervention and State Building* 1(1): 87–106.

Kaldor, M. (1999) *New and Old Wars: Organised Violence in a Global Era*. Cambridge: Polity Press.

Luetchford, M. And Burns, P. (2003) *Waging the War on Want: 50 Years of Campaining Against World Poverty*. London: War on Want.

Lugard, Lord ([1922] 1965) *The Dual Mandate in Tropical Africa*. London: Frank Cass.

Macmichael, H.A. (1923) *Indirect Rule for Pagan Communities*. Sudan Archive, University of Durham, 586/1/1–55.

Maffey, J.L. (1927) *Minute of His Excellency the Governor General*, Khartoum: Governor General's Office.

Mehta, U.S. (1999) *Liberalism and Empire*. Chicago: University of Chicago Press.

Morel, E.D. (1920) *The Black Man's Burden*. Manchester and London: The National Labour Press Ltd.

Paris, R. (2001) 'Human Security: Paradigm Shift or Hot Air?' *International Security* 26(2): 87–102.

Patel, R. and Mcmichael, P. (2004) 'Third Worldism and the Lineage of Global Fascism: The Regrouping of the Global South in the Neoliberal Era'. *Third World Quarterly* 25(1): 231–54.

Roberts, A. (1993) 'Humanitarian War: Military Intervention and Human Rights'. *International Affairs* 69(3): 429–49.

Seeley, Sir J.R. (2005[1883]) *The Expansion of England: Two Courses of Lectures*. New York: Cosimo Classics.

Smith, R. (2006) *The Utility of Force: The Art of War in the Modern World*. Harmondsworth: Penguin Books.

Solana, J. (2003) *A Secure Europe in a Better World: European Security Strategy*. Paris: The European Union Institute for Security Studies.

Strategy Unit (2005) *Investing in Prevention: an International Strategy to Manage Risks of Instability and Improve Crisis Response*. A Strategy Unit Report to the Government. London: Prime Minister's Strategy Unit, Cabinet Office.

Sylvester, C. (2004) 'Bare Life as a Development/Postcolonial Problematic'. *The Geographical Journal* 172(1): 66–77.

UNDP (1994) *Human Development Report, 1994*. New York and Oxford: United Nations Development Programme/Oxford University Press.

Van Creveld, M. (1991) *The Transformation of War*. New York: Free Press.

Wilson, H. (1953) *The War on World Poverty*. London: Victor Gollancz.

1

The Exceptional Inclusion of 'Savages' & 'Barbarians'
The Colonial Liberal Bio-politics of Mobility & Development

MATTHEW MEREFIELD

Introduction

This chapter addresses mid-nineteenth-century British liberalism as it engaged with the crisis of the Morant Bay Rebellion (1865), following the 'great experiment' of emancipation in the British colony of Jamaica from 1833 onwards. The chapter uses that legacy to reflect upon limits of liberal government in the pursuit of security and the facilitation of freedom, including freedoms of mobility and the facilitation of developmental capabilities. While it is primarily concerned with the partial extension of liberal government to the post-emancipation population of Jamaican-African peasants in the period 1833–1865, the concluding section reflects on the legacy of this phase of liberal-colonial government for the contemporary framing of 'southern populations'.

In focusing on emancipation and rebellion in Jamaica, I am concerned with the British government's extension of liberal 'tuition' to Jamaican subjects, where Britain attempted the incorporation of 'surplus population' within the free yet disciplined realm of liberalism. In conceptualising the Jamaican population in terms of surplus population, I am following political economy and developmental paradigms belonging to the nineteenth-century (Cowen and Shenton, 1996: 150–3). The term 'surplus' refers to the way in which the freedwomen's and men's migration from the agricultural-and-industrial plantation system to small-holding was surplus to the requirements of a profitable land-labour ratio in the colonies, and constitued a ready supply of cheap labour (Wakefield, 1834). Here Marx's taxonomy of floating, latent and stagnant labour is relevant in the domain of political economy (Marx, 1928:711). Like Marx's stagnant labour, the Jamaican population proved resistant to incorporation into the ostensibly 'free' labour market. In the domain of colonial government and political liberalism, this surplus population also appeared within racialised taxonomies and political technologies. As I show below, Foucault's taxonomies of subjectivisation are also relevant, as the problem of resistant surplus population appeared in the domain of differential capacities requiring sovereign, disciplinary and regulatory strategies of incorporation.

In this discussion of liberal strategies of incorporation my specific focus is on J.S. Mill's utilitarian and imperialist approach to problems of colonial government. Mill was greatly concerned with the equality of British subjects, whether they resided in the colonies or in Britain itself, and he sought to extend the rule of law to British Jamaican subjects in the event of the suppression of the Morant Bay Rebellion. As

Uday Singh Mehta (1999:3) notes, liberals like Mill endorsed 'the empire as a legitimate form of political and commercial governance', justified and accepted 'its largely undemocratic and non-representative structure' and invoked 'history, ethnicity, civilisational hierarchies, and occasionally race and blood ties as politically relevant categories'. Mill also wrote that lesser races held a potential for equality that could be furthered via the 'tuition of a paternal leadership grounded in the use of force' (Mill, 1991[1861]:45–51,316, 345–8). Mill was concerned with anthropological limits to the practice of liberalism, and sought to delineate the forms of tutorage that could be used to bring 'immature' populations towards the state of rational autonomy necessary to liberal practice. Here, in the context of colonial government, Mill the political philosopher met Mill the political economist, for the predominant form of tutorage Mill envisioned was participation in the disciplines of the free labour market.

Philip Cole (2000) has noted that while Mill's liberal political philosophy is central to normative political theory, the colonial practice of liberalism has been neglected. Beate Jahn (2005:599–600) also notes that the discipline of International Relations has neglected the colonial aspects of Mill's works, preferring to focus instead on the principles of non-interference he advocated amongst the (European) nations representing mature civilisation (Mill, 1984[1878]:109–24). My discussion draws upon recent scholarship in Politics and International Relations that addresses Mill's works in terms of their liberal colonial legacies, including studies by Uday Singh Mehta (1999), Eddy M. Souffrant (2000), and Jennifer Pitts (2005). While these works point to the historically contingent limits of practices and theories of liberalism, there is also a growing body of work utilising Foucauldian analysis in terms of colonial legacies. Here there has been a shift from an early and effective study of colonial discourse and governmentality, such as Edward Said's *Orientalism* (1995), to an engagement with Foucault's later works and, particularly, the idea of the modern development of bio-politics governing the relations between sovereign, population, and territory such as Ann Louise Stoler's (1995) *Race and the Education of Desire: Foucault's History of Sexuality and the Colonial Order of Things*.

This chapter's consideration of legacies of Millian liberal-colonialism reflects on the Morant Bay Rebellion (1865) as an example of a crisis over the incorporation of colonial subjects within the sphere of liberal norms and law, and examines Mill's involvement in the subsequent controversy over Governor Eyre's imposition of martial law and brutal suppression of the rebellion. The rebellion and its aftermath have been the subject of sustained academic interest, particularly amongst historians of British colonialism who view the rebellion as the culmination of the problems of the early period of emancipation. I draw upon Bernard Semmel's (1956) *Jamaican Blood and Victorian Conscience: the Governor Eyre Controversy*, which maps the contest between liberal (Mill) and authoritarian (Carlyle) modes of British responses to the suppression of the rebellion. Jennifer Pitts (2005) provides a useful critique of the racialised limits of Mill's attempt to restore British law in the colonial context. Catherine Hall's (1992) account of the politics of emancipation and the rebellion, examines the event's pivotal place in the shift from cultural to biological racism in Britain and amongst colonialists. In the Jamaican context, Gad Heumann's *The Killing Time: the Morant Bay Rebellion in Jamaica* (2000) recounts the politics of the conflict in Jamaica itself, paying careful attention to the organised 'populist legitimism' of the rebellion, pointing to the rebels' use of notions of the rule of law and membership rights in framing their grievances, claims and actions. Heumann's works, like that of Thomas C. Holt (1992), usefully address the socio-political problems of the post-emancipation society leading to conflict. This context is a necessary consideration in regard to Mill's attitudes to the position of the Jamaican population in terms of development, progress, and order.

In the post-9–11 context, reflections on the colonial government of security could be derived from the Jamaican crisis in the mid-Victorian period. One such significant account is given in Nasser Hussain's critical-legal study *The Jurisprudence of Emergency* (2003), where the rebellion and its suppression through martial law are analysed for their appearance as moments of 'sovereign exception' (Georgio Agamben: 2005), providing a test of the very authority of the rule of law in the colonial context. Hussain's work opens up a space in which one could usefully think of the post-9–11 shift to authoritarianism, securitisation, and a 'politics of fear', given in the emergence of Britain's terror laws as correlated moments for the sovereign exceptionality belonging to a colonial-liberal government's suppression of 'savages' and 'barbarians'.

My account here relates to Hussain's work in asking what constitutes the logic and practice of government from which a state of exception was drawn. I am concerned with the manner in which this period represents a shift from the inclusive movement of emancipation whereupon free Jamaicans were subject to incorporation within the workings of the free labour market through to the socio-political resistance and 'barbaric' revolt of the Morant Bay Rebellion that I argue represented claims for recognition under the rule and norms of British law. My specific interest lies in the way that Mill's efforts to include colonial subjects within the sphere of British justice constituted a liberal strategy that conflicted with the anthropological limits and racialised view of progress that framed his views on colonial rule.

In the first section I outline the relevance of Foucault's theories of governmentality and bio-politics in terms of colonial modes of the government of mobility and development. I seek to show how Foucault's conceptions of bio-politics and the supplementary relationship between sovereign, disciplinary and regulatory powers provide a framework for an analysis of liberal strategies promoting progress, order, and development. In the process I apply his notion of state racism to the development of a bio-politics of mobility in the colonial context. In the second section I use this theoretical framework to analyse Mill's liberal-colonial approach to the problem of surplus population in the example of the Morant Bay Rebellion and the Controversy of Governor Eyre. In the concluding remarks I reflect on the legacies of the liberal-colonial past for contemporary government.

A Liberal-Colonial Bio-politics

The nineteenth-century movement towards emancipation was a key component of a discourse of national identity in Britain that depended, in part, on the enactment of a 'civilising mission' in the colonial domain. As British political identity developed in terms of the nation's role as the commercial-and-liberal centre of the world, this discursive space allowed for the promotion of domestic and foreign political and economic freedom as the manifestation of that centrality. Emancipation served to legitimate the status of liberal values as it served to legitimate the status of Britain in the world that Palmerston, fifteen years later, was to describe as standing 'at the head of moral, social, and political civilisation' (Pemberton 1954:141).

The Emancipation Act was taken as validification of the parliamentary reforms of 1832 (the Great Reform Act), as it demonstrated the new-found strength of the innately liberal middle class (Hall 1992:208). In Britain the Emancipation Act was followed by the Poor Law Act (1834) which facilitated a utilitarian strategy to develop the moral and productive capacity of the domestic surplus population. Catherine Hall observed that one form of progress that the anti-slavery movement and, in particular, the missionary groups sought was to be manifest in the form of a 'free' Jamaica, a 'Christian, civilised, capitalist, free labour economy with democratic institutions'. It was therefore a vision of 'a country based on their own version of the British model' (Hall 1992:121). The abolition movement was built on a contradiction belonging to the civilising mission, where the tendency to regard the African slaves as naturally equal was contradicted by a corresponding view of African society as backward.

In Britain, a gradual swing in public opinion developed away from the cultural racism of the 1830s towards a 'biological' racism revolving around bourgeois anxieties about domestic social disorder and imperial decline in the 1850s and 1860s. At this juncture a constellation of colonial and foreign forms of resistance, the popular patriotism of Palmerston, and the rise of newly scientific theories of 'racial' difference combined with domestic anxieties about the working-class threat to social order to produce a sense of crisis that was both imperial and national. In the colonies, the India Mutiny (1857) saw the remilitarisation of the British empire in India, and also led to the increasing legitimation, at home, of a militant colonial expansion tied to a renewed sense of racial supremacy, for the Mutiny was taken to have shown that the 'backward' were intrinsically 'barbaric' and thus incapable of the rationality necessary to incorporation within the liberal sphere. In this context the Morant Bay Rebellion (1865) and the subsequent controversy over Governor Eyre's suppression of the rebellion were key events in the shift towards a racialised British nationality and a liberal-imperial paradigm.

While the Reform Act and the Emancipation Act marked the political ascendancy of the British middle class, the latter, in Foucauldian terms, was emblematic of the shift from the dominance of the juridical sovereignty of the *ancien régime*, just as the demise of the whip represented the diminishment of spectacular corporeal punishment as a key political technology. For Foucault this shift was not one of absolute disjuncture; sovereign power did not disappear with the emergence of disciplinary techniques and discourse producing docile subjects, nor with the emergence of a regularising bio-politics promoting the security and prosperity of the population (Foucault 1991a:102). The emergence of bio-politics signifies the development of a different but complementary power over life (Foucault 2003:243), which works to regularise the population at the level of the mass, thereby supplementing the disciplinary techniques that work at the level of the individual. Emancipation heralded a sea change in Jamaica, with the new governing concern for the social reproduction of the black Jamaicans; henceforth they became a 'population' that was the object of a colonial bio-politics. Here, as Ann Louise Stoler notes, power was 'no longer lodged in the sovereign right 'to kill and let live' but rather in "the reverse of the right of the social body to ensure, maintain or develop its life"' (Stoler 1995:83; Foucault 1998:136). The 'right' that was to be enjoyed here, moreover, was one of a right of intervention into "the manner of living, in 'how' to live"' (Stoler: *op. cit*; Foucault 1991b:46).

In his lectures of 1977–78, Foucault provides a sketch for a bio-politics of mobility (Foucault 2007). For the modern state, the government of the relationships between sovereignty, people, and territory is central to the work of bio-politics (Foucault 1991a:102–3). This triangulation is relevant to the development of the modern European state and its government of colonial mobility. The rationale of a bio-political government of mobility is the optimal arrangement of the relations between circulation and stasis and the well-being of the population (Foucault 2007:18–19). The colonial government of mobility was concerned with the relationship between different categories of circulation and stasis, as was evident in the colonial concern for the correct balance between land, labour, and capital. Colonial administration in Jamaica, for example, was concerned to rectify a deficit of static labour (labour available to the plantation system) through the remedy of Afro-American and European labour immigration in the 1840s (Holt 1992:198). Colonial government was concerned for the complete array of mobilities; thus alongside finance and commodities such as sugar and coffee, and sources of labour, the government of mobility extended to the circulation of social values in, for example, the provision of Christian belief systems, labour tutorage and 'moral' education, and politics in, for example, the provision of guidance for the 'responsible' use of newly-won freedoms and the containment of their abuse.

Bio-politics proceeded via state racism, where what is established is a 'positive relationship between the right to kill and the assurance of life'; what modern government posits is that 'the more you kill [and] ... let die, the more you will live' (Stoler 1995:84). Assuming a broad definition of mobility encompassing the social and geographical, we can also correlate Foucault's conceptualisation of the statisation of bio-politics with that of mobility; in the first regard, Foucault notes that the 'fostering of the life of some is dependent on "disallowing" the life of others' (Foucault 2004:65). Within the modern bio-political state, technologies of security rework the sovereign right to 'kill and let live' in order to enhance the 'right of the social body to ensure, maintain, or develop its life'; here, the sovereign right to kill appears as an 'excess of bio-power that does away with life in the name of securing it' (Foucault 1998:138; Stoler 1995:84; Foucault 2003: 238–9). This positive right of the modern bio-political state is polyvalent: it applies to all of the 'degenerate' or 'abnormal' categories representing internal and/or external threats to the well-being of the population.

The bio-political right applies to circulation insofar as this affects the well-being and prosperity of the population. Foucault states that government should provide a 'milieu' in which it is possible to 'maximilise good circulation and diminish the bad' (Foucault 2007:18), for example setting a *laissez-faire* milieu in which the 'freedom' of mobility should be exercised. In combination, Foucault's ideas on the bio-political right and circulation could be reformulated in the following terms: *the fostering of the mobility of some is dependent on disallowing the mobility of others.* Moreover, as noted above, the government of mobility applies to the relationship between different categories of circulation and stasis. Thus, for example, the healthy flow of finance and trade may require, at some point, the stasis of labour, rather than its further circulation. This was the case in Jamaica in the post-emancipation era, when sugar and coffee plantations required the stasis of newly free labour, and sought means to disallow its exodus.

In the context of the shift from slavery to emancipation, the colonial extension of free labour mobility, given the rise in the mid-nineteenth century of *laissez-faire* political economy, was the correlate of colonial labour strategies such as those of Edmund Wakefield. Wakefield's ideas about colonisation, labour and migration were based on utilising labour mobility and stasis to produce the most profitable relationship between land, labour and capital. Previous forms of colonisation had failed, argued Wakefield, because wages had been set at too high a rate in relation to capital and land. The result was that free migrant labourers tended to desert the fields of capitalist production as soon as their savings allowed them to set up as independent smallholders. In this instance, British surplus labour was wasted by being employed in smallholding instead of large-scale capitalist agriculture. The solution Wakefield proposed was to set the rates of land value at a 'sufficient price' to exceed the labourer's savings (Semmel 1993:27–8).

By violating the principle of non-interference in the workings of the market, capital investment would be attracted to the colonies by the prospect of a constant supply of affordable labour. This strategy was unsuccessfully sought by the plantation class in Jamaica, which failed to attract significant numbers of Afro-Americans or Europeans to the plantations after emancipation. Wakefield advised that his system should be extended to the United States where the use of market regulation to bind 'pauper labourers' to productive farming would provide an alternative to the use of slave labour, and result in the greater exchange of cheaper corn for British manufactures. In the colonies, Wakefield added, the working class could be rendered as 'comfortable, satisfied and wise at least, as the working class in America' (Wakefield 1834:120–1). Yet it was the tendency of the American working class to disperse from the site of capitalist production that he wanted to overcome by raising the price of land. In extending the bondage of labour to a longer period of capitalist-intensive production, Wakefield's proposals, which were intended to coerce the labour-migrants into a form of stasis, can thus be seen as an attempt to create the appropriate milieu for a regime of indentured labour that operated as 'free labour'.

These examples of mobility regularisation demonstrate the contingent nature of the extension of liberal freedoms and the interdependence of free-flowing circulation upon forms of stasis. Foucault's conceptualisation of bio-political recipricocity is matched by liberal theory where, in the context of British colonialism, the interdependence of freedom for some and restriction for others is clear. Eddy M. Souffrant (2002:112) observes that J.S. Mill's utilitarian liberalism was primarily concerned with the freedom of the *national* population. 'Barbarian' populations were largely of concern to the extent that they affected the interests of the 'civilised' national population. 'Barbarian' populations had their internal correlates in those non-deserving elements of the poor identified by Marx as the paupers, vagrants and criminals comprising the stagnant population. Frequently addressed by the governing elites in racialised terms, such populations constitute those that Foucault describes as a 'criminally delinquent' threat to the state.

For the liberals civilised society was justified in taking punitive measures in the interests of protecting the pursuit of freedom amongst autonomous rational actors. The Poor Law, the workhouse and the penitentiary, for example, were disciplinary technologies designed to promote the proper circulation of labour and capital and thus help secure the prosperity of the population. Such actions may have been directed at threats that were internal or external or both at the same time. Moreover, liberalism's staged theory of development allowed despotic government of 'immature' populations to be justified as a means of their own improvement (Mehta 1999: 30–3). For Mill, savagery and barbarism were followed by slavery before a society might reach the modern state of civilisation best represented by Britain. These civilisational categories match modes of government. Despotic government was necessary for those societies remaining in the natural state of savagery. Despotic government was also required for barbarian populations which were distinguished from savage populations by their violent opposition to civilisation.

Slavery, as a mode of government, was suitable for teaching obedience to immature societies and required forced stasis and mobility. Thereafter, the paternal tutorage of despotic government was a suitable means of developing the potential of immature populations whose mobility should, where possible, be channelled into the freedom of the labour market. This is where newly emancipated populations figured for Millian liberal colonialism: for such formerly savage 'developing' nations Mill recommended guidance:

> [A] people in that condition require to raise them out of it a very different polity from a nation of savages ... The step they will have to take, and their only path to improvement, is to be raised from a government of will to one of law ... What they require is not a government of force but one of guidance. Being, however, in too low a state yet to yield to the guidance of any but those to whom they look up as the possessor of force, the sort of government fittest for them is one which possesses force, but seldom uses it. (Mill 1991:49–50)

Sovereign power must visibly exist, yet, if used at all, was to be educative and thus aid the disciplining of the immature population. The Millian hierarchy of capabilities and government correlates with the (primarily) disciplinary power that organises social life in relation to the figure of the autonomous rational liberal norm. In Mitchell Dean's account of Foucault's schema, these include those who

> (b) need assistance to maintain capacities for autonomy ...; (c) ... are potentially capable exercising liberal autonomy but who are yet to be trained in the habits and capacities to do so; (d) .. having reached maturity of age, are for one reason or another not yet or no longer able to exercise their own autonomy or act in their own best interests; and (e) ... are permanently criminally delinquent or dedicated to the destruction of the state. (Dean 2002:48)

Disturbing a simple ranking of categories of class and 'race', examples here might include the 'deserving poor' (b), colonial subjects and the idle poor (c and/or d), and rebellious colonial subjects and the criminal poor (e). Ranging from nearly autonomous to deliberatively incapable, each category is subject to different modes of sovereign and disciplinary power. Here, the pursuit of liberal progress and the prosperity of the population requires the 'normation' (Foucault 2007:58–9) of these groups towards a state of productive rationality. The majority excluded from the freedom of the liberal norm through varying degrees of incapacity or resistance will be subject to greater degrees of disciplinary and regulatory power within regimes of mobility. Bio-politics is concerned not only with the specific range of interventions appropriate to each category, but also with the proper ordering of the relations between them. For example, categories (b) and (c) consist of subjects who are guided in a movement towards the eminently governable figure of the liberal norm. Category (e) consists of those subjects (individuals, states) which threaten to disrupt this progressive movement on which the way of life of a particular bio-politics is dependent. Thus the 'criminally delinquent' (e) must not be allowed to corrupt the governmentality of those who actively move towards, or own the capacity for, autonomous self-government (a-c).

While colonial-liberalism constituted a bio-politics that facilitated progress inasmuch as it furthered the prosperity of the (British) population, emancipation allowed the development of formerly enslaved populations, bringing them within the realm of the exercise of choice, rationality and individuality via the disciplines of the institutions of the labour market, the church, and the (European) family. Nonetheless, such a population still required subjection to colonial order until the point at which they might eventually demonstrate the capacity for self-government. Representative government and unregulated mobility were only suitable for populations already capable of exercising the freedom and responsibility of autonomous rationality. In this context, the liberal development of immature populations formed a strategy providing a bridge between the colonial pursuit of progress and order. The shift from slavery to emancipation was part of a liberal strategy which was to redeem the progressive order of colonial rule.

Freedom & Exodus (Jamaica 1833–1865)

Emancipation marked a point at which the forced mobility and stasis of plantation labour reliant of spectacular and real violence gave way to an extension of the freedoms and disciplines on the labour market. In Jamaica emancipation developed in the form of the apprenticeship system in 1833 before giving way to a free labour market system in 1838. British policy was initially set in the Glenelg doctrine (1837), which stated that 'the apprenticeship of the emancipated slaves is to be immediately succeeded by personal freedom, in that full and unlimited sense of the term in which it is used in reference to other subjects of the British Crown' (Holt 1992:179). As Thomas Holt observed (*op. cit.*:180), the doctrine pointed the Jamaican people towards political equality, equality before the law, and equality within the labour market, but also contained an expectance that Jamaican subjects would prove capable of the exercise of freedom.

Under apprenticeship the freed slaves were to work the major part of the week on their former master's plantations in return for their customary perquisites (food, clothing, housing and medical care). In their 'spare time', however, they were encouraged to hire themselves out at market rates, or to cultivate their own lands in order to trade in the market. Whilst achieving a constant labour supply for the plantations, the apprenticeship system represented a largely unsuccessful attempt by the Colonial Office to guide directly both newly freed slaves and the plantation masters in the capabilities and responsibilities necessary for liberal freedom. Whilst the Home government continued to attempt to exert influence in the interests of the broader liberal project after 1838, its task was complicated by the Jamaican conditions where there was low population density and vast areas of uncultivated land in the interior (Holt 1992:43). As the Colonial Office clerk Matthew Taylor noted, freed slaves might have little compulsion to work the plantations when subsistence could be achieved from one day's work on their own plots (Holt, *op. cit.*). The solution that was pursued followed the principles of profitable land-labour ratios set out by Wakefield (see above) and was provided by the Colonial Secretary, Lord Glenelg, who stated that

> [T]he minimum price of land ... should be high enough to leave a considerable portion of the population unable to buy it until they have saved some capital out of the wages of their industry, and at the same time low enough to encourage such savings by making the possession of land a reasonable object of ambition to all. (Glenelg 1936; Holt 1992:75)

The strategies of liberal colonial government had been designed, in part, to encourage the emergence of a self-governing population whose experience in the plantation system would be matched by their suitability for the free labour market. Whilst restricting the freed Jamaican's ability to make an 'irrational' choice, the system guided them in the sensible allocation of time and rational calculation of self-interest necessary to inculcate market values. The 'failure' of this project of subjectivisation was evident in the significant migration to the Jamaican hills where, by 1860, some 50,000 small-holdings were being farmed by freed women and men (Semmel 1963:33). For many of the former slaves the possession of land had become the very definition of the real meaning of freedom in the post-emancipation context (Heumann 2005:111–13). Yet rejection of plantation labour did not necessarily imply a blanket rejection of the 'moral values' required for responsible freedom. Some measure of the meaning of freedom was given in the petition that the poor people of St. Anne's sent to Queen Victoria in 1865, pleading that, if provided with land at low rent, they would

> Put our hand and heart to work, and cultivate coffee, corn, cane, cotton and tobacco and other produce [;] we will form a company for that purpose if Our Gracious Lady Victoria our Queen will also appoint an agent to receive such produce as we may cultivate ... (Heumann 2000:49)

Here the residents of St. Anne's endorsed market values, albeit in the pursuit of communal autonomy rather than of individual profit. Their address, moreover, was framed in terms of a plea for the recognition of membership rights as full British subjects. Here, then, there was no simple rejection of the lessons of post-emancipation tutorage, but rather a form of counter-conduct utilising a critical appropriation of those lessons.

A large share of responsibility for the failure of incorporation belonged to the white colonial planter class. Following emancipation, the plantocracy retained political and economic power, and 'the population of over 400,000 negroes remained under the legislative control of a 47–man planter oligarchy chosen by fewer than 2,000 electors' (Newsinger 2006:31). In addition, the Jamaica Assembly retained great autonomy from the Home government, which was limited to the negative power of vetoing unacceptable Jamaican legislation. This autonomy aided the plantocracy's subversion of the liberal strategies of emancipation belonging to the Colonial Office, as they preferred to maintain or reinvent, where possible, key elements of the coercive political technologies established under slavery. The intensity of this subversion increased with the gradual increase of the sugar economy's difficulties. The dire situation in which the people of Jamaica found themselves by the 1860s had slowly gathered force over the preceding two decades. In 1946 the *laissez-faire* British government equalised the sugar duties, thus withdrawing protection from the Jamaican plantation industry. In response to the ensuing crisis the planters reduced wages on their estates by as much as 25 per cent (Heumann 2005:114). The sugar economy also declined in the face of competition from producers in Brazil and Cuba, as well as from falling productivity in the Jamaican plantations. By 1865 half of the estates operating at emancipation had closed, and unemployment was rife throughout the island (Heumann 2000:46).

While hardship and dissent became evident throughout the 1830s to 1860s, the response of the British government and the plantocracy to the non-compliance of the black Jamaicans worked within the logic of a bio-politics that bridged across liberal, mercantilist and racialised epistemes and political strategies. The Colonial Office and successive British Governors supported the Jamaican Assembly as it enacted restrictive regulations including vagrancy laws and tenure and taxation systems designed both to coerce the black Jamaicans back into the poorly-paid plantation system (Semmel 1963:33) and to protect the interests of the plantation owners.

These measures of coercion mirror the black Jamaicans' objects of protest, since their main concerns lay with the lack of political representation, restricted, unfair or prohibited land tenure, punitive rates of duties on necessities and excessive taxation, the injustices of the judicial system, low pay rates on the plantations, and a lack of support for diversification. Neither the British government nor the Jamaica Assembly was prepared to extend measures of support to the diversified smallholder agriculture, nor to extend any alleviation of the onerous taxation system. The Jamaican movement to smallholder farming represented a regression that transgressed the developmental logic of progress belonging to political science, and was regarded by the plantocracy as a return to the natural state of 'idleness' purportedly belonging to the African 'race'. Both the liberal episteme requiring participation in the free labour market and the more mercantilist interest of the plantocracy necessitated a rejection of the exodus from the stasis of the plantation system.

Crisis & Liberal Paradox

In 1862 Edward Eyre became Governor of Jamaica in the context of general economic distress and socio-political conflict. As Gad Heumann (2000:48, 54–5) notes, both the Governor and the Colonial Office supported the position of the plantocracy and shared their belief that 'poverty and crime in the colony was due to the apathy and indolence of the community'. Eyre quickly found himself in conflict with George William Gordon, the leader of the left-wing Town Party. Gordon, the son of a white planter and and enslaved woman, was one of the coloured members of the Jamaican Assembly and served as a spokesperson for the settlers in the hill country and the pauperised Afro-Jamaicans in the towns and sugar estates. Gordon' political activity provided support for the reinvented practice of freedom sought by the critical elements of the black population.

The dissent and organised protests of the 1860s erupted in the form of the Morant Bay Rebellion in 1865, which was led by the Baptist leader Paul Bogle in the parish of St. Thomas. Eyre's response was to send out reconnoitring parties, which proceeded to flog or hang the blacks they found. In addition, martial courts were convened to try captured prisoners who were summarily found guilty and hanged. In all, some 499 people were killed, 600 men and women flogged, and 1000 cottages burnt to the ground (Dutton 1967:295). Eyre also moved quickly to issue a warrant for Gordon's arrest claiming that, although not directly involved in the riots, he was 'ultimately the chief cause and origin of the whole rebellion' (Semmel 1967:52). Tried under martial law and prevented from presenting a defence, Gordon was summarily found guilty and hanged.

In Britain the reaction to Eyre's suppression was initially positive, as it was assumed that he had taken effective action to restore law and order. It was believed that the rebellion had held potentially catastrophic consequences, as recent memories of the revolt in Haiti and the India Mutiny led to a belief in the 'barbaric' qualities of colonial populations. Yet controversy soon surrounded the issue of the necessity of the imposition of martial law, and the summary trial and execution of Gordon in particular (Hussain 2003:111). Liberal pressure persuaded the government to establish a Royal Commission which went on to criticise the use of martial law and the unwarranted violence of the suppression but also found that the rebellion had been a real threat and that Eyre had been right to take vigorous defensive action. Subsequently, the newly fledged 'Jamaica Committee' led by J.S. Mill pressed the government to prosecute Eyre for the murder of Gordon. As Nasser Hussain shows, the failure of this prosecution shifted the definition of necessity onto a racialised basis, thus endorsing Eyre's perception that the barbaric character of the black Jamaicans had, in this instance, constituted an actable emergency (Hussain 2003:114; Hall 1996).

In seeking the prosecution of Eyre, Mill had echoed the Glenelg doctrine in recognising the extension of the equality of all British subjects under the rule of law. At the same time, however, Mill's liberalism was deeply rooted in an imperialist ideology. As noted earlier, sovereign power underlies the extension of the rule of law to subject populations, as well as the strategies of discipline aiding their tutorage and the regularisation promoting bio-political security for the European way of living. In terms of liberal philosophy the inclusion of emancipated colonial subjects requiring their equality under the rule of law was a necessary component of their tutoring towards a state of mature autonomy. Equally, the gradual introduction of moral education was thought necessary for the production of a well-ordered labour force (Brion Davis 1984:169). Mill's choice of intervention is indicative of this logic, for Gordon – a slave-and-master-descended subject who had become a Member of Parliament – represented the moral development that Mill regarded as resulting from the benevolent extension of liberalism. Gordon's status as an educated, propertied professional demonstrated the ownership of rational autonomy that could potentially be exercised by subject races. He represents, in other words, the sort of liberal individual development that should reconcile the pursuit of progress and order (Cowan and Shenton 1996:40).

Mill's arguments at the time were carefully colour-blind, approaching the problem as one of the murder of a British subject, as a problem of law that seemed to exist outside of the racial and political context in Jamaica (Semmel 1963:56–80).The liberal and colonial philosopher did not engage in a broader criticism of the government of Jamaica nor in the merits of the Rebellion itself. His idea of a 'government of leading strings' included a strategic tolerance of cultural diversity that was intended as a tutorage in liberal values and the rule of law (Mill 1991:350–2). That tolerance, however, met its limit in the combined requirements of liberal political economy and the liberal developmental imperative. Mill had been an enthusiastic believer in Edmund Wakefield's idea that colonial 'labourers must be prevented from becoming peasant proprietors' (Brinley 1973:7), and could not have approved of the Jamaicans movement towards smallholding. Here there is no liberal paradox between the economic and political domains: rather, Mill's economic liberalism agrees with his political liberalism. For the imperative of the productive use of colonial labour agrees with both Mill's racial ranking and the utilitarian imperative for communities to progress: the Jamaican movement thus belongs to an unproductive recidivism that tends backwards towards the state of savagery. This recidivism undoes the development of individual freedom and rationality that disciplined labour facilitates, and thereby reverses the immanent process of development that the post-emancipation incorporation of colonial subjects in the labour market should bring.

Such a regression and the corresponding rebellion would seem to be precisely the sorts of grounds that Mill believed justified the despotic rule of subject populations (Mill, 1991). Yet, for Mill this did not provide justification for Eyre's turn to martial law. The implication here was not the opposition of liberalism to despotism, since Mill clearly supported despotic government in the colonial context, but that government should lawfully provide the necessary tutelage to the subject population. Eyre's actions, in this view, transgressed the proper relationship between progress, order and development by an exceptional and illegal use of sovereign power. They threatened a British regression to the rule of the *ancien regime*, and denied the work of development that should, eventually, re-produce Jamaican society as a self-governing population.

The liberal strategy informing the guiding extension of discipline and regulation contained its own contradictions, however. Colonialism was deemed a utilitarian good that served the prosperity of the population. The colonial bio-politics of liberal development in the Jamaican colony, premised on racialised beliefs, comprised a punitive incorporation of the Jamaican blacks within the free labour market, wherein regularising rent and tax rates restricted the transformation in the terms of freedom that the black Jamaican people sought. The pursuit of order in the colony included restriction of mobility via vagrancy laws, and restrictions of political and judicial rights for the yet-to-mature subject population. The pursuit of progress via development and order led not to a steady supply of well-ordered labour but to economic crisis and revolt constituting threats to the bio-politics of the governing population and its liberal milieu. As John Ruskin observed, the radical liberal's philosophy of political science required the use of despotic violence that Mill sought to criminalise as a transgression of the rule of law (Semmel 1963:111).

Postscript: Legacies of Colonial Liberal Bio-politics

I noted above that, after the emancipation movements of the first half of the nineteenth century, the mid to late nineteenth century witnessed the rise of Britain's imperialist nationalism. Liberalism defined the leading role that Britain presented to the 'international community' that consisted, for Mill, of modern civilised nation states as opposed to barbarian or savage peoples. The (then) Chancellor Gordon Brown recently revisited that legacy, stating that

> [t]he days of Britain having to apologise for its colonial history are over ... We should talk ... about British values that are enduring, because they stand for some of the greatest ideas in history: tolerance, liberty, civic duty, that grew in Britain and influenced the rest of the world. Our strong tradition of fair play, of openness, of internationalism, these are great British values. (Brown, cited in Younge 2005)

Reinventing British imperialism as the benevolent extension of liberal values, contemporary British government expresses its aim in terms of the benefits and risks of globalisation. Political discourse involving the pursuit of a leading global role via humanitarian interventionism invokes the liberal tradition of the 'civilising mission' as a moral duty (Jahn 2005:615). The intention to 'reorder the world around us' is qualified by representations of reference to Britain as a 'beacon nation', a provider of moral education for a global community defined in terms of its capabilities or propensity to share 'our way of life' (Blair 2001). A vision of a nationally globalised community has been promoted where 'our self interest and our mutual interest are woven together'; accordingly, the new 'power of community will transform domestic as well as international politics, because globalisation shrinks the distance between domestic and international issues' (PMSU 2005). The form of 'global social inclusion' envisioned is a sphere in which principles of tolerance, democracy, and the rule of law are to be extended through humanitarian intervention into crisis zones and neo-liberal regulation to the world's poorest countries. The space of inclusion marks a 'community' in which global citizens share 'needs, mutual responsibilities, and linked destinies' (Brown 2000:3).

This extension of equitable liberal inclusion operates within categories which mirror Mill's hierarchy that continued from 'savages' and 'barbarians' through to the civilisation of the mature nation state. The contemporary continuum starts with the 'pre-modern' state, progresses to the 'modern' state, and culminates in the 'post-modern' state. The first (most progressive) category consists of those 'postmodern and postimperial' states that 'no longer think of security primarily in terms of conquest', and potentially forms a new 'commonwealth'. This category of 'trading states' includes the nations of the European Union that form a realm of progressive interdependence, but also any states that uphold values of political and economic liberalism. The second category consists of 'traditional "modern" states that follow

Machiavellian principles and *raison d'état'*, such as Pakistan, India and China. Their statecraft is represented as an anachronistic form of repressive power that falls short of the primarily non-coercive postmodern power.

The final category takes the form of a 'pre-modern' zone in which the (primarily postcolonial) state has failed and a Hobbesian war of all against all exists (Cooper 2000:12). This realm is held to be the source of global threats such as the networks of terrorism and 'South to North' migration. Arguably, these populations have become subject to a bio-political government of human security, where social cohesion within Britain is thought to be dependent upon the containment of chaos without. 'Undesirable' categories of south-to-north migrants function in a manner akin to the place of colonial subject people for J.S. Mill. 'Pre-modern' by virtue of their membership of 'chaotic' societies, they threaten to disrupt the liberal imperative to progress that facilitates the prosperity of the population and its milieu – the operation of a liberal way of life and government. The contemporary bio-political securitisation of the 'northern' population works through a partnership between the developmental 'root causes' approach to the problem of 'south to north' migration and a strategy of migration restriction designed to contain the 'southern' population in its region of origin. Here the 'freedom' that is extended via neo-liberal development programmes is increasingly conditional on the willingness of the 'southern' state to contain its own 'surplus' population.

Mill's colonial-liberal legacy is evident where the contemporary discourse of 'liberal imperialism' frames foreign relations, international development, and migration policy. The contemporary bio-politics is utilitarian rather than racialised, yet draws not only on ideas and practices of liberal inclusivity, but also upon those of 'community', 'progress', 'order' and exclusion that were developed in the operation of a racialised colonial bio-politics.

Bibliography

Agamben, G. (1995) *States of Exception*. Chicago: University of Chicago Press.
Blair, T. (2001) 'Speech to the Labour Party Conference'. Brighton, 2 October.
Brinley, T. (1973) *Migration and Economic Growth: a Study of Great Britain and the Atlantic Economy*. 2nd edn. Cambridge: Cambridge University Press.
Brion Davis, D. (1984) *Slavery and Human Progres*. Oxford: Oxford University Press.
Brown, G. (2000) 'Gilbert Murray Memorial Lecture'. Oxford: Oxfam.
Cole, P. (2000) *Philosophies of Exclusion: Liberal Political Theory and Immigration*. Edinburgh: Edinburgh University Press.
Cooper, R. (2002) 'The Postmodern State', in Leonard, Mark (ed.) *Re-ordering the World*. London: Foreign Policy Centre.
Cowen, M.P. and Shenton, R.W. (1996) *Doctrines of Development*. London: Routledge.
Dean, M. (2006) *Governmentality: Power and Rule in Modern Society*. London and New York: Sage.
Duffield, M. (2005) 'Getting Savages to Fight Barbarians: Development, Security and the Colonial Present'. *Conflict, Development and Security* 5(2): 141–57.
Dutton, G. (1967) *The Hero as Murderer: The Life of Edward John Eyre, Australian Explorer and Governor of Jamaica, 1815–1901*. Sydney and Melbourne: Collins & Cheshire.
Foucault, M. (1991a) 'Governmentality'. In Burchell, G., Gordon, C., and Miller, P. (eds) *The Foucault Effect: Studies in Governmentality*. London: Harvester Wheatsheaf, pp. 87–104.
Foucault, M. (1991b) 'Faire vivre et laisser mourir: la naissance du racisme'. *Les Temps Modernes* February: 37–61.
Foucault, M. (1998) *The Will to Knowledge: The History of Sexuality Volume I*. Harmondsworth: Penguin.
Foucault, M. (2003) *Society Must be Defended: Lectures at the Collége de France, 1975–7*. Harmondsworth: Penguin.
Foucault, M. (2004) *Securité, territoire, population: cours au Collége de France, (1977–8)*. Paris: Gallimard Seuil.

Foucault, M. (2007) *Security, Territory, Population: Lectures at the Collége de France, 1977–78*. Senellart, Michael (ed.), trans. Graham Burchell. Basingstoke: Palgrave Macmillan.

Glenelg, Lord, (1836) 'Glenelg to the Governors of the West Indies Colonies, 30 Jan,' *Parliamentary Papers* (166) 48: 58–60.

Hall, C. (1992) *White, Male, and Middle Class: Explorations in Feminism and History*. London: Polity Press.

Hall, C. (1996) 'Imperial Man: Edward Eyre in Australasia and the West Indies, 1833–66'. In Schwarz, B. (ed.) *The Expansion of England: Cultural History of Race and Ethnicity*. Abingdon, Oxford: Routledge, pp. 130–71.

Heumann, G. (2000) *The Killing Time: the Morant Bay Rebellion in Jamaica*. Knoxville, TN: University of Tennessee Press.

Heumann, G. (2005) 'Is This What You Call Free? Riots and Resistance in the Anglophone Caribbean'. In Heumann, G. and Trotman, D.V. (eds) *Contesting Freedom: Control and Resistance in the Post-Emancipation Caribbean*. Oxford: Macmillan, pp. 104–18.

Holt, T.C. (1992) *The Problem of Freedom: Race, Labor and Politics in Jamaica and Britain, 1832–1938*. Baltimore, MD: Johns Hopkins University Press.

Hussain, N. (2003) *The Jurisprudence of Emergency*. Ann Arbor, MI: University of Michigan Press.

Jahn, B. (2005) 'Barbarian Thoughts: Imperialism in the Philosophy of John Stuart Mill'. *Review of International Studies Association* 31: 599–618

Marx, K. (1928) *Capital*. London: Allen and Unwin.

Mehta, U.S. (1999) *Liberalism and Empire: a Study in Nineteenth Century British Liberal Thought*. Chicago: University of Chicago Press.

Mill, J.S. (1984[1861]) 'A Few Words on Non-Interference'. In Robson, J.M. (ed.) *The Collected Works of John Stuart Mill, vol. XXI*. Toronto: University of Toronto Press, pp. 109–24.

Mill, J.S. (1991) *Considerations on Representative Government*. New York: Prometheus Books.

Newsinger, J. (2006) *The Blood Never Dried: A People's History of the British Empire*. London: Bookmarks.

Pemberton, W.B. (1954) *Lord Palmerston*. London: Batchworth Press.

Pitts, J.A. (2005) *Turn to Empire: the Rise of Imperial Liberalism in Britain and France*. Princeton, NJ: Princeton University Press.

PMSU (Prime Minister's Strategy Unit) (2005) 'Investing in Prevention: An International Strategy to Manage Risks of Instability and Improve Crisis Response'. London: TSO.

Said, E. (1995) *Orientalism*. London: Penguin.

Semmel, B. (1963) *Jamaican Blood and Victorian Conscience: The Governor Eyre Controversy*. Cambridge: Riverside Press.

Semmel, B. (1993) *The Demons of Empire: Theories of imperialism from Adam Smith to Lenin*. Baltimore, MD: Johns Hopkins University Press.

Souffrant, E. M. (2000) *Formal Transgressions: John Stuart Mill's Philosophy of International Affairs*. Lanham, MD: Rowman and Littlefield.

Stoler, A.L. (1995) *Race and the Education of Desire: Foucault's History of Sexuality and the Colonial Order of Things*. Durham, NC and London: Duke University Press.

Wakefield, E. (1833) 'England and America', and (1834) 'Notes upon Wealth of Nations'. In Pritchard, Lloyd (ed.) (1968) *Collected Works of E.G.W. Wakefield*. Glasgow: Collins, pp. 93–117.

Younge, Gary (2005) 'Cruel and Usual: The Outrages at Camp Breadbasket are Consistent with British Colonial Rule – Brutal, Oppressive, and Racist'. *The Guardian* (1 March).

2

Empire, International Development & the Concept of Good Government[1]

VERNON HEWITT

Introduction

This chapter sets out to look at the term 'good government' and to examine its contemporary meaning in comparison with its usage during the British Empire (Robinson, 1994; Leftwich, 1996). It seeks to draw parallels in the use and evolution of the term, not as a matter of historical curiosity, but in order to increase awareness of the origins of this form of governmentality (or, as Duffield calls it, a liberal strategisation of power) and to highlight parallels with its contemporary use.

From the mid-1930s onwards, good government was improvised and redefined as a strategy of imperial control, following earlier attempts to 'control at a distance' through free markets, and then in the wake of various experiments with indirect rule using (or actually inventing) native administration. It then transformed itselfby a familiar transformation: from a simple belief in financial solvency and 'minimum' governance, through conceptions of trusteeship and self-governance, to an extraordinary commitment to social engineering and constitutional change. So redefined, good government sought to combine British economic interests, with both emergent humanitarian concerns and strategic competition for territory with other Powers. By the mid-1940s, the tenacity and elasticity of the term disguised differences of opinion and usage within the British Empire and within the international community. It was used both by Fabian socialists calling for a new charter of colonial welfare, and by leading conservatives of the day (notably by Malcolm Hailey 1939) as a propaganda tool to placate opponents of empire abroad by explicitly linking Empire to social and economic progress.

The re-emergence of the term began in the wake of the World Bank's 1994 report, *Governance and Development* (World Bank 1994a) and proceeded to evolve from then on. Applied with increasing sophistication throughout the 1990s, and by an increasing number of agencies and actors, the term good government continued to mutate from a technical debate about efficiency, transparency and anti-corruption strategies within an overall 'crude' market strategy, towards an implied process of democratisation and a softening of attitudes towards non-market institutions (World Bank 1996). Perhaps unintentionally, it informed a wider debate on new institutionalism and civil society. In general, good government is taken by many commentators on the Post-Washington Consensus to posit some relationship between capitalism and democracy. While it remains quintessentially free market, it conceptualises the problems of market failure, and recognises the wider socio-economic and cultural processes in which market transactions ought to be situated in order to be legitimate and successful.

Are these parallels merely coincidental, meaningless, or revealing of wider linkages between an understanding of Empire and the contemporary World system in which international development constitutes a vast array of institutions and actors, and provides a wide range of justifications for intervention? (Hardt and Negri 2000). In conclusion, this chapter argues that the international economic order maintained by the United States in complex interaction with international institutions, the European states, China and East Asia, etc., can and should be compared with the socio-economic management of the British Empire, not simply as an analogy, but as a derivative set of actors and agencies structured in part by the same ideology of development, and the same strategisation of power. As a project, international development can be defined as a product of empire, a universal language of 'improvement' and civilisation acted out through a series of complex – and contradictory – processes and interactions.

Colonial Usages of the Term Good Government

For the British, the term good government is associated with conceptions of liberty and the emergence of civil society during the sixteenth century (Greene 1999; Steele 1999). Good government had clear usagein the eighteenth century within wider Whig conceptions of the good life, and the perceived nature of British constitutionalism. It reflected a commitment to 'ancient' parliamentary privileges, the financial, legal and 'natural' responsibilities of a landed nobility, and a significant degree of local autonomy from central government and Crown privileges. Such prejudices structured views within Britain's elite of their own 'exceptionalism' – that is, the apparent superiority of English government over other European models (Porter 1982:14).

English liberties were, however, infused with the mistrust of popular government, and upheld notions of an enlightened elite defined by class, tradition and, increasingly, race. In origin, the ambiguity of good government's relationship to democracy is instructive. It exemplified the liberal concern over mass politics and majoritarianism, and the belief that specific classes were gifted to rule others for their *mutual* benefit. Extended abroad, the term shaped forms of colonial intervention in a variety of ways contingent on the configuration of geographical area and local and metropolitan interests.

After 1778, within the settler colonies, good government cautiously evolved towards representative assemblies – appointed and elected – working alongside colonial appointees (Holmes and Szechi 1993; Conway 1999). In areas of the so-called informal Empire, good government was initially defined with reference to free trade policies, and the general 'openness' of foreign economies to British traders (Lynn 1999). Following the collapse of 'legitimate trade' and the onset of annexation in South and South-East Asia, West and Southern Africa, the term good government became initially associated with indirect rule, as well as with trusteeship as a doctrine of social protection and conservation. Despite the apparent economic and strategic interests that compelled annexation, colonialism needed first and foremost to protect 'native' interest and its cultural and social way of life in order to be morally defensible. As such, until the late 1920s, good government informed the basic doctrines of Lugard's dual mandate, and the logic of indirect rule (Perham [1937]).

Yet there remained deep-seated controversies as to where native interests lay and how they should be articulated by good government as a policy (Metcalf 1994; Bayly 1996:365–76). Where colonialism drew native populations into a commercialised, increasingly economic and capitalist life, good government could not adequately shield indigenous societies from the impact of trade and the subsequent erosion of their traditional identities. Where it effectively created a dualist economy, with a modern sector in the hands of European traders and companies, and a subsistence-based peasant economy, colonialism arguably failed both its moral and socio-economic rational. By the mid-1930s, amid the evident squalor and under-provisioning of the 'Bantu' state model, it became increasingly argued that colonial authorities should provide indigenous society with the skills to benefit from the impact of trade and commerce, from urbanisation and from social migration. Anthropologists, field researchers and Christian activists in Africa were increasingly critical of the justification and ability of the British to protect 'traditional society', particularly from the modernising impact of capitalism and foreign trade, and especially in areas influenced by white settler interests (Beinart 1989). Such protection was good neither for imperial finances nor elite conceptions of moral responsibility, in that it abandoned indigenous society to a sort of traditional 'rural ideal' of increased poverty and squalor, and denied or sought to restrict peasant-based economic activity that would arguably compete with settler interests.

The period from 1929 until 1935 was one of widespread debate within Britain as to how best to run its colonies. Changes in attitude were also furthered by a slow-down within the British economy which acted to undermine social paternalism and widen the meanings and definitions of good governance. The after-effects of World War I generated overwhelming economic pressure to review colonial policy from the perspective of creating tangible gains for the British economy against enhanced European competition. As such, the British state was forced to re-evaluate explicitly the role that the colonial hinterland played in maintaining British industry, both with reference to potential raw materials and as a market for British goods. British colonial policy could no longer ignore the economic costs of defending (often unproductive) agrarian elites from the predations of local settler interests, and manipulating so-called 'native' authorities who were not interested in, or capable of, responding to changing economic needs. The pressures on colonial conservativism and preservation were further increased by World War II (Darwin 1988).

By the time of the Atlantic Charter in 1941, it was no longer a question of how Britain should administer its colonial empire, but why and on what moral basis it should have one at all. War and conflict changed not just the economic logic of Empire but also the moral framework in which Empire had to be defended. The World War I generated international regimes to uphold liberal (and potentially democratic) principles of intervention, and a growing agenda to hold imperial powers responsible for the development of their territories for eventual democratic self-rule (Louis 1984). The Mandates Commission of the League of Nations, although chaired successively by two key British imperialists (Lord Lugard, and then Lord Hailey), could not prevent international pressure from scrutinising – or seeking to clarify – the meaning of British policy.

The Paris Peace Treaty of 1919 established a broad principle of trusteeship under Article 22 of the League of Nations Covenant, which was applied to the Middle East, Tropical Africa and the island dependencies of the Pacific. Despite its limited application, Article 22 brought to the concept of trusteeship an implicit universal language of liberty and equality, and directly associated good government with notions of democracy and independence for the first time. The League provided a key forum in which British imperial concerns could be internationalised, especially with reference to the Middle East (Louis 1977; James 1994). During World War II, these ideas would feed directly into allied war aims, and the then founding of the United Nations.

This combination of economic and political pressure dramatically accelerated the pace of reform. Michael Lee has noted that, for the generation of British administrators that came of age in the 1930s, 'their most perplexing dilemma was whether to aid the transformation of colonial society or to preserve the traditional order' (Lee 1967:3). Facing growing economic crisis at home, and humanitarian criticisms from Christian, Labour and foreign governments – especially from the United States, the British opted to recast and enlarge the concept of good government in a radical direction to accommodate domestic and foreign critics. By 1941, the British official classes had undergone a total revolution in their ideas on development: 'The new development philosophy required more conscious and collective actions in preparing indigenous peoples for industrial and political life. It meant a commitment to the total, if gradual transformation of colonial society' (Lee *op.cit.*).

Lord Hailey & the *African Survey*

No colonial document better encapsulates this transformation than Hailey's *African Survey*, a near exhaustive study that reads both as an inventory of British possession and also as a statement of necessary reform. Hailey's work was the culmination of the inter-war generation's debates on the African problem, and on the future and responsibility of the empire (Cell 1992:217; Flint 1989:220). Hailey's undertaking was in essence the brainchild of Joseph H. Oldham, founder of the International Institute of African Languages and Cultures, and secretary to the British Missionary Society and the World Council of Churches. Oldham argued that, having failed to shield indigenous societies from the impact of capitalism, Britain's imperial responsibility lay in adequately – and thoroughly – preparing them to adapt to modernity. The concept of modernity as westernisation writ large had become part of the new meaning of trusteeship, one in which metropolitan and peripheral society were no longer seen as being in conflict, but a partnership within development. This emphasis on quality and team work shifted the post-war emphasis from Empire to a conscious use of the term Commonwealth, and ultimately the phrase 'commonwealth of nations'.

In 1933, the choice of Malcolm Hailey as potential director of the *Survey* appeared an odd one to spearhead a revolution in development thinking for Africa. Hailey (1872–1969) had spent his entire career in the Indian colonial service. His own conception of good government centred on identifying a prosperous yeomanry who could produce for the market, pay taxes for land settlement, and act as a respected and legitimate elite for an agrarian society. Hailey had experienced at first hand the need to offer responsible government to a growing urban social constituency, amid fears that the Indian middle-class intelligentsia would not prove representative of, or responsible to, social diversity (Darwin 1999; Cell 1999). Hailey accepted the post in 1934, and began consulting a wide range of non-state actors and pressure groups, such as activists working for the Fabian Colonial Bureau, the Empire Marketing Board, the Royal African Society and many missionary activists. He sought to create a consensus around a conception of good government that drew both the Right and the Left into a commitment to colonial reform. In doing so, it went a long way towards removing colonial issues from the heat and dust of British party politics, especially once the wartime coalition government collapsed after 1945. The *Survey* even found common ground with emergent nationalist opinion (Lee 1967:505).

Along with W.H. Macmillan and Oldham, and later views of Margery Perham, Hailey came to recognise that the peasant basis of African society established by indirect rule was part of a cycle of indebtedness and social poverty. The *Survey* set out, in stark terms, the belief that indirect rule was ideologically incompatible with British moral responsibility to develop self-rule, and also with British economic needs. In a talk at Chatham House in 1939, Hailey noted that 'It is the growing of cash crops, the earning of wages, the travelling back and forward to the mines that is the most potent solvent of the old customary life' (Hailey 1939:196). It was in managing this change, and not resisting it, that the future of the colonies and of Empire lay. The *Survey* called for administrative reform and devolution, capital investments in modern industry, the development of modern agricultural colleges and extension services, and a huge expansion in education, especially in the tertiary sector. It opened up what was to be a sustained and devastating attack on the principle of sequestering the natives away from the impact of colonialism. Land reform was necessary to remove obstacles to modernising African farming practices with greater individual access to resources and markets. Hailey was particularly concerned about the failure to define and enforce land tenure rights needed to encourage capitalist investment.

To sum up, by the 1940s good government had come to represent the totality of social and economic change, known later as westernisation and then modernisation (Rostow, 1990). Development now required the education of Africans to take their rightful place within their own administrations, and to gain valuable experience within the colonial civil service. Such an emphasis foresaw eventual self-government *within the empire*, in which individual colonies would be granted dominion status. The *Survey* reflected emerging views over the role of the state in economic management that were deemed as applicable to Africa as they were to Britain and the US. This would require enormous investment, carried out over an extended timeframe. Ideas of good government fed directly into the passing of a series of Colonial Development and Welfare (CDW) Acts from 1940 onwards. In the light of the *Survey*'s findings, these acts saw the need to reverse the flow of capital back to the colonies, and to include, where necessary, the cancellation of debt to London, especially where such repayments remained highly improbable and where, if made they discouraged capital investment in infrastructure and resources in specific colonies.

Yet while the onset of the war encouraged some of these trends, it miligated against others. Even contemporary critics noted that outward investment was undermined by assets frozen in London and used for the British balance of payments. Moreover, as Britain itself encountered capital scarcity, the sheer scale of the problem proved too much. It has been calculated that, from 1870 to 1938, a mere £1222 million had been sent in the African colonies, almost half of which had been borrowed by hard-up public authorities for non-development expenditure, and the rest as equity investment to the South African mines (cited in Rimmer 2000:239). From 1940 until 1944, Hailey himself presided over an advisory committee located within the Colonial Office that vetted proposed economic projects for Africa. In 1945 alone, the CDW Acts directed £120 million to Africa (Freund, 1998), but these tended to gravitate to specific colonial exports considered crucial for the build-up of dollar reserves (Lee 1967:31; Darwin 1988).

The weakness of the CDW Acts was not just in the scale of the capital investments undertaken, but in the modesty of their goals. The acts provided grants in aid for social development and specific small-scale projects that would not in themselves earn revenue, but which would provide solid foundations for (increasingly uncertain) future investment. Very little financial provision was made for 'national' or regional development projects, although resources were increased in 1950. The creation of the Nigerian Local Development Board in 1946 to assist local authorities to create small-scale industrial projects was typical of the ethos behind a development strategy that was some what brutally summarised as 'economics before politics and local before central'.

The links between local government, self-determination, and the gradual advancement towards 'national' democracy remained obscure in the *Survey* itself, as they did among the British official classes committed to policy formulation. Hailey expanded on these views in his Report on Native Administration and Political Development (Kirk-Greene 1979), and even here it was left to others to spell out exactly what democratic advancement might mean in policy terms. Hailey was prepared to commit British financial resources to construct and, where it already existed, to augment a social class able to manage an urban, industrialised economy in partnership with the metropolitan core. But detail was vague. Hailey was reluctant to specify what these wider democratic institutions would be and when exactly they would be put in place. He believed that the British must give the emergent elites within the dependent empire the chance to modernise their societies and reform their 'local' economic and political systems first, but the process of graduating to the national level was obscure.

In effect, the general use of the term good government from 1941 fudged the distinction between local and national, dominion status and independence, empire and Commonwealth. Lee states that 'Good Government was rarely defined in detail, although nationalist politicians were obliged to listen to frequent repetition of these two words which, by 1948, appeared in the Secretary of State for Colonial Affairs' own job description' (Lee 1967:13). This vacuity was full of risk. In conflating good government with self-government outside the settler/dominion context, the British were 'chasing two hares at once, good government meaning they must stay, and self government meaning they must quit' (Thornton 1999:619). Yet the conflating was in large part not the work of colonial reformers themselves, but of powerful actors within the international order (the US), and increasingly assertive sections of colonial and nationalist opinion within the dependent empire itself. Hailey's particularistic endorsement of good government was in fact a commitment to an open-ended reform process that the British would not be able to control (Flint 1983).

The political disruption created by education, social reform and the recognition of labour rights fuelled particular types of colonial resistance, even though it was designed to assist in the emergence of a modem and competent colonial elite (Falola and Roberts 1999). The British discovered that the empowerment of societies within the wider restrictive structures of empire, requiring as it did the *increase* in colonial supervision, led to a growing sense of impatience and potential violence. In such circumstances, and amid growing US hegemony, an emphasis on local government at the expense of national institutions could not be sustained. Where elite pressure was well developed, little interest was shown in local initiatives unless they provided a key route to the controlling of national institutions and state power. In such circumstances, and as British power failed, London was pressurised to make concessions to somewhat shadowy national bodies that had, in fact, rarely grown up from within local cultures or from emerging social movements.

From Good Government to International Development

Post-war conceptions of international development and industrialisation were the direct legatees of Britain's state-based project of socio-economic engineering. Development economics emerged into the 1960s committed to a dominant role for the state in the allocation of economic resources, reforming agriculture and directing social and political change. Colonial parastatal organisations and marketing boards were retained after independence, and primary exports were increased to pay for import substitution. The economic plan set out to diversify the economy and to complete the task of producing an integrated market that could provide consumers for internally produced goods as well as a citizenry able to pay taxes and participate in national democratic institutions. Although the political endgame of Rostow was not spelt out, it was evident that the post-'take-off' phase merely substituted conceited views on English exceptionalism with American views on their own constitution and its universal relevance.

Yet the inheritance could not bear the strain. Nationalist elites that came to power through the auspices of 'colonial reform' were incredibly limited, ethnically divided, and inexperienced. Their apprenticeship had been brutally shortened by the collapse of British power, as were the subsequent resources placed at their disposal (Fieldhouse, 1986; Leys, 1996). Lee cited a Colonial Office Memorandum of 1951 warning that 'too precipitate a rate of advance [in decolonisation] might result in handing over an immediate electorate consisting of a large number of more or less primitive [*sic*] people to a small number of the educated class who have insufficient experience to exercise power in a democratic manner' (Lee 1967:173). The elites' control of the state, the territorial basis of which was often open to question, lacked legitimacy in any meaningful civil society in the conventional Western sense of the term. As the principal economic hub, the state became the focus of serious ethnic rivalries and political violence, and economic activity slowed appreciably by the end of the 1960s (Chabal 1986; Clapham 1996; Mosley *et al* 1991).

In response to these failures, international development theory shifted towards a more market-based strategy that depicted the state as the main cause of socio-economic collapse. Through a series of macroeconomic policies aimed at removing the state and reducing the public sector, Structural Adjustment Programmes (SAPs) sought to restore international competitiveness and efficiency, and control over 'sovereign' governments was exercised through stringent economic conditions and the belief that reductions in social expenditure would restore equilibrium. Yet by the 1990s there was a growing, if mute, recognition within the Bretton Woods institutions themselves that the results of structural reform had been at best disappointing, at worst a singular failure.

It began, as a attempt within the neo-liberal paradigm, to address two analytical puzzles associated with the shift towards market supremacy. First, why had the private sector not been able to take advantage of the new policy environment? And, second, how was it possible to explain and thus accommodate public hostility to the SAPs? Taken together, both indicated a sustained attempt by the Bretton Woods institutions to evolve a more sophisticated and inclusive agenda for implementing pro-market strategies that would not prove hostile to regulation and investment, nor appear to be anti-democratic. The IFIs initiated an engagement with ideas of civil society and social capital, and acknowledged that restarting economic activity was not just about getting the prices right, but involved re-thinking what type of institutional support was needed to sustain market-based activity and how it could be brought about. Such a rethink implied *more* conditionality, not less, and a more intrusive form of intervention in aspects of broad socio-economic policy now defined as necessary for allowing markets to function. (Weiss and Gordenker 1996). Good government was a term that came, as it had during the British period, to encapsulate broad-based institutional reform aimed at political, economic and social improvement.

Two specific influences were important here, and again merit direct comparison with the processes that affected Hailey's *African Survey*. One was the rise of NGO activity that had, to a large extent, been mobilised around the failures of SAPs and the impact of structural adjustment policies on the poor (Chabal 1998; Makumbe 1998). The second influence could be traced to developments in international politics. Following the collapse of the Soviet Union, the UN assumed an increasingly assertive role, shifting away from what Weiss calls the Westphalian conception of sovereignty, which drew a stark line between domestic politics and foreign policy, towards an idea of sovereign responsibility that legitimated international concerns over issues such as human rights and the rule of law. Within international political forums, debates on global governance and the ethics of humanitarian intervention latched onto the term good governance as a means of promoting liberal political values and democratic forms of governance both in their own right and also as a necessary condition for market-based growth. Much liberal writing on globalisation also naively furthered the apparent twinning of capitalism and liberal democracy (Fukuyama 1992).

The combined result of NGO pressures and increased international concerns over democratisation pushed the World Bank's minimalist definition of good government in a new direction (Stiglitz 2002; Thirkell-White 2003). The emphasis on rolling back the state's role in economic activity shifted in the direction of more complex strategies. World Bank thinking started to debate the economic consequences of differing types of political regimes, the processes through which economic authority was exercised (and indeed legitimated), and the capacity of governments to design, implement and monitor the success of specific development policies (Weiss 2000). Despite the Bank's articles of association which prohibited it from adopting a more direct approach to 'politics', it nonetheless sought to extend institutional reform beyond economics (narrowly defined) to areas of civil society and local government. By the late 1990s, the World Bank was discussing the role that institution building could play in enabling *polities* to facilitate development – most notably in its 1997 *World Development Report*, which was subtitled *The State in a Changing World.*

The Policy Implications of Good Government

The moral and ethical connotations of the phrase good government encouraged NGOs to engage in more radical, 'political' activity, while creating an apparent overlap with thinking in the UN's increasing emphasis on 'sovereign responsibility', which sanctioned direct and sustained liberal intervention against irresponsible and 'failing' governments. Both NGO activity and UN-speak on responsible sovereignty stressed the centrality of good governance (Mingst and Karns 2000). Yet, like the British term in the late 1940s, the shift within the international financial institutions towards a social and political agenda for development was never free from wider concerns with international financial stability and the need to ensure global growth, and the conviction that globalisation was a virtuous circle for all national economies, despite increasing evidence that suggested the vulnerability of African economies to globalisation and underlined the weakness of global institutions themselves to direct sustained intervention into their domestic affairs.

Between 1997 and 2003 the World Bank expanded its conception of good government to touch on wider and overtly political aspects of reform, especially during Joseph Stiglitz's tenure as the Bank's chief economist (Weiss 2000:803). The 1997 *World Development Report* (*WDR*) spoke candidly of the need for state institutions to support the growth of markets and, with reference to the East Asian 'tigers', saw the importance of regulatory structures to monitor markets during periods of adjustment and instability. Criticism shifted from the state to the need to replicate, where possible, the variant of the developmental state that had supported the East Asian miracle. Significantly, the report recognised that there may well be a rationale for an increase in state *capacity* to ensure the delivery of high-quality services, implying a necessary increase in the state's resource-base as well (Harriss *et al.* 1995). Indeed, the Asian financial crisis of 1997 highlighted the benefit of short-term capital controls in moments of crisis and the need for strong financial regulatory structures to prevent collapse.

From 1998 onwards, additional ideas were attached to the agenda of good governance. In the 1999/2000 *WDR*, subtitled *Entering the 21st Century* (World Bank 2000), the Bank consciously summarised its views on good government as 'socially inclusive and responsive processes' of decision-making. Its goal was the transformation of *over-centralised* states through the empowering of sub-national and local governments. The report also emphasised the importance of NGOs, seeing them as a promising facet of civil society capable of pressuring states to take account of public concerns. The Bank also noted the need to cancel external debt where there was no hope that it would be repaid, and where the resulting debt overhang discouraged economic activity or the ability to restructure specific institutions – a point which would have been well understood by Hailey, and which led to a series of conditional high debt cancellation programmes.

Both the 2002 and the 2004 WDR returned to, and elaborated, these themes, which represented a widening and deepening of the idea of good governance to the point where it seemed almost to breach the neo-liberal obsession with the market itself. In practice, however, there was significant disagreement within the Bank over the degree of emphasis on institutional reform and rebuilding, as well as between the World Bank and the IMF, and between the senior Bank management and the US Treasury (Stiglitz 2002). Many NGOs were increasingly critical of what they saw as the World Bank's cooptation of the good government concept: the Bank was seen as having adopted the term to increase its control over aid-recipient states as well as over the international development agenda more broadly. It was critically seen as a way of deepening neo-liberalism, not abandoning it. Yet, whatever its agenda, the World Bank could not prevent others from seeing good government as a call for, and an instrument of, democratisation. Many NGOs and bilateral donors advocated electoral reform, press freedom, constitutional change and social pluralism well ahead of the Bank's cautious agenda on local government, tax reform and changes to the regulation of state-owned assets.

These tensions closely resembled those played out during the closing stages of British colonial rule. It is instructive to recall that Lord Hailey spent a great deal of his time trying to sell British colonial policy to the Americans by emphasising democratisation and downplaying the attempt to reconstitute and secure British power. Like British colonial reform, World Bank thinking on decentralisation had to stress its administrative rather than political role, despite the fact that local government reform was almost always conceived of as democratic decentralisation, in which local bodies would be elected. Ironically, the need for this fig leaf was grounded in the fears (of radicalism and social violence) expressed by aid-recipient states. Yet until central institutions were reformed, local government was unlikely to radically alter the terms of either social or political relations. Indeed, NGOs pointed out that unless the World Bank was prepared to monitor and enforce demands for democratic inclusion, local government structures were easily subverted by elites and resources directed away from the poor.

Again, like earlier British initiatives, the language of participation and empowerment risked inciting dissent over policies. Radical thinkers argued that, like British ideas on good government, the Bretton Woods institutions could never commit themselves to a genuinely democratic agenda because it would undermine their own hegemony and expose the contradictions between global capitalism and the welfare of people in post-colonial states (Greene 2004). Just as the British could not square for themselves the tensions between empire and democracy, the World Bank and the IMF have found it difficult to reconcile the interests of global capitalism with the needs of African states, and the nature of the state as it had emerged in colonial and post-colonial Africa. Perhaps the most substantial parallel with the British experience is the paucity of theorising about the precise relationship between capitalism and democracy within the term good government, as well as the place of good government within wider debates on globalisation.

This confusion is critical, in that the Bank, like the British, seeks not only to empower but also to control, and sees no contradiction between the economic and political processes of change it is encouraging. As Ursula Hicks remarked over the scope of colonial reform in Africa in the 1940s, 'defined as democracy, good governance was distressingly naive, implying that local government is a good thing, and that economic development is a good thing, and that their common virtues draw them together' (Hicks cited in Lee 1967:186). It was even more naive when envisaged as a historical dynamic for the still recently formed states of sub-Saharan Africa in an era of global capital. Johnson has recently remarked that

> Perhaps the most deceptive aspect of globalisation [is] its claim to embody fundamental and inevitable technological developments rather than the conscious policies of Anglo-American political elites trying to advance the interests of their own countries at the expense of others. (Johnson 2004:260)

This is a point that could be made directly with reference to British 'expert' aid after 1938. There is more than a passing resemblance between the language and layout of the *Survey* and the ostensibly 'non-ideological' nature of the *Reports*. Even the 1997 *Report's* comments on the newly industrialising countries NICs had avoided a debate on the exact role the state had played in the East Asian miracle, and the cultural and social variables that might make the difference between a strong and a weak state. Cut off from wider academic debates over the causal relationship between capitalism and democracy, civil society and the state, the World Bank used the term good government to indicate an alleged consensus on the development process as objective and neutral. (Harriss 2001).

The democratisation project implicit within the term good government also remains profoundly ethno-centric and conditional on capitalism, despite its commitment to seeing institutions in specific regional and cultural contexts. British ideas on social engineering in the African colonies were undertaken with the minimum amount of knowledge about local cultures and customs, and with an overall philosophy based on European experience' (Lee 1967:186) and stress economic growth at all costs. Much the same could be said of contemporary scholarship on the subject. There is little evidence that the new approach has really influenced development thinking. Rather, it reasserts the old orthodoxy that rationalised external intervention, firstly through the markets. In this regard, current thinking on good government is the unacknowledged offspring of British colonial reform, and a modem manifestation of even older notions of trusteeship and responsible government devised for Africa by international powers.

Conclusions

The use of the term good government as devised by the British colonial authorities in the early twentieth century is remarkably similar to the term used by the World Bank from the early 1990s onwards. Without acknowledgement or attribution, the term underwent a parallel trajectory in each of these two periods, from a technical, minimalist definition towards a more expansive, social and institutional conception of development. Like the British, the Bank sought to 'depoliticise' the term by stressing technical issues such as legal reform, local and 'regional' institution building, and public sector reform. In seeking to grasp the links between market reform, political institution building and the successful development of capitalism, the World Bank, like the British, sought to invoke good governance as the missing link capable of establishing a virtuous circle, in which capitalism and democracy become mutually self-reinforcing within a global market. More broadly defined, the development community has rearticulated this ambitious 'colonial' agenda of socio-economic change, *despite* the change in international context, away from the hegemony of ideas on Empire towards an system of sovereign, interdependent states.

Is this significant, or is like being compared with unlike? Do these similarities disguise underlying differences between what is being compared? There are obvious differences between these periods that also need to be recognised. It is *not* being suggested, for example, that the international financial institutions are a formal Empire, with the US economy at the hub. The Bretton Woods institutions obviously lack the monopoly of territorial control that the British had, and their membership remains formally equal between nation states. Yet territorial control is not itself a precondition for empire. Indeed ongoing colonial historiography has long questioned the efficiency of direct control over the informal but arguably cheaper structures of markets and trade (Lynne 1999).

While their control of capital (and the role of the Bank and the IMF as gate keepers to the flow of international private capital and investment) is obvious, their position over the implementation of policy in recipient states is less direct, and much evidence suggests the existence of 'slippage' or imaginative non-compliance with donor conditionality. Weiss has noted that the IMF controls a mere four per cent of global liquidity, yet this disregards its hegemonic ability to direct private capital flows and to pitch its influence against states that can be disciplined not by gun boats but by capital flight. In this regard the financial resources of the Bretton Woods institutions are massive compared with those of Britain from the mid-1930s onwards, and the fact that they are made operational in a radically different context of global capital in which ideas of empire cannot be publicly supported, or territory annexed and controlled, is arguably much less significant than it at first appears.

Recent historical revisionism on the British empire has stressed the de-centred nature of political and social control, and the sheer hybridity of cultural forms that shaped both the colonial and metropolitan milieus. Even a clear and sustained emphasis on the economic rationale of empire is hard to sustain free from ideas of trusteeship and international responsibility, elements the British took seriously as part of their mission in different places and at different times. In terms of the nature of governance, and the strategisation of power, the British Empire was not homogenous, hermetically sealed, or capable of being directly coerced. The use and differentiation of the term good governance perfectly illustrate this and were integral to the operation of that power.

Likewise in the 1990s, the dynamics that led to a widening scope of conditionality towards a more open-ended, ideological agenda, can be seen as attempting to further the controlling position of the Bretton Woods institutions while simultaneously making these institutions vulnerable to outside forces. The issue is again one of power. When the British undertook the restructuring of their colonies they were in decline, and their power was swiftly ebbing. This decline explained both the language of colonial reform and its failure. Does the same dynamic hold true for the US, and/or the powers of the World Bank and the IMF in the opening decades of the twenty-first century? Is the shift in the meaning of the term good government evidence of a crisis within globalisation, a reorientation of policy to ensure that it continues?

It would be intriguing to press for a more explicit debate on the utility of empire as an analytical tool for understanding the role of the IFIs. Current scholarship is in ferment with regard to former empires and their contributions to the modem world, as much as over the role of the US in the twenty-first century (Ferguson 2004). It was common in the 1960s to discuss empire as a form of US neo-colonialism, in which the US strove to ensure, through Soviet containment and a universal commitment to democracy, a world safe for global capital and, within a capitalist order, its own national interest. Recent work has reiterated these themes, including the idea that the US strives, especially, to articulate its own particular capitalist interests as vital for global peace and stability (Harvey 2003). In some specific debates, Empire is no longer even a bogy word, but reclaimed to its seventeenth-century usage as enlightened and civilised union. It becomes a synonym of a modernised 'civilised' power whose power for good is undermined only by a perverse Anglo-American habit of needless introspection (Roberts 2006).

As with ancient Rome, conceptions of the 'modern west' are seen by most of those who live within it as synonymous with the civilised democratic world. Outside are barbarians who, if they attack or reject the Empire, can be motivated only by envy, bitterness, the refusal to accept the obvious superiority of its values. And those values are superior not for any ethnocentric or nationalist reason. On the contrary, their greatness lies in their universality. (Howe 2002:116–117)

Hardt and Negri's unusual book *Empire* suggests that international relations in an era of globalisation is moving 'back' towards a de-centred 'empire', defined as a civilisational idea premised on access to universal norms of citizenship made flesh through the UN and other institutions of global governance. Unlike previous orders, contemporary empire is defined by inclusion and participation through novel forms of government and information flow. It is profoundly misleading, Hardt and Negri maintain, to read this version of empire merely as a form of US hegemony or even as necessarily 'imperialist' (Hardt and Negri 2000). Central to their understanding of this emerging form of order are the powers of the Bretton Woods institutions and their links with other international organisations as well as transnational NGOs and social movements. Empire here is reclaimed, indirectly, not as a hierarchical or ethnically exclusive order, but again in terms of Roman cultural synergy and mobility. Moreover, Empire, like Marx's praise of capitalism, restores a specific dialectic to ideas of social change and progress that are replete with crisis and contradiction but also potential. There is, oddly, a curious convergence between left-wing historiography and politics on Empire and current liberal and even right-wing debates on global capitalism, that has been brought about, in the main, by the use of the term good government itself.

If such a thing were possible, Hailey, and the generation of British colonial officials who came of age between 1937 and 1957 would understand immediately why such a convergence has taken place.

Bibliography

Bayly, C.A. (1996) *Empire and Information: Intelligence Gathering and Social Communication in India 1780–1870*. Cambridge: Cambridge University Press.

Beinart, W. (1989) 'W.M. Macmillan's Analysis of Agrarian Change and African Rural Communities'. In Macmillan, H. and Marks, S. (eds) *Africa and Empire. Macmillan, Historian and Social Critic*. London: Temple Smith, pp. 68–191.

Cell, J.W. (1992) *Hailey: A Study in British Imperialism 1872–1969*. Cambridge: Cambridge University Press.

Cell, J.W. (1999) 'Colonial Rule'. In Brown, J. and Louis, W. R. (eds) *Oxford History of the British Empire: Volume IV The Twentieth Century*. Oxford: Clarendon Press, pp. 232–54.

Chabal, P. (ed.) (1986) *Political Domination in Africa: Reflection on the Limits of Power*. Cambridge: Cambridge University Press.

Chabal, P. (1998) 'A Few Considerations on Democracy in Africa'. *International Affairs* 74(2): 289–304.

Clapham, C. (1996) *Africa and the International System: The Politics of State Survival*. Cambridge: Cambridge University Press.

Conway, S. (1999) 'Britain and the Revolutionary Crisis 1763–1791'. In Marshall, P.J. (ed.) *Oxford History of the British Empire: Volume II The Eighteenth Century*. Oxford: Clarendon Press, pp. 325–46.

Darwin, J. (1988) *Britain and Decolonisation: The Retreat from Empire in the Post War World*. London: Macmillan.

Darwin, J. (1999) 'A Third British Empire? The Dominion Idea in British Politics'. In Brown, J. and Louis, W.R. (eds) *Oxford History of the British Empire: Volume IV. The Twentieth Century*. Oxford: Clarendon Press, pp. 64–87.

Escobar, A. (2004) 'Beyond the Third World: Imperial Globality, Global Coloniality and Anti-globalisation Social Movements'. *Third World Quarterly*. 25(1): 207–30.

Falola, T. and Roberts, A.D. (1999) 'West Africa'. In Brown, J. and Louis, W.R. (eds) *Oxford History of the British Empire: Volume IV The Twentieth Century*. Oxford: Clarendon Press, pp. 515–29.

Ferguson, N. (2004) *Colossus: The Rise and Fall of the American Empire*. London: Allen Lane.

Fieldhouse, D.K. (1986) *Black Africa 1945–1980 Economic Decolonisation and Arrested Development*. London: Unwin Hyman.

Flint, J.E. (1983) 'The Failure of Planned Decolonisation in Africa'. *African Affairs* 82: 398–411.

Flint, J.E. (1989) 'Macmillan as a Critic of Empire: The Impact of a Historian on Colonial Policy'. In Macmillan, H. and Marks, S. (eds) *Africa and Empire: H.M. Macmillan. Historian and Social Critic*. Aldershot: University of London Press, pp. 212–31

Freund, B. (1998) *The Making of Contemporary Africa: The Development of African Society since 1800*. Basingstoke: Macmillan.

Fukuyama, F. (1992) *The End of History and the Last Man*. London: Hamilton.

Greene, J.P. (1999) 'Empire and Identity from the Glorious Revolution to the American Revolution'. In Marshall, P.J. (ed.) *Oxford History of the British Empire: Volume II. The Eighteenth Century*. Oxford: Clarendon Press, pp. 208–30.

Hailey, M. (1939) 'Some Problems Dealt with in *The African Survey*'. *International Affairs* 18(3):194–210.

Hardt, M. and Negri, A. (2000) *Empire*. Cambridge, MA: Harvard University Press.

Harriss, J. (2001) *Depoliticizing Development: The World Bank and Social Capital*. New Delhi: Leftword.

Harriss, J., Hunter, J. and Lewis, C. (eds) (1995) *The New Institutional Economics and Third World Development*. London: Routledge.

Harvey, D. (2003) *The New Imperialism*. Oxford: Clarendon Press.

Holmes, G. and Szechi, M. (1993) *The Age of Oligarchy: Pre-Industrial Britain 1722– 1783*. London: Longmans.

Hopkins, A.G. (1999) 'Development and the Utopian Ideal 1960–199?'. In Winks, R.W. (ed.) *Oxford History of the British Empire: Volume VI Historiography*. Oxford: Clarendon Press, pp. 635–52.

Howe, S. (2002) *Empire: A Very Short Introduction*. Oxford: Clarendon Press.

James, L. (1994) *The Rise and Fall of the British Empire*. New York: Little, Brown & Company.

Jenkins, R. (2001) *Churchill*. Basingstoke: Macmillan.

Johnson, C. (2004) *The Sorrows of Empire: Militarism, Secrecy and the End of the Republic*. London: Verso Press.

Kiernan, V. (1969) *The Lords of Human Kind: European Attitudes to Other Cultures in the Imperial Age.* London: Weidenfeld & Nicolson.

Kirk-Greene, A.H. (ed.) *Africa in the Colonial Period: The Transfer of Power.* Oxford: Committee for African Studies.

Lee, J.M. (1967) *Colonial Development and Good Government: A Study in the Ideas Expressed by the British Official Classes in Planning Decolonisation 1939–1964.* Oxford: Clarendon Press.

Leftwich, A. 1996 (ed.) *Democracy and Development: Theory and Practice.* Cambridge: Polity Press.

Leys, C. (1996) *The Rise and Fall of Development Theory.* Oxford: James Currey.

Louis, W.R. (1977) *Imperialism at Bay 1941–1945: The United States and the Decolonisation of the British Empire.* Oxford: Clarendon Press.

Louis, W.R. (1984) 'The Era of the Mandates System and the Non-European World'. In Bull, H. and Watson, A. (eds) *The Expansion of International Society.* Oxford: Clarendon Press, pp. 201–16.

Lynn, M. (1999) 'British Policy, Trade and Informal Empire in the Mid-Nineteenth Century'. In Porter, A. (ed.) *Oxford History of the British Empire: Volume III The Nineteenth Century.* Oxford: Clarendon Press, pp 101–21.

Makumbe, J.M. (1998) 'Is There a Civil Society in Africa'. *International Affairs* 74(2): 305–18.

Metcalf, T.R. (1994) *Ideologies of the Raj.* Cambridge: Cambridge University Press.

Mingst, K. and Karns, M. (eds) (2000) *The United Nations in the Post Cold War Era.* Boulder, CO: Westview Press.

Mosley, P., Harrigan, J. and Toye, J.F.J. (eds) (1991) *Aid and Power: The World Bank and Policy Based Lending. Vol. One.* London: Routledge.

Perham, M. ([1937]1962) *Native Administration in Nigeria.* Oxford: Oxford University Press.

Porter, A. (1999a) 'Trusteeship and Humanitarianism'. In Porter, A. (ed.) *Oxford History of the British Empire: Volume III The Nineteenth Century.* Oxford: Clarendon Press, pp. 198–221.

Porter, A. (1999b) 'Religion, Missionary Enthusiasm and Empire'. In Porter, A. (ed.) *Oxford History of the British Empire: Volume III The Nineteenth Century.* Oxford: Clarendon Press, pp. 222–46.

Porter, R. (1982) *England in the Eighteenth Century.* London: Allen Lane.

Rich, P.B. (1986) *Race and Empire in British Politics.* Cambridge: Cambridge University Press.

Rimmer, D. (2000) 'African Development in Economic Thought'. In Rimmer, D. and Kirk-Greene, A. (eds) *The British Intellectual Engagement with Africa in the Twentieth Century.* London: Macmillan, pp. 231–60.

Roberts, A. (2006) *A History of the English Speaking Peoples Since 1900.* London: Folio Society.

Robinson, M. (1994) 'Governance, Democracy and Conditionality: NGOs and the New Policy Agenda'. In *Governance, Democracy and Conditionality.* Oxford: INTRAC, International NGO Training and Research Centre, pp. 119–30.

Rimmer, D. (2000) 'African Development in Economic Thought'. In Rimmer, D. and Kirk-Greene, A. (eds) *The British Intellectual Engagement with Africa in the Twentieth Century.* Basingstoke: Macmillan, pp. 231–60.

Rostow, W.W. (1990) *The Stages of Economic Growth: A Non-Communist Manifesto.* Cambridge: Cambridge University Press.

Steele, I.K. (1999) 'The Anointed, the Appointed and the Elected: Governance of the British Empire 1689–1784'. In Marshall, P.J. (ed.), *Oxford History of the British Empire: Volume II The Eighteenth Century.* Oxford: Clarendon Press, pp. 105–27.

Stiglitz, J. (2002) *Globalisation and its Discontents.* Harmondsworth: Penguin Books.

Thirkell-White, B. (2003) 'The IMF, Good Governance and Middle-income Countries'. *The European Journal of Developmental Research* 15(1):90–125.

Thornton, A.P. (1999) 'The Shaping of Imperial History'. In: Winks, R.W. (ed.) *Oxford History of the British Empire: Volume V Historiography.* Oxford: Clarendon Press, pp. 612–34.

Weiss, T. and Gordenker, L. (eds) (1996) *NGOs, the UN and Global Governance.* Boulder, CO: Lynne Rienner.

Weiss, W.G. (2000) 'Governance, Good Governance and Global Governance: Conceptual and Actual Challenges'. *Third World Quarterly.* 21(5): 795–814.

World Bank (1994a) *Governance and Development.* Washington, DC: World Bank.

World Bank (1994b) *Adjustment in Africa: Reform, Results and the Road Ahead.* Oxford: Oxford University Press.

World Bank (1996) *World Development Report 1996: From Plan to Market.* Washington, DC: World Bank.

World Bank (1997) *World Development Report 1997: The State in a Changing World.* Washington, DC: World Bank.

World Bank (1998) *Assessing Aid: What Works, What Doesn't, and Why.* Oxford: Oxford University Press.

World Bank (2000), *World Development Report 1999/2000: Entering the 21st Century.* Oxford: Oxford University Press.

Note

1 Hewitt, V.M. (2006) 'A Cautionary Tale: Colonial and Post-Colonial Conceptions of Good Government and Democratisation in Africa', *Commonwealth and Comparative Studies* 44 (1): 32–48.

3

Empire: A Question of Hearts? *The Social Turn in Colonial Government, Bombay c.*1905–1925

HENRIK ASPENGREN

Introduction

By the turn of the twentieth century, British colonial government in Bombay became serious about sustaining the life of its subjected population, rather than treating it with indifference. The shift was not clear-cut. But the records produced by British administrators and their Indian colleagues tell of an emerging social sensibility and a growing concern over social conditions. This concern stuck with colonial state discourse up until a more repressive agenda began to sideline it by the mid-1920s. So, at this juncture, not at all brief in time, colonial officials in Bombay began to use a social vocabulary, engage social projects, and implement socially informed legislation. They did so as they grappled with how to govern a modern, yet colonial, industrial society. They did not, however, believe in political self-government and freedom for the Indians. Among administrators in Bombay, and in the British Empire more generally, colonial government was not in question. On the contrary: empire was still seen as the best way to organise India's inter-national and domestic political and commercial relations.

Yet slowly, under the period here under review, views of the imperial connection with India were being rethought by some of those thinking about the working of the colonial state. In their view, social reform under colonial rule could enhance progress in India. And sifting through the archives produced at this time, reveals that colonial governments now began elaborating agendas of state-guided reform of the social environment, manifested by programmes of housing, sanitation and primary education. As the then Under Secretary of State for India put it, empire was becoming 'not a question of land, but of hearts' (Montagu [1912] 1917). In what follows I shall explore how the entering of a social language in colonial state discourse, and the elaboration of socially informed colonial policies, formed a part of a globalising approach stressing the need for reform of the social environment. This kind of movement is often analysed in terms of how the colonial state in India enforced disciplinary power and domination through 'social control' (Legg 2007). But, at this time the colonial state struggled to do more than simply dominate – if by domination we mean to ignore or attempt to crush the capacity for action of the dominated.

Therefore, I also intend to indicate how the ideology which sustained this turn to the social, as well as the design of actual and placed policy, began to expand the limits of political power. In other words, when the modern colonial state formalised the social domain for whatever reason, and included it in its repertoire, it acknowledged a space for politics within that domain (Rose 1999:114–17). Ideas about how to govern effectively began at this time to recognise a capacity for action of the governed, in this case colonised, population, within a social space. The ability to adjust governing practices to this capacity became an objective of colonial state discourse. In order to carry this out, to govern now implied trying to understand what mobilises the population – and then act upon those issues and forces (Rose *op. cit.*:4). In colonial Bombay social concern was a very real foundation for popular mobilisation in the minds of colonial administrators. In order for them to govern this situation successfully, it became imperative to act, perhaps only rhetorically, upon the social environment.

Subsequently, the first section of this chapter will discuss the social-political thought and political language which underpinned the turn to the social. By revisiting the formation of ideology and political language at this juncture, we step right into a contemporary debate which helped to shape what was then seen as the limits to what was politically possible (Skinner 1998:104–6). The line of thought discussed in this section emerged in the latter part of the nineteenth century. It was embraced by a large section of liberal and socialist thinkers and practitioners. Their views on the social reform of modern industrial society entered discussions about imperial relations as an extension of the classically conceived moral commitment of the British in India. However, the limit to what was politically possible did not only take shape through principles parcelled out by elevated thinkers. It was also formed through the friction generated when those principles engaged a grounded socio-historical reality (Mehta 1999:9–10). The reality with which this socially informed ideology engaged was highly imperial, and, partly as a consequence of the connections of empire, marked by the globalisation of modern industrial society (Bayly 2004). Therefore, in the second section of the chapter, I shall highlight one instance where ideas of how to govern a colonial industrial society through socially informed policy were actually projected, materialised and embedded. The chapter will discuss educational, legislative and spatial projects which came out of this social turn between 1905 and 1925 in the Bombay Presidency – the most industrialised area in the most important British colony.

Social Reform & Colonial Government

The wide tradition of thought and practice which may best be categorised as British liberalism developed in close relation to the proliferation and consolidation of the second British Empire. With lineages in seventeenth-century republican thought feeding into eighteenth-century ideas about freedom under commercial empire, this process of mutual constitution between liberal ideas and empire fermented over the nineteenth century (Sartori 2006). Sometimes in dissent, but often enough supportive, this relationship became embodied and expressed by towering nineteenth-century British liberal thinkers like Jeremy Bentham and James and John Stuart Mill (Pitts 2005). In the late nineteenth century, continuing in the first quarter or so of the twentieth – a period connecting the dusk of high imperialism with the dawn of decolonisation – British liberal thought, action and governing practices were partly reformulated. From this reformulation emerged a socially orientated strand of liberalism which greatly influenced the politics of the time (Cain 2002).

This form of British thought acknowledged the fabric of society put under stress by the entrenchment of the modern industrial system. Now activists and commentators, many of whom oscillated between socialist and liberal positions, contrary to their recent tradition, found much more extensive social interventions justified. Initially, this socially informed liberalism claimed to identify and act upon social evils, and found in state-led social reform one of its more defining expressions. Very soon, however, this line of thought turned into a distinct view of progress, freedom, civics and ethics, stressing the need for a moral and practical reformation of society. Ideologically it went beyond contemporary views of mere amelioration of the conditions of the poor. Instead, in an original way, its more theoretically informed proponents conceived of a distinct social domain as a location for the realisation of freedom for the whole of society. This social focus called for nuanced social thought and, in the field of action, an elaborate social policy in order to 'govern from a social point of view' (Rose 1999:114–33).

Alarmed by the squalor of modern industrial society, political commentators began to question why, in their view, material progress did so little to create a morally advanced and socially orientated society. Instead, they found that years of rapid development of modern industry had not improved, but rather worsened, the conditions under which society evolved (Hobson 1920). New surveys of industrial towns in Britain provided telling evidence, they argued, that conditions actually arrested progress. Acknowledging that there was something wrong in the working of the industrial system itself, political observers found that, in order to enhance development, a moral and material reformation of society was needed. Keen observers of contemporary society, such as the members of the Sociological Society, combined biology, statistics and ethnography with social philosophy into the new discipline 'sociology' – the 'science of society' (Collini 1980). Sociology provided both a methodology and an ideational framework for action-oriented policy. This was also the purpose of the first sociological department in British India, which was established inside Bombay University soon after World War I and was led by a member of the Sociological Society, Professor Patrick Geddes (Hazareesingh 2000).[1]

Consequently, beginning in the late nineteenth century, liberal concepts of 'freedom' and 'progress' came to operate within a new discourse of social reform. This discourse was self-conscious and sensitive to the socio-historical context in which it took shape, and a wide group of practitioners and thinkers dispersed it through the liberal press. The wide scope of the reform agenda elaborated at this time actually expressed a significant expansion of liberal frameworks (Alden 1919). The shift concerned the central conceptualisation of how societal progress would actually come about. With the emergence of a more socially informed liberalism and its practical action-oriented reform agenda, focus was expanding from individual self-development to the collective development of conditions as a prerequisite for individual self-development. It was argued that, unless the conditions in which the individual acted were improved, individual self-development was of little use. Subsequently, it was becoming a shared notion among liberal commentators in the early twentieth century that social progress was dependent not only on the reduction of constraints on the individual, but also on the possibilities for all to engage actively and wholly in social life. Only through collective effort would individuals be able to realise their full potential (Muirhead 1910). Societal progress had become a social affair, demanding the active participation of the state (Hobhouse 1966). However, the way socially oriented liberals and other reformers conceptualised 'social reform' was multidimensional, and often vague. The meaning given to the concept could include technical ideas of how to ameliorate the conditions of the poor and labouring classes through housing and education, as well as philosophical discussions of how to bring long-term material and moral progress to the whole of society. Reform practitioners began to view social reform as an ongoing process – and as such never fully realisable. And so, the reformation of the social domain turned into an end in itself; it became an ethical process as much as a social-political one (Hobhouse 1911:41).

For a commentator like Robert Gunn Davis it was modern commerce and industrialisation, by materialising tastes and entrenching inequalities, that 'have created impediments to moral and intellectual awakening, and so the development of widespread social freedom and happiness' (Davis 1909). This, in turn, had developed into a full-blown obstacle to progress; and this obstacle lay not in the political organisation of contemporary industrial society. In fact, Davis was not at all enthusiastic about democratic reforms (Davis 1911). Nor was it an economic problem which impeded development; it was a 'social problem'. This 'social problem' had to be resolved at its root causes through the use of political power. And it was here, he argued, that the charity-oriented nineteenth-century liberal conceptualisations of social amelioration went wrong. They did not systematically and scientifically attack the social evils preying on social relations in modern industrial society.

Davis found that 'the self-sacrificing labours of many of these good people have been in vain, and have seriously hindered reform'. The social problems, he suggested, could not subsequently be resolved at the level of the individual, by, for example, doling out food or clothing to the poor. Instead, the problem to be solved was 'chiefly a problem of conditions, and not a problem of individual regeneration apart from or independent of conditions' (Davis 1906). The close connection between human development and the development of conditions in which humans act underpinned an action-oriented agenda, including demands for minimum wages secured by the state, the nationalisation of certain industries,the improvement of housing conditions, and a minimum of economic security for workers and their families in the case of accidents. But it also included calls for creating 'minimum opportunity for the development of human personality', expressed through the shortening of working hours (Rowntree 1919).

How, then, did the social turn described above relate to the grounded socio-historical realities of the British Empire? Clearly, empire in relation to social development in industrialising societies continued to be debated in the wider liberal press of the time (Himmelfarb 1994:44). And both the so-called Morley-Minto and Montagu-Chelmsford reforms, aimed at changing very moderately the political organisation of British rule on the Indian subcontinent, spurred debates over India's 'level' of social development in relation to the possibility of its becoming politically self-governing.

Generally speaking, just government could not be guaranteed within an extensive empire, according to those who were anti-imperialist on principle. Moreover, such an empire threatened the stability of Britain in two ways. First, it naturally militarised government, as new areas were conquered by the sword, rather than trade (Armitage 2000:142). Also, they argued, homecoming administrators and officials had no sense or experience of democratic politics from their practice in the colonies or dependencies, and they therefore corrupted political relations on their return to Britain. A second argument against imperialism was that empire diverted interest to imperial relations from the pressing need for social reform in Britain itself (Hobhouse 1908). Yet many British liberals still found empire in general and British rule in India to be a moral commitment (Harris 1917).

Although they had done so already during the Evangelical reformist phase of the 1820s–30s, now, in the late nineteenth century, the emphasis on religiosity had slowly given way to a stress on secular moral action (Metcalf 1995:28–65). Indeed, this moral impulse was recognised by active imperialist practitioners as a 'secular religion, embodying the most sacred duty of the present' (Curzon 1908). It was with reference to this secularised morality that calls for the socialisation of policy in the empire became attached. This notion was expressed by the prominent liberal coterie The Rainbow Circle, when it met for its session in 1899–1900.

The theme for the session was 'Liberalism and Imperialism' (Rainbow Circle [1899–1900] 1989:70). Herbert Louis Samuel, Liberal Party man and writer, who later became High Commissioner for Palestine between 1920 and 1925, opened the discussion on 'Imperialism in relation to Social Reform'. Samuel describes two ways which make 'Empire the most valuable ally of Social Reform'. The argument he produced was of the economic as well as moral kind. First, he says, colonial expansion improves England's trade position. The creation of wealth contributes to the national ability to reduce poverty in England. Secondly, the empire 'subserves the welfare of other peoples. We can protect small nations from attack or govern them, giving them the fruits of our own experience...In the white colonies the Empire serves as a cause of social reform by protecting them; in other cases...it uplifts the native' (*ibid*:74). Thus with an active reformist policy, members of the Circle argued, these could be developed, between 'ourselves & our subject peoples', a bond of 'moral responsibility – a kind of imperial strength which no other empire has enjoyed' (*ibid*:71).

It was partly through social programmes in the globalising industrial society that this lofty ideal would find its practical application. Socially informed commentators of the early twentieth century began to describe empire as a platform for launching, in their view, progressive social projects as an extension of the programmes attempted in Britain. It took only a few years of social legislation and action in Britain for commentators in the liberal press to proclaim that 'interest in humanity need not stop with the shores of England'. Instead, they found that '[e]mpire offers a magnificent field for social experiment' and that 'Liberal Imperialism goes hand in hand with social reform' (Cook 1914). These commentators attached to both empire as an ideal, and to colonial bureaucracy as a structure, a capacity to rise above sectional interests to act upon social evils. They increasingly found the *laissez-faire* approach unable to deal with the many problems facing modern capitalist societies, wherever those societies might be located (Kylie 1911).

Hence by the turn of the twentieth century the vision of establishing a comprehensive modern imperial, and capitalist, industrial system of production, consumption and exchange, was increasingly understood as encompassed by a wider set-up of relationships, manners and morals. As such, modern industrial relations were neither exclusively economic nor determined by the economy; they were social and political as well. Moreover, many British liberals and socialists argued, the emergence of this set-up of modern industrial relations reflected a stage in the historical progress of societies. The ability to influence, supervise, and when necessary directly intervene in this process, became the aim of statecraft. But contrary to the early nineteenth century, India of the early twentieth century was no longer seen by British officials as a laboratory for reforms impossible to carry out in Britain. Instead, on the one hand, the image of industrialising areas outside Britain – such as Bombay – was now put up as mirroring Western progress. This helped to cement the notion of the primacy of Western ideas. In fact, versions of many of the new reform programmes of the period here under review had been established in Britain only a few years earlier. Contemporary developments in both places were often compared. On the other hand, Bombay was understood to be a pioneering case in British India. Reforms tried out there were later attempted not only in Calcutta or Rangoon, but also elsewhere in the empire.

During the years connecting both sides of World War I a more socially oriented view of government gradually established itself within the colonial administration of the Bombay Presidency. Bombay was now discussed as the foremost expression of industrial society in the Indian context. However, contemporary social relations in Bombay had to be further aligned in order for this phase in history to be wholly realised, administrators agued. Moreover, conditions were not always conducive to this development taking place, they suggested.[2] Just after his arrival in Bombay, the new Governor of the Presidency, George Lloyd, regretted that he had not been more studious on the parliamentary social reform committee.[3] Facing the problems of Bombay, he thought he ought to have studied issues of housing and education in much more depth. This did not, however, prevent him from calling for social reform while speaking to the Legislative Council of the Bombay Presidency:

> I desire now to say a few words in regard to the general question of social reform, especially in regard to housing, sanitation, primary education...I conceive that there is no greater thing a Government can accomplish, no greater task that a Government can apply itself to, than that of attempting to ameliorate the lot of the great mass of the work people who labour in its urban and rural areas. Rhetoric on these questions is apt to be cheap...It is far more difficult to find a remedy for evils which have been allowed to grow up and be fair to wreck the very foundations of the social life in our midst. Better conditions are useless without better education...The problems...can only be solved by the cooperation of all concerned. I have only this to say...that Government alone cannot solve these problems. It can, it must, and it will provide the impetus for reform. It will go further; it will assist in practical manner those public bodies who attempt to make these reforms...[4]

It was a fine balance, thought colonial administrators. On the one hand, they must embrace the emergence of modern industrial society as an inevitable expression of history in progress. On the other hand, they clearly conceived of the social fabric of the Presidency to being put under stress by the trajectory of modern industrial development. And so there was a sense of risking the progress they thought they and their predecessors had accomplished in the region, intermingled with worries that the pressure of modern industrial society would stir local feelings towards social unrest. This delicate situation lent a new sensation of mission to the colonial administration. In a letter Montagu writes to Lloyd that the latter 'went to Bombay...with an enthusiasm for the progressive development of your Presidency and I had hoped that your time would be devoted almost exclusively to this fascinating problem'.[5] It was against this background that a social language of the colonial administration consolidated. The notion of reformed social relations encompassed ideas of how to create an environment which would foster the character of a conceived modern and industrious, yet colonised individual. The crude character of this vision was cushioned by the hope that a benevolent colonial administration would guide the Presidency towards greater wealth, but preventing a repetition of the social consequences experienced by the West in its recent industrial history. As such, ideas about social reform coalesced with a discourse on how to govern Bombay.

Reforming The Social Environment: Bombay *c.*1905–1925

Lloyd delivered his speech in the Legislative Council at a time when Bombay City had gone through a long period of expansion. The trade in the port had made the urban area grow fast. As the British opium trade ceased, Bombay-based, and to a large extent, indigenous capital was re-directed into the cotton textile industry. After the first mill was erected in the 1850s, the industry soon exploded in activity. The City of Bombay became, along with New York and Liverpool, the biggest market place for the cotton trade, and in the early 1870s Bombay City became the second largest city of the empire. Between 1897 and 1915 the number of mills in Bombay Presidency rose significantly; in 1915, 184 mills were in continu0us production. The same year well over 280,000 people were recorded as working in larger factories in Bombay, the vast majority of them men.

The social texture of the urban setting was a product of the migration patterns of workers and the lower middle classes. Mostly manual workers arrived from the Konkan area of the Presidency, and many skilled artisans came from Punjab. When coming to Bombay, around 80 per cent of the workers and artisans incurred debts.[6] On the whole, living and working conditions for sections of the society, especially the Indian middle- and working classes, were abysmal. In fact, already during the 1890s the Municipal Health Commissioner had complained about the conditions in particular areas of Bombay City.[7] The monthly earnings of a whole family was just under 26 rupees a month, 22 rupees of which were on average, spent on food and everyday necessities, leaving less than 4 rupees for occasional expenses such as medical help and clothing.[8] Yet, for a long time government and municipal expenditure had been directed towards the development of urban commercial infrastructure, and very little had been done for the improvement of social conditions. In fact, conditions were steadily deteriorating, and after George Lloyd had moved on to a High Commissionership in Egypt, they still, to use Stanley Reed's words, 'sadly perplex the industrialist, the humanitarian and the sociologist' (Reed 1925).

The years surrounding the World War I saw much industrial action. Before 1914, writes Chandavarkar, strikes in the cotton textile mills occurred, but were not co-ordinated. However, between 1919 and 1940 the mill industry in Bombay experienced 8 well co-ordinated general strikes. Soon Bombay, the most important area for modern industry in India, turned into what Chandavarkar calls 'the most dramatic centre of working-class political action' (Chandavarkar 1994:6).

Montagu, then Secretary of State for India, involved in the peace negotiations at Versailles, wrote worried letters to the Governor of Bombay from Paris, suggesting that he should perhaps persuade the trade unionist John Burns to go to Bombay and organise the workers properly.[9] Indeed, a sense of urgency had also crept into Lloyd's private communications with London. He found that a section within the administration shared the view that the social problem in Bombay had been left unchecked, owing to the inaction of his predecessors. Administrators now worried about Bombay becoming increasingly ungovernable.[10] However, to promote the changes they had in mind, they needed to refine their policy. Writing to Montagu months before he spoke in the Legislative Council, Lloyd commented on the work ahead with a touch of his usual paternalistic despotism: 'I honestly don't want to do popular work so much as good work, though I do not ever for one moment ignore that in dealing with children you can achieve much more through their affection than through stern cold justice.'[11] In this crucial time of the emergence of industrial society, officials argued, government must be truly engaged. Political power was imperative, they believed, in order to reform the social environment.

Hence, although for different reasons, administrators and the indigenous intelligentsia began to link issues such as intemperance, lack of education, bad housing, sanitation and social discontent. Housing and primary education were singled out as pressing issues to address on the part of the administration. Local elites, as well as administrators, had begun to view these two specific areas as keys to steady progress.

It was argued that better housing, public amenities and elementary education would improve the general health of the population, increase its industrial output and stabilise neighbourhoods and social structures. Now, officials began to think about reform in these areas as closely linked to their future ability to govern the Presidency. The government sensed, and recognised, strong public opinion forming around these issues. It also sensed that the press, as well as business, increasingly viewed it as a responsibility of the state to extend its reach into those areas where social discontent could mobilise. Before, newspapers had found that employers of labour must take charge of both the education and housing of their workers; now, instead, they called for a reorientation of general government policy to make it more favourable to reforms and public responsibility. As one newspaper pointed out:

> In almost every country in the world, the State has a recognised function in respect of social and moral progress. Such progress should...proceed largely from non-official effort, but there are some matters where State aid is essential and in all matters the moral support of the State is of the greatest value. In British India, the reformer not only received no countenance from the State, but oftentimes, he finds the State ranged on the side of obstruction.[12]

In the following two sections we shall see how debates over housing and primary education – over time – became framed by new social concerns and emerging views on the need to use political power to reform the social environment. We shall also see how in this process social reform measures became interlinked with other practices of government.

Housing

Government representatives gave witness of the conditions on which they would later act. 'Although I have observed a good deal of poverty in my walk through life and in many countries,' wrote consultant surveyor A.E Mirams in his memorandum to the Indian Industrial Commission, 'I confess', he continued, 'I did not realise its poignancy and its utter wretchedness until I came to inspect the so-called homes of the poorer working classes of the town of Bombay.'[13] This observation was made almost eighteen years after the Government of Bombay established an Improvement Trust (1898) in order to 'open up' congested areas.[14] The Trust, which did little to alter housing conditions, was set up after a plague epidemic severely interrupted local trade and production (Kidambi 2007). Nevertheless, despite the attempts made by the Trust, poor housing condition for workers, artisans and lower-middle-class clerks made industrial progress slow, the Government of India suggested.[15] And as long as these conditions were not ameliorated, other reforms would have no real impact.[16] Moreover, to reduce hours of work, and not simultaneously improve housing, could create unstable neighbourhoods. In the fact that workers spent their time not at home, but on the streets, officials saw a symptom of their disorganisation.[17]

However, an important question needed to be resolved. Who was responsible for the housing of the urban population in expanding industrial centres? The Bombay mill owner Dinshaw Wacha put this question repeatedly to the government of India in 1918–19. Did the government, he asked, recognise it as a principle of a 'civilised State' to provide suitable housing for the working classes?[18] Or did industrial enterprise involve a responsibility to uphold social welfare for employees? For a long time colonial officials had argued that it was up to big employers of labour to house their own employees; it was not for the state to intervene.[19] The view within business was divided as late as 1914. In fact, large employers of labour had a very poor track record when it came to arrangements for housing their employees.[20] In response to this,

E.S Montagu drew on the British experience: 'the experience of housing difficulties in this country indicates that private enterprise cannot be relied on to provide the adequate remedy.'[21] The government of Bombay calculated a shortage of 64,000 such one-roomed tenements. And to this end, the administration said, the provision of housing by the Bombay Improvement Trust and private enterprise was 'utterly inadequate'.[22] State intervention was thus understood as a necessity. An Industrial Housing Scheme was set up to house 'the industrial classes'. This diffuse segment included workers, the lower middle classes, and sometimes the middle classes as well. The scheme was placed under a newly established governmental department, the Bombay Development Department. Now 50,000 tenements were planned to house 250,000 people in compartmentalised industrial areas in Bombay City.[23] And by allowing for recreational grounds and shops when planning the outlay, administrators hoped to keep the population off the streets. When the programme was closed, only 16,000 tenements had actually been built.

Between 1913 and 1915 the average rent for one-room tenements had risen by over 70 per cent.[24] Subsequently, it was suggested that if rents in the newly built *chawls* were set below yhe economic rent people would freely migrate to newly built areas, which would lead to a loss for the colonial administration. To resolve the deficit it imposed a Town Duty of 1 rupee on every bale of raw cotton travelling through Bombay City. Money generated by the duty was to diverted to cover the losses on rent.[25] However, rent levels were set far above what average working-class families could possibly pay, resulting in a low occupancy rate in the newly built *chawls*.[26] Along with the general price rise due to World War I, already strained workingclass and lower-middle-class household budgets were now on the verge of collapse. Administrators expressed the view that a *laissez-faire* approach would fail under the extraordinary conditions caused by the War. However, according to the records, it was disturbances in the poor quarters of Bombay City that tipped the Government of India in favour establishing new provisions to regulate rent. These provisions were made under the Defence of India Act of 1915.[27]

They were installed 'for the purpose of public safety', and cleared for the control and regulation of the housing of labourers and artisans.[28] When made into provincial legislation, two Rent Acts were passed.[29] These were, in scope and character, related to the Rent Acts put in place in Britain at the same time. One major difference was that, in the Bombay context, there was no fixed and guiding 'standard of living'.[30] The intervention was enforced by the establishment of a Rent Controller.[31] The Rent Controller had the powers of a civil court, but there was no appeal against his decisions. On his instance, for example, premises which he found to be withheld from occupation for 'no good reason', could be confiscated by the government and rented out. Geographically the provisions under the Rent Act could be applied wherever the Government of Bombay deemed appropriate. In this way it came to constitute a means of confiscating property without liability.[32]

The Acts were not initially debated among colonial officials. They were conceived as emergency measures, which would serve their purpose throughout the war. But as the war came to an end, only a minority of colonial officials argued for their abolition; a majority wanted to see them kept. As a former Municipal Commissioner put it, 'I have heard from the highest police authority in Bombay that the Rent Act has had a very good effect, and more especially a sedative or soothing effect,'[33] The Acts would address discontent among the majority of the population. Accordingly, administrators found that the Acts 'were always political'.[34]

Free & Compulsory Primary Education

The introduction of compulsory primary education in England was hailed as a manifestation of a new socially oriented form of government. From the mid-1890s the debate as to whether to introduce such education into the Bombay Presidency intermingled with general discussions concerning the reform of the social environment. Over the period here under review, primary education became linked to the success of other reforms. Local pressures were imperative for this shift in views to come about; it also stemmed from changing views inside the administration. By the end of the period discussed here, the principle of compulsory primary education for boys had been established within the repertoire of the modern colonial state.

In 1894 and 1896 the question was raised as to whether the Government of Bombay ought to introduce free and compulsory primary education into the whole of Bombay Presidency. The government found the suggestion impractical and rejected it. However, in 1906 the issue resurfaced as the Government of India outlined its intention to make primary education free, but not compulsory, when (or if) the country's finances agreed.[35] The Government of Bombay began to receive petitions on the matter from underprivileged groups. The question was put to Collectors in the districts of the Presidency as to whether to pursue this policy. Very few agreed.[36] Some local administrators argued that the introduction of free education into the Presidency would only benefit the well-to-do classes, who already sent their boys to school. The poorer classes and agriculturalists would not send their children to school even though fees were remitted: they could not afford the cost of books, and, more importantly, they needed every hand they could muster to contribute to the household.[37] In order to have an effect, free education could only be introduced along with compulsion, district collectors argued. However, on the other hand, they rejected compulsion in education on both practical and political grounds. Local administrators argued that, were compulsion to be introduced, poor parents would end up being penalised by the district magistrate over and over again for withholding their children from education, as of necessity they were employing them elsewhere. The ensuing discontent would have political implications, the Education Department noted.[38] The debate did not lead to any substantial policy change on behalf of the administration, but the idea that it was among the responsibilities of the state to provide free and compulsory education had gained considerable ground.[39]

Between then and the outbreak of World War I, the issue of compulsory primary education intermingled with the question of whether it was the responsibility of the state to educate children employed in factories.[40] As was the case with housing, this question related to the responsibilities of the state in relation to its subjects as well as to industrial capital. A special committee reported in 1913 on whether free and compulsory education could be granted children working in factories. Three official members and the chairman suggested that children employed as half-timers, that is, those who worked 6 hours, should have their shift divided into two parts; in the interval they could study basic arithmetic, reading and writing.[41] One objective when introducing compulsion into the education of factory children was that the children could be better supervised, and consequently their migration between Bombay and the villages could come to a halt. The minority of the committee, three millowners, complained that this would increase the price of child labour, and that children in need of money, would look for work elsewhere during that interval. The Government of Bombay had made up its mind long before the publication of the report: the 'very qualified support' given by the committee would make it impossible for the government to decide 'in favour of a measure of so highly controversial a character'.[42] There were also general political and economic risks involved in pursuing such a policy, argued some administrators. Education among artisans or peasants could lead to a contempt for manual labour. One deputy collector wrote: '[e]ncourage education by all means in the masses, but please note that...an educated son of a peasant...becomes a permanent loss to agriculture'.[43] This could increase the shortage of factory and rural labour, they contended.

However, by the time of the end of World War I the debate over free and compulsory education inside and outside factories had taken a new turn. The debates surrounding the so-called Patel Bill in 1917–18 indicated shifting views as to whether compulsory primary education was a public responsibility.[44] By 1922 a consensus seemed to emerge that the introduction of such education was needed and the colonial state must take an active role.[45] In doing so, the state would now begin to control the relationship between parents and children. This was something new, argued colonial officials: domestic concerns had previously been left outside the scope of government. Nonetheless, one official witness stated in his evidence before the Compulsory Education Commission: 'Education is one of the most important functions of the State and the State cannot afford to let it pass out of its cognisance or supervision.'[46] Several factors had come into play, altering the framework for debate.

The War had proved a potential in Indian manufacturing, but it had also pointed towards certain conceived weaknesses in the system. One such weakness, according to colonial officials, was the instability of the labour force. It was now argued that primary education could help steady labour in the long term. The Indian Industrial Commission put it bluntly: 'if the children of workers are provided with education under tolerable conditions of life, a new generation of workers will grow up, who will learn to regard millwork as their fixed occupation.'[47] Moreover, it was now clear to many of the industrial capitalists in Bombay that an educated workforce could increase productivity.[48] But the rhetoric also pointed towards social and political ends. Here the indigenous intelligentsia and the colonial administrators came to a shared view: education was becoming politicised. Here was an 'opportunity for Government to introduce compulsory education and satisfy the demands of the people and by doing so they will allay the unrest'.[49] Moreover, primary education could help alleviate illiteracy, which was a major obstacle to progress, some officials argued. Without elementary education, attempts to improve sanitation and industrial skills would also fail, they suggested. And a system of primary education could help them spread moral education much more effectively.[50] The introduction of compulsory primary education would clearly benefit the reform of the social environment they had in mind.

Conclusion

This chapter has explored the emergence of a socially informed approach to how to govern a colonial society, and discussed its application in Bombay in the first quarter of the twentieth century. The first part of the chapter attempted to place the turn to the social in colonial government within a wider framework of social-political thought. The second part pointed towards the actual socially informed programmes of housing and education elaborated in the Bombay Presidency, then the most industrialised area in the most important British colony. At this time, questions of housing and primary education became incorporated into the wider conceptualisation of a social environment. Colonial officials viewed a favourable social environment as imperative for future progress. Poor housing conditions and poor education now signified a deteriorating social environment, which put development at risk and could foster discontent. Consequently programmes and technical projects were designed to amend social conditions, in order to make the social domain more conducive to progress, and less a cause for discontent. In this respect, the social turn within the Bombay Presidency is a good example of how, rather than being just a post-Cold War phenomenon, the development-security nexus is both historically entrenched and intimately associated with colonial forms of government.

However, the actual debates and policies discussed here have also served as illustrations to indicate a more general point: the extension of the limits to political power taking place at this time through both discourse and practice. When political commentators and, later, colonial officials began to discuss and actually design programmes for reforming the social environment, they had to rely on political power for that reform to come about. As such, they increasingly formalised the social environment and placed it within the repertoire of the state. And at this point when the colonial state was making headway into the social domain, it became more entrenched into colonial society than it had ever been before. But by extending its reach into areas previously unregulated by political power, it came to acknowledge a space for politics within that domain. However, it was a particular form of politics – a politics that accepted continuing colonial rule. The social turn was encouraged insofar as it produced grateful and politically docile colonial subjects. Given the impervious nationalist demand for independence, the social turn did not survive much beyond the mid-1920s. In view of the contemporary interest in the development-security nexus, the case of the Bombay Presidency suggests that security in this context is primarily the security of governing power and the minimal social reforms deemed necessary to maintain that power.

Bibliography

Alden, P. (1919) 'A New Liberal Programme: Liberalism and Labour'. *Contemporary Review* [*CR*] April 115: 396–403.

Armitage, D. (2000) *The Ideological Origins of the British Empire.* Cambridge: Cambridge University Press.

Bayly, C.A. (2004) The *Birth of the Modern World, 1780–1914.* Oxford: Blackwell.

Cain, P. J. (2002) *Hobson and Imperialism: Radicalism, Imperialism and Finance 1887–1938.* Oxford: Oxford University Press.

Chandavarkar, R. (1994) *The Origins of Industrial Capitalism in India. Business Strategies and the Working Classes in Bombay, 1900–1940.* Cambridge: Cambridge University Press.

Collini, S. (1980) 'Political Theory and the "Science of Society" in Victorian Britain'. *The Historical Journal* 23(1): 203–31.

Cook, E.T. (1914) 'Eight Years of Liberal Imperialism', *CR* 105 January: 1–11.

Curzon, Lord (1908) 'The True Imperialism'. *Nineteenth Century* 63 January: 151–65.

Davis, R.G. (1906) 'Slum Environment and Social Causation'. *Westminster Review* [*WR*] 167 September: 249.

Davis, R.G. 1909) 'Some Obstacles to Progress'. *WR* 171 June: 639–45.

Davis, R.G. (1911) 'Equality: A Study in Social Philosophy'. *WR* 175 June: 648–53.

Harris, J.H.(1917) '"Empire Resource Development" and Britain's War Debt'. *CR* 112 July: 65–71.

Hazareesingh, S. (2000) 'The Quest for Urban Citizenship: Civic Rights, Public Opinion, and Colonial Resistance in Early Twentieth-Century Bombay'. *Modern Asian Studies* 34 (4): 797–829.

Himmelfarb, G. (1994) *The De-moralization of Society. From Victorian Virtues to Modern Values.* New York: Vintage Books.

Hobhouse L.T. (1908) 'The Prospects of Liberalism', *CR* 93 March: 349–58.

Hobhouse, L.T. (1911) *Liberalism.* London.

Hobhouse, L.T. (1966) *Sociology and Philosophy. A Centenary Collection of Essays and Articles*. London: London School of Economics.
Hobson, J.A. (1920) 'The New Industrial Revolution', *CR* 118 November: 638–45
Kidambi, P. (2007) *The Making of an Indian Metropolis: Colonial Governance and Public Culture in Bombay, 1890–1920*. London: Ashgate.
Kylie, E. (1911) 'Liberalism and Empire', *CR* 99 January: 71–6.
Legg, S. (2007) *Spaces of Colonialism: Delhi's Urban Governmentalities*. Oxford: Blackwell.
Mehta, U.S. (1999) *Liberalism and Empire. A Study in Nineteenth-Century British Liberal Thought*. Chicago: Chicago University Press.
Metcalf, T. R. (1995) *Ideologies of the Raj*. Cambridge: Cambridge University Press
Montagu, E.S. ([February 12, 1912] 1917) 'Liberalism and India'. In Montagu E.S. *Speeches on Indian Questions*. Madras: Nateson.
Muirhead, J.H. (1910) 'Liberty-Equality-Fraternity'. *Sociological Review* 3 (3): 197.
Pitts, J. (2005) *A Turn to Empire: the Rise of Imperial Liberalism in Britain and France*. Princeton, NJ: Princeton University Press.
Rainbow Circle ([1899–1900] 1989) 6th Session 1899–1900, Minutes 47–54. In Freeden, M. (ed.) *Minutes of the Rainbow Circle 1894–1924*. Camden fourth series No. 38. London: Offices of the Royal Historical Society.
Reed, S. (1925) 'Introduction'. In Burnett-Hurst A. R., *Labour and Housing in Bombay. A Study in the Economic Conditions of the Wage-earning Classes in Bombay*. London: P. S. King & Son, p.v.
Rose, N. (1999) *Powers of Freedom: Reframing Political Thought*. Cambridge: Cambridge University Press.
Rowntree, B. S. (1919) 'Prospects and Tasks of Social Reconstruction'. *CR* 95 January: 1–9.
Sartori, A. (2006) 'The British Empire and Its Liberal Mission'. *The Journal of Modern History* 78, September: 623–42.
Skinner, Q. (1998) *Liberty Before Liberalism*. Cambridge: Cambridge University Press.

Notes

1 Government Order, Education, no. 97, 13 Jan 1915; Education Department [ed.]. Indian Economics and Sociology, Compilation [Comp.] 360, 1919. Maharashtra State Archives [MSA], Mumbai.
2 A.E Mirams, 'An address to Members of the Municipality and Citizens of Poona on The Bombay Town Planning Act of 1915', Poona 1916; J. P. Orr. 'Social Reform and Slum Reform: Bombay Past and Present". A lecture delivered to the Social Service League', Bombay, 8 October 1917. Oriental and India Office Records [OIOC], London.
3 Lloyd to Hallifax, Private Letter, 22 December 1918, Lloyd Papers, B158. OIOC.
4 In Lloyd to Montagu, private letter, 18 March 1919, Montagu Collection, Coll. 24. OIOC.
5 Montagu to Lloyd, private letter, 1 May 1919, Coll. 22. OIOC.
6 A.E. Mirams, 'Memorandum of Evidence [Memo.]', Indian Industrial Commission 1916–17, p. 22. OIOC.
7 Report of the Municipal Health Commissioner in the Annual Report of the Municipal Commissioner for the City of Bombay, 1894–96. OIOC.
8 A.E. Mirams, 'Memo.', pp. 2, 12, Appendix F.
9 Montagu to Lloyd, private letters 8 April 1920 and 29 January 1919, Montagu Collection, Coll. 22. OIOC.
10 Lloyd to Montagu, private letters, Montagu Collection, Coll. 24 and 25. OIOC.
11 Lloyd to Montagu, private letter, 30 April 1920, Montagu Collection, Coll. 25. OIOC.
12 *Indian Social Reformer*, 23 May 1909. In Report on Indian Newspapers published in the Bombay Presidency 1909, January-June.
13 A.E Mirams, 'Memo.', pp. 4–5.
14 'Administrative Reports of the Bombay Improvement Trust 1899–1905'. OIOC.
15 H. Sharp, Letter No 628,12 August 1920. G.D. House Accommodation. Compilation No. 1258, Box 43, 1920. See also: Annual Report Department of Industries (Bombay Presidency) 1919–20, p. 6. MSA.
16 T. Holland, 'Proceedings of the Indian Legislative Council, 19 February 1920'. MSA.
17 Witness no. 278 C. N. Wadia. Oral evidence 12 November 1917. Minutes of Evidence taken before the Indian Industrial Commission, 1916–18. Vol. 4, Bombay. Parliamentary Papers, Vol. 16. London: HMSO.
18 D. Wacha, 4 September 1918. 'Proceedings of the Indian Legislative Council', Vol LVII, 1918–19. MSA.

19 'Report of the Bombay Development Committee 1914'. OIOC.
20 Secr. Government of Bombay [GoB] to Secr. Government of India [GoI], 13 March 1918. General Department [G.D]. Housing. Compilation 1142, Box 26, 1918, MSA.
21 Despatch from the Secretary of State for India, no. 85 Rev, 26 October 1917. In Proceedings Bombay Development Department [BPDD]. OIOC.
22 Secr. GoB to Secr. GoI, Department of Education, 30 Sept. 1919. BPDD. OIOC.
23 Annual Report of the Development Department, 1921, OIOC.
24 A.E. Mirams, 'Memo.', p. 24.
25 Administrative Report of the Municipal Commissioner of Bombay City for the year 1919–20.
26 Report of the Special Advisory Committee on the Industrial Housing Scheme, Government of Bombay 1924.
27 Letter GoB to E.S. Montagu, 8 February 1918. G.D. Rent Acts. Comp 1136, Box 40, 1920, MSA.
28 Memorandum, GoB Judicial Department, 17 February 1918 in G.D Rent Act. Comp 1136, Box 26, 1918. MSA.
29 Bombay Rent Act No. I, Act No. III of 1918; Bombay Rent Act N.o II Act No. VII of 1918. MSA.
30 Letter from the Collector and Rent Controller, Bombay Suburban District, 19 February 1924, G.D. Bombay Rent Act. File no. 1432 (iii) – (a), Box 24, 1925. MSA.
31 Letter from municipal officer to Controller of Prices [n.d]. G.D. Rent Act. Compilation 1136, Box 26, 1918, MSA.
32 P.A. Desai, BLC, 30 July 1918. MSA.
33 R.R. Cadell, BLC, February 1918. MSA.
34 Letter from the Controller of Rent, Bombay Suburban Division, 19 February 1925. G.D. Bombay Rent Act. File no 1432 (iii) – (a), Box 24, 1925. MSA.
35 GoI, Home Department (Education) letter No. 882, 22 Nov. 1906. MSA.
36 Collector of Ahmedabad to Secr. GoB, E.D, Letter no. 1419 of 1907, 31 March 1907. MSA.
37 Selby to Secr. GoB, E.D, Letter no. 4466 of 1907–08. E.D. Primary Education, Vol. 54, Comp. 78 I, 1908. MSA.
38 Gilles to Quin, Departmental Note, 14 January 1906. E.D. Primary Education, Vol. 42, Comp. 78, 1906. MSA.
39 See: E.D. Primary Education, Vol. 49, Comp. 78, 1912. MSA.
40 E.D. Education of Factory Children, Comp. 447, Box 12, 1916.
41 G.D. Resolution No. 8051, 8 October 1914, in E.D. Education of Factory Children, Comp. 447, Box 15, 1914. MSA.
42 GoB to GoI, G.D. letter No. 7762, 16 November 1912. In E.D. Education of Factory Children, Comp. 447, Box 12, 1916. MSA.
43 K. K. Lakori, in Land Revenue Administration Report of the Bombay Presidency including Sind part II for the year 1915–16.
44 E.D. Primary Education. Comp. 78 I, Box 3, 1917.
45 Compulsory Education Committee, Written and Oral Evidence, 1922. MSA.
46 Witness No. 133 F.G Pratt. Oral evidence 9 December 1921. Compulsory Education Committee, 1922. MSA.
47 Report of the Indian Industrial Commission, 1919. London: HMSO, p. 179.
48 Witness No. 280 N B Saklatvala. Written evidence, Indian Industrial Commission 1916–17.
49 Witness No. 47 R.R Kale. Oral evidence 21 January 1922. Compulsory Education Committee, 1922. MSA.
50 E.D. Moral Training. Comp. 272, 1916. MSA.

4

'Conflict-Sensitive' Aid & Making Liberal Peace

SUTHAHARAN NADARAJAH

Introduction

The notion of 'conflict sensitivity' has become increasingly integral to the provision of international humanitarian and developmental assistance to countries afflicted by political and communal violence. On the one hand, the principle of 'do no harm' (Anderson 1999) has been taken up by donors and agencies with the ethos that efforts to administer humanitarian relief or facilitate development should not exacerbate existing tensions or create new ones. On the other hand, going actively beyond this and driven by the now common, if contested, wisdom that underdevelopment and poverty lead to violence (OECD 2001), donors have sought to actively use aid to intervene in 'internal' conflicts in order to end ongoing violence, ameliorate its perceived causes and, thereby, to 'build peace'. While 'conflict sensitivity' is an evolving concept with different interpretations (Barbolet *et al.* 2005), its essence is captured in a definition put forward by a coalition of NGOs, drawing on experiences from different conflict sites. Conflict sensitivity is the capacity of an actor to:

> understand the (conflict) context in which it operates; understand the interaction between its operations and the (conflict) context; and *act upon the understanding* of this interaction in order to avoid negative impacts and maximise positive impacts on the (conflict) context. (Resource Pack 2004, emphasis added)

The imperative for 'conflict sensitivity' thus comes from the laudable demand that external actors should not exacerbate conflict and, indeed, should actively work to ameliorate both its effects and its causes. Emerging from advocates' desire to politicise 'apolitical' approaches to development in conflict countries, this normative imperative has consequently led to attempts to use international aid, one of the primary modes of external engagement with conflict sites, to end ongoing violence and 'build' peace. Donors have thus sought to shape their projects to ease perceived tensions between communities, for example through 'equitable' development, as well as to use aid to get conflict parties to the negotiating table through incentives (offers of aid) and sanctions (withholding aid) and, thereafter, to compel political agreements from them through 'peace conditionalities' (Boyce 2002) on aid disbursement. However, although 'conflict sensitivity' is based on, and indeed implies, the adoption of more constructive and nuanced approaches to aid provision, its practice turns crucially on donors' *own* subjective, even ideologically shaped, understandings and assumptions as to the causes and dynamics of present and potential conflicts. As such, donors' stated intent and efforts to be 'conflict-sensitive' do not necessarily mean that the effects of their actions will be so. Indeed, as discussed here, donors' use of their financial leverage to shift power balances or shape developmental patterns within conflict countries are no less likely to fuel violence than their past, supposedly conflict-insensitive, approaches.

Most importantly, contemporary international efforts to end intra-state conflicts take place within the framework of establishing what Mark Duffield (2001) has labelled a 'liberal peace', the central tenets of which are 'market sovereignty and democracy' (Goodhand and Klem *et al.* 2005:65). This global project, increasingly undertaken in the past two decades by powerful Western liberal states and their organisations, institutions and agencies, posits economic interdependence, democracy and the rule of law as constituting the sustainable foundations for world peace (Willett 2005). Theeffects of the liberal core to pacify the global periphery, moreover, are now based on converging conceptualisations of poverty, conflict, development and security: while poverty and underdevelopment are blamed for eruptions of violence, conversely, enduring conflict is deemed to retard development and, thus, the consolidation of peace. In short, 'there will be no lasting security without development and no effective development without security and stability' (G8, cited in Willett 2005).

The normative goal of establishing global liberal peace is thus deemed to require not only the development of the periphery but also ending the conflicts (i.e. ensuring security) within it. It is in this context, as well as the claimed immanence of violence along unpredictable faultlines, that the imperative for aid flows into the liberal peace's borderlands to be 'sensitive' to conflict has arisen. Consequently, rather than representing a light-touch approach to aid provision, 'conflict sensitivity', as a mode of liberal intervention, has become integral to the ongoing 'securitisation of development'. Taking development as a set of governmental practices for managing populations in poor countries and, thus, as a central aspect of global liberal governance, it is argued here that the notion of 'conflict sensitivity' has, through its micro- and macro-level implementation, come to reify a specific strategic logic that shapes, legitimises and facilitates donors' interventions in the pursuit of *preferred outcomes* to intra-state conflicts. Conflict sensitivity is thus an emergent technology of governance which is concerned less with either 'doing no harm' or non-intrusively promoting peace than with the wider project of integrating violent borderlands into the global liberal order.

An examination of donor policies and actions during the past decade of Sri Lanka's conflict illustrates the subjective nature and questionable promise of 'conflict sensitivity' as well as the security-driven interventionary logic it now embodies. The donor-backed, Norwegian-led peace process which began in 2002 with the signing of a ceasefire agreement between the government of Sri Lanka (GoSL) and the armed opposition movement, the Liberation Tigers of Tamil Eelam (LTTE), came after two decades of increasingly intense fighting interspaced by four abortive peace attempts. This extensive external intervention to end one of South Asia's longest-running conflicts brought several major state and multilateral donors together in what has been described as a 'more robust and multi-faceted international response to conflict and peace dynamics than has historically been the case' (Goodhand, Klem *et al.* 2005:10). Moreover, many of the donors not only claimed to 'have calibrated their assistance according to the broader objective of building peace' (*ibid*:iii), but were deemed to 'have become increasingly sensitive to conflict issues and how they relate to aid programming' (Burke and Mulakala 2005:5).

The chapter begins with an overview of the 'liberal peace' and its conceptualisations of intra-state conflict, peace and, especially, the ideal form of the modern state. After discussing the role of the postcolonial Sri Lankan state in shaping ethnic tensions, it considers how the notion of 'conflict sensitivity' fed into donor policy during the armed conflict and later during the Norwegian peace process. Examining donor conduct in the years preceding and following the 2002 ceasefire, the chapter outlines how donors' conceptualisation of Sri Lanka's crisis, and hence how it ought to be resolved, led to policies that served not to entrench peace but instead to reinforce the asymmetries and dynamics that underpin the conflict. In conclusion, it argues that 'conflict sensitivity' is a relation of global liberal governance, constituting intervention in the peripheral state's management of its internal security *as well as* its development.

Conflict & Liberal Peace

To begin with, the ultimate goal of liberal peace is stability (Duffield 2001:34). To produce stability in any part of the periphery is also to contribute to global stability, a logic which has come to the fore especially after 11 September 2001. Moreover, since 'instability anywhere is instability everywhere', no part of the periphery can be left indefinitely outside the reach of liberal peace. This is how the 'War on Terror' became a 'global' struggle, drawing disparate conflicts in different locations into a single conceptual framework based on Manichean – good/evil, liberal/illiberal, etc. – battle lines. For example, despite acknowledging that the LTTE's armed struggle for independence is waged solely against the Sri Lankan state, most Western liberal states have now proscribed the organisation as a terrorist group and included it in domestic counter-terror actions. This goal of global security – and hence global stability – has also rationalised the increasing use of sometimes massive violence, such as in Iraq and Afghanistan, in pursuit of liberal peace (Dillon and Reid 2000). Thus, global liberal governance, while still conceptualising conflict as an 'exogenous shock' to development (Willett 2005:573), does not see the process of ending conflict as merely engineering a return to an earlier status quo so that stymied development can resume but, rather, as the *transformation* of state and society into a new mesh of internal and external relations in which the re-emergence of violent conflict is actively precluded.

As such, the liberal peace is 'irrevocably linked to the territorially sovereign state as an umbrella for political community' (Richmond 2007:13). Global liberal governance aspires to an ideal of the modern state which, once rendered ubiquitous, it is argued, would lead inexorably to the emergence of a pacific, liberal world order. The imperative for liberal peace is therefore to 'change the dysfunctional and war-affected societies it finds on its borders into cooperative, representative and, especially, stable entities' (Duffield 2001:11). This 'radical mission to transform societies as a whole, including the attitudes and beliefs of the people within them' (*ibid*:258) turns on an implicit assertion that political identities are malleable. Thus, just as local 'conflict entrepreneurs' are deemed to have mobilised ethnicity into violently antagonistic formations, liberal peace must dismantle these regressive groupings and remobilise their members into a multicultural and pluralist collective with a civic identity – one centred, moreover, on a responsive and robust state equipped with mechanisms for peacefully resolving disputes.

It is in the pursuit of this 'mission civilisatrice' (Paris 2002) that, at its boundaries, the liberal peace comes to confront institutions, norms and practices that differ violently from its own (Dillon and Reid 2000:117). Creating the ideal modern state entails the 'construction of liberal democracy, with a free market and globalised economy, progressive development strategies, and guaranteed human rights' (Richmond 2004:132). It is no matter that few developing states currently meet this standard. Engendered by a belief that 'conflict in the South is best approached through a number of connected, ameliorative, harmonizing and, especially, *transformative* measures' (Duffield 2001:11 emphasis added), the project takes a universal, problem-solving approach. In other words, it matters less how the states or societies in question reached their present state of disfunction and instability than how they *respond* when engaged by the numerous technologies of global liberal governance. Moreover, no state or society is too far beyond the pale to be engaged and transformed; the only question is *how* this is to be achieved.

International humanitarian and developmental aid is an essential tool – deployment of which is now sometimes preceded by the use of massive interventionary force – in the production of liberal peace. Economic conditionalities on aid have long been part of global liberalism's efforts to coopt the developing state into entrenching the Washington Consensus, sometimes violently, within its borders. Whilst the mandates of the World Bank and other international financial institutions required them to stay clear of 'political' matters amid the problematic claim that politics and economics are somehow separate domains, the merging of security and development, which accelerated during the 1990s, has radically changed this. In 1997 the OECD's Development Assistance Committee (DAC) issued what it described as its 'ground-breaking' guidelines on 'Conflict, Peace and Development Cooperation on the Threshold of the 21st Century.' These were incorporated in 2001 into the guidelines on 'Helping Prevent Violent Conflict'. The new document is of particular interest in contexts like that of Sri Lanka, since it 'relates primarily to collective conflict – conflict among groups within or across nations. It also covers, *to some extent*, state violence against groups or individuals' (OECD 2001:17, emphasis added). The rationale behind the new doctrine is that development agencies 'now accept the need to work in and on conflicts rather than around them, and make peacebuilding *the main focus* when dealing with conflict situations' (*ibid.*, emphasis added).

In practice this, the OECD points out, is 'a significant step toward long-term engagement and away from an earlier short-term concentration on post-conflict recovery and reconstruction efforts' (*ibid.*). Development agencies, moreover, are now 'accepting the risks of moving more deeply into this sensitive *political* terrain' (*ibid.*, emphasis added). From the outset, agencies are to work towards the future integration of the developing state into the global liberal order, even bringing their own governments into shaping the recipient's policies in 'trade, finance and investment, foreign affairs, defense, and development cooperation' (*ibid.*) In preparation, therefore, donors must 'address democracy, security and better governance as major issues' (*ibid.*:18). In terms of preventing conflict, agencies must pursue the 'mutually reinforcing goals of social peace, respect for the rule of law and human rights, and social and economic development' (*ibid.*:17). They should also 'promote multiculturalism and pluralism' and 'strengthen democratic systems'. Given that the state could be serving particularistic interests, donors must focus on 'influencing and reinforcing *state policies* of social inclusion based on principles of equality and non-discrimination (specifically addressing gender-based discrimination)' (*ibid.*:62, emphasis added). As for armed opposition, donors should 'recognise how important it is for countries to form political parties' and support this 'as a way to promote the transformation from violent conflict to peace' (*ibid.*:18).

Crucially, however, donors 'need to maximise opportunities to *help strengthen state capacity to respond appropriately to conflict*' (*ibid.*:62, emphasis added). Donors must thus seek to engage with the recipient country at multiple levels to produce 'a legitimate state authority and a healthy civil society' (*ibid.*:15). Engagement is the priority even when 'the state takes on an oppressive and predatory role in relation to society, foments internal conflict and abrogates its core functions as "protector"' (*ibid.*:20). Admitting that engagement with oppressive regimes can be 'problematic', the OECD nevertheless warns against donor withdrawal, as it 'may have negative impacts and be read as a signal of external indifference' (*ibid.*). In a section titled 'situations of repressive or divisive governance', the OECD, insisting that 'experience suggests donor countries should seek opportunities for continued engagement with such states', argues that *withdrawal* 'risks encouraging state actions contravening human rights standards, possibly leading to state collapse, or denying humanitarian assistance to affected populations' (*ibid.*:62).

The DAC guidelines exemplify global liberal governance's conceptualisation of 'ethnic' conflicts within developing states. Irrespective of whether the armed conflict stems from tensions between ethnic communities or persecution of a minority by a majoritarian state, the solution is ultimately the same: a democratic state with strong liberal institutions, a civic polity and an open economy. Crucially, moreover, the way to achieve this goal is to stabilise, restructure and reform the *existing* state; in particular, to build institutions to support 'democracy, security and better governance' and to forge a national society based on 'multiculturalism and pluralism'. Even in the context of popular minority demands for self-rule, what is not desirable is the 'fragmentation' of the state along 'ethnic lines'. Crucially, therefore, armed movements, including those fighting for self-determination, are first and foremost a threat to the stability of the state and must be encouraged or compelled to disarm and seek redress for the grievances they claim to represent through (newly institutionalised or to be improved) democratic mechanisms, perhaps becoming political parties in the process: 'the problem of peace is that first war must be eradicated or managed' (Richmond 2007:3).

A Contemporary Experiment

Sri Lanka, a developing country gripped by ethnic violence yet enjoying consistent economic growth, has increasingly become an important site for the expansion of global liberal governance. Despite the strong welfarist traditions of all post-independence governments, the country has since 1977 been a model economic reformer, embracing the open economic model and complying, albeit at a slower pace than demanded, with donors' other neo-liberal conditions (Shastri 2004). Furthermore, Sri Lanka has held regular elections since independence in 1948, and developed a private media industry and an active 'civil society' ethos. Donors' appreciation of all this has not been dulled by their awareness that patronage politics, electoral malpractice and violence, and corruption are common (Rampton and Welikala 2005:58) or that the island's communities – the majority Sinhalese and the minority Tamils, Upcountry Tamils and Muslims – are sharply polarised along ethnic lines that cut through electoral politics (De Votta 2004), media (Nadarajah 2005) and civil society (Orjouela 2003).

Despite these latent factors and the deprivations of two decades of high-intensity conflict, international actors were nevertheless of the view in 2002 that Sri Lanka was an opportunity for 'an internationally supported success story in liberal peacebuilding' (Goodhand, Klem *et al.* 2005:67). However, the Norwegian-led initiative did not succeed in moving the country from a ceasefire to a permanent peace. Sporadic violence from mid-2004 escalated into open, if undeclared, war by 2006. Whilst the focus here is on donors' policies, these must necessarily be considered against the foil of the peace process which they explicitly sought to support, especially as this is recognised as one of the contemporary experiments in liberal peace building (*ibid.*, 2005:65). In short, differences in emphasis amongst them notwithstanding (*ibid.*:68–69), donors 'believed that the promotion of a liberal market economy and strengthening of liberal institutions and values was the way forward for peace and prosperity in Sri Lanka' (Bastian 2005:5). A peace deal between the GoSL and the LTTE was deemed necessary for this, but – despite donors' insistence on a 'home-grown' solution to the conflict – its terms were required to fall within the liberal peace, and aid was consequently deployed at various levels to engineer this specific outcome.

Sri Lanka is 'historically one of the highest per capita recipients' (Goodhand 2001:10). All the donors concerned, especially the three biggest – Japan, the World Bank and the Asian Development Bank (which collectively provide over 75 per cent of Sri Lanka's aid) – have been involved in the island for many decades prior to the 2002 Norwegian peace process. Aid flows to the island began before long simmering resentments in the Tamil areas in the Northeast erupted into armed conflict after the 1983 anti-Tamil pogrom. Indeed, soon after the United National Party (UNP) came to power in 1977 with an economic model which 'emphasised the private sector, markets and opening up to the global economy' (Bastian 2005:11), 'aid flows into Sri Lanka became a veritable flood, making the country the world's leading aid recipient' at the time (Arunatilake *et al.* 2001:1485). In the subsequent three decades, even as the conflict escalated, turning into an intense, conventional war with the LTTE running a de-facto state (Stokke 2006) in parts of the Northeast, Sri Lanka has continued to receive generous international aid (Ofstad 2002; JBIC 2003). It was the governments's failure to crush the LTTE and the severe economic disruption of its efforts to do so that eventually led in the late 1990s to donors prioritising 'a political solution' to Sri Lanka's ethnic question (Ofstad 2002:168; JBIC 2003:S-9).

Donors' commitment to a 'liberal peace' vision for Sri Lanka engendered an ahistoric and formulaic approach to engaging with the conflict and the state. The notion of 'conflict sensitivity' consequently had specific interpretations. The building of liberal peace necessarily entails a central role for the state, which is held responsible not only for restructuring itself but also for taking the steps necessary to defuse communal tensions and preclude their return by building a civil, multi-ethnic polity. Despite controlling up to 30 percent of the country, the LTTE was excluded from donors' strategic planning before the 2002 ceasefire (JBIC 2003:58) and, as discussed below, afterwards. Donor ambitions for what a future Sri Lanka ought to be, and confidence that such a vision could be realised, served to preclude serious consideration of the historical and ongoing role of the postcolonial state as the primary vehicle for the Sinhala nationalist project (Krishna 1999; Rampton and Welikala 2005) which since independence has inexorably marginalised the Tamils politically, culturally and economically. Instead, donors believed that, provided the *violence* could be kept frozen by the 2002 Ceasefire Agreement (CFA), aggressive liberalisation and 'equitable' development would, albeit over time, ameliorate communal tensions and undermine the 'competing nationalisms' (Goodhand, Klem *et al.* 2005:7) held responsible for the ongoing conflict. In other words, 'limited peace would lead to a transformative peace' (*ibid.*:8).

Just as global liberal governance privileges the sovereign territorial state, it is hostile to violent challenges ('terrorism') to state authority. Thus, while armed ethno-political opponents of the state draw international ire, ethnocentric or otherwise exclusive, even repressive, regimes can, as the OECD DAC insists they should, expect continued international support. International actors saw Sri Lanka's conflict as an ethnonationalist, terrorist challenge to a multi-ethnic, 'vibrant democracy' (World Bank 2003) rather than armed resistance to state repression. Donors have thus been preoccupied with containing the LTTE's armed struggle, but are demonstrably less concerned that 'decades of potent socialisation through familial, religious, educational, and media practices have resulted in a Sinhala Buddhist nationalist hegemony that spans the political, socio-economic and cultural landscape of Sri Lanka' (Rampton and Welikala 2005:57). The goal of Tamil independence is also seen as a demand for a 'mono-ethnic' state, rather than a vehicle for emancipation from racist oppression. That the main Sinhala political parties, increasingly sensitive to international opinion, were becoming 'careful how they expressed themselves on the ethnic issue' (Shastri 2004:88) further enabled the characterisation of Sinhala majoritarianism as a mirror of Tamil nationalism and both as the preserve of an 'extremist' few.

As a consequence, international efforts to deploy developmental and humanitarian aid to preclude a return to violence, encourage a restructuring of the state and promote communal amity centred around stabilising the state and supporting it against its 'terrorist' adversary. While the logic of 'conflict sensitivity' implies the principle of subsidiarity, whereby interventions should seek, through affirmative action, to eradicate structural asymmetries underpinning conflict, donor action in Sri Lanka instead exacerbated these and also upset the fragile power balances which had precipitated the space for peace efforts in the first place. For example, when the peace process started in 2002, the Tamil-dominated Northeast had been utterly devastated by two decades of the state's escalating efforts to destroy the Tamil rebellion by military force and economic blockade. The Sinhala South had enjoyed consistent growth in that time and, whilst enduring significant poverty, was nonetheless far better-off than the Northeast. This disparity was widely recognised, with even the state citing the destruction in the Northeast while demanding increased donor assistance.

Yet 'conflict-sensitive' international intervention resulted in the imposition of 'peace' conditionalities on rehabilitation aid for the Northeast, while delivering unprecedented developmental aid and economic support to the South. Positing the LTTE as the reluctant participant in the peace process, international actors actively reinforced the state – whose failure to crush the LTTE had resulted in the negotiating process in the first place – in military, political and economic terms. Thereafter, whilst sustaining this massive power imbalance at the table, the international community insisted that both sides 'negotiate a political solution' to end the conflict – one moreover, in keeping with the 'liberal peace' i.e. a single state with a single, civic polity.

The Postcolonial State

To begin with, the Sri Lankan state is a colonial construct. Whilst there is scholarly disagreement over its precolonial history, the imposition of a single administrative structure for the entire island was a British colonial decision, following centuries of incremental – Portugese, Dutch and British – conquests of its parts. Nonetheless, at independence in 1948, Sri Lanka, with high human development indicators and well-developed infrastructure, was expected to become a model democracy. Instead, as Camilla Orjuela puts it, 'Sri Lanka could be seen as a textbook example of an ethnic conflict, where economic, political and cultural deprivation and grievances of a minority have provoked a violent rebellion against a state that has come to be seen as representative of only the majority ethnic group' (2003:198). Inexorable Sinhalisation of the postcolonial state has resulted in a state bureaucracy, judiciary, police and military with an entrenched majoritarian ethos. Even by the mid-1970s, well before the armed conflict began, Sri Lanka 'had regressed to an illiberal, ethnocentric regime bent on Sinhala superordination and Tamil subjugation' (De Votta 2004:6). It's governments have meanwhile been led alternatively by the two main Sinhala parties, the rightist UNP and the leftist SLFP (Sri Lanka Freedom Party), 'with diametrically opposed approaches to economic policy, but sharing a tendency to compete for votes ... by appealing to Sinhala chauvinist sentiment' (Winslow 2004:32), a process Neil De Votta (2004) has termed 'ethnic outbidding.' Thus 'at the heart of the Sri Lankan crisis is a crisis of the state' (Goodhand 2001:30).

The multi-faceted discrimination against the Tamils by the Sinhala-dominated state has been discussed in several scholarly works (Bose 1994; Krishna 1999, etc.) and even in some recent donor studies (World Bank 2003; JBIC 2003). The embedding of majoritarian chauvinism in state structures resulted in policies such as the imposition in 1956 of Sinhala as the official language (inplace of English) and later the exclusion of Tamils from state jobs (then the largest employment sector) and from access to universities (Goodhand 2001; JBIC 2003:12–17). A policy of recruiting only Sinhalese into the military was introduced in 1962, the beginning of today's 'ethnically pure army' (Blodgett 2004:54), while state-sponsored Sinhala colonisation (Manogaran 1994) sought to radically alter the Northeast's demography and undermine minority claims for autonomy (Rampton and Nadarajah 2008). Apart from this escalating structural violence, post- independence history has been 'punctuated by bouts of annihilatory violence directed against the Tamils in 1956, 1958, 1977, 1981 and 1983' (Krishna 1999:67). By the 1950s Tamils were agitating through mass protests and civil disobedience for greater autonomy and in the mid-1970s the demand for federalism became a call for independence. When the state responded with military force, simmering militancy turned into armed struggle, especially after the 1983 state-backed anti-Tamil pogrom (Bose 1994:74).

Nonetheless, some authors deny any *intentionality* behind these processes of racial marginalisation by the state. Sirimal Abeyaratne, for example, rejects the 'narrow focus' on ethnic relations, and argues instead that the conflict 'has its roots in the post-independence *development* process, resulting from policy *errors*' (2004:1313 emphasis added). Linking the LTTE's struggle and uprisings (1971 and 1988–89) in the South by the Sinhala-nationalist Jantha Vimukthi Perumana (JVP) as 'two major facets' of a single political conflict, he argues that 'widespread social exclusion in a stagnant economy ... created a fertile ground for ... political conflict'. '[This] was exploited and frustrated youth mobilised into the twin political conflict' (*ibid.*). Ethnicity is therefore posited as merely a mobilisation device for economic grievances. Furthermore, Abeyaratne argues, liberalisation after 1977 did not have 'adequate time to neutralise the fertile ground for conflict created by three decades of economic stagnancy'. The resonance these arguments have with the rationales underlying 'traditional' donor approaches to Sri Lanka's conflict is unmistakable.

However, other scholars disagree with this denial of intentionality. Jonathan Goodhand notes how 'state-led development in the post-colonial period operated in a framework of dominant nationalism and *favoured* one ethnic group over another' (2001:34 emphasis added). Deborah Winslow observes that 'never, in independent Sri Lanka, has economic policy been isolatable from issues of ethnicity' (2004:31). Examining the state's economic decisions since independence, V. Nithiyanandam argues that successive Sri Lankan governments enacted policies which transferred resources to the majority at the expense of the minorities (2000:294–5).

Aid Amidst War

The essential point here is that the primary cause of Sri Lanka's ethnic crisis is exclusion, marginalisation and repression of the Tamils by the majoritarian state, of which economic discrimination is only one aspect. Liberalisation and substantial inflows of aid exacerbated, rather than reduced, ethnic tensions (Herring 2001; Gunesinghe 2004; JBIC 2003:41), especially as most foreign aid was directed to the South (Goodhand, Klem *et al* 2005:78; JBIC 2003:8–13) except for Sinhala colonisation in the Northeast (JBIC 2003:41; Rampton and Nadarajah 2008). Even in the late 1970s, despite the Tamils now demanding independence and militancy emerging, there were no changes in government policies or insistence on any by donors. Not that the donors, who had become 'extremely influential in policy making' (JBIC 2004:37), were unaware of the deteriorating situation; for example, from 1977 to 1990 alone, there were at least ten World Bank studies on Sri Lanka (Nithiyanandam 2000:296). However, despite the military repression and the period from 1977 to 1983 being 'one of incessant ethnic rioting' (Gunesinghe 2004:100), donors were competing to find high-visibility projects in Sri Lanka (Herring 2001:150).

In a study of donor responses to the now high-intensity armed conflict in the late 1990s, Arve Ofstad (2002:167–8) identifies four 'strategic patterns': the 'traditional development agency approach' (Japan, the World Bank and the ADB), the 'comprehensive approach' (UN agencies and most bi-lateral donors, exemplified by the medium-sized donors, such as the Netherlands, Germany and Britain), the 'human rights approach' (such as that of Canada) and the 'pro-active approach' (Norway and Sweden). While all donors claimed to promote a peaceful solution to the war, only Sweden and Norway sought to reorient their whole aid programme to this end (*ibid.*). The 'comprehensive' approach entailed maintaining 'a regular aid program in collaboration with the government, but also provided a substantial humanitarian program with an expressed concern for [displaced people] and other civilians affected by the war on all sides' (*ibid.*). The rare 'human rights approach' entailed a decision not to provide direct development support to the government (except for governance and human rights institutions) and instead to fund NGOs. However, the 'traditional approach' – adopted by the three largest donors – was 'to practically disregard the war and provide development assistance *as if the war did not exist, except to avoid all conflict-affected areas in the north and east*' (*ibid.*, emphasis added). This policy was, notably, consistent with the state's own exclusionary developmental patterns (JBIC 2003:41; Rampton and Nadarajah 2008), while the other donor approaches also supported and legitimised the state.

All donors accepted the state's policy on the conflict – to isolate the LTTE from the Tamils and militarily destroy it, while devolving limited powers to *all* the provinces (rather than recognise the Tamil homeland) – and saw no reason to alter their aid strategies (Ofstad 2002:168). Even the severity of the humanitarian effects of the state's blockades and its human rights abuses were not considered sufficient to reduce aid (*ibid.*:169). All donors, however, expressed their concern over the impact of the continuing violence on the economy (and on development) and called for a political solution, but agreed with the government that the LTTE had forced the war on it (*ibid.*:168). However, as the military struggled to crush the LTTE and the escalating conflict increasingly disrupted the economy, donor disquiet mounted. There was particular frustration at the government's continuing failure to put forward a political solution and the slow pace of post-conflict reconstruction in the captured areas (*ibid.*:169). As the economy deteriorated amid the seeming impossibility of the government winning the war, foreign aid slowed (Burke and Mulakela 2005:15) until the ceasefire was signed by the newly elected UNP government in 2002.

Although the range of donor responses to the escalating conflict suggests a diversity of rationales, their collective approach, especially when considered against the OECD DAC guidelines, were broadly consistent with the liberal peace framework. Throughout the conflict, irrespective of the state's repression, donors maintained aid flows through the state, funded development projects (albeit only in the South) and, to a very limited extent, supported human rights institutions and 'civil society'. Whilst there was increased humanitarian assistance to the Northeast, this was channelled into the state's counter-insurgency: whilst LTTE-held areas – the main war zones – received some assistance through NGOs, most was directed through state structures for areas recaptured by the military (JBIC 2003:8–9, 30, 53), thereby supporting the government's 'hearts and minds' effort. Donors readily accepted the state's restrictions on aid agencies and development in both LTTE- and GoSL-controlled parts of the Northeast (Ofstad 2002:166). Most importantly, while donor aid was for developmental and thus non-military purposes (the military separately received substantial foreign assistance), it constituted an integral part of the overall resource base of the state and, being fungible, allowed more state resources to be redirected to the war (JBIC 2003:37; Ofstad 2002:169). In effect, donors collectively reinforced the state and its 'War for Peace' until an attritional military stalemate emerged.

Aid for Peace

The 2002–6 Norwegian-led peace process has been the most coordinated and sustained international intervention in Sri Lanka's conflict to date. The donor community, led by the United States, the European Union, Japan and Norway, engaged in a broad and sustained effort aimed at transforming Sri Lanka's state, polity and social order. In this regard, donors felt they had a willing partner in the new UNP government (Goodhand, Klem *et al* 2005:67–68). The landmark 'Tokyo Declaration' signed in June 2003 by 70 bilateral and multilateral donors as they pledged a massive US$4.5 billion sets out their 'market democracy' vision for Sri Lanka – and even a roadmap to get there (MOFA 2003). The Norwegian initiative was thus not a radical break in international approaches (Goodhand, Klem *et al* 2005:67). Given the tenets and underlying assumptions of the liberal peace, all forms of aid, including the now resumed flood of developmental aid, could in theory be said to contribute to 'building peace' in Sri Lanka. There was, however, new emphasis by donors on two peacebuilding elements: rehabilitation aid for the Northeast and, to a lesser extent, funding for promoting civil politics – inter-ethnic harmony, human rights, media independence, etc. (Burke and Mulakala 2005). Furthermore, international engagement was characterised by the heavy use of sanctions, incentives and conditionalities to compel both sides to reach an agreement on restructuring the state along federal lines – a solution endorsed by donors as a suitable compromise between a unitary state and separation.

Reflecting the underlying assumptions of the liberal peace, donors saw the LTTE as an unwilling and cynical participant in the peace process (Nadarajah and Vimalarajah 2008). This was not least because they regarded the 'authoritarian, violent' LTTE's 'extreme' goal of an independent state for the Tamils as an 'ethnonationalist, secessionist' project directly at odds with their 'market democracy' vision of a united, multi-ethnic Sri Lanka. In contrast, donors saw the UNP government, which welcomed the international intervention in Sri Lanka (Goodhand, Klem *et al* 2005:66), especially the security guarantees against the LTTE's armed struggle that came with it, and enthusiastically embraced the neo-liberal reforms demanded of it, as sincerely sharing their goals. These perspectives profoundly shaped the international community's engagement (Nadarajah and Vimalarajah 2008). The main tools to 'keep' the LTTE in the peace process included threats of further international proscriptions, peace conditionalities (i.e. linkages to 'progress' towards a federal solution) on aid for the *Northeast* and, at least initially, support for joint LTTE-GoSL initiatives on reconstruction and development there. There was also substantial international, particularly US, support for rebuilding the military and reviving the war-shattered economy. The state had to contend with the customary (and largely superfluous, given the UNP's leanings) neo-liberal economic conditionalities.

While donors' newly emphasised goal of building peace appeared unproblematic, it was in its implementation that inherent contradictions emerged. Apart from coercive measures against the LTTE, precluding a return to war was thought to require creating a 'peace dividend' for 'all communities' in the island. Conflict-sensitive peacebuilding therefore meant providing the South with economic improvements to ease the cost of living, while in the Northeast it called for rebuilding the war-shattered region and resettling the hundreds of thousands of (mainly Tamil) internally displaced. However, there was also a concomitant and contradictory strategy of compelling the LTTE towards a federal solution by withholding rehabilitation aid for the Northeast. The 'peace dividend' for the war zones was thus blocked by the 'peace' conditionalities. Some rehabilitation aid did flow, especially after the devastating December 2004 tsunami, primarily through INGOs, but nowhere near what was needed even before the disaster.

However, development aid for the state (i.e. the South) was not subject to peace conditionalities. Even after talks stalled in 2003 when the LTTE 'temporarily suspended' their participation, protesting the government's non-implementation of agreements reached on rehabilitation of the Northeast and their exclusion from a key donor conference, developmental aid to the South continued while reconstruction aid to the Northeast remained frozen. This policy did not change even when the LTTE, putting forward proposals for an interim administration to rebuild the Northeast, called for talks and the government refused (insisting that talks must address 'core' political issues, while the LTTE argued that the humanitarian crisis could not remain unresolved pending a permanent solution). The impact of massive flows of development aid to the South meanwhile was reinforced by the immediate economic improvements from the cessation of hostilities: tourism and trade expanded and foreign investment began to arrive.

The net effect of the international intervention in Sri Lanka was therefore to revive the Southern economy and reconstitute the military, thereby removing key factors that had compelled the state to abandon a military approach and pursue negotiations. Despite disgruntlement amongst Sinhala voters over the UNP's neoliberal reforms, the state was on the whole soon in a much better position than during the war. International bias against the LTTE had other consequences in the Northeast, apart from precluding the upliftment of the region. While the ceasefire provided some much needed respite, as did the lifting of the economic embargo, crucially the military refused to implement the 'normalisation' clauses of the CFA. These required the armed forces to vacate tens of thousands of homes as well as schools and places of worship they were occupying. An estimated 800,000 people remained in homeless limbo. The military also arbitrarily reimposed restrictions on fishing and farming, disrupting revival of the Northeastern economy. Although the LTTE repeatedly protested at these standing violations of the CFA, there was little international pressure on the state to implement the normalisation clauses. Donors largely accepted the state's arguments, for example that the armed forces' withdrawal from the occupied civilian sites would militarily advantage the LTTE.

Whilst the bulk of donor funding – primarily from Japan, the World Bank and the ADB – went through the state, other (mainly small, Western) donors sought to support 'peacebuilding' through a myriad of piecemeal projects implemented by NGOs aimed at promoting ethnic harmony, human rights, media freedom and other aspects required to foster a liberal, multi-ethnic polity. Donors also sought to encourage 'civil society' in the Northeast and the South, as a space for political participation and non-violent pursuit of conflicting interests. The strategic logic of these initiatives sought to undermine the LTTE's nation- and state-building project around the concept of an independent 'Tamil Eelam'. However, the effects of these ad hoc and limited projects are questionable, not least given the ethnic polarisation amongst Sri Lankans, a point underscored by the ease with which strident Sinhala nationalist sentiments reemerged amongst the southern populace when the conflict resumed in 2006 (Rampton with Welikala forthcoming).

While donors had an aversion to dealing with the 'terrorist' LTTE, circumstances made this difficult to avoid. Not only were the LTTE the state's formal 'partner in peace', the movement was in control of a substantial territory with hundreds of thousands of residents whose humanitarian needs, after decades of fighting and government embargo, were particularly acute. The exigencies of 'conflict sensitivity' meant that it could not be 'business as usual'. Some donors funded INGO-implemented projects in the Northeast, accepting that these would be regulated by the LTTE, the 'local' authority. Others sought to work through the main 'local' NGO in the Northeast, the Tamil Rehabilitation Organisation (TRO). Whilst seen as 'close to' or even 'an arm of' the LTTE, the TRO was also registered as a charity in Sri Lanka, which sanitised donor funding (TRO 2004). Some donors, including the World Bank and the ADB, were prepared to talk with the LTTE, given that key Northeastern projects they had begun prior to the ceasefire now required, from an 'even-handed' approach, implementation on both sides of the border.

In general, however, donors could not overcome the inherent contradictions between characterisations of the LTTE as 'partner in peace' and 'terrorists'. These tensions became acute after the December 2004 tsunami. Amid heavy loss of life and widespread destruction in both LTTE- and GoSL- controlled parts of the Northeast, donors sought to overcome their dilemma by demanding that both sides agree on an aid-sharing mechanism. Such a structure, involving the state, would legitimise donors funding it, would meet their requirement to be seen as 'even-handed' and, from a peacebuilding perspective, constitute a site of negotiation. However, although a deal was signed after six months of acrimonious talks, most donors, led by the US, refused to use the mechanism anyway.

Conclusion

Sri Lanka has long been on the frontline of liberal governance's expansion into the global periphery. However, the failure of international efforts to transform the island from a state of ethnic crisis to one of liberal peace has as much to do with how donors have operationalised their goals as with 'internal' dynamics. As Sri Lanka's recent history demonstrates, provided the peripheral state is working towards its eventual integration into the global liberal order, for example by following donors' neo-liberal prescriptions and adopting procedural democracy, it can escape censure for using massive force to crush rebellions against its authority. To this end, even repressive states can enlist in the 'War on Terror' and draw on the support of powerful liberal states and like-minded actors for pacifying their internal borderlands. It is in the context of the peripheral state failing to secure its internal security and stability and its efforts proving disruptive either to its own economy or to that of the region (i.e. undermining development), that international 'peace' interventions emerge.

These constitute, therefore, the peripheral state's surrender of its responsibility for 'internal security' to international custody, whereupon the process of 'building liberal peace' (i.e. reimposing security and resuming development) can be taken more closely in hand. The gradual withdrawal since 2005 of many donors from the project of making peace in Sri Lanka takes place in the context of the state resuming and making advances in its military campaign against the LTTE. In other words, having reconstituted and enhanced the capability of the Sri Lankan military and ensured the country's economic stability, global liberal governance has returned responsibility for containing the Tamil rebellion (i.e. providing internal security) to the state. Donors' undisguised eagerness in mid-2007 to resume development in the East of the island, as soon had the military had recaptured the region after a particularly brutal campaign that destroyed most of the Tamil settlements and displaced their residents, is a case in point.

The principle of 'conflict sensitivity', whilst based on the laudable goal that external intervention must alleviate human suffering and avoid its exacerbation, can be seen to have produced perverse effects when interpreted by donors through the specific framework of securitised development that underpins the liberal peace. Turning on the creation of an ideal state form, this global project engenders an ahistoric and formulaic, 'problem-solving' approach to internal conflict and the peripheral state. Consequently, donors' ambitions of transforming the postcolonial Sri Lankan state into a market democracy with a civic polity have precluded serious consideration of its historical and *ongoing* role as the primary vehicle for majoritarian hegemony. Consequently, 'peace building' in Sri Lanka has translated into an imperative to support the state, contain and discipline its armed non-state challenger, the LTTE, and undermine the 'Tamil Eelam' project's nation- and state-building efforts. Conflict sensitivity this operationalised is less about either 'doing no harm' or non-intrusively promoting peace than about international intervention in the state's management of its internal security *as well as* its development. Conflict sensitivity therefore constitutes a relation of global liberal governance, shaping interpretations and understanding of the dynamics of internal conflict and organising the deployment of developmental and humanitarian aid alongside international military assistance and other political technologies, including internationally-led conflict resolution, towards the goal of transforming the peripheral state into an ideal form and integrating it into the global liberal order.

Bibliography

Abeyaratne, S. (2004) 'Economic Roots of Political Conflict: The Case of Sri Lanka'. *The World Economy* 27(8):1295–1314.

Andersen, M.B. (1999) *Do No Harm: How Aid Can Support Peace – or War*. Boulder, CO: Lynne Rienner.

Arunatilake, N., Jayasuriya, Si. and Kelegama, S. (2001) 'The Economic Cost of the War in Sri Lanka'. *World Development* 29(9): 1483–1500.

Barbolet, A., GoldwyN, R., Groenewald, H. and Sheriff, A (2005) *The Utilities and Dilemmas of Conflict Sensitivity*. Berlin. Berghof Research Center for Constructive Conflict Management. Available at www.berghofhandbook.net/uploads/download/dialogue4_barbolet_etal.pdf.

Bastian, S. (2005) *The Economic Agenda and the Peace Process*. San Francisco/Washington, DC: The Asia Foundation. www.asiafoundation.org/resources/pdfs/SLEconomicsofPeace.pdf.

Blodgett, B. (2004) *Sri Lanka's Military: The Search for a Mission: 1949–2004*. San Diego, CA: Aventine Press.

Bose, S. (1994) *States, Nations, Sovereignty: Sri Lanka, India and the Tamil Eelam Movement*. London: Sage.

Boyce, J. (2002) 'Aid Conditionality as a Tool for Peacebuilding: Opportunities and Constraints'. *Development and Change* 33(5):1025–48.

Burke, A. and Mulakala, A. (2005) *Donors and Peacebuilding in Sri Lanka*. San Francisco/Washington, DC: The Asia Foundation: www.asiafoundation.org/resources/pdfs/SLDonorsandPeacebuilding.pdf.

De Votta, N. (2004) *Blowback: Linguistic Nationalism, Institutional Decay, and Ethnic Conflict in Sri Lanka*. Stanford, CA: Stanford University Press.

Dillon, M. and Reid, J. (2000) 'Global Governance, Liberal Peace and Complex Emergency'. *Alternatives* 25(1):117–45.

Duffield, M. (2001) *Global Governance and the New Wars*. London: Zed Books.

Goodhand, J. (2001) 'Aid, Conflict and Peace Building in Sri Lanka'. London: The Conflict, Security and Development Group.

Goodhand, J. and Klem, B. with Fonseka, D., Keethaponcalan, S.I. and Sardesai, S. (2005) *Aid, Conflict, and Peacebuilding in Sri Lanka, 2000–2005*. San Francisco/Washington, DC: The Asia Foundation: www.asiafoundation.org/resources/pdfs/fullsrreport.pdf.

Gunesinghe, N. (2004) 'The Open Economy and its Impact on Ethnic Relations'. In Winslow, D. and Woost, M.D. (eds) *Economy, Culture, and Civil War in Sri Lanka*. Bloomington, IN: Indiana University Press.

Herring, R.J. (2001) 'Making Ethnic Conflict: the Civil War in Sri Lanka'. In Esman, M.J. and Herring, R.J. (eds.) *Carrots, Sticks and Ethnic Conflict: Rethinking Development Assistance*. Ann Arbor, MI: University of Michigan Press.

JBIC (2003) *Conflict and Development: Roles of the JBIC – Development Assistance Strategy for Peace Building and Reconstruction in Sri Lanka*. Research Paper No. 24. Tokyo: Japanese Bank for International Cooperation.

Krishna, S. (1999) *Postcolonial Insecurities: India, Sri Lanka & the Question of Nationhood*. Minneapolis, MN: University of Minnesota Press.

Manogaran, C. (1994) 'Colonization as Politics: Political Use of Space in Sri Lanka's Ethnic Conflict'. In Manogaran, Chelvadurai and Pfaffenberger, B. (eds) *The Sri Lankan Tamils: Ethnicity and Identity*. Boulder, CO: Westview Press, pp. 84–125.

MOFA (2003) *Tokyo Declaration on Reconstruction and Development* of Sri *Lanka*. Tokyo: Ministry of Foreign Affairs,. www.mofa.go.jp/region/asia-paci/srilanka/conf0306/declaration.html.

Nadarajah, S. (2005) *Sri Lanka's Vernacular Press and the Peace Process*. The Asia Foundation: www.asiafoundation.org/resources/pdfs/SLMediaSurvey.pdf.

Nadarajah, S. and Vimalarajah, L. (2008) 'The Politics of Transformation: the LTTE and the 2002–2006 Peace Process in Sri Lanka'. *Transitions* No. 4. Berlin: Berghof Research Center for Constructive Conflict Management. www.berghof-center.org/uploads/download/transitions_ltte.pdf.

Nithiyanandam, V. (2000) 'Ethnic Politics and Third World Development: Some Lessons from Sri Lanka's Experience'. *Third World Quarterly* 21(2):283–311.

OECD (2001) *The DAC Guidelines: Helping Prevent Violent Conflict*. Paris: OECD. www.oecd.org/dataoecd/15/54/1886146.pdf.

Ofstad, A. (2002) 'Countries in Violent Conflict and Aid Strategies: The Case of Sri Lanka'. *World Development* 30(2):165–80.

Orjuela, C. (2003) 'Building Peace in Sri Lanka: A Role for Civil Society?' *Journal of Peace Research* 40(2):195–212.

Paris, R. (2002) 'International Peacebuilding and the "Mission Civilisatrice"'. *Review of International Studies* 28(4):637–56.

Rampton, D. and Nadarajah, S. (2008) 'Development, Colonization and Pacification in Sri Lanka'. Paper presented at British Association of South Asian Studies Conference, Leicester, March 26–28.

Rampton, D. and Welikala, A (2005) *The Politics of the South*. San Francisco/Washington, DC: The Asia Foundation: www.asiafoundation.org/resources/pdfs/SLPoliticsoftheSouth.pdf

Rampton, D. with Welikala, A. (forthcoming) 'Colliding Worlds: Sinhala Nationalism and Populist Resistance to the Liberal Peace'. In Goodhand, J., Korf, B. and Spencer, J. (eds.) *Caught in the Peace Trap? Conflict, Aid and Peacebuilding in Sri Lanka*. London: Routledge.

Resource Pack (2004) 'Conflict-sensitive Approaches to Development, Humanitarian Assistance and Peacebuilding.' Available at www.conflictsensitivity.org.

Richmond, O.P. (2004) 'The Globalization of Responses to Conflict and Peacebuilding Consensus'. *Cooperation and Conflict* 39(2):129–50.

Richmond, O.P. (2007) *The Transformation of Peace*. Basingstoke: Palgrave Macmillan.

Shastri, A. (2004) 'An Open Economy in a Time of Intense Civil War: Sri Lanka, 1994–2000'. In Winslow, D. and Woost, M.D. (eds) *Economy, Culture, and Civil War in Sri Lanka*. Bloomington IN: Indiana University Press, pp. 73–93.

Stokke, K. (2006) 'Building the Tamil Eelam State: Emerging State Institutions and Forms of Governance in LTTE-controlled Areas in Sri Lanka'. *Third World Quarterly* 27(6):1021–40.

TRO (2004) *Reconstruction and Rehabilitation towards Peace-building: Challenges, Opportunities and Engagement of the Diaspora*. Colombo: TRO.

Willett, S. (2005) 'New Barbarians at the Gate: Losing the Liberal Peace in Africa'. *Review of Political Economy* 106:569–94.

Winslow, D. (2004) 'Introduction to Part I'. In Winslow, D. and Woost, M.D. (eds) *Economy, Culture, and Civil War in Sri Lanka*. Bloomington, IN: Indiana University Press, pp. 31–40.

5

Development, Poverty & Famines
The Case of British Empire

RICHARD SHELDON

Introduction

It is now well known (despite little mention in recent major works, including the current *Oxford History of the British Empire*) that anything between 30 and 40 million persons died in the wake of famine in India in the half-century following Britain's final military conquest of the Indian subcontinent in 1857. The earlier stages of the conquest and colonisation under the East India Company had also been marked by large-scale famines, in particular the shocking Bengal famine of 1769–70 in which something like 10 million people, or a third of the population, perished. The famines of 1784 (upper India), 1803–6 (Bombay), the 1830s (North India), 1854 (Madras), 1861 (North West), 1865 (Orissa), and 1876–8 (South and North-east) are only now finding an established place in the historiography of India. Although precolonial India had certainly known famine, their frequency, scale and magnitude expanded dramatically and seemingly in line with the disruption to indigenous social and economic structures that accompanied colonial interference and extractions, especially the heavy and unpredictable cost of land revenues.

Cornelius Walford the Victorian demographer calculated that British India experienced 34 separate famines, compared with only 17 recorded instances in the prior two millennia of Indian history. An early critic of British rule complained in 1776, anticipating a major plank of later Indian nationalism, that 'famine, pestilence and the English have covered our land with horror and desolation' (Arnold 1999: 99). A case against British rule was made by Dadabhai Naoroji in his *Poverty and Un-British Rule in India* (1901):

> How strange it is that the British rulers do not see that after all they themselves are the main cause of all the destruction that ensues from droughts; that it is the drain of India's wealth by them that lays at their own door the dreadful results of misery, starvation, and the death of millions. (Naoroji 1901: 212)

This indictment was backed up in detail by the economic history of R.C. Dutt, but has sometimes been challenged in more recent revisionist histories, especially that of Charlesworth (1982, see also Bayly 2008 for a more complex picture).

Dominion under the British Empire came with the promise of a short cut to modernity, prosperity and civilisation. How can and how have such claims stood next to the appalling figures of famine-related mortality? Whilst contemporary European commentators routinely blamed a malignant nature manifest in successive waves of climatic disaster or in unavoidable Malthusian 'checks', Mike Davis's recent work has seen the famines as products of the age of imperialism: it was not the absence of modernity and development which made these lands 'subject to famine', rather it was the very process of incorporation into a global capitalist economy that gave the famines their terrible potency (Davis 2001).

This chapter is a study of the background to colonial development theory and the dual role of famines inside that body of knowledge. India, Ireland and other parts of the empire were portrayed as lands of famine, partly as a strategy of domination, partly as a legitimating notion for colonialism. India was backward because it was subject to famine; enlightened imperial governance provided the only escape route. How did liberal imperialism in its golden age deal with the question of poverty and famines, and with what legacy for the present? Its focus is on the framing and representation of famine in the mainstream discourse of colonial development. Thus, it has little to say about actual economic change, save, briefly, that the record of empire in development is mixed, to say the least. To consider just one example: around 1750 Britain was an importer of Indian textiles, but a century later India was clothed by Britain, entirely to the loss of the Indian producers. By 1900 India had been eclipsed in world markets largely due to the aggressive protectionism of the colonial state. Britain did invest in infrastructure that would eventually assist Indian development: roads, railways, telegrams and electric grids were all financed under British rule, but not, of course, without a downside, and not always to the advantage of the Indian people as a whole. For the mid-Victorian generation there was no more vivid marker of European progress and Asiatic backwardness than the railways.

The efforts began under the governership of Dalhousie in the 1850s: major railway construction schemes, the construction of the Ganges canal in 1854. The foundation of a Department of Public Works in the same year marked a new attitude and sense of purpose to the modernisation of India that was reinforced by the uprising of 1857. In Trevelyan's exuberance:

> These two thin strips of iron, representing as they do the mightiest and most fruitful conquest of science, stretch hundreds and hundreds and hundreds of miles across the boundless Eastern plains – rich, indeed, in material products, but tilled by a race far below the most barbarous of Europeans. (Trevelyan 1866:22)

Later economic histories have given a similar prominence to the role of rail in Indian development, but the issue can be seen in another light. Canals and irrigation works were more often called for by Indians themselves. Improvements in information, helping to free up blockages in supply and even out prices, came with the telegram, but the transition from local and regional patterns of marketing and supply to the world economy did not progress smoothly, and these new instruments of trade took note and responded to the stimulus of effective economic demand, not need. The railway and the steamship could in any case even be used to remove food from the areas most in need.

Railways also served strategic purposes as well as those of development, and profits from successful enterprises such as the East India Railway were not kept or reinvested for India. Commentators such as Strachey were also frank about the importance of improved communication and transport in military strength and maritime supremacy in the Empire leading him to conclude that no 'combination of hostile powers should dangerously threaten our dominion' (Strachey 1903:216). By 1900, after the opening of the Suez Canal and the penetration of Chinese markets, as other world powers erected tariff barriers against British goods, the Indian market integrated by rail and lined to the global marketplace became more important. The appointment of Curzon, previously best known as a writer on the territorial threat of Russia, as Vicreoy of India in 1899 underlines the growing importance of military-strategic considerations in imperial development.

Industrial infrastructure was almost always constructed in order to exploit Indian raw materials and markets in favour of British manufacturers. Literacy remained low (17 per cent), public health was largely neglected and life expectancy at the time of independence a miserable 32.5 years. Using the data assembled by Angus Maddison, we can say that India experienced zero per capita growth between 1600 and 1870. Growth in the period 1870 to 1947 was just 0.2 per cent (cited in Sachs 2005 173–6). This is not the place to engage in counter-factual speculation, but it is easily conceivable that India would have developed left to its own resources. Japan provides an alternative model to that of Western-led growth. India's retreat from the process of industrialisation cannot be understood as a 'failure' or as a consequence of 'under-development', unless that concept is understood as an active process shaped from the imperial core.

Enlightenment, Poverty & Famines

Today it is all too apparent that 'development' is an ideologically freighted concept. Whilst not denying that there are arenas in which it makes sense to work critically with development paradigms, we should also consider the theory as a prescriptive and hegemonic formation: a language of technological mastery and scientific control, a way of seeing nations and colonies as wholes, a way of theorising and sometimes misrecognising difference through concepts such as 'backwardness', 'overpopulation' etc. In the language of development, or civilisation, there is, as postcolonial writers and critical theorists of development have noted, a certain 'violence of representation at play' (Escobar 1995:103). In imposing European expectations and assumptions about the uses and ownership of the land, the appropriation and exploitation of nature, the relationship between different social groups and the state, British theorists engaged in a form of wilful misrepresentation and recoding. They sought to apply concepts derived from the historic experience of northern Europe, especially the decline of feudalism and the process of agrarian improvement, and thus forced colonial possessions into a straitjacket of historical expectations.

Development economics as currently taught in higher education and practised in international organisations emerged only in the mid-twentieth century, but there is little anachronism involved in asserting that the theory, or a markedly similar conceptual construct, one in which the central concerns of development economics can already be seen, emerged in the middle decades of the eighteenth century from the comparative economics of the Scottish and French enlightenments and their discourses on 'improvement' and political economy (Hobsbawm 1980; Barber 1975). In fact, I argue that there is much to be gained from setting up this story in a longer timeframe, especially as the older paradigm is increasingly subjected to critique.

With the developments in economics and historical sociology that emerged in the middle decades of the eighteenth century from Paris, Glasgow and Edinburgh came the first 'development theory', one that still leaves a discernible genetic imprint on its later models. Very simply, the French and Scottish schools theorised four-stage models of development from the rudeness or barbarity of hunter-gatherer societies, through pastoralism, then agriculture, ending up with the polished citizens of commercial societies. With each shift in what the Scottish historian Robertson first termed 'the mode of production' evolved a corresponding shift in the laws and political institutions (Meek 1976).

In the beginning, as Locke said, all was America (meaning native North America as a hunter-gatherer society); towards the end of the story were the polite and commercial civilisations of northern Europe. Although the theory was based on universal models of human psychology, and thus suggested that all peoples could advance, in practice it began to lend itself to a view of a hierarchy of civilisations and notions of cultural, later racial, superiority. In general, European conceptions of India held that it was predominantly an agrarian civilisation, with large backward zones. Europe, or at least its northern zones, by contrast had progressed into a new world of commercial society, with a consequent increase in the forms of knowledge and government that they labelled civil society. 'Asiatic' began to emerge as a term synonymous with backwardness or stagnancy. Adam Smith, the best known writer of this tradition, may have been free of prejudice against non-Europeans, but as Pitts writes, 'his theory of development may have left an ambivalent legacy: that the categories and historical arguments he introduced were deployed by others to justify civilizing imperial rule' (Pitts 2005:26).

Around 1800 enlightenment economics were transplanted from the backward soils of the Limousin and Highland Scotland to the fertile plains of Bengal. Locke's view had been that the original Indian was poor because of a want of improvement in the land by way of labour. Real improvement would only emerge with rights of private property and the end of the commons, as had occurred in the English countryside. The Colonial Secretary, Goderich, asked rhetorically in 1831: 'Without some division of labour, without a class of persons willing to work for wages, how can society be prevented from falling into state of almost primitive rudeness' (Thompson 1991:167). 'Permanent settlement' of the land in Bengal was proclaimed in 1793, hoping to transform the zemindar class of indigenous 'landlords' into an English-style agri-capitalist gentry. Settled ownership, it was projected, would lead to the replication of schemes for enclosure and improvement that had transformed the landscape and markets of rural England. Although a shift in the early nineteenth century saw attempts to place land with the cultivator rather than landlords, it was attempted with little more understanding or respect for existing agrarian customs and local factors.

It is not often appreciated just how concerned, intellectually and professionally, many of the key personnel of British political economy in its first generations were with India. Sir James Steuart was commissioned by the East India Company in the early 1770s to examine and make representations on the monetary system of Bengal. James Mill and his better known son John Stuart made long careers in the company (Mill senior unsuccessfully attempting to bring his friend David Ricardo onto the Company's board of directors). Malthus became the first professional teacher of economics in the Company's employment at the Haileybury College, and was followed in that office by Richard Jones, largely on the basis of his theoretical work on the subject of peasant rents. (Later, Marshall wrote and gave official testimony on the Indian economy; Keynes spent eighteen months working for the India Office; Beveridge was born in Bengal, the son of a sessions judge in the Indian Civil Service.)

The unique institutional status of British political economy in the early nineteenth century lent it an unrivalled primacy in debates about colonial development. Its doctrines regarding famines give matters a special and historically significant twist. In the nineteenth century, famine became a marker separating the rude from the advanced nations. The continuation of famines was taken as a sure symptom of backwardness. For Whately, who oversaw the Irish Poor Law inquiry a generation before the Great Famine, the only real means of preventing a famine lay in 'agricultural improvement, accumulation of capital, commercial resources, and the other results of national wealth' (Whately 1832:14). Backward, uncapitalised lands without the benefit of scientific farming remained subject to famine. For Nassau Senior, in the West where 'society is better constituted', the threat of famine receded. But in the 'uncivilised, or partially civilised, nations' famine retained all its awful potency: 'in a barbarous, and consequently a poor and non-commercial people, they are among the most frightful forms of national calamity' (Senior 1854:3, 3, 21). He later declared, drawing on his experience of the Irish famine, that famine was 'a calamity which cannot befall a civilised nation': 'When such a calamity does befall an uncivilised community ... things take their own course; it produces great misery, great mortality, and in a year or two the wound is closed, and scarcely a scar remains' (Brantlinger 2003:103). The preliminary remarks to Mill's *Principles of Political Economy*, the settled synthesis of economic lore for the mid-Victorian generations, associated famines with Europe's pre-industrial past and with 'Oriental' countries in his own day (1921:19).

On the level of ideology, Indian incapacity to combat the new famines became a key issue in the justification of colonialism. The colonial state would also disparage the pre-existing protocols of famine avoidance and relief, pushing its own projects of public utility and economic development; at the same time and through the same mechanisms, it was able to strengthen and deepen its own control of the land. In terms of practice, mechanisms for the better understanding and control of famine – statistics, surveys, reports and inspection – became technologies of domination. Physical monuments to development and famine avoidance such as the great canals played a similar role in both spheres (Sharma 2001: *passim*).

In the eighteenth century new lines of argument disputed received notions of the cause and remedy of famine and dearth, displacing forever traditional and providentialist views. The modern economic view of famines emerged in the period 1750–76, its main theorists being the Frenchmen Turgot and Condorcet, alongside Adam Smith who travelled in France and corresponded with Turgot. Turgot, who served as an administrator in a backward region of France, would be celebrated for his practical efforts and remembered as a working model for the conquest of backwardness throughout the nineteenth century. French economists of the 1750s, '60s and '70s (in part basing their case on what they saw as the more successful agrarian model of Britain) argued for free trade based on free internal circulation, the end of customs zones inside France, and the dismantling of administrative systems for price controls designed to protect the poor in times of hardship. The spirit of these campaigns is best captured in a condensed manifesto for free trade appearing as part of Condorcet's *Life of Turgot*. Condorcet described the anti-famine measures instituted by Turgot in the Limousin (1761–74). Turgot was entirely convinced

> [T]hat unrestricted liberty and protection to magazines and to the speculations of commerce, were the only means to prevent or repair this mischief. The scarcity of provisions, by raising their price, augments the interest which each proprietor has to carry them where the scarcity is the greatest: while laws of police, forced sales, and regulations of price only oppose barriers to this natural impulse, and deprive the public of this resource. Besides the evil they produce of themselves, they contribute to expose the trader to the vexations of petty officers, and to the violence of the populace, whose terror and disquietude are excited or kept up by the spectacle of a restless and turbulent legislation. (Condorcet cited in Baker 1975: 61–2)

Markedly similar conclusions were reached in Adam Smith's Wealth of Nations. Smith defended all branches of the corn trade and denied that there was any conflict of interest between them and the consumer. The trade was too diverse and competitive to act in concert, and as there was no advantage to be gained from attempts at market rigging they were unlikely to take place. Laws and restrictions on the grain traders only encouraged the suspicion and hostility often expressed by the common people towards them. Smith's views were uncompromising: there had never been a famine other than those caused by clumsy attempts at market interference by unenlightened governments. Even the recent Bengal famine of 1770 was the product of East India Company bungling and of ill-judged attempts to control markets (Smith (1976)[1776]:524–43). Turgot's views, especially as represented in popular essays by liberal writers including John Morley, carried huge influence, as we shall see. To give any credence to ideas of speculation was to follow the mob and their unenlightened conspirators into the persecution of middlemen, to believe in the myths of 'artificial scarcity' or even a 'pacte de famine', a plot to starve the people.

Free trade and the guaranteed security and liberty of traders and middlemen provided the only route away from dearth and hunger. The views of the poor themselves on subsistence were congenitally ill-informed and generally an obstacle to progress. Popular fears of market manipulation could be compared to belief in witches or to religious prejudice. What had appeared first as an enlightened defence of commerce, as a pathway out of misery and hunger, hardened into a theoretical orthodoxy, which blinkered subsequent generations of economists, politicians and administrators. A kind of intellectual absolutism also legitimated decades of suspicion and distrust of the poor's ability to understand and act upon their own predicament

The militant rationalism of enlightenment thought forged in the struggles against the old regime in Europe carried an instinctive hostility towards the poor. Turgot's only fault was in not realising that the unenlightened were unable to make the right choices and had to be helped along. A significant feature of his reputation is not so much that his reform measures worked, but rather that they failed. Following service in the Limousin, Turgot was appointed controller general of French finances between 1774 and 1176 and presided over a *laissez-faire* experiment in which an attempt was made to liberalise and free up the trade in grains across France in one 'big bang' single stroke. The result, in short, was debacle: food riots, confusion, soaring prices and finally a return to the regulatory model of the *ancien regime*. Despite, or even precisely because of, this, Turgot became a tragic heroic figure in the liberal imagination: the enlightened reformer who attempted to cut off the flooding course of the French Revolution but who was betrayed by the unenlightened, vested interests, privilege and superstition.

Condorcet was scathing of the monarchy's lack of will to use its power in the service of progress and enlightenment. 'To do good one must have at least as much power as goodwill' he had written to Turgot early in his period of office (Baker 1975:56). Government needed strength and a clear vision in order to overcome the deeply ingrained prejudices of the popular imagination and its captive servants in the lower ranks of administration and the decaying branches of the aristocracy and church. Where conditions of development did not permit the exercise of democratic government in the service of a virtuous republic, then the offices of the monarchy had to be appropriated for the cause. Thus was born an authoritarian strain of economic liberalism which would profoundly influence the colonial development theories of the nineteenth century.

Smith, Turgot and later J.S. Mill all took up the case for free trade as progressives, motivated by genuine sympathy for the plight of the poor: each spoke from an optimistic moment of liberalism. But they all espoused an enlightenment liberalism tempered with authoritarianism, rather than a sentimental concern. Free trade and the spread of enlightenment promised progress: mankind was perfectible. But revolution, war and the threat of famine towards the end of the eighteenth century led to a bleaker 'Malthusian moment'. Enlightenment optimism was succeeded by a moment of pessimistic liberalism. For Malthus, Smith and Turgot were correct about the need for free trade, but there was no guarantee of security or improved living standards for the poor as Smith had forecast.

Malthus's original case was put across as science (as with many of its later variants), but also in explicit opposition to the insurgency of the poor marked by the radical decade of the 1790s. Not only were the progressive thinkers of the high enlightenment deluded, even utopian, in seeing a prospect of material amelioration for all, their speculations had fostered a dangerous disposition amongst the poor to claim a entitlement to the produce of the earth, as Jacobins and others took heart from the declaration of Liberty, Equality and Fraternity. The *Essay on the Principles of Population* had its sights set on the liberal Condorcet as well as the English plebeian radical Tom Paine, whose *Rights of Man* had outlined a national system of welfare support for the poor. All such speculations were deluded attempts to 'reverse the laws of nature'. 'At nature's mighty feast' there was no room for the poor man. 'A man who is born into a world already possessed, if he cannot get subsistence from his parents ... and if the society do not want his labour, has no claim of right to the smallest portion of food, and, in fact, has no business to be where he is' (Malthus 1803:249). Ironically, given Malthus' opposition to Condorcet's political ideas, their views on the question of the free market as arbiter of rights and entitlements to food were equally stringent.

Political circumstances dictated that adherence to a strict version of political economy became a test of political will and character around 1800. During the wars with revolutionary France young men of the ruling class were sent north, rather than off on the Grand Tour, to Edinburgh to learn their political economy at the feet of Dugald Stewart, Adam Smith's successor. The political battles of the late eighteenth century: first against the *ancien regime*, then against revolutionary insurrection from below marked political economy with an unflinching opposition to interference with the trade in provisions.

'A Good Stout Despotism': British Rule in India

Jennifer Pitts has considered the question of the strange about-face of advanced opinion between the age of enlightenment and the flowering of liberalism. In the late eighteenth century liberals often opposed empire and happily predicted its downfall. By the middle of the nineteenth century, however, few thinkers held to the old line, indeed prominent figures such as John Stuart Mill and Alexis de Tocqueville actively promoted the project of imperial consolidation and expansion. A strengthened confidence and sense of mission in Europe was undoubtedly one key element in explaining this. This confidence was in large part based on 'the extraordinary surge in economic and technological development' that occurred in Britain. Argue as economic historians may about the balance sheet of empire, part of the surge in Britain owed its origins and momentum to the exploitation of colonial raw materials. On the other hand, 'the stagnation attributed to the Indian economy by nineteenth century Britons was due in part to the effects of British rule itself' (Pitts 2005: 1, 17).

This intellectual transition in liberalism can be seen in the evolution of the thought of James and John Stuart Mill. James Mill the Scottish philosopher and father of John Stuart, was a late product of the Scottish enlightenment – a movement he attempted to graft onto Benthamite utilitarianism. His *History of British India* – a book that would win a senior administrative post for himself and later his son in the London headquarters of the East India Company – was an attempt to place India in the 'scale of civilisation', and to assess its prospects for development under the benign tutelage of a more advanced conqueror. His assessment of Hindu and Muslim culture was damning – a 'hideous state of society', inferior to Europe 'even in its darkest feudal age'.

Mill set out explicitly to counter the view that Hindu India had formed a notable world civilisation. Pro-Oriental scholars such as Sir William Jones were his particular target. The *History* is a signal work in a broader trend, which saw enlightenment cosmopolitanism replaced by views which we can characterise as straightforwardly 'orientalist' in the sense famously put forward by Edward Said. Never having visited India, Mill felt his disinterested stance justified such severe views (Stokes 1959:53). What was required was 'a simple form of arbitrary government, tempered by European honour and European intelligence'. After all, 'even the utmost abuse of European power is better, we are persuaded, than the most temperate exercise of Oriental despotism' (Mill 1966:387).

As Stokes makes clear, James Mill shunned the earlier optimism of liberalism, holding a gloomy view of human capabilities in general, and those of 'asiatics' in particular (1959:57). Free trade was indeed indispensable, but could promise no certain prospects for improvement in the condition of the poor. The prospects for an Asian catch-up could be postponed almost indefinitely. His testimony to a Parliamentary Select Committee on the affairs of the east India Company in 1831 captures well his synthesis of cheap, effective, government with a view of European racial superiority. The 'great concern of the people of India is, that the business of government should be well and cheaply performed, but that it is of little consequence to them who are the people that perform it.' (Mill 1966:441). Following 1857, vast tracts of India came under direct rule. Some commentators now entertained serious doubts about the capability of 'barbarians' for progress but others including many of the officers of the Indian Civil Service still retained an ethos of reform and improvement. As Metcalf puts it, India then became a 'laboratory for the creation of a liberal administrative state' (Metcalf 1994:29).

In John Stuart Mill's essay *On Liberty* an immaturity analogy appeared in support of an authoritarian variant of liberalism appropriate to the age of empires. Mill wrote:

> It is perhaps hardly necessary to say that this doctrine is meant to apply only to human beings in the maturity of their faculties. We are not speaking of children or young persons below the age which the law may fix as that of manhood or womanhood. Those who are still in a state to require being taken care of by others must be protected against their own actions as well as against external injury. For the same reason we may leave out of consideration those backward states of society in which the race may be considered as in its nonage. The early difficulties in the way of spontaneous progress are so great that there is seldom any choice of means for overcoming them; and a ruler full of the spirit of improvement is warranted in the use of any expedients that will attain an end perhaps otherwise unattainable. Despotism is a legitimate mode of government in dealing with barbarians, provided the end be their improvement and the means justified by actually effecting that end. (Mill 1859:69)

This argument elegantly summed up and underlay the broad thrust of imperial development theory. He later argued, in a line which became the credo of many a late Victorian imperialist, that British rule in India represented 'not only one of the purest in intention, but one of the most beneficial in act, ever known among mankind' (quoted in Strachey 1903:502)

Around 1800 a battle was fought and won over the direction of East India Company policy and British rule. A hybrid dynamism, forged from utilitarianism, religious evangelism and progressive liberal belief in the civilising powers of 'commercial society', came to the fore. The learning of Indian languages and language skills was no longer to be supported by the Company. In the debates about the best means of training company servants we can see clearly the direction of change. Charles Grant, evangelical Christian and member of the Clapham sect of reformers, chairman of the court of directors of the East India Company moved to close down the company's college in Calcutta, which was felt to be too pro-oriental, and shifted operations to a new college at Haileybury in England. The new ethos of the company servants echoed a new seriousness and commitment in politics and religion at home, and gave birth to what Bayly terms 'a new moral racism' abroad (Bayly 1989:115). Interest in Indian languages and customs declined and a conviction took hold that India needed to be led by a more advanced civilisation. Examinations in London became the basis for entry to company service; with Indians themselves only allowed to take up subaltern positions. This triumph of the liberal revolution in government was characterised by one Bengali writer as merely 'despotism tempered by examinations' (Bates 2007:53).

The Company college at Haileybury was established to remove corrupting influences from students and to refocus training away from engagement with Indian culture and languages, towards modern European sciences, especially political economy. The plan of education was designed to fortify the students against 'erroneous and dangerous opinions' (Cohn 1988:526). Malthus took an active role in the organisation and intellectual culture of the college, becoming known to generations of students as 'Old Pop'. Among the school's alumni was Charles Trevelyan, whose career would progress through a twelve-year stint with the EIC, to an appointment as Assistant Secretary at the Treasury (during which time he took executive control over British policy in Ireland during the Great Famine of 1845–50), to the Governorship of Madras. Malthus established a syllabus based on prevailing economic orthodoxies and thus equipped generations of future company servants and later members of the Indian Civil service, including the famous brothers John and Richard Strachey, with a ready-made set of ideas about poverty, development and famines.

The Indian Famine Commission

Little systematic attention was paid by Britain to the question of Indian famine until the Orissa famine of 1866. Political unrest and controversy over famines in the 1870s, in part stirred up by the humanitarian reaction to press coverage in Britain and India, including documentary photographs of starving and emaciated Indians, led Disraeli to call for an inquiry into Indian famines. Arguments between the administrations of different provinces had run for some time, leading to calls for the application of a uniform policy. The result of this was the first of a series of reports drawn up for Parliament in the shape of the Indian Famine Commission. Richard Strachey and Sir Charles Elliott were directed by Lord Lytton to examine and report on the question of famine and famine relief. From the 1880 Commission came a Famine Code, arguably representing the world's first modern anti-famine policies. Strachey, as an experienced administrator with his own strong views on famine policy, was determined to rig the outcome of the Commission and Code, in particular to outmanoeuvre the proponents of irrigation and large-scale public works, and also to prevent setting any precedence in controls in the market for food. It was ultimately 'a political exercise to produce a favourable report, rather than a measured response to one of the most significant problems of the Government of India' (Brennan 1984:108)

Unsurprisingly, the Reports bear the imprint of their times, including the utilitarian psychology that underlay the English Poor Law of 1834, the Smilesian ideology of self-help and a liberal dose of Malthusian prejudice expressed as warnings against the 'ill-directed and excessive distribution of charitable relief'. Ill-judged famine action, it was argued, might, like the 'unreformed' English Poor Law, do more harm than good. As colonial rule was believed to have reduced the potency of positive checks to population such as war and infanticide, there was scope for populations to grow more rapidly, thereby 'calling more frequently on famine as the ultimate check.' (Caldwell 1998:681). Empire had, 'with so many of the latest appliances of civilisation and science at its command ... fundamentally changed the position of the people for the better'. But the 1980 Report also needed to warn that 'all such advantages tend to favour the increase of population, and to add to the pressure on the means of subsistence'. It was, therefore, 'especially important that the Government, when it has to deal with calamities such as famines, should so frame its measures as to avoid every tendency to relax in the people the sense of the obligation which rests on them to provide for their own support by their own labour' (Famine Commission 1880:35).

Thus, for the framers of the Famine Codes, it was 'the cardinal principle of their policy that their relief should be so administered as not to check the growth of thrift and self reliance among the people' (Strachey 1903:226). The view grew that gratuitous relief would only work in the long run to increase the number of poor Indians subject to famine, a prospect which the leading British statistician, assistant editor of *The Economist* and later chief of the Board of Trade, Sir Robert Giffen decried 'from the point of view of civilisation and progress' (quoted in Caldwell 1998:683). Again famines and development placed India in a double bind: development, it was claimed, led to increasing numbers, which made India more vulnerable to famine.

Lord Lytton, the Viceroy and Governor General, spoke in 1878 in defence of British policy forged in accordance with these principles and found encouragement in a wider and longer tract of history: 'if you embrace in one view our own history with the past history of other countries in other climates, you will find that the principles on which we have lately acted ... have been found no less applicable, no less efficient, in other countries similarly affected, than they have proved to be in this country, wherever they have been intelligently understood and loyally carried out.' There was, he continued:

> no more striking illustration of this truth than the history of the scarcity that occurred in Central France during the year 1770–1. That great statesman, M. Turgot, was then minister. His administrative ability was equalled by his philosophical power of thought; and, fighting with difficulties in many respects almost identical with those which we ourselves have lately had to deal with – difficulties partly material, but greatly aggravated by the prevalence of extremely erroneous economical conception – Turgot conceived, developed, and in the face of great opposition, carried into effect, views no less identical with those which have guided our own action, as to the essential importance of guarding the perfect freedom of inland trade in grain, of improving the internal communications of the country, and of providing relief works of permanent utility upon which to employ the suffering population.(Indian Famine 1878:90)

It was a common view, expressed here by Strachey, that Indians were 'intensely conservative and intensely ignorant, wedded, to an extent difficult for Europeans to understand, to every ancient custom'; as such, none were fitted for high office in the legal system or government of India. Strachey, who even believed himself to be a victim of unenlightened prejudice from his critics, argued the need 'to govern India with unflinching determination on the principles which our superior knowledge tells us are right, although they may be unpopular' (Strachey 1903:504 506). Addressing the Royal Institution in 1877, he pointed to a possible means of combating the 'worst results' of a hostile environment and climate in India by 'the progress of civilisation'. But he was careful also to caution that the 'moral qualities' of 'self-sacrifice' would also need to be developed in the Indian colonial subject

> Experience in India leads to exactly the same conclusions as those arrived at elsewhere, that a system of public relief in time of distress, not guarded by the sense of specific local financial responsibility, is a source of grievous abuses, misery, and demoralisation; and it is my earnest hope that no selfish (if I may be allowed so to apply the term) effort to escape at any cost the pain of witnessing it, may be permitted to stand in the way of that real benevolence which is founded on sound principles, drawn by dispassionate intelligence from the lessons of experience, principles which I am glad to believe have been adopted by the highest authorities concerned in the government of India. (Strachey 1878:425–26).

The Famine Commission Report of 1880 describes Turgot as 'a great administrator of famine relief in modern times' (Famine Commission 1880:36), whilst the Victorian liberal commentator John Morley, in an essay on Condorcet, explained that Turgot could be compared to 'a chief commisioner' in India, forced 'to deal with a famine, just as the English civilian has to do in Orissa or Behar' (Rothschild 2002:74). John Stuart Mill once told Morley that he would in his youth regularly return to the writings of Condorcet for inspiration and a lifting of his spirits (*ibid.*:2002:215). Mill believed every bit as fervently as Condorcet had before him that enlightened administration in the cause of the common good was preferable to the exercise of immature or untutored democracy. Writing to John Nichol, he admitted 'I myself have always been for a good stout despotism – for governing Ireland like India. But it cannot be done. The spirit of democracy has got too much head there, too prematurely' (Ambirajan 1978:5).

Lyall, who had become an authoritarian following his experiences during the Indian Mutiny, promoted a view of British rule in India as 'a highly organised machine, so powerful, and so complicated in its functions that scientific management and control of them is indispensable'. 'Foreign dominion must necessarily be more or less autocratic for some time after it has been acquired'; in fact 'no other form of rulership has ever been attempted in a purely Asiatic state' (Lyall 1916:387, 388). This view of poor Indians being chained by superstition and taboo to unsuitable and impractical food preferences had a long imperial afterlife. The technologicalisation of the question of hunger in the 1930s led to the forming of scientific bodies such as the Committee on Nutrition in the Colonial Empire which complained again of the problem of 'innate conservatism, prejudice, religious scruples and taboos', which acted as 'a barrier to progress' (Vernon 2007:114)

The Vernacular Press Law of passed by the governing council of India on Lyton's urging suppressed the freedom of the Indian press by requiring printers and publishers 'to enter into a bond not to print or publish anything likely to excite feelings of disaffection to the government...' Although passed following a flurry of criticism of the ill-fated and costly invasion of Afganistan, it was also quickly felt to be a barrier to effective criticism of famine responses. The extracts from Indian papers published to justify the government's actions contained an excerpt from the newspaper *Shwaji* (16 November 1877) complaining that 'the English rulers of India are possessed of excessive pride and despise the natives as utterly worthless... the English are subjecting them to a treatment which even beasts will not bear patiently. They are enacting the most vexatious laws. The people have become so poor, that a single year's failure of rains exposes them to starvation' (Dacosta 1878:2, 10). Such was the outcry against censorship the Press Law proved unworkable.

The importance from the 1870s onwards of an Anglo-Indian public sphere comprising pro-Indian Englishmen such as Digby and Hyndman and 'anglicised' Indians including Dadabhai Naoroji and R.C. Dutt should not be neglected. Digby, in 1878, and Dutt in 1897 were able to make much of the contrast between lavish expenditure on Imperial ceremonies and niggardly amounts of poor relief whilst famine conditions continued. Although an admirer of British letters and politics, Dutt firmed up the nationalist critique of the economics of empire, a thesis that can be pithily summarised as 'the evil of a perpetual economic drain from India' has made the country 'a land of poverty and famines' (Arnold 1988:116–7). In the early twentieth century, the Indian National Congress reminded government 'of its solemn duty to save human life and mitigate human suffering', arguing that the existing measures were 'inadequate and oppressive' (Bhatia 1991:273).

Growing opposition in India symbolised by the emergence of the *Swadeshi* movement for home rule, and in the UK, criticisms from abroad of British policy including hostile coverage in the Russian press and the formation of subscriptions for famine relief, led to two further Famine Commissions in 1898 and 1901 as well as an Irrigation Commission in 1903 and review of land revenue policy. Eventually the idea of *laissez-faire* as famine policy ebbed. Scarcity remained a regular occurrence but this was no longer accompanied by famine mortality. Conditions for development were in place, the railways allowed much greater mobility of labour, and finally large annual imports of foodgrains established by the 1920s meant that India no longer suffered mass starvation, outside of the extraordinary circumstances of Bengal in 1943 (Bhatia 1991: ch. 10).

Admitting that the famine of 1896–7 was 'not well managed, and the mortality was very heavy', an unabashed admirer of British empire in its twilight hour asserted that 'British officials worked with their usual devotion', and drew attention to the inscription upon a cross at Jabalpur. 'To the memory of the officers of the Central Provinces who sacrificed their lives to their duty in the struggle to save life during the great famine of 1896–1897' (Rawlinson 1948:163). The cross at Jabalpur and the sacrifices it marked reappears in histories of empire sympathetic to the imperial project (most recently in Gilmour 2005:116–117; see also Woodruff 1954:114) and help maintain a cosy view of the Raj. Lives were laid down for humanitarian purposes, but none of this should deter us from the wider sociological and historical analysis of famine.

Conclusion

After 1989 neo-liberal prescriptions for the alleviation of poverty gained the ascendancy. After 11 September 2001 we have witnessed the re-emergence of an impatient and authoritarian form of Christian-humanitarian imperialism. A 'roadmap to a more prosperous and secure world', even to 'the end of poverty', has been offered to the current generation from a liberal capitalist vantage point, one that explicitly seeks to appropriate the eighteenth-century progressive mantra of Condorcet, Turgot and Smith: those 'awe-inspiring geniuses of the Enlightenment, who first glimpsed the prospect of conscious social actions to improve human well-being on a global scale' (Sachs 2005:348). Commercial society is often represented as the only model for the poor left standing today, but let us at least remember the mixed record of that movement in practice as well as some of the unintended consequences of its impatience and lack of regard for the views of its subjects.

Bibliography

Ambirajan, S. (1978) *Classical Political Economy and British Policy in India.* Cambridge: Cambridge University Press.

Arnold, D. (1988) *Famine: Social Crisis and Historical Change.* Oxford: Blackwell.

Arnold, D. (1999) 'Hunger in the Garden of Plenty: The Bengal Famine of 1770'. In Johns, A. (ed.) *Dreadful Visitations: Confronting Natural Catastrophe in the Age of Enlightenment.* New York: Routledge, pp. 81–112.

Baker, K.M. (1975) *Condorcet.* Chicago: University of Chicago Press.

Barber, W.J. (1975) *British Economic Thought and India, 1600–1858.* Oxford: Clarendon Press.

Bates, C. (2007) *Subalterns and Raj: South Asia Since 1600.* London: Routledge.

Bayly, C.A. (1989) *Imperial Meridian: The British Empire and the World 1780–1830.* London: Longman.

Bayly, C.A. (2008) *Indigenous and Colonial Origins of Comparative Economic Development: The Case of Colonial India and Africa.* Policy Research Working Paper 4474. Washington, DC: World Bank.

Bhatia, B.M. (1991) *Famines in India.* New Delhi: Konark Publishers.

Brantlinger, P. (2003) *Dark Vanishings: Discourse on the Extinction of Primitive Races, 1800–1930.* Ithaca, NY: Cornell University Press.

Brennan, L. (1984) 'The Development of the Indian Famine Code.' In Currey, B. and Hugo, G. (eds) *Famine as a Geographical Phenomenon.* Dordrecht: D. Reidel.

Caldwell, J.C. (1998) 'Malthus and the Less-Developed World: The Pivotal Role of India'. *Population and Development Review* 24: 675–96.

Charlesworth, N. (1982) *British Rule and the Indian Economy, 1800–1914.* London: Macmillan.

Cohn, Bernard S. (1988) *An Anthropologist Among the Historians and other Essays.* New Delhi: Oxford University Press.

Dacosta, J. (1878) *Remarks on the Vernacular Press Law of India.* London: W.H. Allen.

Davis, M. (2001) *Late Victorian Holocausts: El Nino Famines and the Making of the Third World.* London: Verso Press.

Escobar, A. (1995) *Encountering Development: The Making and Unmaking of the Third World.* Princeton, NJ: Princeton University Press.

Famine Commission (1880) *Report of the Indian Famine Commission. Part I. Famine Relief.* London: George Edward Eyre and William Spottiswood for HMSO.

Gilmour, D. (2005) *The Ruling Caste: Imperial Lives in the Victorian Raj.* London: John Murray.

Hobsbawm, E. (1980) 'Scottish Reformers of the Eighteenth Century and Capitalist Agriculture'. In Hobsbawm, E. *et al.* (eds) *Peasants in History. Essays in Honour of Daniel Thorner.* Calcutta: Oxford University Press, pp. 3–29.

Indian Famine (1878) *The Indian Famine of 1877. Being a Statement of the Measures Proposed by the Government of India for the Prevention and Relief of Famines in the Future.* London: C. Kegan Paul and Co.

Lyall, A. (1916) *The Rise and Expansion of the British Dominion in India.* London: John Murray.

Malthus, T.R. ([1803] 1992) *An Essay on the Principles of Population.* Cambridge: Cambridge University Press.

Meek, R. (1976) *Social Science and the Ignoble Savage.* Cambridge: Cambridge University Press.

Metcalf, T.R. (1994) *Ideologies of the Raj.* Cambridge: Cambridge University Press.

Mill, James (1966) *Selected Economic Writings.* Winch, Donald (ed.). Edinburgh: Oliver and Boyd.

Mill, J.S. ([1848] 1921) *Principles of Political Economy.* London: Longman.

Mill, J.S. (1859) *On Liberty.* Harmondsworth: Penguin.

Mill, J.S. (1990) *Writings on India.* Toronto: University of Toronto Press.

Naoroji, D. (1901) *Poverty and Un-British Rule in India.* London: Swan Sonnenschein.

Pitts, J. (2005) *A Turn to Empire: The Rise of Imperial Liberalism in Britain and France.* Princeton, NJ: Princeton University Press.

Rawlinson, H.G. (1948) *The British Achievement in India: A Survey.* London: William Hodge & Co.
Rothschild, E. (2002) *Economic Sentiments: Adam Smith, Condorcet, and the Enlightenment.* Cambridge, MA: Harvard University Press.
Sachs, J. (2005) *The End of Poverty: How We Can Make it Happen in Our Lifetime.* Harmondsworth: Penguin.
Senior, N.W. (1854) *Political Economy.* 3rd edn. London: Richard Griffin and Co.
Sharma, S. (2001) *Famine, Philanthropy and the Colonial State: North India in the Early Nineteenth Century.* New Delhi: Oxford University Press.
Strachey, J. (1903) *India. Its Administration and Progress.* London: Macmillan.
Smith, A. (976)[1776] *The Wealth of Nations.* Oxford: Oxford University.
Stokes, E. (1959) *The English Utilitarians and India.* London: Oxford University Press.
Strachey, R. (1878) 'Physical Causes of Indian Famines'. *Proceedings of the Royal Institution.* (January): 407–26.
Thompson, E P. (1991) *Customs in Common.* London: Merlin Press.
Trevelyan, G.O. (1866) *The Competition Wallah.* London: Macmillan.
Vernon, James (2007) *Hunger: A Modern History.* Cambridge, MA: Harvard University Press.
Whately, Richard (1832) *Introductory Lectures on Political Economy.* London: B. Fellowes.
Woodruff, Philip (1954) *The Men Who Ruled India: The Guardians.* London: Jonathan Cape.

6

Plain Tales from the Reconstruction Site
Spatial Continuities in Contemporary Humanitarian Practice

LISA SMIRL

Introduction

The idea of a 'pure' or natural disaster is a pervasive one. The occurrence of an 'Act of God' appears to be the one instance where international intervention is beyond criticism: the blamelessness of the victims translates into an ethical imperative for action on the part of the 'international community' to alleviate the resultant suffering (Edkins 2000). While it is possible to point to many instances of critique of political interventions (Mamdani 2007; Pugh 2005; Chandler 2006) and others who criticise the efficacy or appropriateness of certain modes of disaster relief (Duffield 1991; Edkins 2000; Keen 1994; De Waal 1997), there are few authors who have problematised the basic premise that the international community has a responsibility to provide assistance to those affected by a natural disaster (Bankoff 2001; Hewitt 1995). Yet authors such as Smith (2006), Davis (2000), and O'Keefe *et al.* (1976) stress that while natural hazards exist, the severity of their impact on human settlement is determined by human decisions: where and how to build; access to preventive measures; the existence and knowledge of escape routes.

While a direct, and unique, causal link between geography and social development (Landes 1998; Diamond 2005) is highly disputed, the link between underdevelopment and increased risk of natural disasters is well documented. According to Ian Davis (1978:11), 'the study of disasters is almost by definition a study of poverty within the developing world.' Even within high-income countries, those groups which are structurally impoverished, or underprivileged, experience a higher vulnerability to disasters (Cutter 2006; Giroux 2006). Nevertheless, such nuances fail to stop the idea of a 'pure' natural disaster from being held up as an ethical rationale for intervention.

This chapter challenges this assumption by pointing out that, despite the perceived ethical neutrality of post-disaster intervention, particular spatial and material approaches may have similarities to previous colonial practice. Focusing on the way in which the international community moves through and lives in the post-disaster reconstruction sites illuminates power relations and dynamics generally obscured by more abstract discussions over the ethics and modalities of international intervention. The first section of the chapter places contemporary humanitarian intervention within a longer continuum of global North-South relations and looks at why a spatial approach provides a useful heuristic for our examination of colonial continuities. The second section examines two particular examples of such continuities, mobility and separation, in some depth, juxtaposing observations and interviews with contemporary development and humanitarian practitioners with personal accounts from previous Anglo-Indian colonial administrators as described in the classic text, *Plain Tales from the Raj*, by Charles Allen (2006).[1]

A Spatial Genealogy of Response: Locating the Humanitarian Imaginary

According to Craig Calhoun, the idea of an Emergency Imaginary is an important part of the Western social imaginary (Calhoun 2004; Taylor 2005; Castoriadis 1987). The 'notion of "emergency" is produced and reproduced in social imagination, at a level that Professor Charles Taylor (Taylor 2002) has described as between explicit doctrine and the embodied knowledge of habitus' (Calhoun (2004:7). Calhoun goes on to say that the 'production of emergencies, and the need to address them, has become one of the rationales for assertion of global power' (Calhoun 2004:9; Klein 2007; Duffield 2007). An important part of the discourse is the perceived unusual nature of the emergency: '"[e]mergency" is a way of grasping problematic events, a way of imagining them that emphasises their apparent unpredictability, abnormality, and brevity, and that carries the corollary that response – intervention – is necessary. The international emergency, it is implied, both can and should be managed' (Calhoun 2004:6).

An important part of this emergency imaginary is the ability to *locate* the emergency, the event, in a particular geography or spatial imagination (Hewitt 1995). The 'assertion of global power' that Calhoun points to must be asserted over someone or something; it must be asserted *from* some position of (perceived) security, and *over* another place of (perceived) insecurity. The 'common practices' that underpin Charles Taylor's understanding of a particular social imaginary happen somewhere; they are locatable, they are grounded. One specific, yet under-examined way in which this is done is in the day-to-day material and spatial practices of international humanitarian workers who come to a disaster or reconstruction site. This is important because, although humanitarian policy and discourse expresses the desire to frame individuals and communities affected by disaster in terms of empowerment rather than victim-hood, the material practice and spatial dynamics of intervention may work against this. Despite an increasing focus in humanitarian literature on 'downward accountability' to 'clients' (beneficiaries), the material practices of aid delivery demonstrate disturbing continuities with previous colonial approaches. While such continuities can be observed across the spectrum of relief to development assistance, this chapter focuses on the particular space of the reconstruction site. This is due both to the privileged position of the emergency within the larger humanitarian imaginary and because the immediacy of its conditions strips away the rhetoric that couches the majority of longer-term development practice, allowing the material and spatial practices to be brought to the fore.

The term 'reconstruction sites' refers to geographic locations that have been or are being physically reconstructed, with external assistance, after experiencing a crisis that overwhelms the ability of the affected society to respond. 'External assistance' refers to the provision of physical and/or financial resources by individuals and agencies that normally reside outside the geographic boundaries of the reconstruction site and have been brought there specifically by the event of the disaster. The precise geography of the reconstruction site will differ depending on whose perspective we are considering. The mapping of the disaster is often one of the easiest and best executed aspects of a post-disaster intervention (Davis 1978). Careful attention is paid to the location and categorisation of victims, beneficiaries, types and location of damaged buildings and infrastructure. But the lens of analysis is rarely, if ever, turned back upon the implementing actors. While there is widespread informal acknowledgement amongst development practitioners that the rapid influx of hundreds or thousands of foreign workers has feedback effects (Collier 2007), these are dramatically under-examined. This is partly explained by the fact that the reconfiguring of space and the reconstruction of the built environment are not seen as political and socially transformative in themselves, but just a basic, and largely neutral, component of a reconstruction process (Graham and Marvin 2001).

However, the dissemination of work by Bourdieu (1990), Bourdieu and Nice (1977), Lefebvre (1991), and de Certeau (1988) highlighted the subjectivity and relativism in the designation and construction of particular physical and social spaces. This work contributed to and coincided with two major disciplinary shifts in the social sciences at large. First, in those disciplines which were already engaged with ideas of space and materiality such as geography and urban planning, it led to a re-examination and problematisation of the ontological pre-eminence of an independent materiality that could be mapped, designed, shaped and built. Second, in disciplines such as anthropology and sociology, it contributed to the recognition of the need to consider space and materiality both as a potentially causal variable in the societies under examination, and also as an inextricable part of the embodied experience of research, and of the construction of knowledge itself (Crang 2000).

The 1990s saw the application of the 'spatial turn' to a wide range of enquiry from discourse analysis (Tuathail 1996) to economic geography (Barnes 2003). However, it did not have a significant impact on development or humanitarian studies, nor, by extension, on post-crisis relief or reconstruction which focused on the level of the individual and its aggregate – society. Issues of governance, local livelihoods, civil society, capacity building, human security and anti-corruption filled the agenda in the 1990s and 2000s (Pupuvac 2005) – an agenda that assumed the solution, liberal, democratic peace, had already been found and only the instruments required perfecting (Paris 2006; Hoogvelt 2006).

This overlooks the way in which post-disaster reconstruction evolved. From its modern post-World War II inception, international humanitarian assistance was conceived in spatial terms (Slater 1997). The categories and binaries by which it defined itself as an activity were fundamentally geographic: First, Second and Third worlds; developed and underdeveloped countries; the global North/global South. Direct links to the process of European decolonisation can also be found (Duffield 2007). Fred Cuny (1983) attributes the rise of disaster response as an industry within the global north to the rapid, post-1945 decolonisation process which left the former colonies without either the human or financial capacity to respond. The 'apolitical' international system of NGOs and multilateral agencies was seen as preferable to the reassertion of control by former colonial powers. However, through the application of spatial considerations, it is possible to see how contemporary material and spatial practices of humanitarian response may continue to invoke and reproduce colonial power relations. If the social imaginary is interlinked with the material practices of the everyday, it is necessary to consider the impact of the material expression of particular places and practices (Bourdieu 1990; de Certeau 1988; Merleau-Ponty 1962).

An initial application of the 'spatial turn' to the realm of post-crisis reconstruction points to several areas which are immediately problematised. There are five such areas of immediate interest. First, the need to consider that the space of a reconstruction site is not a *tabula rasa*, and that what is produced is immediately and inextricably politicised and used in different ways by different groups, for different ends (Lefebvre 1991). Second, space is relative and relational. Spatial and material designations, mappings and representations of needs and responses may not be in keeping with other scalar designations or social categories such as the idea of the 'local', in the policy designs of the international community; or the programmatic separation of certain categories of beneficiaries such as post-conflict vs. post-disaster (Scott 1998; Ferguson 2006; Escobar 1994).

Third, that knowledge is embodied – predicated upon 'cognitive (mental) and physical (corporeal) performances that are constantly evolving as people encounter place' (Hubbard *et al.* 2004:6). These 'geographies of embodiment' are therefore implicated in the subsequent production and reification of categories of class, gender and, in the case of humanitarianism of donor/beneficiary and saviour/victim. In the case of post-conflict reconstruction, this embodiment will be the result of the social and cultural environments that humanitarian workers have come from (their countries of origin) as well as the environments that they find themselves in during the reconstruction process. According to Bourdieu (1990), it is impossible to separate subjects from their *habitus* (the practices and games of their surroundings) either present, past, or possibly future (Massumi 2002). This means that the responses of particular individuals and agencies are conditioned as much by previous experiences both of their place(s) of origin and of previous reconstruction sites, as they are by the immediate emergency to which they are responding. Further, as discussed below, the precise material circumstances experienced while in a reconstruction site may also be significant.

These linkages point to the fourth insight of the spatial turn for post-crisis reconstruction: that the presence of international humanitarian agencies in the country of intent, must always be read contrapuntally with their space of origin (Inayatullah 2004; Said 1995). The activities, practices and places of the international community in reconstruction sites are as closely networked to their spaces of origin as they are to their proximate physical environments (Castells 2000; Sassen 2000; Appadurai 1997) and may need to be considered as particular, embodied instances of larger global processes (Beck and Ritter 1992; Harvey 2001). As such, their representational consequences need to be taken into consideration. How are these international practices and spaces understood and interpreted by the groups and individuals in their immediate physical surroundings? Does this impact on or affect the tactics (de Certeau 1988; Scott 1998) that may be used in their interactions with the international donor community?

A fifth area of consideration is how the spatial and material circumstances of humanitarian relief workers are related to temporal considerations. How do differential spaces affect the way in which the time of response and intervention is conceived (Massey 2006)? The differential rates of mobility and speed between the international community and the target population are rarely examined, yet lie at the heart of some of the most problematic aspects of the ineffectiveness of humanitarian assistance. While the previous discussion has focused on the applicability of the spatial turn to contemporary post-crisis reconstruction, the foregrounding of space and materiality also highlights the continuities of contemporary practice with previous modes of colonial governance and the unequal practices associated with it. In particular, two major continuities can be identified: mobility and separation. The next section will look at these two continuities in more depth.

Spatial Continuity A: Mobility

A key feature of contemporary humanitarian intervention is the mobility with which aid workers move to and from, and between, response and reconstruction sites (Telford 2006). The nature of an emergency requires the rapid deployment of staff. The relatively short period of time that is required for the response and post-crisis reconstruction; the frequency of disaster events and the scarcity of qualified professionals mean that staff are only present in one place for a limited time: anywhere from a few weeks to, at most, a few years. Likewise, within contemporary development practice, the (necessary) introduction of transport networks dedicated to the movement of international staff and associated goods creates a parallel space of movement, maintaining physical difference between the individuals who have come to assist, and those who are being assisted.

These differential spaces of travel and movement are important in several ways. First, they are significant in that they are securitised and separated, either literally or symbolically. This will be further explored below, under the theme of separation. Second, a key aspect of humanitarian assistance and post-crisis reconstruction is timing, as the space of response and reconstruction necessarily has a higher velocity than its surroundings (Virilio 1991). Long debates have taken place on the so-called 'relief-to-development' continuum, i.e when humanitarian assistance ends and long-term development assistance begins. While the current consensus in policy circles is for the need to link the two to ensure that humanitarian assistance is sustainable in development terms, an unavoidable distinction remains: humanitarian assistance must arrive as soon as possible after an emergency in order to achieve its stated aim of saving lives. The introduction and use of parallel transport systems for staff, and parallel delivery systems for food and non-food-items (NFIs) such as tents, medicine, blankets are justified on the grounds that a slow humanitarian response invalidates the rationale for providing assistance.

But the ends of timeliness and efficient delivery require certain sacrifices at the level of process, i.e. it may be deemed necessary to bypass national systems in the delivery of aid. For example, in the case of the international humanitarian response to the 2004 tsunami, the World Food Programme (WFP) instituted almost daily flights up and down the coast of Aceh to transport humanitarian staff and equipment. This was justified on both the basis of need (efficiency) and staff security. However, the perception among some Acehnese was that, particularly in the post-emergency stage of the recovery effort, the WFP travel department operated more as a tour operator than a development agency, ferrying consultants, visitors from headquarters, and well-off disaster tourists from disaster site to disaster site. The flights cost exponentially more than domestic carriers, and therefore were out of reach for the average Indonesian. They were also temporary, and will not leave a sustainable transport infrastructure behind, to be used by the Acehnese, upon the departure of the international community. In the larger picture, the timeliness of delivery is also an important proof of the technical superiority and ability of the global North to respond to and manage emergencies.[2]

The differential rates of mobility also emphasise the different metrics that are used to assess the risk conditions of humanitarian staff versus those of the target communities. While, within the emergency imaginary, a disaster is a unique and unusual event which can be gone to, managed, and left, for the populations that are being assisted, risk (or the potential vulnerability to similar disasters) is part of the fabric of daily existence. But for the humanitarian (and development) aid workers, the ability to leave the reconstruction site at any point, is always an option, a condition of their employment. Many medium-term, high-risk postings also contain the guarantee of regular periods when staff are expected to leave their place of work and go to another physical location to relieve the pressure of living in confined and dangerous surroundings. This emphasises the feeling of impermanence of location amongst the staff, and the emotional and cultural distance from their immediate physical environment. It also highlights the centrality of travel and movement to the experience of humanitarian assistance.

While often identified as a feature of contemporary globalisation (Bauman 1998; Appadurai 1997), such impermanence and mobility have a much longer history (Hirst and Thompson 1999). Significant work has been done on the pivotal role played by ideas and experiences of travel under colonialism (Pratt 1992; Gowans 2006; Kearns 1997). As heard in Allen's testimonials, constant travel also characterised the life of colonial administrators and their families: '[F]requent transfers and movements over great distances were recurrent themes in the "Anglo-Indian" experience: As official people we were constantly on the move' (Allen 2006:57). Allen's interviewees describe the boat voyage to India as a central part of the colonial experience: a space where professional and social networking took place and where relationships and partnerships were formed and solidified (see also Gowans 2006).

Striking comparisons can also be drawn between contemporary and colonial experiences of arrival: '[r]eceptions varied according to status and connections. Those of high degree or with connections were garlanded and their luggage seized by *chaprassis* in scarlet uniforms. Some were met by shipping agents and shepherded through customs. Others had less auspicious introductions' (Allen, 2006:54–5).[3] Such a scene could equally well describe the arrival of international aid workers at a reconstruction site. Those who belong to a high-level international agency such as the United Nations or the World Bank are often quickly guided through customs by their agencies' operations staff, whisked into a large, radio-equipped sports utility vehicle (SUV) and driven away in power-locked and air-conditioned security, while those who are from a smaller organisation or travelling as individuals may face long queues at the visa window and frustrating negotiations with local cab drivers.

Regardless of the hierarchical position of the agency or organisation in question, an under-examined aspect of the reconstruction effort remains the types of individuals that it attracts. Across generations and cultures, the idea of the unknown and the 'other' is appealing to certain segments of a population. The idea of a reconstruction site has been imbued with poetic, often romantic notions (Kenny 2005). According to Ian Davis, the process of rebuilding after a disaster combines preoccupations of social awareness, advanced technology, mobility and impermanence (Davis 1978), and may attract individuals who seek a life that is perceived as more adventurous, unpredictable and emotionally and professionally fulfilling than could be found in their country of origin (Cain 2004). This allure of the foreign was clearly seen in the types of NGOs and aid personnel that arrived in South-East Asia after the 2004 tsunami (Kenny 2005).

Such desires are also found in the descriptions of the types of individuals who were drawn to the colonies. As described by the Prince of Wales in his opening address to the 1886 Colonial and Indian Exhibition in London, 'the Colonies...are the legitimate and natural homes, in future, of the more adventurous and energetic portion of the population of these Islands' (British Parliamentary Papers 1886). Indeed, within the person of the aid worker, the embodied links between colonial administration and contemporary humanitarianism can be clearly identified. Duffield (2007:59–60) describes how during the 1950s and '60s the 'expanding overseas voluntary sector' relied on 'people who, through colonial administration, military service, missionary societies or the business world had come of age within the Empire'. While the types of individuals who were attracted to the overseas voluntary sector were initially different from the previous colonial administrators in their desire to give something back, the subsequent merging of NGO and donor processes has meant, once again, a reintegration and exchange of state and non-governmental personnel, through, among other things, the merging of career paths (Duffield 2007:64–5).

On a psychological level, continuities also exist between the two groups over their conflicted emotions surrounding ideas of 'home'. British colonists in India were, on the one hand, living far away from their official domicile. '"We never thought of England as home," recalls Nancy Foster. "It never occurred to us that our home wasn't India"' (Allen 2006:35). On the other hand, their 'home' in the colonies was the bi-product of employment, and therefore subject to uprooting at any moment. This contributed to a feeling of impermanence (*ibid.*:87; see also Blunt 1999). 'For instance, flowers grew very beautifully in the north of India but you knew when you planted some daffodil bulbs that you'd never see them come up' (Allen 2006:87). For some countries, rapid rotation of the diplomatic corps was a precautionary measure against their 'going native' and losing their emotional ties to the metropole. While no such official policy is behind contemporary development practices, the institutionalisation of certain programmatic approaches and categories (for example, the categories of 'relief and response' or 'rapid reaction teams') means that the individuals occupying these positions will find themselves quickly rotated from job to job, from emergency zone to emergency zone. The feeling of impermanence may also account for the iconic role played by the ex-pat hotel in both the colonial and contemporary post-crisis setting (Wrong 2000; Dallaire and Beardsley 2003; Allen 2006).

The impact of this constant mobility is two-fold. First, rapid staff turnover may lead to the impression on behalf of 'local' interlocutors and staff that the international agencies are not truly committed to fostering a long-term relationship with the beneficiary country. It may lead to short termist programming, a lack of institutional memory, and a disproportionate amount of resources going into staff recruitment and relocation. Secondly, this rapid mobility from one disaster site to another makes it difficult for the international staff to engage with their surroundings, leading staff members to turn more easily towards their fellow aid workers than towards their physical surroundings. The institutional structure of international relief and development also creates conditions that promote collusion amongst aid agencies at the field level, by encouraging them to spread the risk of non-delivery among themselves and concentrate on promoting collective successes rather than individual failures (Easterly 2002).

While Easterly concentrates on the negative economic consequences that this has on the inefficient delivery of aid, the sociological impact of such behaviour is also worthy of attention. By creating an environment that encourages intensive networking through frequent meetings, coordination and information exchange, the emotional and intellectual worlds of the international community are arguably defined more by its own needs and demands than by local beneficiaries. Although current policy agendas of international relief and development organisations include the need for increased feedback and input from the target beneficiaries of the aid, it is worth considering the material and spatial circumstances of the way in which this feedback is sought and collected. While participatory planning processes have long been an integral part of humanitarian assistance, they are problematised when we take into consideration the physical and material circumstances in which the processes are held, which may themselves account for the identified inability of beneficiaries to provide feedback (*ibid.*:244). In the same way that the location of peace talks may influence the outcome of a fragile negotiation, so could the location of consultative meetings influence the coordination of particular relief sectors or aid frameworks.

Spatial Continuity B: Separation

The previous section has looked at the common theme of mobility in both the colonial and contemporary development settings. The differential rates of movement between humanitarian aid workers and target beneficiaries will influence programmatic choices such as where and how to build, and who to assist. Intensified by the notion of an 'emergency' of which the ethical imperative for action may justify normally inappropriate decisions, this leads to a situation in which response strategies are determined, in part, by a temporary and short-termist logic. This creates one type of separation. However, within the reconstruction site there also exist built forms of separation between the aid workers and the beneficiaries: forms that evoke colonial patterns and practices. In this section, two particular forms will be examined: the space of the home and the space of the vehicle.

The Space of Home

The living conditions of humanitarian aid workers are often compared informally to architectural and visual typologies of the fortress, the compound, the camp, the cantonment. But how applicable are these allusions? Can comparisons be drawn with colonial approaches to the built environment?

The particular physical type of building will depend significantly upon the circumstance of the particular reconstruction site. Where the built environment has been seriously damaged or destroyed, temporary accommodation may be provided in the form of tents, the few remaining hotels, or rental of select, often premium, properties. Where security is of immediate and significant concern, the built form of the compound may be used. While the camp, or compound, is by no means the only type of physical experience of the international community in a reconstruction zone, it is an evocative one – a place that often becomes the focus of 'ex-pat' meetings and leisure activity, whether or not it is truly representative of the international sentiment at large. Authors such as de Chaine (2002), Ek (2006) and Edkins (2000) have pointed to the physical, bounded structure of the international compound (or 'camp') as having unique and potentially affective properties on the bodies they contain and exclude (Clough and Halley 2007). Descriptions of the US Green Zone in Iraq increasingly point to the implications of conducting a 'reconstruction' from within a walled compound; however, the analysis is not taken beyond the point of journalistic or anecdotal observation (Chandrasekaran 2006). This is particularly surprising when we consider the instrumental role played by the colonial home under British Imperialism.

According to Blunt and Dowling (2006:150), the space of the Anglo-British colonial home was important in the reproduction of the 'domestic, social, and moral values legitimating rules'. It was partly through the example of what a quintessentially British household was supposed to be, that the civilising mission was to be achieved (Gowans 2006). British superiority was to be defined by the degree to which its civility and order differed from the chaotic and unregulated space of the native, and vice-versa (Said 1995). Allen (2006:63) describes the British section of Calcutta as 'a world apart', with residential areas reflecting the social divisions of the colonial administration.

> There were the old parts of central Calcutta where the old palatial *burra* sahibs' houses had been built, left as a legacy to those who came on afterwards, and around them came the new buildings, blocks of flats where the young sahibs lived when they first came out. But as you became more senior and you wanted tennis courts and more servants, you moved into what was called the suburbs. Ballygunge was the second stage, and Alipore, built under the wing of the Belvedere, which had been the old vice-regal lodge and which therefore contained that air of sanctity, was the final stage. (*ibid.*:63–4).[4]

Even within the colonial cantonment, racial demarcations 'reproduced on a domestic scale the racial distancing that underpinned colonial urbanism' (Blunt and Dowling 2006:152). However, the space of the colonial home had at least three further functions. First, the placement of particular settlements or hill stations was useful for purposes of oversight and control of populations (Duncan and Lambert 2004). Second, the adoption of 'European models of household organisation and domesticity' was a central part of assimilationist strategies (*ibid.*: 392). Finally, the linking of metropole to the colonies was a key part of the domestication of empire. Not only did this involve bringing the colonies 'home' through exhibitions, scientific studies and even the import of exotic plant species (Duncan and Lambert 2004; Blunt 1999), but aslo through the transference of architectural styles, aesthetic trends, and legal and educational systems, brought the metropole to the colonies. In this way, the space of the home played a central part in colonial governance and nation building. However, its exclusivity and racial segregation may have also 'provoked racial antagonisms between rulers and ruled, and ultimately contributed to the decline of the British Empire' (Blunt and Dowling 2006:150).

In a contemporary humanitarian context, this resonates with the rental of the most expensive houses in a reconstruction site by internationals, at greatly inflated prices.[5] Similarly, while the names, locations, and political economy of particular hotels, restaurants and clubs may be meaningless to new humanitarian arrivals, they may evoke a material legacy of previous colonial patterns of domination (Sudjic 2005; King 1990; Vale 1992).

The Space of the Vehicle

The separate living spaces of humanitarian workers can be seen to extend to the realm of the vehicle. Few visual images are as evocative of the international community as the white UN SUV. It can be observed across reconstruction settings, often in a caravan with several others, parked outside a particular office complex, bar or restaurant. Even in countries where it is not necessary, it is often used.

The form of the SUV has been extensively analysed within a North American and European context (Bradsher 2003). Edensor (2004:117) describes how cars 'are part of the mediated imaginaries, mundane geographies and everyday practices that inhere in the formation of national identities'. Work on the social impact in the United States of the SUV suggests that its rise parallels a model of citizenship that values safety and inviolability of person above all else (Mitchell 2005; Campbell 2005). If we apply this to a humanitarian context, the material practice of the international community may be seen to constitute an 'attempt at self-imposed exclusion from the wider neighbourhood, as well as the exclusion of others' (Atkinson and Flint

2004:178), reinforcing the observations from local residents that the objectives of the international community are different from those of the community they are assisting.

Such a delimitation from the wider physical context is also found within colonial experience. A description of the 'highly hierarchical' railway carriages, that reflected the social structure of British India reads thus:

> [a] four-berth carriage had been reserved for us with a self-contained toilet compartment with a shower....Furthermore, the windows, which were in triplicate – glass, venetian blinds and gauze – were also latched, so you were in a pretty impregnable position. We asked what would happen if anybody else tried to come into our compartment and were assured that nobody would turn up. No Indian would dare to attempt to come into our compartment so long as he saw more than one European therein. (Allen 2006:59)

This allowed its travellers to ride comfortably, undisturbed and separate from the surroundings they were there to assist. More broadly, the very possibility of travel was imbued with notions of freedom versus 'unfreedom', distinctions which continue to resonate within contemporary humanitarian practice (Grewal 1996).

Implications

This chapter has discussed how continuities exist in the material and spatial practices of the international community with previous Anglo-Indian colonial experiences. The initial examination indicates two ways in which this might be significant. First, even where no obvious barrier exists between the international community and the intended beneficiaries of the assistance, the material practices and spatial dynamics create a bounded microcosm of international activity. Such separation inevitably affects the way in which the international aid workers interact with and understand the target community. This will influence perceptions of what types of response strategies are needed and, through path dependence and 'lessons learned', what types of interventions are used in future reconstruction sites.

Second, particular material and spatial arrangements have an observed impact on the individuals that they are intended to assist. The tropes of the white SUV, the ex-pat hotel, the UN transport planes have become clichés, but their persistence, denigration and targeting indicate their importance in the overall impression of humanitarian intervention. By reinforcing ideas of exclusivity, transience and inaccessibility, neo-colonial categories of us-them; local-international; North-South are reinforced and perpetuated.[6]

How exactly particular material forms or designated places (Cresswell 2004; Agnew 1997) are implicated in and related to larger categories of space (Lefebvre 1991) is the subject of much study. Contemporary theories of cultural geography emphasise the importance of materiality and lived experience in the construction of such abstract, scalar, concepts as the international. For example, in their work on the nation, Jones and Fowler look at the importance of local spaces in the reproduction of the nation. They argue that localised places can become '"metonyms" of the nation' through their abstract and generic representation of national messages, symbols and ideologies (Jones and Fowler 2007:336). Citing Penrose and Jackson (1994), they 'stress the potential for localised places to be key sites for generating ideas and sentiments that can ultimately reproduce the nation' (*ibid.*). But what happens if we extend this to the category of the 'international'? How do particular practices of the international community contribute to creations of larger ideational categories? The classic texts of post-disaster intervention point to the military spatial heritage of humanitarian relief and reconstruction: the tents, the conception, layout and organisation of refugee and relief camps (Kent 1987; Cuny and Abrams 1983; Davis 1978). However, they do not include an examination of older continuities – those that may exist between the built forms of colonial occupation and contemporary relief efforts.

Conclusion

In the current processes and practices of international assistance, the lived experiences and built environment of the international community are rarely examined despite their contributions to the humanitarian imaginary. They may also be an important aspect of the way in which the international community is understood and interpreted at the local level. In this way, although many theorists have cautioned against drawing historical continuities where none exist (between development and colonialism), this analysis suggests that these parallels may be stronger than hitherto suggested and worthy of further sustained examination. The material and spatial practices of these groups will not only inform the immediate and long-term direction of the reconstruction project, but may, ultimately, contribute to the larger social imaginary – both in terms of how the international community sees itself, and how the international community is viewed by others. It is within reconstruction sites and other humanitarian spaces that particular key relations are crystallised, produced and reproduced.

Bibliography

Agnew, J.A. (1997) *Political Geography: A Reader.* London: Arnold.

Allen, C. (2006) *Plain Tales from the Raj.* London: Abacus.

Appadurai, A. (1997) *Modernity at Large: Cultural Dimensions of Globalization.* Minneapolis, MN: University of Minnesota Press.

Atkinson, R. and Flint, J. (2004) 'Fortress UK? Gated Communities, the Spatial Revolt of the Elites and Time-Space Trajectories of Segregation'. *Housing Studies*, 19: 875–92.

Bankoff, G. (2001) 'Rendering the World Unsafe: "Vulnerability" as Western Discourse'. *Disasters* 25: 19–35.

Barnes, T.J. (2003) 'The Place of Locational Analysis: A Selective and Interpretive History'. *Progress in Human Geography* 27: 69–95.

Bauman, Z. (1998) *Globalization: The Human Consequences.* New York: Columbia University Press.

Beck, U. and Ritter, M. (1992) *Risk Society: Towards a New Modernity.* London: Sage.

Blunt, A. (1999) 'Imperial Geographies of Home: British Domesticity in India, 1886–1925'. *Transactions of the Institute of British Geographers* 24: 421–40.

Blunt, A. and Dowling, R.M. (2006) *Home.* London: Routledge.

Bourdieu, P. (1990) *The Logic of Practice.* Cambridge: Polity Press.

Bourdieu, P. and Nice, R. (1977) *Outline of a Theory of Practice.* Cambridge: Cambridge University Press.

Bradsher, K. (2003) *High and Mighty: The Dangerous Rise of the SUV.* New York and Oxford: Public Affairs and Oxford Publicity Partnership [distributor].

British Parliamentary Papers (1886) *Report of the Royal Commission of the Colonial and Indian Exhibition.* London.

Cain, K. (2004) *Emergency Sex (and Other Desperate Measures): [True Stories from a War Zone].* London: Ebury.

Calhoun, C. (2004) 'World of Emergencies: Fear, Intervention, and the Limits of Cosmopolitan Order', 35th Annual Sorokin Lecture. University of Saskatchewan.

Campbell, D. (2005) 'The Bio Politics of Security: Oil, Empire, and the Sports Utility Vehicle'. *American Quarterly*, 57: 943–72.

Castells, M. (2000) *The Rise of the Network Society*. Oxford: Blackwell.
Castoriadis, C. (1987) *The Imaginary Institution of Society*. Oxford: Polity Press in conjunction with Blackwell.
Chandler, D. (2006) *Empire in Denial: The Politics of State-Building*. London: Pluto.
Chandrasekaran, R. (2006) *Imperial Life in the Emerald City*. New York: Alfred A. Knopf.
Clough, P.T. and Halley, J.O.M. (2007) *The Affective Turn: Theorizing the Social*. Durham, NC and Chesham: Duke University Press and Combined Academic [distributor].
Collier, P. (2007) *The Bottom Billion: Why the Poorest Countries are Failing and What Can be Done About It*. Oxford: Oxford University Press.
Crang, M.A.N.T. (2000) *Thinking Space*. London and New York: Routledge.
Cresswell, T. (2004) *Place: A Short Introduction*. Oxford: Blackwell.
Cuny, F.C. and Abrams, S. (1983) *Disasters and Development*. New York: Oxford University Press.
Cutter, S. (2006) *The Geography of Social Vulnerability: Race, Class and Catastrophe*. London: Social Science Research Council.
Dallaire, R.O.A. and Beardsley, B. (2003) *Shake Hands with the Devil: The Failure of Humanity in Rwanda*. Toronto: Random House Canada.
Davis, I. (1978) *Shelter After Disaster*. Oxford: Oxford Polytechnic Press.
Davis, M. (2000) *Late Victorian Holocausts: El Nino Famines and the Making of the Third World*. London: Verso Press.
De Certeau, M.D. (1988) *The Practice of Everyday Life*. Berkeley, CA: University of California Press.
De Chaine, D.R. (2002) 'Humanitarian Space and the Social Imaginary: Médecins Sans Frontières and the Rhetoric of Global Community'. *Journal of Communications Inquiry*, 26: 364–69.
De Waal, A. (1997) *Famine Crimes: Politics and the Disaster Relief Industry in Africa*. Oxford: James Currey.
Diamond, J.M. (2005) *Collapse : How Societies Choose to Fail or Survive*. London: Allen Lane.
Duffield, M.R. (1991) *War and Famine in Africa*. Oxford: Oxfam.
Duffield, M.R. (2007) *Development, Security and Unending War: Governing the World of Peoples*. Cambridge: Polity Press.
Duncan, J.S. and Lambert, D. (2004) 'Landscapes of Home'. In Duncan, J.S., Johnson, N.C. and Schein, R.H. (eds) *A Companion to Cultural Geography*. Malden, MA and Oxford: Blackwell, pp. 382–403.
Easterly, W. (2002) 'The Cartel of Good Intentions: The Problem of Bureaucracy in Foreign Aid'. *Policy Reform*, 5: 223–50.
Edensor, T. (2004) 'Automobility and National Identity: Representation, Geography and Driving Practice'. *Theory, Culture & Society*, 21: 101–20.
Edkins, J. (2000) *Whose Hunger? Concepts of Famine, Practices of Aid*. Minneapolis, MN and London: University of Minnesota Press.
Ek, R. (2006) 'Giorgio Agamben and the Spatialities of the Camp: an Introduction'. *Geografiska Annaler, Series B* 88: 363–86.
Escobar, A. (1994) *Encountering Development: The Making and Unmaking of the Third World*. Princeton, NJ and Chichester: Princeton University Press.
Ferguson, J. (2006) *Global Shadows: Africa in the Neoliberal World Order*. Durham, NC & London: Duke University Press.
Giroux, H.A. (2006) *Stormy Weather: Katrina and the Politics of Disposability*. Boulder, CO and London: Paradigm.
Gowans, G. (2006) 'Travelling Home: British Women Sailing from India, 1940–1947'. *Women's Studies International Forum* 29: 81–95.
Graham, S. and Marvin, S. (2001) *Splintering Urbanism: Networked Infrastructures, Technological Mobilities and the Urban Condition*. London: Routledge.
Grewal, I. (1996) *Home and Harem: Nation, Gender, Empire, and the Cultures of Travel*. Durham, NC and London: Duke University Press.
Harvey, D. (2001) *Spaces of Capital: Towards a Critical Geography*. Edinburgh: Edinburgh University Press.
Hewitt, K. (1995) 'Sustainable Disasters? Perspectives and Powers in the Discourse of Calamities'. In Crush, J. (ed.) *Power of Development*. London: Routledge, pp. 111–24.
Hirst, P.Q. and Thompson, G. (1999) *Globalization in Question: The International Economy and the Possibilities of Governance*. Cambridge: Polity Press.
Hoogvelt, A. (2006) 'Globalization and Post-modern Imperialism'. *Globalizations* 3: 159–74.
Hubbard, P., Kitchin, R. and Valentine, G. (2004) *Key Thinkers on Space and Place*. London: Sage.
Inayatullah, N.A.D L.B. (2004) *International Relations and the Problem of Difference*. New York: Routledge..
Jones, R., and Fowler, C. (2007) 'Placing and Scaling the Nation'. *Environment and Planning D: Society and Space* 25: 332–54.
Kearns, G. (1997) 'The Imperial Subject: Geography and Travel in the Work of Mary Kingsley and Halford Mackinder'. *Transactions of the Institute of British Geographers* vol. 22 (4): 450–72.

Keen, D. (1994) *The Benefits of Famine: A Political Economy of Famine and Relief in Southwestern Sudan, 1983–1989*. Princeton, NJ and Chichester: Princeton University Press.
Kenny, S. (2005) 'Reconstruction in Aceh: Building whose capacity?' *Community Development Journal* 42: 206–21.
Kent, R.C. (1987) *Anatomy of Disaster Relief: The International Network in Action*. London: Pinter.
King, A.D. (1990) *Urbanism, Colonialism, and the World Economy: Cultural and Spatial Foundations of the World Urban System*. London: Routledge.
Klein, N. (2007) *The Shock Doctrine: The Rise of Disaster Capitalism*. London: Allen Lane.
Landes, D.S. (1998) *The Wealth and Poverty of Nations: Why Some are so Rich and Some so Poor.* London: Little, Brown and Company.
Lefebvre, H. (1991) *The Production of Space*. Oxford: Basil Blackwell.
Mamdani, M. (2007) 'The Politics of Naming: Genocide, Civil War, Insurgency'. *London Review of Books* 29(5): 1–9.
Massey, D. (2006) *For Space*. London: Sage.
Massumi, B. (2002) *Parables for the Virtual: Movement, Affect, Sensation*. Durham, NC: Duke University Press.
Merleau-Ponty, M. (1962) *Phenomenology of Perception*. London: Routledge & Keegan Paul.
Mitchell, D. (2005) 'The S.U.V. Model of Citizenship: Floating Bubbles, Buffer Zones, and the Rise of the "Purely Atomic" Individual'. *Political Geography* 24: 77–100.
O'Keefe, P., Westgate, K. and Wisner, B. (1976) 'Taking the Naturalness out of Natural Disasters'. *Nature* 260: 556–7.
Paris, R. (2006) *At War's End: Building Peace after Civil Conflict*. Cambridge: Cambridge University Press.
Penrose, J. and Jackson, P. (1994) *Constructions of Race, Place and Nation*. Minneapolis, MN: University of Minnesota Press.
Pratt, M.L. (1992) *Imperial Eyes: Travel Writing and Transculturation*. London: Routledge.
Pugh, M. (2005) 'Peacekeeping and Critical Theory', In Bellamy, A.J.A.P.W. (ed.) *Peace Operations and Global Order.* London and Oxford: Frank Cass and Routledge, pp. 39–58.
Pupuvac, V. (2005) 'Human Security and the Rise of Global Therapeutic Governance'. *Conflict, Security & Development* 5: 161–81.
Said, E.W. (1978) *Orientalism*. Harmondsworth: Penguin.
Sassen, S. (2000) *Cities in a World Economy*. Thousand Oaks, CA and London: Pine Forge Press.
Scott, J.C. (1998) *Seeing like a State: How Certain Schemes to Improve the Human Condition have Failed.* New Haven, CT and London: Yale University Press.
Slater, D. (1997) 'Geopolitical Imaginations Across the North-South Divide: Issues of Difference, Development and Power'. *Political Geography* 16: 631–53.
Smith, N. (2006) *There's No Such Thing as a Natural Disaster*. London: Social Science Research Council.
Sudjic, D. (2005) *The Edifice Complex: How the Rich and Powerful Shape the World.* London: Allen Lane.
Taylor, C. (2002) 'Modern Social Imaginaries'. *Public Culture* 14: 91–124.
Taylor, C. (2005) *Modern Social Imaginaries*. Durham, NC and London: Duke University Press.
Telford, J.A.J.C. (2006) *Joint Evaluation of the International Response to the Indian Ocean Tsunami: Synthesis Report*. London: Tsunami Evaluation Coalition.
Tuathail, G. (1996) *Critical Gopolitics: The Politics of Writing Global Space*. London: Routledge.
Vale, L.J. (1992) *Architecture, Power and National Identity*. New Haven, CT and London: Yale University Press.
Virilio, P. (1991) *The Aesthetics of Disappearance*. New York: Semiotext(e).
Wrong, M. (2000) *In the Footsteps of Mr Kurtz: Living on the Brink of Disaster in the Congo.* London: Fourth Estate.

Notes

1 Empirical work for this chapter is based upon open-ended interviews with subjects working in and on the post-crisis reconstruction in Aceh and Sri Lanka. The themes are part of a doctoral dissertation at the University of Cambridge, Centre for International Studies entitled: 'Post-Crisis Built Environments of the International Community'. For their comments and suggestions, the author would like to thank Mark Duffield, Vernon Hewitt, Tarak Barkawi, David Nally and Arran Gaunt.
2 This is part of the reason why the inability of the US to respond to Hurricane Katrina was so disturbing. It drew into question the ability, and therefore the legitimacy, of the US to respond to overseas emergencies.
3 Allen translates *chaprassi* as 'office servant' or 'messenger'.
4 Allen translate *burra sahib* as 'great man'.

5 According to Allen's interviewees, bachelors would typically live in a shared household, with a cook, and basic rented furniture. Such themes can be easily translated into the social divisions in contemporary development practice, with young, unattached emergency workers living in shared, rented accommodation, while heads of station and senior staff of bilateral and multilateral agencies will be put in large, often grand houses suitable for diplomatic functions; their furniture shipped by their agency from a previous duty station.

6 For example, the representative significance of the form of the white SUV can be seen in its violent targeting in a variety of humanitarian and developmental contexts. In certain situations (Afghanistan) non-governmental organisations purposefully defaced their white SUVs to make them less conspicuous. Elsewhere, development organisations have recently forgone the traditional white SUV in favour of local taxi cabs (Darfur), and mini buses (Liberia).

7

The International Politics of Social Transformation
Trusteeship & Intervention in Historical Perspective

DAVID WILLIAMS
& TOM YOUNG

Introduction

The premise of this chapter is that colonialism was always in part about social transformation. Despite the tendency in recent history and social science writing to play down the idea of the '*mission civilisatrice*' (for fairly obvious ideological reasons), its plausibility is prompted by a number of considerations. Firstly, the ending of the slave trade and the relative failure of 'legitimate commerce' provided the setting for the colonial experiment. Very crudely thinking about these matters was shaped by understandings of 'civilisations' and the absence of such in an Africa characterised by petty despotisms and endemic (quasi-criminal) conflict that was unable to sustain the minimum requirements of order and commerce, including the 'internal' order needed to finish off the slave trade. The pervasive sentiments of superiority, however repulsive to modern liberal ears (in part because of their not infrequent racial gloss), are understandable in the historical context (extreme technological disparities between African and European societies, widespread pseudo-Darwinian assumptions, etc.) and it is implausible to see them as (mere) rationalisations of conquest (Klein 1999; Colley 1994), or, in more recent vein, that the reproduction of 'difference' was a form of oppression of the 'other' (Said 1978; Todorov 1993). This obscures the very strong assertions of the universality of human nature throughout the modern period, even with regard to Africa, tempered, of course, by all sorts of quasi-evolutionary assumptions (Bell 2006).

Secondly, there are the remarkable parallels between colonialism as a civilising mission and a domestic strategy focused on the discipline of mass populations within the framework of the nation-state; the contemptuous rhetoric directed towards the domestic masses at the least rivalled that directed at colonial natives. This is not a new point but it has not perhaps been fully explored. It is instructive to recall that in France even in the 1870s standard French was a foreign language for half the population; that the country did not use standard time till 1891; that wall-maps of France were not used in schools till the 1880s, with the first nationality law and universal military service in 1889. The project of turning 'peasants into Frenchmen' is familiar, as is the way in which successive French governments unified the country (extension of the railway and education systems; nation-wide banking system; military service; public support for symbolic capital and so on) (Weber 1976).

The French case is, of course, well-known as is the prominent role of the state. But the processes, and even the timing were perhaps not so different in the English case.

Popular customs had, of course, been targeted by elites at least since the sixteenth century but the English elite moved decisively against the 'rough' elements of popular culture in the last quarter of the nineteenth century. Rowdy festivities and traditions, loud music and forms of popular justice, all were effectively eroded not least by their appropriation by middle-class elites which drained them of their popular content. And where popular culture was not appropriated it was replaced, particularly by organised sport managed through bureaucratic and national processes. The role of the central state seems less prominent in England but it is a domestic civilising mission nonetheless. A historian writing of this period suggests that, 'Religion in general, and the civilising mission in particular, worked to strengthen the distinction between a "cultivated", Christian and philanthropic middle class and an ignorant, heathen, and morally irresponsible mass' (Gunn 1996). But he is talking about Manchester, not Africa. A kind of practical historicism was by no means limited to exotic 'others', but informed thinking and practice about Ireland, Scotland and England itself. There were widespread doubts about the possibility of applying general laws and a greater concern with apparently historically specific practices and institutions (Dewey 1974; Lustick 1993).

Thirdly, both these factors played some role in shaping the emergence of an international order comprising competitive nation-states but increasingly seeing themselves as sovereign within a framework of like states, and those same states lording it over 'inferior' peoples, defined as outside a 'standard of civilisation' (Hegel 1952). This latter came in degrees, of course, as can be seen in the relative treatment, of say, Turkey and China compared with outright colonies. Colonial conquest of Africa, though undoubtedly fuelled by great power rivalries, also, from the beginning, had an element of international tutelage. At various international gatherings the colonising powers committed themselves not merely to bringing the 'blessings of civilisation' (Berlin Conference) but also controlling the arms and alcohol trades. The notoriously brutal and really extractive (private) regime of Leopold II in the Congo was eventually terminated through pressure from the major powers (Koskenniemi, 2001).

Thus it can be argued that, while colonial conquest involved violence and domination, it was not a purely exploitative, extractive or nationalist project. It did take place under definite conditions which shaped its precise trajectory – notably economic and political rivalries between western nation-states as well as contingent factors, particularly technological developments (in armaments and medicine). It was shaped also by the particular institutional and other exigencies of the states embarking on it; clearly, therefore, local institutional differences (the positions of the army or the ministry of finance) made a difference to colonial policy as it developed. But it retained a strong element of domination in order to effect transformation in the dominated object. Colonialism involved full-scale political control: there were to be no half-way-house deals with existing African sovereignties; nor were African polities to be treated as equals (or indeed recognised as states) in the realm of international power politics (none were invited to the Berlin Conference). These two facts alone suggest the implausibility of narrowly economic understandings of the phenomenon, since other forms of informal control had proved workable before (indeed, forms of formal control at least over parts of states were not uncommon in the nineteenth century, cf. the Greek and Ottoman public debt). Finally, colonialism was never reducible to the actions of states but included other forces, also, notably missionaries but later more secularly orientated 'experts', often concerned to distance themselves in significant ways from colonial states; the precursors of what we now call international organisations, and so on.

All these features left their mark on colonial practice, but of the complex sets of constraints and imperatives the following seem to stand out. Firstly, the tension between the maintenance of order at minimal cost (Sara Berry's 'hegemony on a shoestring') and a commitment to effecting change. Secondly, the management of the direct and indirect effects of colonial rule itself. And thirdly, the different analyses and agendas of those involved in the colonial project – different kinds of officials, missionaries, business interests, metropolitan lobbies. We suggest that the outcomes of these tensions may be characterised in three ideal types and that actual colonial rule was always a mixture of these:

1. In more conservative mode the maintenance of order is the overwhelming priority and often involved close relations with local intermediaries ('indirect rule') of a quasi-collaborative type and considerable reluctance to upset local social arrangements. This was sometimes allied to a rather nostalgic regard for elements of non-industrial society and resistance to perceived agents of change such as missionaries.

2. The construction of the colonial territory and state had unavoidable effects; limiting the points to the political area, these included the very idea of a tightly defined territory with an identity of a kind, e.g. a 'capital', the physicality of power (colonial buildings etc.), a single system of law (at least supreme over customary law), in principle a single currency. Another effect was the creation, not least for reasons of cost, of a new class of natives as state employees: court clerks, interpreters, later teachers and minor officials who to a degree internalised the values of the colonisers (language, personal names, modes of dress and marriage etc.) and arguably in the more advanced colonies comprised elements of a 'civil society' (press and public debate) (Ibhawoh 2002).

3. In more progressive mode characterised by both a commitment to some notion of development which clearly tracked metropolitan norms (wage labour, housing, welfare and family structures, education) and therefore involved confrontation with, or at least disapproval of, practices 'repugnant to civilisation' (female circumcision, polygamy, bride price, elaborate funeral ceremonies, widowhood practices etc. cf. the British abolition of *sati* in 1829) and a more positive attitude towards the 'educated African' not necessarily in the sense of being entitled to political independence but in the sense of being a potential citizen. Colonial legal history provides considerable evidence of efforts to create a modern legal system which will eventually supersede the tactical concessions to native custom. Even the codification of 'customary law' was not intended to preserve the status quo but to evolve with changing circumstances. Customary courts were placed under increasing supervision from 'modern' judicial authorities (Gocking 1997).

Conklin concludes for French West Africa that 'the Government General's long-term objective remained, in Africa as in France, a free labour economy, in which the self-directed laborer worked to satisfy ever-expanding wants'(Conklin 1998). There is a general point here that colonial bureaucracies, while subject to political control, were by no means uniform, and different sections of them could and did pursue different agendas. 'Specialist' officials did not necessarily acquire colonial service 'attitudes'. In the realm of education, for example, it is simply not true that the objective was the inculcation of a slave mentality. The designer of the history syllabus for Gold Coast talked of syllabuses designed for the 'cool and well-balanced citizen of a modern State'. Again, while some school textbooks took standard positions about the worthlessness of African history, others did not. Somervell, a writer of officially sanctioned school textbooks, wanted an 'Africo-centric history syllabus' (Zachernuk 1998). What seems undeniable is that the discourses and practices the colonisers brought with them inevitably brought about social change – colonial rule then was much more than domination; it was the transfer of new forms of social order.

Sovereignty, Development & the Liberal Order

Even before World War II, colonialism, either because it had succeeded or because it had failed, was coming to be seen as something of an historical anachronism. Old ideas of civilisation were increasingly discredited, new notions of sovereignty made it possible to conceive of, and allow the creation of, weak states that had negative rather than positive sovereignty (Jackson 1990). This was strongest in Britain, which had a long constitutional tradition of conceding self-government to colonies. The principle of territorial annexation was increasingly questioned and resulted in the colonies of the defeated powers in World War I being transformed into mandates. (Callahan 1999). The major powers were also engaged in building an international architecture which, while it remained, in important ways, crippled by Great Power or Cold War confrontation, nevertheless institutionalised notions of the juridical equality of people, states and 'cultures' – 'religion, or the controversial test of degree of civilisation, has ceased to be, as such, a condition of recognition of statehood'.(Zhang 1991). The ILO, for example, had long taken an interest in colonial questions and, while not confrontational towards colonial powers, had already placed them under pressure to make further progress in areas like disguised forms of servile labour. This partial internationalisation predates World War II but was, of course, enormously reinforced by that conflict, the ideological terms of which, however ignored in the immediate post-war period, allowed only a remnant of colonialism in the form of trusteeship.

Thus, while much of the pressure for decolonisation came from within the colonies themselves, the anti-colonial struggle in Africa was in a sense, and of course with exceptions, something of a false combat. Colonialism had, in all sorts of ways not necessarily explicit or intentional, paved the way for a modernising elite, much of the discontent amongst whom concerned neither the direction nor the destination but the somewhat leisurely pace of the journey. As Nkrumah put it in 1961, the people had to be liberated 'from the bondage of foreign colonial rule and the tyranny of local feudalism'. Beyond identification of the enemy, African nationalism comprised deep resentment of 'backwardness', understood largely in terms of wealth and power, allied with an equally strong conviction that the way to overcome that backwardness was to emulate the Western state as closely as possible, with all its attendant representational, bureaucratic and juridical modes insofar as these expedited modernisation. African nationalism was about the securing of power in already demarcated territories, the control and consolidation of already existing states and the (if necessary) ruthless subjection of heterogeneous societies to the processes of modernisation.

In all of this Western states and the multilateral institutions promised to assist. In other words, the project of social transformation becomes, with decolonisation, 'internalised' to the newly independent states. At the same time, the institutions of the liberal international order undertake to assist states in the achievement of this project, and in so doing the project becomes 'multilateralised'. The achievement of state sovereignty in the post-war world was, then, distinctly double-edged. Sovereignty represented the institutionalisation of a notion of collective freedoms (captured under the name 'self-determination'); but it also represented a set of expectations about what countries were to do with their new-found freedom; and, in turn, a set of expectations about what the governments of these countries were to do for their people. To use Reus-Smit's phrase, development had become one of the 'moral purposes' of the state: 'legitimate statehood and rightful state action were ... increasingly tied to the augmentation of individuals' purposes and potentialities' (Reus-Smit, 1999). Into the normative structure of international politics had emerged the view that it was, in the end, individual persons and their well-being that provided the only legitimate foundation for state sovereignty.

In the immediate post-war period, the pursuit of development became not just a moral obligation; it became wrapped up with the broader aims of the architects of the post-war order (Craig and Porter 2004). A concern with economic development was central to the aims of the liberal order established under US hegemony (Deudney and Ikenberry 1999; Ruggie 1982; Latham 1997). As the US State Department put it, 'this work as a whole required consideration of the political, territorial, military, economic and social conditions essential to enduring peace'.(Burley 1993). American planners drew the traditional liberal connection between economic prosperity and peace. To be sure, much of this was initially driven by a reflection on the conditions of pre-war Europe, where it was argued that economic crisis had led directly to political violence (Latham 1997:130). The concern to ensure economic prosperity was manifest in the stress on economic openness (at least within certain limits) and the establishment of a regulatory order that would ensure international economic stability. It was also given an immediate institutional embodiment in the Marshall Plan, albeit in this case yoked to an anxiety about the vulnerability of European states to Communist influence.

But it was also, and importantly, expressed in the establishment of multilateral development institutions such as the World Bank. The obvious tensions here were, for a time at least, obscured by a view of the development process, and a view of the role of external agents in assisting that process, that focused largely on the transfer of capital and relatively large-scale, capital-intensive projects. The sovereign state was to be the primary agent of development. For example, the vast bulk of Bank lending at this time was for infrastructure projects (Mason and Asher 1974). The primary domestic problems were seen by the Bank to be the lack of infrastructure necessary for private enterprise to flourish and the lack of domestic savings to finance infrastructure development; hence the need for Western capital.

Taken together, these shifts shaped the way Western states and development agencies related to their borrower countries. Both the new nationalist leaders and the Western states agreed on the necessity and urgency of social transformation; nationalist leaders promised to make good the promise of sovereignty by pursuing the project; and Western states and development agencies promised to assist states in this project. The tensions here are obvious. First, there was a tension between sovereignty as freedom and sovereignty as obligation, especially given that international institutions like the World Bank were committed to assisting countries fulfil their developmental obligations. This established the possibility that when states became seen as having failed in this obligation, sovereignty would be trumped by the pursuit of development by international agencies like the World Bank. Second, and related, while development agencies concerned themselves with only a narrow range of issues, their development thinking was powered by the idea that they really did know what was best for these countries. There is the possibility here that, should development agencies start to concern themselves with a much wider range of issues, they would feel justified in pursuing much more interventionist development policies.

Some of this started to happen in the late 1970s and early 1980s. The debt crisis and the more general development crisis that began to engulf many developing states during this period coincided with a rethinking of development theory and development policy among the major Western donors, and especially in the IMF and World Bank (Toye1987). The result – a new stress on the centrality of the market mechanism – was pursued through structural adjustment lending (Mosley *et al.* 1995). But while structural adjustment lending was certainly more intrusive than the development practices of the 1960s and 1970s, it remained nonetheless broadly within the sovereignty model: Governments established quasi-contractual relations with the Bretton Woods institutions according to which they were supposed to undertake policy changes in return for loans.

As the 1980s wore on the extent and depth of the economic crisis, particularly in Africa became clearer, as did the fact that structural adjustment was not producing its expected results. At the same time the economistic logic of neo-liberalism became applied to politicians and bureaucrats (Kreuger 1992). The World Bank's 1988 *Annual Report* argued that 'individuals whether in or out of government use the resources at their disposal to further their own private interests' (World Bank 1988: 49–51). As Craig and Porter have put it, this view is one of 'bad policemen and greedy officials, abusing power to oppress the poor' (Craig and Porter 2004:8). Seen in this way, these arguments provided a powerful justification for increasingly intrusive development strategies, for in any developmental accounting the real economic interests of society would take preference over the detrimental actions of a small number of self-seeking politicians and bureaucrats (Hawthorn and Seabright 1993). It was here that the sovereignty model started to erode. For, according to this logic, politicians and bureaucrats could not be relied upon simply to pursue the project of social transformation; rather they would do so only if they were constrained within political and institutional structures – i.e. good governance. In this way the promises of nationalism were recast as empty rhetoric.

The post-war era had, then, been characterised by a deep ambiguity. On the one hand, it had produced an order with genuine elements of sovereign equality in which all states were recognised to be juridically equal (Chandler 2000). They were assisted with fairly generous allocations of aid and allowed considerable leeway as to their domestic economic, social and political arrangements. No doubt these elements were more salient in the African case because, with the exception of the Horn and South Africa, the continent remained relatively insignificant strategically speaking. On the other hand, it had implanted the elements which could produce a new kind of hierarchy between states.

Social Change 'at a Distance'

The balance between these two changed dramatically with the end of the Cold war. Two conceptual shifts seem to be central concerning sovereignty and rights. Contemporary discourse on these matters has shifted towards (or back?) to restricted notions of sovereignty no longer as something inheremt in states but in states in relation to their populations. This suggests, of course, a revival of older notions of trusteeship etc. which, as already suggested, carry strong quasi-evolutionary assumptions about progress. However, because the connection between states and individuals is articulated in a strongly universalistic idiom of rights, such evolutionary assumptions are no longer plausible or indeed even available.

This rather explosive combination then sanctions interference in states by other states on behalf of the population of the target state (Williams 2005). But such a combination precludes the resurrection of overtly colonial modes of administration (despite a degree of nostalgia for them in certain liberal circles) and produces the tricky terrain of effecting social transformation 'at a distance' without direct local control. Worse, the shrill urgency of 'rights' and the absence of evolutionary reassurances generate pressure for very rapid change.

Both the logic and the means of interference would inevitably be re-shaped by global changes. New forms of interference would therefore be framed by wider processes of deterritorialisation and the undermining of state sovereignty and the construction of new kinds of global institutional architecture in which states would be enmeshed – practices which Western states were already busily engaged in imposing on themselves. And as, in a truly global system, it is conceptually, and even empirically, difficult to treat some countries differently, to these has been added a third objective, relatively novel but not without precedents, namely, the construction of appropriate states. Thus new forms of intervention, both direct and indirect, have come to shape Africa policy.

Direct intervention has tended to take four forms. The first is intervention which directly impinges on the sovereignty of states and relies in part on recent problematisations of the notion of sovereignty or explicit attempts to place new limits on it. Of these the most dramatic, and politically problematic, have been interventions of the 'humanitarian' kind using coercive force and armed peace-keeping operations. The second is the development of a whole new raft of conditionalities aimed at shifting the behaviour of states but which are not the stuff of traditional state-to-state relations. These are not usefully understood as in the interest of more powerful states but are designed to effect policy changes within target states. The third takes the form of enmeshing states in new global architectures, of which the most important are the economic and the quasi-legal. The fourth is the attempt to reshape political and administrative elites to sustain these various regimes and conditionalities.

A first essential shift in the contemporary era is the practice of 'humanitarian intervention'. The Great Powers have now used armed force or waged open war against states or political forces within states on a number of occasions in which 'humanitarian' motives have been claimed. It is common to dismiss these claims as bogus, as little more than a cover for other more traditional *Realpolitik* motives, but this is a mistake. The distinction between traditional state 'interests' (themselves never given and always subject to discursive construction) and ethical motives fails to capture the sense in which Western elites increasingly regard their interests as served by the, if necessary, forcible reconstruction of whole societies (Paris 2002). The shrill chorus of support for this amongst civil society, NGO organisations and 'progressive' forces gives the lie to any notion of a deep disagreement between Western states' elites, multilateral agencies and self-proclaimed civil society groupings. There are, however, political constraints on such violent incursions and political risks in participating in them. Their justification to wider domestic constituencies may involve large-scale mendacity (as in the recent war against Iraq) which comes to haunt its promoters (and their claques in academia and the media), and their legitimation in terms of human sympathies may run up against the notoriously fickle limitations (and ignorance) of Western public opinion.

The extent and the modalities of conditional lending have changed dramatically from narrowly agency-state-related and specific conditionalities associated with structural adjustment to the multilateralisation of conditionality via mechanisms like the Comprehensive Development Framework and Poverty Reduction Strategy Papers (PSRPs). At the same time, there has been the development of various forms of political conditionalities. There has been an increasing willingness to impose all sorts of conditionalities, including political conditionalities, on states hitherto regarded as sovereign (Williams 2005). Even as early as the second half of the 1980s the World Bank turned increasingly towards the use of sectoral adjustment loans (SECAL) rather than more general structural adjustment loans. SECALs were designed to pursue the objective of economic policy reform at a sectoral rather than economy-wide level, and as such they usually involved smaller amounts of money and tended to have fewer conditions attached to them. This made them easier for the Bank to implement and monitor, and they could be undertaken when the Bank and the borrower government could not agree on an overall programme of macroeconomic policy changes. Most important of all, SECALs proved to be a more effective instrument for the pursuit of economic restructuring (Jayarajah and Branson 1995).

Despite these, serious problems of both implementation and outcomes became apparent. Even when short-term macroeconomic balance had been achieved, the supply-side response of adjusting economies was very much slower. The expected improvements in investment, productivity and output were in many cases so slow in coming that they potentially endangered the whole adjustment effort, since neither interest groups nor politicians would receive substantial benefits in the short or even medium term from structural adjustment (Mosley *et al.* 1995). For the World Bank, it became clear that a major reason for the poor private sector response to adjustment, especially in the non-export sector, was the institutional framework within which the private sector operated. This led the Bank beyond the issue of unnecessary government regulation of the economy, to such issues as the legal system, the regulatory framework, contract enforcement, the predictability of government policy, the banking and financial systems, and the lack of accurate and timely economic information. It was becoming clear that much more detailed institutional engineering was necessary to produce a dynamic market economy. What was significant about the focus on institutional reform was that it required that the day-to-day workings of individual bureaucrats, as well as entire bureaucracies, and their relations with politicians and clients, be brought into view.

At the same time, there has been an inadequately studied but very significant shift whereby development agencies, both bilateral and multilateral, as well as many development NGOs, have become more integrated into a single 'development community'. Dissenting voices among significant development institutions have almost vanished (Jokinen, 2004). Many of the various aid agencies are linked together through formal and informal arrangements. NGOs, for example, are often used as implementing agencies by larger aid organisations. The various organisations at work in any one country often engage in (more or less successful) coordination of their development activities. There is a pattern of rotation of staff from one agency to another (de Waal 1997). Many organisations have relationships of various kinds with academics, researchers, 'development consultants' and government officials. It is this that leads James Morton to call the 'aid machine' a 'bureaucratic-academic complex' (Morton 1996).

In theory the PRSP process is supposed to lead to greater country 'ownership' of development programmes by encouraging 'participation' in the process of defining development objectives and designing development strategies. In reality, the content of the poverty reduction strategies that emerge from this process have been almost identical with the development strategy advocated by the World Bank and, in addition, there are good reasons to be sceptical about the extent and impact of 'participation' within this process (Whitfield 2005). Rather than regarding the PRSP process as a way of overcoming the problems of accountability and legitimacy associated with extensive external intervention in political, social and economic life, it might be better seen as a way of increasingly legitimating this intervention. What this means in fact is, first, that lots of other donors are pursuing projects with the same ambitious scope and the same level of detail, and second that, at the level of development strategy, recipient countries are increasingly facing aid donors as a unified bloc. Under these conditions it is not clear that 'sovereignty' means very much for states in Africa (Williams 2003).

Regimes & Reform Coalitions

Here we designate attempts to make permanent a latticework of conditionalities in a form that is internalised by states and eventually political elites, that is to say, new ways of enmeshing states in new kinds of international architectures as well as regional variants of those architectures. An economic example may suffice. The Asian financial crisis led the World Bank, in tandem with the IMF, to embrace an agenda of far-reaching financial-sector institutional reform with the explicit aim of developing surveillance and governance regimes that would (in theory) ensure the stability of domestic financial systems (Wade and Veneroso 1998). In 1999, they established the Financial Sector Assessment Program (FSAP), the aim of which is to 'monitor financial system soundness ... to assess the effectiveness of various aspects of monetary and financial policies and to promote the *harmonization* and *international convergence* of key financial policy areas' (World Bank 2005). The assessments themselves examine the extent and quality of domestic surveillance practices, the extent and quality of domestic regulatory and supervisory institutions, and the extent and quality of the financial system infrastructure (legal system, accounting and auditing framework, disclosure regime, reporting requirements, and so on). They are also explicitly concerned with assessing the extent to which domestic financial governance regimes comply with international standards and 'best practices' (*ibid.*). Financial sector reform becomes concerned with the creation of a 'framework of governance linkages that cut across national borders', as a World Bank staff member has put it (Kaufmann 2004).

A final form of direct intervention may be called the construction of 'reform coalitions' or, if we want to recall the historical precedents, the reinvigoration of modernising elites. Western agencies have not, of course, hesitated to engage in various ad hoc pressures on ruling elites, most usually requiring them to concede open elections, but this has been subject to various political hazards and has lacked consistency and continuity (Gibson 1999; Brown 2001). These experiences have promoted a readiness to commit long-term support to elite groups within certain countries who are deemed to have internalised the liberal project agenda (Kelsall 2002). This support is aimed at certain sections of the bureaucracy, notably the Ministry of Finance and the political elite more generally. The latter have benefited from huge flows of resources not merely to keep their state afloat (Uganda relies on external finance for 50 per cent of its budget) but also to fuel their own accumulation strategies (Harrison 2001).

Harrison talks about social coalitions, minimally pliant governing elites. When faced with what it sees as a recalcitrant and incapable bureaucracy, one of the World Bank's favourite tactics has been to work with bureaucratic 'enclaves'. This is where the Bank works closely with a select group of politicians and bureaucrats, often in the Ministry of Finance. The idea behind this is to obtain the support of certain influential bureaucrats in the hope that they will be able to use their political power to get the rest of the bureaucracy to fall into line. 'Donors have tended to unduly personalise relationships they have with a number of institutions when they have found individuals competent and cooperative' (Aryeetey and Cox 1997:105). It is a reasonable surmise that, for all the talk about transparency and accountability, this is regarded by the Western powers as a price that has to be paid, at least in certain cases, for the reconstitution of the domestic modernisers (Hanlon 2002).

The achievements of direct intervention strategies remain, for their promoters at least, alarmingly elusive, and subject to a variety of instabilities, stemming not least from those very promoters. The multiplicity of goals and the continuing rivalries of Western states, the sometimes uneasy relations between those states and a burgeoning realm of non-state agencies and international organisations, and the still uncertain forms of coordination across these many forces which have so far been constructed, have all ensured that the process of transformation has been, for many, tortuously slow. Beyond that, in a whole series of areas the external promoters of change have encountered not just the obvious obstacles like the sullen non-cooperation, if not active hostility, of target elites, but also unexpected effects and unanticipated consequences. Target elites and social groups more generally have not been slow to spot new spaces for manoeuvre and new resources to be accessed (Rakner 2003). So the relative failure of these strategies, in an environment of increasingly open contempt for the sovereignty of the weak, has prompted a new raft of policies and instruments designed to refashion states and societies not so much by constraining them from without as by effecting changes from within, such that they become fit for and fit into the newly developing global architectures.

There is a kind of ineluctability to these policies, an almost gravitational pull, such that, as each policy area is seen, if not to fail, then to be inadequately configured on its own, yet another policy front has to be opened up. If macroeconomic policy is irrational, this may require the training of new economists who speak the right language and pressures on the local state to heed their voices; but this in turn requires a capacity for policy debate and for the provision and diffusion of information; but this will be worthless without an accountable state which has internalised the need to hear these debates; but an accountable state is inconceivable without a political force, something like a civil society, holding it to account; but such a civil society must be capable of sustaining political organisations; such organisations may indeed come into existence but may in fact be completely ineffectual and therefore may need direct support…At each of those nodal points the demands for intervention radiate outwards to comprise an extraordinary range of forms of internal restructuring. Reconstructing the state can come to involve, at least in principle, massive interventions across every aspect of social life. At their most ambitious, indeed, nothing may escape the Western gaze or eventually elude the demands of progress (Ahlberg 1994).

Something like this process can, we suggest, be traced in the discourse of an institution like the World Bank. The stress on institutions, as already noted, was a significant step towards the idea of 'good governance'. In his address to the 1997 Annual World Bank Conference on Development Economics, Joseph Stiglitz outlined his understanding of the process of economic development, and the role of the state. He said that a 'striking lesson' to have emerged from the experience of the East European countries was 'how difficult it is for markets to get established – there is a rich institutional infrastructure, much of which requires government action to establish and maintain', and 'it may take a strong government to establish a strong market' (Stiglitz 1997:3). For development to be successful, government must take responsibility for creating laws and legal institutions, establishing clearly defined property rights, ensuring effective competition, enforcing contracts, and regulating the financial sector. This will require improving the performance of governments, through accountability, incentive mechanisms, use of market surrogates, improving the composition and quality of government employees, and improving systems of hiring, training and promotion. In conclusion, he argued that 'an essential part of the new development strategies involves the creation of institutions and the changing of cultures – the movement to a culture of change and science, where existing practices are questioned and alternatives constantly explored' (*ibid.*:18). This is a dramatically expanded vision of the kind of social transformation required for 'development' (Stiglitz 1998). As Stiglitz finally concluded 'in the end, the transformation of society entails a transformation of the way *individuals* think and behave' (*ibid.*:27).

But the difficulties that attend such grandiose attempts at internal change are legion. The instabilities that characterise external strategies are multiplied. There is even less consensus about how to proceed with a project of what might be called social transformation at a distance, and even more fragile means to coordinate it. To these must be added the absence of any kind of plausible calibration. The external demands can at least be registered according to some criterion: a policy announced, an election held, legislation passed. The policy may be bogus, the election rigged and the new law stillborn, but at least there are benchmarks. But in the world of social transformation at a distance, without direct control, it is difficult to know whether projects and policies have succeeded, indeed whether they have had any effect at all, and whether any limits, including, and especially, any limits of time, can be placed on the volume of effort and resources that might be required.

Conclusion

Nevertheless Western agencies have become committed to such a project and, although each of these policy areas has developed in different ways, been promoted by a variety of agencies, and remains subject to contestation and tactical calculation, a number of key themes can be discerned. A first bundle of instruments, which at its loosest may be termed 'development', concerns not so much the macroeconomic policies of states but rather the constitution of rational economic actors. A second, whose slogan is roughly 'governance', focuses not so much on state compliance with external demands for performance and so on, but rather on the repositioning of the state in relation to the constitution of a liberal capitalist order. This is complemented by a third, comprising both the elaboration of a buttressing 'civil society' that will sustain 'governance' and a 'democratisation' understood as the minimum necessary form for that civil society to function. This is considered appropriate at least for urban middle-class Africa (which is already converted to democracy). Finally, the whole 'rights' project, its own self-assessment notwithstanding, is a language ideally suited for the legitimation of the kind of deep structural change deemed appropriate for rural Africa.

Taken together, these interventions constitute a massive effort of social transformation at a distance without direct political control, and at their heart lies a common project consisting of three major clusters of analysis and policy, all of which have only fully developed over some two decades. The first of these concerns the state about which it is clear that, certain one-sided or polemical formulations notwithstanding, the trick is not more or less state but the right kind of state. Secondly, this formulation inevitably raises the question of how the right kind of state is to be attained, and here governance, despite its slightly archaic and formal ring, signals that holding the state to account means wholesale restructuring of what has increasingly come to be known as civil society. Thirdly, it is impossible, or so we suggest, from within this set of propositions and practices to avoid their extension to the level of the individual self, though this implication tends to be avoided in the current mainstream academic and policy literature. Thus, simply put, what is at the heart of the liberal project in Africa is the formation of the right kind of state, the right kind of civil society and the right kind of individual (Williams and Young 1994).

Bibliography

Ahlberg, B.M. (1994) 'Is there a Distinct African Sexuality? A Critical Response to Caldwell *et al.*'. *Africa* 64(2): 220–42.

Aryeetey, E., and Cox, A. (1997) 'Aid Effectiveness in Ghana'. In Carlsson, J., Somolekae, G. and van de Walle, N. (eds) *Foreign Aid in Africa: Learning from Country Experiences.* Uppsala: Nordiska Afrikainstitutet, pp. 65–111.

Bell, D. (2006) 'Empire and International Relations in Victorian Political Thought'. *Historical Journal* 49(1): 281–98.

Brown, S. (2001) 'Authoritarian Leaders and Multiparty Elections in Africa: How Foreign Donors Help to Keep Kenya's Daniel Arap Moi in Power'. *Third World Quarterly* 22(5): 725–39.

Burley, A.-M. (1993) *Regulating the World.* New York: Columbia University Press.

Callahan, M.D. (1999) *Mandates and Empire: The League of Nations and Africa 1914–1931.* Brighton: Sussex Academic Press.

Chandler, D. (2000) 'International Justice'. *New Left Review* 6: 55–66.

Colley, L. (1994) *Britons Forging the Nation 1707–1837.* London: Pimlico.

Conklin, A. (1998) 'Colonialism and Human Rights, A Contradiction in Terms? The Case of France and West Africa'. *American Historical Review* 103(2): 419–42.

Craig, D. and Porter, D. (2004) *Development Beyond Liberalism? Governance, Poverty Reduction and Political Economy.* London: Routledge.

Craig, D., and Porter, D. (1988) *Development Beyond Neoliberalism: Governance, Poverty Reduction and Political Economy.* London: Routledge.

de Waal, A. (1997) *Famine Crimes: Politics and the Disaster Relief Industry in Africa.* Oxford: James Currey.

Deudney, D. and Ikenberry, J. (1999) 'The Nature and Sources of Liberal International Order'. *Review of International Studies* 25(2): 179–96.

Dewey, C. (1974) 'Celtic Agrarian Legislation and the Celtic Revival: Historicist Implications of Gladstone's Irish and Scottish Land Acts 1870–1886'. *Past & Present* 44(1): 30–70.

Gibson, S. (1999) 'Aid and Politics in Malawi and Kenya: Political Conditionality and Donor Support to the "Human Rights, Democracy and Governance" Sector'. In Wohlgemuth, L. *et al.* (eds) *Common Security and Civil Society in Africa*, Uppsala: Nordiska Afrikainstitutet, pp. 192–207.

Gocking, R. (1997) 'Colonial Rule and the "Legal Factor" in Ghana and Lesotho'. *Africa* 67(1): 61–85.

Gunn, S. (1996) 'The Ministry, the Middle Class, and the "Civilizing Mission" in Manchester, 1850–1880'. *Social History*, 21(1): 22–36.

Hanlon, J. (2002) 'Are Donors to Mozambique Promoting Corruption?' Paper Presented at a Conference on 'Towards a New Political Economy of Development', Sheffield.

Harrison, G. (2001) 'Post-conditionality Politics and Administrative Reform: Reflections on the Cases of Uganda and Tanzania'. *Development and Change* 32: 657–79.

Hawthorn, G., and Seabright, S. (1993) 'Where Westphalia Fails: The Conditionality of the International Financial Institutions and National Sovereignty', Ca (mimeo). Cambridge: Politics, Psychology, Sociology and International Studies Faculty Library.

Hegel, G.W.F. (1952[1821]) *Philosophy of Right.* Oxford: Oxford University Press.

Ibhawoh, B. (2002) 'Stronger than the Maxim Gun Law, Human Rights and British Colonial Hegemony'. *Africa* 72(1): 55–83.

Jackson, R.H. (1990) *Quasi-states: Sovereignty, International Relations & the Third World.* Cambridge: Cambridge University Press.
Jayarajah, C. and Branson, W. (1995) *Structural and Sectoral Adjustment: World Bank Experience, 1980–92*, Operations Evaluation Study. Washington, DC: World Bank.
Jokinen, J. (2004) 'Balancing between East and West: The Asian Development Bank's Policy on Good Governance'. In Boas, M. and McNeil, D. (eds) *Global Institutions and Development: Framing the World?* London: Routledge, pp. 137–50.
Kaufmann, D. (2004) 'Corruption, Governance, and Security: Challenges for the Rich Countries and the World'. In World Economic Forum, *Global Competitiveness Report 2004/5.* Geneva: World Economic Forum, pp. 83–100.
Kelsall, T. (2002) 'Shop Windows and Smoke-filled Rooms: Governance and the Repoliticisation of Tanzania'. *Journal of Modern African Studies* 40(4): 597–620.
Klein, H.S. (1999) *The Atlantic Slave Trade.* Cambridge: Cambridge University Press.
Koskenniemi, M. (2001) *The Gentle Civiliser of Nations: The Rise and Fall of International law, 1870–1960.* Cambridge: Cambridge University Press.
Kreuger, A. (1974) 'The Political Economy of the Rent-seeking Society'. *American Economic Review* 64(3): 291–303.
Latham, R. (1997) *The Liberal Moment: Modernity, Security, and the Making of Postwar International Order.* New York: Columbia University Press.
Lustick, I.S. (1993) *Unsettled States Disputed Lands.* Ithaca, NY: Cornell University Press.
Mandler, P. (2000) '"Race" and "Nation" in mid-Victorian Thought'. In Collini, S. *et. al.* (eds) *History, Religion and Culture: British Intellectual History, 1750–1850.* Cambridge: Cambridge University Press, pp. 224–44.
Mason, E.S. and Asher, R.E. (1974)*The World Bank Since Bretton Woods.* Washington, DC: The Brookings Institution.
Morton, J. 1996) *The Poverty of Nations: The Aid Dilemma at the Heart of Africa.* London: Tauris.
Mosley, P., Harrigan, J. and Toye, J. (1995) *Aid and Power: The World Bank and Policy-based Lending.* Routledge: London.
Paris, R. (2002) 'International Peacebuilding and the "Mission Civilisatrice"'. *Review of International Studies* 28(4): 637–56.
Rakner, L. (2003) *Political and Economic Liberalisation in Zambia 1991–2001.* Uppsala: Nordiska Afrikainstitutet.
Reus-Smit, C. (1999) *The Moral Purpose of the State: Culture, Social Identity, and Institutional Identity in International Relations*, NJ: Princeton: Princeton University Press.
Ruggie, J. (1982) 'International Regimes, Transaction, and Change: Embedded Liberalism in the Postwar Economic Order', *International Organization* 36(2): 195–231.
Said, E. (1978) *Orientalism.* Harmondsworth: Penguin.
Stiglitz, J. (1997) 'An Agenda for Development in the Twenty-first Century', Annual Bank Conference on Development Economics, Washington, DC, April 30–May 1.
Stiglitz, J.E. (1998) 'Towards a New Paradigm for Development: Strategies, Policies, and Processes'. Prebisch Lecture, October 19. Geneva: UNCTAD, pp.1–46. http://www.worldbank.org/html/extdr/extme/prebisch98.pdf
Todoro, V.T. (1993) *On Human Diversity, Nationalism, Racism and Exoticism in French Thought.* Cambridge, MA: Harvard University Press.
Toye, J. (1992) 'Interest Group Politics and the Implementation of Structural Adjustment Policies in Sub-Saharan Africa'. *Journal of International Development* 4(2): 183–97.
Toye, J. (1987) *Dilemmas of Development.* Oxford: Blackwells.
Wade, R. and Veneroso, F. (1998) 'The Asian Crisis: The High Debt Model versus the Wall Street-Treasury-IMF Complex'. *New Left Review* 228: 3–23.
Weber, E. (1976) *Peasants into Frenchmen: The Modernisation of Rural France 1870–1914.* Stanford, CA: Stanford University Press.
Whitfield, L. (2005) 'Trustees of Development from Conditionality to Governance: Poverty Reduction Strategy Papers in Ghana'. *Journal of Modern African Studies* 43(4): 641–64.
Williams, B. (2005) *In the Beginning was the Deed.* Princeton, NJ: Princeton University Press.
Williams, D. (2000) 'Aid and Sovereignty: Quasi-States and the International Financial Institutions'. *Review of International Studies* 26(4): 557–573.
Williams, D. (2003) 'Managing Sovereignty: The World Bank and Development in Sub-Saharan Africa'. *Mondes en Développement* 31(3): 5–22.
Williams, D. and Young, T. (1994) 'Governance, the World Bank and Liberal Theory'. *Political Studies* 42(1): 84–100.
Wolfensohn, J. (1999) *A Proposal for a Comprehensive Development Framework.* Washington, DC: World Bank

Publications.
World Bank (1981) *Accelerated Development in Sub-Saharan Africa: An Agenda for Action.* Washington, DC: World Bank.
World Bank (1988) *Annual Report 1988.* Washington, DC: World Bank.
World Bank/IMF (2005) *Financial Sector Assessment: A Handbook.* Washington, DC: World Bank/IMF.
World Bank/IMF (2005), *Financial Sector Assessment: A Handbook*, Washington, DC: World Bank/IMF.
Zachernuk, P.S. (1998) 'African History and Imperial Culture in Colonial Nigerian Schools'. *Africa* 68(4): 484–505.
Zhang, Y. (1991) 'China's Entry into International Society Beyond the Standard of "Civilization"'. *Review of International Studies* 17: 3–16.

8

Liberal Interventionism & the Fragile State
Linked by Design?

MARK DUFFIELD

Introduction

Following the international interventions in Afghanistan and Iraq, a number of aid-related ideas concerned with working in *difficult environments*, or engaging with countries described as *poor performers*, or indeed the problems of *fragile states* have entered policy discourse (Torres and Anderson 2004; DCD 2004; DFID 2005). They attempt to describe the developmental challenge at a time when, despite the recent step-change in all forms of humanitarian, development and peace interventionism, it is still unclear whether any of these incursions have actually solved the larger political problems that gave rise to them (Smith 2006). Since ideas concerning difficult environments or poor performers are similar in content, the term 'fragile state' is used here as a generic descriptor to denote this discourse. Policy thinking on fragile states presents itself as innovative and forward-looking regarding the problem of state reconstruction in circumstances where local administrative capacity and political will are absent or limited (DFID 2005). This chapter's central argument, however, is that, rather than being wholly new, fragile state discourse reproduces some of the key assumptions and relations of colonial bureaucracy, in particular, the liberal practice of indirect rule or Native Administration (Lugard [1922]).

Although Native Administration was concerned with the *tribe*, and the object of fragile state discourse is the *state*, both these entities are understood and acted upon in a similar way. In other words, as taxonomies or hierarchies of different capacities and political will that either support or prevent their fulfilling a liberal ideal of autonomy and independence. In both cases, the challenge for policy is to reduce, shape or somehow streamline administrative tasks and demands to match that limited capacity which does exist. When arranged as a series of evolutionary stepping-stones, each more demanding than the last, these capacity-building tasks function to encourage the bureaucratic maturation or development of the tribe or state concerned. Rather than such similarities being accidental, this chapter argues that they are examples of a recurrent liberal problematic of security.

Native Administration emerged in the context of the so-called New Imperialism of the closing decades of the nineteenth century (Hobson [1902]). Often associated with the Scramble for Africa but geographically wider in scope, it was a time when the world's last remaining independent territories and populations were forcefully brought under colonial administration. Compared with earlier settler colonies, this act of closure created a new governmental challenge. That is, the need to effectively administer the autonomous and, in terms of their basic biological, economic and social needs, largely self-reproducing populations acquired through conquest. Native Administration, with its underlying developmental logic (Cooke 2003), emerged as a liberal alternative to the exterminatory impulse driving the rapacious 'insane imperialism' that had unthinkingly produced this challenge to govern (Hobson [1902]; Morel 1920).

While history does not repeat itself, fragile state discourse emerges in not dissimilar circumstances. The unprecedented international interventionism, at least in recent times, of the post-Cold War period has succeeded in reducing the number of ongoing civil wars in the world's crisis zones (HSC 2005). The present post-interventionary epoch has emerged, among other things, from the relative ease of changing the incumbents of ineffective states. At the same time, however, the intractable difficulties of winning the peace among the people, a contest in which military force has little utility (Smith 2006), has also been exposed. For the international community of effective states, this ongoing process of post-interventionary pacification has called forth responsibilities to protect and reconstruct (ICISS 2001) that have a familiar ring when viewed against the history of liberal interventionism (Jahn 2005). It is in relation to contemporary security concerns over the existence of ungoverned space and the corresponding need to reconstruct fragile states that the underlying assumptions and techniques of Native Administration appear to occupy once more the political foreground. This chapter examines the current understanding of the fragile state, indicates how this interleaves with key tenets of liberal imperialism and concludes with a review of existing interventionary technologies.

From Failed to Fragile States

In its present outing, the concept of the fragile state is a post-9/11 updating of the 1990s idea of the *failed* state. This reworking, however, does not relate to content, that is, what failed or fragile states are thought to be; they are both experienced as a more or less sovereign void and, in relation to legitimate rule, an ungoverned political space. The difference between them is in how effective states relate to this incomplete and illegitimate condition. In terms of content, both failed and fragile states epitomise state ineffectiveness and represent the antithesis of what are thought to be effective or successful states (Maass and Mepham 2004). State failure/fragility typically denotes a lack of administrative capacity and political will reflected in economic collapse, social fragmentation, a disregard for human rights and an inability to support human security (Ghani *et al.* 2005). Since they denote the same condition, what marks out a fragile from a failed state is the difference in *the policy tools* and the sense of *priority* with which the international community now problematises the existence of lawless or ungoverned space in the global South. While drawing on earlier antecedents, the failed state as a concept is an early post-Cold War construction. For much of the 1990s, especially in regions of limited strategic importance, failed states ranked low on the international agenda. Pre-9/11 Afghanistan is a case in point (Newburg 1999). The main policy tool associated with state failure was humanitarian aid (Leader and Colenso 2005:38). Towards the end of the 1990s, however, this situation was already beginning to change. In particular, from a relegated position following the global ascendancy of neo-liberal economics during the 1980s, the state or, at least, a particular form of the state, has returned to the foreground of development policy (Stiglitz 1998).

If one takes the changing organisational structure of UN system-wide aid and peace interventions as symptomatic of wider shifts, the post-Cold War period divides into two broad phases. Until at least the mid-1990s, reflecting the prevalence of ongoing civil war, the main system-wide structure was that of *negotiated access* (Karim *et al.* 1996). That is, the procedure whereby a UN lead-agency would, by reaching a negotiated agreement with warring parties, secure international humanitarian access to war-affected populations. By the end of the 1990s, however, as the ambit of pacification grew, system-wide operations had begun to morph into the *integrated mission* (Donini *et al.* 2004). Rather than adjusting to ongoing war, increasingly the concern was to achieve greater coherence between aid and politics, in particular to realign system-wide operations behind the peace formula that had either been agreed or internationally imposed. This political shift problematised the earlier reliance on humanitarian assistance (Macrae 1998). Founded on the principles of neutrality, impartiality and transparency, by its nature humanitarian assistance is uneasy with state power and usually concerned to work around it. Consequently, it is of limited use as a tool of state reconstruction (Leader and Colenso 2005:39). Following the movement of the state back to the centre of development discourse, the concept of the fragile state codifies a new willingness by effective states to engage weak or failed state entities *developmentally*. The declaration of an indefinite state of international emergency following 9/11, however, and the consequent need to strengthen liberalism's external sovereign frontier, have confirmed the importance of state reconstruction.

Unlike the failed state and humanitarian assistance, the developmentally charged fragile state captures some of the institutional experimentation currently taking place in the shift from intervention to a post-interventionary epoch (*ibid*; PRDE 2004; McGillivray 2005; DCD 2004; Picciotto *et al.* 2004). This coexists with a heightened security concern over the porous borders of mass consumer society and the consequent vulnerability of critical public infrastructure to destabilising or predatory forms of global circulation emanating from the world's crisis zones, for example surges of asylum seekers, illicit transborder economies and terrorist networks. Complementing the deepening of immigration control and major restrictions regarding the right to asylum, the choice or ability to intervene and reconstruct fragile states is now an essential part of liberalism's external sovereign frontier.

Fragility & International Instability

There is no agreed list of fragile states. They appear in parts of Latin America, the Caribbean, Africa, the Middle East, Transcaucasia, South-East Asia and the Pacific. Neither are they limited to countries affected by conflict. DFID defines a fragile state as 'those where government cannot or will not deliver core functions to the majority of its people, including the poor' (DFID 2005:7). Although there is no accepted measure, there are thought to be about forty to fifty countries of varying combinations of weak institutional capacity and lack of political will that fall into this category. It is estimated that about 16 per cent of the world's population live in fragile states. Collectively, however, they account for '...35 per cent of the world's poor, 44 per cent of maternal deaths, 46 per cent of children out of school and 51 per cent of children dying before the age of five' (Leader and Colenso 2005:9). Fragile states are the most 'off-track' with regard to achieving the UN's Millennium Development Goals (MDGs) which include the halving of chronic poverty by 2015. Indeed, their existence threatens the achievement of these goals (Benn 2004). People living in fragile states are statistically likely to die young or live with chronic illness; they are unlikely to go to school or receive essential health care; and they have few if any economic opportunities. Chronic poverty and its associated threats to international security are concentrated in these states.

Not only are fragile states an obstacle to reducing global poverty; from a security perspective they are a potential source of global insecurity. Reflecting the move to a post-interventionary era, just as the fragile state has replaced the failed state in policy discourse, the idea of internal *conflict*, a central worry of the 1990s, is now giving way to a more generalised concern with international *instability*. In Britain, the government's Strategy Unit report, *Investing in Prevention* (2005), which complements DFID's work on fragile states (Torres and Anderson 2004:3), signals this important shift. It acknowledges the early 1990s; the long upward trend in the incidence of civil war has now reversed, even in Africa (see HSC 2005; Marshall 2005). This is explained in terms of the major increase in post-Cold War international humanitarian, development and peace interventionism (Strategy Unit 2005:21). The Strategy Unit report points out, however, that the halving of ongoing internal war since the early 1990s does not tell the whole story. Namely, while intervention may have reduced the number of open civil wars, the potential for continuing violence and political instability remains; it is more a question of 'its suppression or containment rather than its resolution' (*ibid*:22). The pacification of post-interventionary society remains incomplete and contingent. For policy-makers, whether there has been a decline in civil war or not, the risk of instability is real and immanent.

It is further argued that if a human security perspective is adopted, that is, a view that takes into account all the factors that threaten life, although there may be fewer actual wars, the situation is argued as being far from comforting. Although battlefield specific mortality may be declining, a human security view '*...suggests that numbers of deaths are increasing*' (*ibid*:22, original emphasis.). In recent African conflicts, for example, on average only around 13 per cent of war-related deaths were attributable to direct acts of violence. The overwhelming majority of fatalities result from the epiphenomena of conflict: mass displacement, lack of sanitation, absence of medical assistance, neglect and malnutrition (IRC 2003). Moreover, such epiphenomena merge into scenarios of generalised insecurity short of war, including sporadic violence, widespread criminality, economic collapse and the degradation of public health and welfare infrastructures. Moreover, when possible future shocks are taken into account, such as the impact of HIV/AIDS, growing environmental stress, climate change, the strategic competition for oil, and the economic isolation of non-integrating countries, it is thought that rising instability '*will be an enduring characteristic of the strategic landscape rather than a temporary phenomenon*' (Strategy Unit 2005:24, original emphasis). It is in relation to this threatening global dystopia that the reconstruction of fragile states gains urgency and relevance.

The Human Security State

Since the state has once again moved to the centre of development discourse, it is worth asking the question, what sort or type of state is actually involved? One can assume that it is not the industrialising, centralising and modernising state once championed by the forces of nationalism and socialism – the state that, for example, sought to achieve economic catch-up with the West. With the exception, for example, of India, China and other parts of East Asia, this modernisation project had all but collapsed over much of the erstwhile Third World by the end of the 1970s. Emerging from this rubble, the envisioned social competence of the fragile state is suggested in the idea of *human security* (UNDP 1994). The *human* part of human security is often thought to signal a progressive turn. In prioritising the security of people over the security of the state, it seems to promise a more universal or inclusive future. However, while policy-makers are clear that the time of absolute sovereignty has passed, especially for states that abuse their powers, they are also equally sure that the state is and will remain the principal means of supporting human security (ICISS 2001). In other words, at the same time as prioritising people, human security also *privileges* the state – or at least the reconstructed or internationally legitimated state – as the supreme juridico-political organisation of power (Duffield and Waddell 2006). In this respect, in terms of the relative competencies at play, human security embodies a distinction between *effective* and *ineffective* states; it signifies and reworks the earlier distinction between developed and underdeveloped worlds. From the point of view of its practical application, human security is an adjunct of cotemporary liberal interventionism: it embodies both *the prioritisation by effective states of the security of people living within ineffective ones* and the privileging of the state as the only body that can legitimately guarantee that security. It contains an expansionary or interventionary logic as well as an urge to reconstruct and consolidate.

Importantly, however, the guarantor of *security* within the ineffective or fragile state does not go beyond satisfying the minimalist basic-needs or self-help approach to human welfare, as represented in existing practices of sustainable development. According to DFID, the most important functions of the state for poverty reduction are 'territorial control, safety and security, capacity to manage public resources, deliver basic services, and *the ability to protect and support the ways in which the poorest people sustain themselves*' (DFID 2005:7, emphasis added). This is a human security view of state competence. In other words, apart from a certain level of physical security and legal redress, the emphasis is upon providing basic public goods and supporting subsistence strategies such that the essential self-reliance of the population – the ability of people to sustain their own self-reproduction – is maintained. When one compares the levels of social protection enjoyed in Europe, for example access to universal health care, comprehensive education, a benefits system and pensions, development appears very different. With its emphasis on sustainability and communal self-reliance, development functions to maintain the developed/underdeveloped divide rather than narrowing it. Reliant upon changing behaviour and attitudes, and encouraging new forms of social organisation, for the majority of its subjects, the non-material bias of liberal development equates with external attempts to maintain a self-adjusting social equilibrium – a condition of stasis, based upon no greater vision than supporting life lived within the limits of basic needs (Pupavac 2005). In the name of global security, never have so many strived to achieve so little.

During the Cold War, in theory at least, the international system was shaped by the principle of territorial integrity and non-interference in domestic affairs. Respect for territorial integrity remains important; liberal interventionism is not about changing borders. Given that liberal states now accept a responsibility for human security within illiberal ones (ICISS 2001), sovereignty over life within the latter has become *internationalised, negotiable and contingent*. While the territorial integrity of the fragile state is upheld, under the post-interventionary conditions of contingent sovereignty, deciding and implementing its core economic and social functions is now integral to what Graham Harrison has called liberalism's external sovereign frontier (2004:26). This frontier of shifting power effects is a site of negotiation, exchange and antagonism, bringing together international actors, state incumbents and civil society groups. For liberal development, social welfare is improved by helping self-reliant communities make the most of free market opportunities. When ideas of 'active citizenship' (see, Harrison 2004:106–7) are grafted on to an assumed communal self-reliance, it is possible to argue that the building of basic public infrastructure like roads and power supplies, together with providing public goods such as basic education and health care, are themselves sufficient to overcome urban/rural inequalities (Ghani *et al.* 2005). By taking advantage of improved market access fostered by such measures, the communities concerned are assumed to be able to lift themselves out of poverty and so secure their own future welfare. As a security mechanism, this self-help approach to human security is even regarded as a force for national unity and able to discourage the formation of other modes of 'opposition identity' (*ibid*:8).

Self-reliance as a technology of security, especially within fragile states, has a number of important implications. Since European-type levels of social protection are not in question, other than a degree of physical security, essential public infrastructure and basic needs, the fragile state is not required to develop extensive, bureaucratic or centralised means for supporting and managing life. Apart from economic and administrative statistics, this obviates the need for the extensive surveying of the population's health and welfare status. Largely geared to emergencies, and albeit in a fragmented fashion, this has become the responsibility of the aid community. As a security mechanism, reducing poverty by promoting sustainable forms of self-reliance is argued to reduce the risk of conflict (Anderson 1996).

Such an approach to security, however, is questionable. Self-reliance tends to privilege the localised relations of kinship, community and culture. Politically it is a centrifugal force, tending to pull apart rather than together (Duffield 2002). This approach to social welfare does not sit readily with the aim of nation-building. Indeed, the continuing difficulties of winning the peace in post-interventionary societies attest to the resilience of centrifugal forces (Smith 2006). This situation has seen a revival of military interest in counter-insurgency (Kilcullen 2006). Under present conditions, counter-insurgency embodies the realisation that ending wars within ineffective states is relatively easy; far more difficult is winning the peace among the people. It is a call for war by other means in which development consciously figures as a major component (Slim 2004). What is less the case, however, is for liberal development, based on self-reliance and basic needs, to be problematised as a *practical* security mechanism. Can such an essentially non-material approach to welfare ever win a battle for hearts and minds? Is war by other means part of an increasingly desperate attempt to maintain the current disastrous formula for sharing the world with others?

The Fragile State & Liberal Imperialism

As a construct of policy discourse, fragile states represent an ungoverned space. Through an absence of capacity and/or will, they lack the ability to become stable aid dependencies. The wherewithal is absent to provide a predictable funding mechanism thus becoming a known part of liberalism's external sovereign frontier. In developing the current approach, policy has tended to work backwards from the nature and types of aid flow argued to have contributed positively to international development (see Harrison 2004). Donor governments tend to fund states judged as good development investments. These are states having an acceptable and sufficient mix of capacity and political commitment. One effect of this 'aid as investment' approach is that fragile states, given their poor social indicators, receive less aid that would be expected. According to a World Bank metric ranking states on their capacity and performance, the bottom 40 per cent account for only 14 per cent of bilateral aid, while the top 40 per cent absorb nearly two-thirds (DFID 2005:12). Moreover, what aid fragile states do receive is volatile, driven by humanitarian crisis and lacking in harmonisation (Ghani *et al* 2005:10–12). From a capacity-building perspective, the aid received is also inefficient. There is a tendency for donors and NGOs to establish parallel structures that replicate and undermine state systems rather than enhancing them. Much of it is humanitarian assistance that 'is delivered outside state structures' (DFID 2005:12). Lacking capacity, fragile states cannot meet donor auditing and accounting requirements, nor can they absorb and disburse aid in an accountable manner. It is consequently argued that fragile states can be reconstructed or developed by increasing flows of good, that is, long-term developmental aid that is predictable, properly harmonised and aligned around appropriate mechanisms that work progressively to increase state capacity, ownership and identity.

However, while appearing new, fragile state discourse, especially when viewed in relation to a liberal problematic of security, has a discernible colonial genealogy. Ungoverned territory, or autonomous peoples or tribes for that matter, constitutes a threat to a risk-based security mentality. This old and recurrent danger has long underpinned a liberal urge to intervene and govern. It makes it possible, for example, to re-discover within fragile state discourse a reworking of the central tenets of the liberal colonial practice of indirect rule or, as formally known within the British Empire, Native Administration. Indirect rule represented a radical break with the militarised, and often genocidal, direct rule that was common during the so-called New Imperialism of the closing decades of the nineteenth century (Hobson [1902]). It involved a rejection of a single, hierarchical model of progress that informed contemporary ideas of race-based social Darwinism. The virtues of indirect rule were cogently expressed in the work of such great liberal imperialists as J.A. Hobson ([1902]), Edmund Morel (1920) and Lord Lugard ([1922]). Indirect rule emerged in parts of India toward the end of the nineteenth century, for example, in the restoration of Mysore to princely rule, before spreading *ad hoc* to other regions of the British Empire, such as the Protectorate over Basutoland in southern Africa and the development of West Africa's cocoa and palm oil industries. By the 1920s, however, spurred by the formation of the League of Nations, indirect rule had been formalised as Native Administration (Lugard [1922]). Variants of indirect rule were also encountered beyond the British Empire, for example, within the Dutch East Indies (Furnivall 1948) and the US Bureau for Indian Affairs during the 1930s and 1940s (Cooke 2003).

To discover fragile state discourse within Native Administration and *vice versa*, current policy prescriptions are discussed under three headings a) *culture and the limits of government*, b) the *necessity of despotism* and c) *adjusting government to culture*. Each of these subsections begins with a few comments on liberal colonial practice.

Culture & the Limits of Government

Native Administration or indirect rule emerged out of the unforeseen consequences of the late nineteenth century's New Imperialism. With regard to the British Empire, when compared with the Old Empire of self-governing colonies such as Canada, Australia and New Zealand, it represented the acquisition of large swathes of tropical and sub-tropical territory. At the time, these acquisitions were argued to contain 'large populations of savages or "lower races"; little of it likely, even in the distant future, to increase the area of sound colonial life' (Hobson [1902]:124). The New Imperialism bequeathed a problem of government that, despite using the biological language of race, still echoes in fragile state discourse. Indeed, although a century of colonialism and independence intervenes between the present and this enunciation, the spatial location of this 'unsound life' and today's fragile states are largely contiguous. As an alternative to extermination, indirect rule was liberalism's tool of choice for addressing the problem of unsound life.

Native Administration embodies the principle that 'progress will take place more and more upon the qualitative plane, with more intensive cultivation alike of natural resources and of human life' (*ibid*:235). It was argued, that rather than one model or standard of social progress, there are many. Edmund Morel, for example, urges that the cultural differences among humanity are taken into account when considering the stable growth of national identity. Moreover, encouraging 'the unfolding of the mental processes by gradual steps is the only method by which the exercise of the imperial prerogative is morally justified' (Morel 1920:205). Central to indirect rule's evolutionary developmentalism was gaining a thorough understanding of the peoples concerned. The study of their languages, customs and social organisation through the emerging discipline of anthropology was encouraged. By promoting tolerance born of a deeper understanding, it encouraged trust on the part of the colonised. Knowledgeable administrators could give 'wider concept to the latent mental powers and spiritual potentialities' of subject peoples (*ibid*:241).

Reproducing the earlier liberal heritage of J S Mill, both Native Administration and fragile state discourse reproduce the liberal identification between culture, or social character, and political existence (Jahn 2005). While the demand that administrators and practioners must understand the societies they work in is as old as the imperial relationship itself, it is nevertheless periodically rediscovered as the acme of effective policy (DAC 1997). It forms the basis, for example, of DFID's (2005) 'drivers of change' approach, the key element of which regarding fragile states is,

> ...the need to understand the history of a country and its people, who holds power and how is it brokered and used, the informal 'rules of the game' (such as how patronage networks operate in government and business), the relationship between these and formal institutions (such as appointments to the executive and judiciary). (*ibid*:14)

While the focus is more institutional than tribal, the intention is the same: through an estimate of social character, to establish the limits of political existence, and once this is decided, to select the most appropriate means of betterment. Fragile state discourse contains the injunction that ineffective states have a *responsibility to develop*. For aid policy, difficult environments are those countries 'where the state is unable or unwilling to harness domestic and international resources effectively for poverty reduction' (Torres and Anderson 2004:3). If fragile states are to become good global citizens, that is, easy environments for international aid organisations to operate in, state incumbents must be willing to use international aid effectively for poverty reduction. Fragile state discourse signals that development is not just a technical matter; it also requires a *political understanding* of the society in question. There 'is a growing recognition of the need to understand the political incentives and the institutions that affect the prospects for reform' (DFID 2005:14). It involves 'an excellent understanding of the political economy' (PRDE 2004:9). In relation to fragile states, DFID's drivers of change approach involves distinguishing between *friend* and *enemy* in terms of the willingness to accept external aid and guidance.

> Effective states depend on effective political leadership equipped with the skills to manage conflicting interests, agree effective policies, and see through structural change. Where insti-

> tutions are weak, personalities often dominate. *In the worst cases, predatory leaders unchecked by institutionalised constraints can steal property, kill people, and ruin the economy.* (DFID 2005:15, emphasis added)

Providing the right type of interlocutor exists, working in difficult environments involves 'being supportive of partner's efforts to create the conditions for political stability, helping build government capacity, encouraging political commitment to stronger policy environments' (PRDE 2004:6). Whereas Native Administration used anthropology to understand tribal society, fragile state discourse relies on political economy to know the state (DFID 2005:14). Once friend and enemy can be distinguished, working in fragile sates is a process of alliance-building with the former. The difficulty, however, is that fragile states often lack effective pro-reform elites. The Iraq and Afghanistan reconstruction programmes, for example, have relied on the diaspora to supply pro-reform elites, already socialised in the boardrooms and campuses of Europe and America, to staff the key positions in the transitional administrations (Herring and Rangwala 2005).

To indicate the range of possible difficult environments, policy documents often give a typology of fragile states based upon different combinations of administrative capacity and political will. DFID (2005), for example, lists four broad types of ineffective state: 'good performers'; 'weak but willing'; 'strong but unresponsive/repressive'; and 'weak-weak' (*ibid*:7–8, also see Torres and Anderson 2005:17–18). Despite such attempts to demonstrate analytic flexibility and openness to social difference, the centrality of pro-reform elites to the development process trumps such nuances; without the right type of political interlocutor, nothing much is going to happen. While such typologies give an air of complexity, in the last analysis, they rest upon a recurrent division of humanity into two main groups, 'the one assumed to be universalistic and progressive, the other supposed irremediably particularistic and primitive' (Balibar 1991:25).

The Necessity of Despotism

From its modern beginnings, liberalism has been characterised by a recurrent paradox. While claiming to govern in the interests of people, freedom and rights, it is willing to accept despotic rule as a necessary transitional stage in achieving wider developmental goals. The case of Afghanistan today, for example, is comparable with liberalism's relationship with imperialism during the nineteenth century (Mehta 1999). Regarding the problems of fragile states, especially the dearth of acceptable interlocutors, the necessity of despotism is at once in the political foreground. Torres and Anderson (2005), for example, query as unreliable and contentious any definition of state failure that draws on an inability to generate legitimate support. They argue that legitimacy and effectiveness are ambiguously related. Weak legitimacy does not automatically equate with weak capacity. Legitimacy, moreover, can be strengthened by pursuing retrospective policies of growth or poverty reduction. At the same time, there is no clear evidence that legitimacy is related to political participation. It is arguable that in many neo-patrimonial states 'it is precisely the pursuit of legitimacy that has made the state a weak partner in poverty reduction' (*ibid*:17). The contemporary rendition of the liberal paradox is eloquently evinced in DFID's (2005) revealing concept of *good enough governance*. Governance reforms need to be achievable and appropriate to their context. In this respect, medium-term realism is needed if long-term development and stability are to be achieved.

> 'Good enough' governance is about effective states fulfilling certain basic functions, including

> protecting people from harm and providing an economic framework to enable people to support themselves. *It may involve practices that would not exist in an ideal government* – corruption may be rife, staff may lack necessary skills, and capacity may be chronically weak and under-funded (*ibid*:20, emphasis added).

There is no agreed threshold separating 'good enough' from 'unacceptable' governance. In its report, *Responsibility to Protect*, the ICISS (2001) places the bar of human suffering very high before a moral responsibility for international actors to intervene within a crisis state is deemed to exist. The report quotes the words of Kofi Annan concerning 'gross and systematic violations of human rights' that affront every precept of a common humanity (*ibid*:vii). It speaks in terms of large-scale loss of life or ethnic cleansing carried out, for example through mass murder, rape and starvation, and operating at an actual or near genocidal level (*ibid*:xi). If this is liberalism's best measure of its own humanity, then good enough governance provides plenty of scope for generalised abuse and oppression that falls short of such 'supreme' emergencies: flawed elections, extra-judicial killings, disappearances, pervasive corruption, routinised human rights abuse, ethnic and religious oppression, dereliction of office, and so on. Good enough governance is the price liberalism is willing to exchange for a stable aid relationship along its external sovereign frontier. Stability, however, is the last thing that good enough governance can deliver.

Adjusting Government to Culture

Liberal interventionism is challenged by the need to adjust the techniques of sound government to the limits set by the social character of the governed (Jahn 2005:601). Native Administration, for example, was based upon devolving appropriate administrative responsibilities such as public works, tax collection, rural courts, local police, primary education, and so on, to indigenous tribal or feudal authorities. In theory, the complexity of the tasks and responsibilities devolved depended upon the level of social organisation encountered. Decentralised tribal groups would be given basic tasks (MacMichael 1923), while feudal kingdoms would be entrusted with a wide remit of local government duties. Through devolving more demanding tasks as lesser ones were mastered, the aim was to progressively move the peoples concerned towards self-determination. To secure this aim, the 'backward races' were not to have an alien model imposed upon them. Rather, they were to be empowered 'by their own efforts in their own way, to raise themselves to a higher plane of social organisation' (Lugard [1922]:215). While the principles of Native Administration were fixed, their application was to vary with levels of social advancement. Moreover, the 'task of the administrative officer is to clothe his principles in the garb of evolution, not revolution' (Ibid:193–194). Native Administration aimed to initiate a process of controlled social change through incremental self-management that maintained social cohesion. While in practice the usual result was to entrench parochialism, in its design and essentials Native Administration was a development policy (Cooke 2003). It is in this sense, of a design of power that fosters maturation through enlightened trusteeship, that indirect rule has a strong affinity with today's fragile state discourse.

Rather than assuming a linear evolution of fragile states into stable and predictable aid dependencies, there is a recognition of the need for specialist measures and frameworks as necessary stepping stones (Leader and Colenso 2005:13–14). In formulating development tools for fragile states, there are three main issues. First, weak administrative capacity; second, weak or absent political will; and finally, the anarchy within an aid system composed of multiple and competing agencies, and 'different perceptions of strategic interest among donors and regional powers' (*ibid*:21). Fragile state policy attempts to address these concerns. The aim is to simplify and reduce the administrative and accounting demands associated with a full-blown Poverty Reduction Strategy (PRS) as encountered in more administratively robust countries (Harrison 2004). Coherence is improved by building in donor harmonisation and alignment from the outset. While often falling short for accountability reasons of the preferred donor aim of funding through the budget, the cut-down tools and frameworks nevertheless aim to engage and socialise fragile state incumbents. Many current aid interventions in the Caribbean, Africa, Transcaucasia, Iraq, Afghanistan, South Asia and East Asia, for example, are laboratories for the development of these technologies (PRDE 2004). It should be emphasised, however, that rather than pioneering new technologies as such, fragile state policy is emerging retrospectively through interpreting and orchestrating initiatives that have often emerged independently in a number of different locations. Recognising that technical details vary according to place, an overview of the main principles behind fragile state policy is given here.

Technologies of Governance

Regarding the lack of capacity, one starting point is the fabrication of standards of competence whose reporting requirements are less demanding than the formal Poverty Reduction Strategies (PRS) agreed with relatively effective states. A good example is the World Bank's Transitional Results Matrix (TRM). Typically, a TRM arises out of a Joint Assessment Mission (JAM) conducted by donors, UN agencies, NGOs and government representatives. Variants have emerged, for example, in East Timor, Liberia, Sudan, Central Africa Republic and Haiti. They set out 'an agreement between donors and the government about how much support will be given to activities in key area' (DIFD 2005:19). As a sort of pre-PRS framework, they 'aim to provide a government and donor road map for prioritisation, coordination and monitoring' (Leader and Colenso 2005:19). In order to develop such technologies, and, at the same time, address international concerns over legitimising unsuitable state incumbents, DFID has introduced the idea of 'shadow alignment' (*ibid*:20). This enables donors to support national competences while, at the same time, not being subject to government priorities. Possibilities include 'putting aid "on-budget" but not "through budget", working with existing administrative boundaries, and providing information to the recipient in terms that are compatible with their national systems such as the budgetary classifications and cycle' (*ibid.*).

Shadow alignment not only adjusts government to existing social conditions; importantly, in the form of a 'shadow budget' or a 'shadow health sector', it attempts to form an externally managed simulacrum of the real thing. As such, it provides a sort of blueprint against which donors, UN agencies and NGOs can harmonise, align and sequence their resources and activities. Regarding NGOs, they have long been accused of further weakening fragile states by establishing a parallel system of service delivery (Ghani *et al.* 2005:10). By emulating national systems, however, shadow alignment can reduce such problems. In offering a simulacrum of national institution, it provides a number of sites where external actors can engage selected state incumbents and engage in controlled capacity-building without legitimating the fragile state as a whole. These points of engagement range from being kept informed, to joint monitoring arrangements, to eventually taking control of the systems concerned. Just as the decentralisation of increasingly demanding administrative tasks under indirect rule was thought to encourage the progressive political maturation of the tribe, fragile states are regarded as capable of eventually growing into and taking over shadow institutions. In this respect, shadow alignment is 'future proof' (Leader and Colenso 2005:20). While Native Administration would eventually lead to tribal self-rule within a colonial state, the end point for fragile states is to form a stable self-governing dependency within a neo-liberal world economy.

Several existing frameworks of engagement lend themselves to techniques of shadow alignment. For example, the *trust fund* has emerged as a way of providing budgetary support to countries 'where fiduciary risk is high while simultaneously building capacity of the state to manage and control its own budget' (PRDE 2005:9). In Afghanistan, for example, the Afghanistan Reconstruction Fund (ARTF) has become the instrument of choice for donors in helping to build trust and capacity. A multi-donor Capacity-Building Support Fund (CBSF) exists in South Sudan to support the recurrent costs of teachers, health workers and administrators in its nascent public administration. In East Timor, a multi-donor Transitional Support Programme (TSP) includes general budget support linked to a framework for service delivery geared to a state in an early stage of formation (Leader and Colenso 2005:23). Sierra Leone and Rwanda have more ambitious donor programmes to support government systems.

Another existing framework is multi-donor *pooled funding* which increases donor harmonisation and allows a more programmatic approach to fragile states. In Burma, pooled funding has enabled the donor community to support a joint HIV/AIDs programme that, while not going through government, has ministry of health officials as 'part of the coordinating structure' (PRDE 2005:9). In Afghanistan, twelve National Priority Programmes (NPPs) serve to pool funds in government-designated priority areas. The National Emergency Employment Programme, for example, is controlled by the Ministry of Rural Rehabilitation and Development, but managed by a special implementation unit staffed by internationals and Afghans and 'is implemented around the country by NGOs and private sector engineering firms' (Leader and Colenso 2005:34).

Another framework lending itself to shadow alignment is the *social fund.* These bring communities, government bodies and donors together to improve 'social protection, service delivery and livelihoods in fragile states' (PRDE 2005:9). The Yemen social fund, for example, has attracted £225 million for the 2004–8 period from the World Bank, the EU, the Dutch, the UK, USAID and the Arab fund. Social funds align with government objectives and attempt not to undermine the state. In Afghanistan, the National Solidarity Programme (NSP) is based on the social fund principle. Donors pay into the NSP fund as a whole and the government, through the auspices of an oversight consultant, releases funds to community groups. Communities have to elect a community development council that is responsible for designing suitable projects. NGOs under contract to the Ministry of Rural Rehabilitation and Development implement the actual projects. The programme is intended to assist communities rebuild assets and improve better community governance (Leader and Colenso 2005: 33). A similar fund also operates in the Ministry of Health where a private American company contracts out health work to international and national NGOs. This relationship involves a foreign private company emulating a ministry as it channels external donor funding to implementing NGOs, many of them international. One of the aims of the NSP is to 'provide a new model of the relationship between state and citizen' (*ibid*:33).

Having examples of many of the fragile state technologies sketched above,

Afghanistan is an important zone of experimentation in shadow alignment. Given the revival of the Taliban, however, and the country's slide into counterinsurgency, one wonders how robust these privatised, multi-agency and externally managed systems are in strengthening the 'relationship between state and citizen'.

Concluding Remarks

Native Administration and fragile state policy are similar, to the extent that both are forms of developmental trusteeship arising out of the governmental challenge posed by life experienced as somehow incomplete. Both share a willingness to accept despotism and, at the same time, in the interests of measured evolutionary change, they adjust the institutions of government to the limits set by culture. They are also dissimilar; although sharing a design or strategisation of power, in terms of the institutions and relations involved, they are different. Native Administration and fragile state discourse book-end the first anti-colonial wave of nationalist resistance. The former problematised an emerging independent state and unsuccessfully sought to mobilise the tribal forces of the countryside against an emerging urban educated elite. Fragile state discourse, however, is concerned with constructing a stable aid relationship out of the rubble of the nationalist project. In other words, with adjusting the mechanisms of government to the capacities of the descendants of that elite while, at the same time, supporting forms of communal life deemed loyal to a contested fragile state. While the West does not threaten the territorial integrity of the fragile sate, it does seek to influence, shape and manage its core economic and welfare functions. Having to confront the new forms of resistance that interventionism itself encourages, the fragile state marks out liberalism's external sovereign frontier.

Bibliography

Anderson, M. (1996) *Do No Harm: Supporting Local Capacities for Peace Through Aid.* Cambridge, MA: Local Capacities for Peace Project, The Collaborative for Development Action, Inc.

Balibar, E. (1991) 'Is There a "Neo-Racism"?' In Balibar, Etienne and Wallerstein, Immanuel (eds) *Race, Nation, Class: Ambiguous Identities.* London: Verso Press, pp. 17–28.

Benn, H. (2004) 'The Development Challenge in Crisis States.' Speech by the Rt. Hon. Hilary Benn MP at the London School of Economics .

Cooke, B. (2003) 'A New Continuity With Colonial Administration: Participation in Development Management'. *Third World Quarterly* 24(1): 47–61.

DAC (1997) *DAC Guidelines on Conflict, Peace and Development Co-operation.* Paris: Development Assistance Committee, Organisation for Economic Co-operation and Development.

DCD (2004) 'Harmonisation and Alignment in Fragile States: Draft report by Overseas Development Institute (ODI), United Kingdom'. *Senior Level Forum on Development Effectiveness in Fragile States, Meeting in London, 13–14 January 2005.* Paris: Development Co-operation Directorate (OECD).

DFID (2005) *Why We Need to Work More Effectively in Fragile States.* London: Department for International Development.

Donini, A., Niland, N. and Wermester, K. (2004) *Nation-Building Unravelled? Aid, Peace and Justice in Afghanistan.* Bloomfield, CT: Kumarian Press.

Duffield, M. (2002) 'War as a Network Enterprise: The New Security Terrain and Its Implications'. *Cultural Values* 6 (1&2): 153–65.

Duffield, M. and Waddell, N. (2006) 'Securing Humans in a Dangerous World'. *International Politics* 43: 1–23.

Furnivall, J.S. (1948) *Colonial Policy and Practice: A Comparative Study of Burma and Netherlands India.* Cambridge: Cambridge University Press.

Ghani, A, Lockhart, C. And Carnahan, M. (2005) *Closing the Sovereignty Gap: an Approach to State-Building.* Working Paper 253. London Overseas Development Institute.

Harrison, Graham (2004) *The World Bank and Africa: The Constitution of Governance States.* London: Routledge.

Herring, E. and Rangwala, G. (2005) 'Iraq, Imperialism and Global Governance'. *Third World Quarterly* 26(4–5): 667–83.

Hobson, J.A. ([1902] 1938) *Imperialism: A Study.* London: George Allen and Unwin Ltd.

HSC (2005) *The Human Security Report 2005: War and Peace in the 21st Century*, Vancouver: Human Security Centre, University of British Columbia.

ICISS (2001) *The Responsibility to Protect: Report of the International Commission on Intervention and State Sovereignty.* Ottawa: International Development Research Centre.

IRC (2003) *Mortality in the Democratic Republic of the Congo: Results From a Nationwide Survey, September – November 2002.* New York: International Rescue Committee.

Jahn, B. (2005) 'Barbarian Thoughts: Imperialism in the Philosophy of John Stuart Mill'. *Review of International Studies* 31: 599–618.

Karim, A, Duffield, M., Jaspars, S., Benini, A., Macrae, J., Bradbury, M., Johnson, D. and Larbi, G. (1996) *Operation Lifeline Sudan (OLS): A Review.* Geneva: Department of Humanitarian Affairs.

Kilcullen, D. (2006) 'Counter-insurgency "Redux"'. *Survival* 48(4): 111–30.

Leader, N, and Colenso, P. (2005) *Aid Instruments in Fragile States.* PRDE Working Paper 5. London: Poverty Reduction in Difficult Environments Team, Department for International Development (DFID).

Lugard, Lord ([1922] 1965) *The Dual Mandate in Tropical Africa.* London: Frank Cass.

Maass, G, and Mepham, D. (2004) *Promoting Effective States: A Progressive Policy Response to Failed and Failing States.* London: Institute for Public Policy Research and Friedrich-Ebert-Stiftung, London Office.

Macmichael, H.A. (1923) *Indirect Rule For Pagan Communities.* Sudan Archive, University of Durham, 586/1/1–55.

Macrae, J. (1998) 'The Death of Humanitarianism? An Anatomy of the Attack'. *Disasters* 22(4): 309–17.

Marshall, M.G. (2005) *Conflict Trends in Africa, 1956–2004: A Macro-Comparative Perspective.* Report Prepared for the Africa Conflict Prevention Pool (ACPP), Government of the United Kingdom. Arlington, VA: Centre for Global Policy, George Mason University.

Mcgillivray, M. (2005) 'Aid Allocation and Fragile States.' Background Paper for the Senior Level Forum on Development Effectiveness in Fragile States. London: Lancaster House.

Mehta, U.S. (1999) *Liberalism and Empire.* Chicago: University of Chicago Press.

Morel, E.D. (1920) *The Black Man's Burden.* Manchester and London: The National Labour Press Ltd.

Newburg, P.R. (1999) *Politics at the Heart: The Architecture of Humanitarian Assistance to Afghanistan.* Global Policy Program, Working Paper No. 2. Washington, DC: Carnegie Endowment for International Peace.

Picciotto, R., Alao, C., Ikpe, E., Kimani, M. and Slade, R. (2004) 'Striking a New Balance: Donor Policy Coherence and Development Cooperation in Difficult Environments'. A Background Paper Commissioned by the Learning and Advisory Process on Difficult Partnerships of the Development Assistance Committee of the OECD. London: Global Policy Project, King's College London.

Prde (2004) *Improving the Development Response in Difficult Environments: Lessons from DFID Experience.* PRDE Working Paper 4. London: Poverty Reduction in Difficult Environments Team, DFID.

Pupavac, V. (2005) 'Human Security and the Rise of Global Therapeutic Governance'. *Conflict, Development and Security* 5(2): 161–82.

Slim, H. (2004) 'With or Against? Humanitarian Agencies and Coalition Counter-Insurgency.' *Opinion.* Geneva: Centre for Humanitarian Dialogue.

Smith, R. (2006) *The Utility of Force: The Art of War in the Modern World.* Harmondsworth: Penguin Books.

Stiglitz, J.E. (1998) 'Towards a New Paradigm for Development: Strategies, Policies, and Processes'. Prebisch Lecture, October 19. Geneva: UNCTAD, pp. 1–46. http://www.worldbank.org/html/extdr/ extme/prebisch98.pdf

Strategy Unit (2005) *Investing in Prevention: An International Strategy to Manage Risks of Instability and Improve Crisis Response.* A Strategy Unit Report to the Government. London: Prime Minister's Strategy Unit, Cabinet Office.

Torres, M. M., and Anderson, M. (2004) *Fragile States: Defining Difficult Environments for Poverty Reduction.* PRDE Working Paper 1. London: Department for International Development, Poverty Reduction in Difficult Environments (PRDE) Team.

UNDP (1994) *Human Development Report, 1994.* New York and Oxford: Oxford University Press for the UNDP.

9

Freedom, Fear & NGOs
Balancing Discourses of Violence & Humanity in Securitising Times

PATRICIA NOXOLO

Introduction

This chapter aims to explore an approach for analysing NGOs' roles in securitisation seen as a form of global governmentality. In recent years, most notably since 9/11 and the so-called 'global war on terror', many writers have noted that global security concerns have changed both in shape and in intensity (Abrahamsen 2004; Duffield, 2002; Higgott 2003), entering many different dimensions of political and economic life (Elbe 2004; Eriksson 2001), and with a range of new or transformed actors (Bislev *et al.* 2001; Leander 2006; Waever 2000). Didier Bigo (2002:63) has combined these insights with a Foucauldian governmentality analysis arguing that, in Europe, 'a continuum of threats and general unease' is created through and around immigration, not by a particular speech act by a particular governmental actor, but by the consonance of global structural trends with the legitimating moves of a range of political actors, and the technological apparatus and expertise of transnational security personnel:

> Securitization, then, is generated through a confrontation between the strategies of political actors (or of actors having access to the political stage through the media), in the national political field, the security professionals at the transnational level (public and private bureaucracies managing the fear), and the global social transformations affecting the possibilities of reshaping political boundaries. (Bigo 2002:75)

Securitisation therefore becomes a form of globalised governmentality, operating through but also across national, regional and global scales.

Many writers have specifically commented on the ways in which NGOs have become linked into increasingly complex relationships with governments, and with the arts of government. Rose and Miller (1992) have shown that alliances between government and NGOs are indispensable to the operation of 'government at a distance', and more recently Morison (2000) has noted that 'compacts' are one of the most recent instruments through which the UK government and the voluntary sector are working out joint rationalities for governing the population. Dean has emphasised the technologies of agency and performance by which NGOs become part of a system of self-managing units 'in which the regulation of services and the management of budgets is undertaken by the polymorphism of the audit and various kinds of accounting' (Dean 1999: 170). Many see the work that NGOs do with client groups as the operation of techniques of the self, 'normalising' or 'responsibilising' (potential) citizens, and transforming people into governable subjects (Bryant 2002; Ilcan and Basok 2004; Larner and Walters 2000).

Networking is increasingly important to NGOs as a way of using scarce resources more effectively, by pooling influence (Yanacopulos 2005) and knowledge (Bach and Stark 2004). NGOs are now multi-scalar networked actors (Demars 2005), networking vertically (for example, local community organisations networking with national, regional and global umbrella organisations), horizontally (with other similar organisations through joint forums and meetings) and diagonally (for example, global actors raising the profile of small indigenous groups). NGOs not only network with each other, but also with government representatives and inter-governmental systems of governance (Willetts 2002), plus a range of other professionals (for example, welfare, legal and security professionals.) Through networking NGOs make policy interventions, share information and provide services. In relation to securitisation as a form of globalised governmentality, therefore, NGO roles are becoming increasingly complex and need to be understood within a framework that is flexible enough to relate to their spatial reach globally as well as their local embeddedness, and to the multi-perspectival diversity of their networked existence, i.e. there is a need to develop a critical approach that can engage with and offer the multiple perspectives both *on* and *from* NGOs.

In the next section this chapter will suggest that a dialogue between postcolonial and Foucauldian theories might be a useful way forward in establishing the multi-perspectival analysis required. In particular, similarities between the critical perspectives of Wilson Harris and Michel Foucault in relation to freedom and (in)security will be identified and related to NGOs' roles in securitisation as governmentality. However, the third section will show that, although both Foucauldian and postcolonial theory emphasise the importance of historicising discourses through time, Harris's work pushes Foucauldian governmentality towards a fuller engagement with associations across space-time. After section four's brief analysis of the ways in which abolitionists balanced freedom and fear in the 'securitisation' and 'de-securitisation' of slaves (as well as the 'counter-securitisation' of planters) (see Waever 1995), the concluding section explores how an engagement with associations across space-time in these two cases – nineteenth-century abolitionism and twenty-first-century anti-terrorism – might illuminate the contribution of securitisation both to the establishment of NGOs and to the shaping and re-shaping of the notion of freedom.

Michel Foucault & Wilson Harris: Shared Perspectives on Freedom & Fear

A starting point to achieve the multi-perspectival approach needed to analyse the roles of NGOs in securitisation is to bring different analytical perspectives into dialogue. A dialogue between Foucauldian and postcolonial perspectives promises to be particularly fruitful. Postcolonial theory has been developing for some time as a critical perspective and takes a variety of forms. In British academic Geography its most noteworthy contribution has been a sustained critique of the historical development of Geography as a discipline that provided many of the visual and intellectual tools that Britain's imperial project put to use (Bell *et al.* 1995; Crush 1994). Postcolonial theory is itself a school of theories with a complex 'mapping' (Sidaway 2000). Quite apart from the obvious fact that historically a range of European, Asian and

African imperial powers have had a range of formal and informal colonial and neo-colonial relationships with a range of vastly different places worldwide, each of those (neo-) colonial relationships has had its own structures of conquest and resistance, forms of exploitation and negotiation, forms of segregation and conviviality, legacies and consequences (Noxolo forthcoming). This diversity sets up a dizzying array of material postcolonial networks, resonances, echoes and contrasts that is indeterminate in terms of boundaries, but that also heavily informs the very contemporary processes of uneven globalisation with which geographers have been engaged for some time (Power *et al.* 2006). The literary routes through which some prominent features of postcolonial theory come are therefore political in an intensely material, corporeally related way, as they express the trauma, pain and intimacy of living with these unequal relationships (Fanon 1967; Gilroy 1993). At the same time, the politics of history, of memory, of who gets to decide where historical narratives mark ruptures, commemorate continuities, or recognise disjuncture, is played out creatively in literary texts and in literary theory (Noxolo *et al.* 2008; Spivak 1992), but is also observed and analysed in political and cultural theory as it manifests itself in brutal wars and banal violence (Duffield 2001; Mbembe 2001).

Related to this is the extremely wide range of postcolonial traditions of thought coming out of these historical circumstances; postcolonial geography is informed by at least the recognition of this range. In terms of European imperialism alone, the different forms of knowledge that colonial powers developed and the range of different kinds of educational strategies that they devised for colonised populations – from the very specific transnational training of Indian elites (Chakrabarty 2000), to the very partial education offered to indigenous Australians (Simon and Tuhiwai Smith 2001), to the deliberate refusal of literacy to enslaved African people (Beckles 1999) – articulated with a wide range of indigenous languages, knowledges and educational practices to inform a range of politicised strategies around the acceptance, adaptation and/or refusal of textuality amongst colonised and formerly colonised people. The implication of this diversity in terms of a materially-routed politics of knowledge is that Euro-American academic disciplines are heavily informed by long-standing colonial relationships, not only in terms of their development as instruments of control, but also in terms of their genesis within varying degrees of intimacy with a range of (subjugated) traditions of knowledge.

Stephen Legg (2007) has noted that a range of postcolonial theorists have engaged critically with Foucault's work, often as a means precisely of exploring these processes of subjugation, including, for example, an ongoing dialogue between Foucault and Edward Said about the question of agency. Recent criticisms of Foucault's work have focused on its eurocentricity, but, for example, Ann Louise Stoler (1995) criticises his lack of engagement with the colonies, which she establishes as a particular and decisive locus for the development of European discourses around sexuality and its boundaries. Similarly, Homi Bhabha (1995:??) criticises Foucault's spatial imaginary of the West (Euro-America) alone as too restricted, necessitating 'homogenising spatial metaphors that do not allow for the different disjunctive temporalities of other cultural articulations'. This is therefore not just a spatial exclusion; it cannot simply be resolved by pulling Foucault into post-colonised settings, i.e. by simply applying governmentality perspectives to development in a range of settings (but, see for example, Huxley 2007; Kalpagam 2000). The time-space limitation that Bhabha indicates means that it is difficult from entirely within Foucault's European-centred analysis to understand the cross-cutting presence of global history seen otherwise and from elsewhere. As a consequence, in relation to NGOs, unless Foucault is subjected to a 'lagging'[1] it will be difficult to use governmentality to appreciate either the cross-cutting multiple perspectives on and of these globalised actors in relation to securitisation as governmentality, or the violent and unpredictable effects of securitisation as governmentality.

The visionary Caribbean novelist and literary theorist, Wilson Harris, carries some of the major themes of postcolonial theory in his work, but also shares with Foucault some highly relevant critical perspectives on modern governmentality, including fear and freedom. There are three elements of Foucault's and Harris's critical perspectives that can be articulated in an analysis of NGOs and securitisation as governmentality. Firstly, their critiques of the forms of freedom experienced by the governed subject are similar, in that both see the forms of action open to the free subject under forms of liberal governmentality as circumscribed by power. Wilson Harris argues that in modern societies individuals are 'locked within block functions' (Harris 1999:77), their actions circumscribed by expectations designed to maintain a stable society by giving what Harris (*ibid.*:78) describes as a 'false clarity', which is the impression that there is only one way of reading or understanding the world, rather than the multiple perspectives of differently situated human beings.

Similarly, Foucault argues that those who govern 'produce' a particular collection of 'freedoms' without which liberal regimes cannot function: free markets, the freedom to buy and sell, the freedom to own property, etc. (Foucault 2004a:65). At the same time, in the very action of producing this set of freedoms, those who govern therefore define the limits within which to be free (*ibid.*). Foucault goes further in relation to securitisation, by suggesting that one 'mechanism' by which freedom is limited is through the invocation of fear and insecurity: 'stimulation of the fear of danger is in some way the condition, the internal psychological and cultural correlative, of liberalism. There can be no liberalism without a culture of danger' (*ibid.*:68, my translation). This tension then, between freedom and 'locking in', through the negotiation of security and fear, recalls analyses of NGOs in relation to governmentality as having important roles in responsibilising and normalising citizens, producing subjects who will use their freedoms responsibly (see for example Lacey and Ilcan 2006). For example, Aradau (2004) has shown how, in the context of a politics of fear, the politics of pity in which NGOs engage in relation to trafficked women merges into a politics of risk, as these women become categorised as possible abusers, and as the end point of NGOs' therapeutic interventions becomes defined as their successful return to their countries of origin.

Secondly, both Foucault and Harris relate this shaping of freedom to processes of subjugation of particular subject positions and of particular groups of people at any given time. Foucault's question at the beginning of *Society Must Be Defended* is a pointed reference to this: 'What types of knowledge are you trying to disqualify when you say that you are a science? What speaking subject, what discursive subject, what subject of experience and knowledge are you trying to minorise...?' (Foucault 2004c:10). Though Foucault in his early work examines how this minorissing of subject positions results in increased disciplining for particular groups (Foucault 2003), the governmentality-derived work of security theorists in relation to the securitisation of immigration illustrates this in a particularly relevant way.

For example, Jef Huysmans (2004) has shown that free movement (broadly defined to include immigration and asylum) into and within the European Union is generally understood within a functionalist framework that understands freedom (understood in terms of fewer constraints)and security as a trade-off: where there is more freedom for the individual, the demand for heightened security restrictions becomes greater, as a corrective to the danger of a destructive 'excess' of freedom that some dangerous individuals might use to harm themselves or others. This is the dominant view within the EU, but Huysmans goes on to explain the process by which this logic leads immigration and asylum to become particularly securitised (see also Huysmans 2000). He describes two layers of technologies of government through which the 'excess' of freedom comes to be defined as a larger object of fear in relation to immigrants and asylum seekers than in relation to other groups. Firstly, territorial/juridical technologies – such as the harmonisation of visa policy, use of detention and the intensification of border patrols – determine not only which groups of people can enter the EU, but also place different conditions around the freedom of movement of non-EU nationals within the region once they enter, thus framing the immigrant or asylum seeker as an *a priori* object of suspicion. Secondly, bio-political technologies – such as using demographic statistics to profile particular sub-sets of the population who 'are considered to have a higher pre-disposition towards sub-optimal or dangerous conduct of freedom' (Huysmans 2004:311) – place different segments of the population along a continuum of risk, with the effect that asylum seekers and immigrants face monitoring, restrictions and controls from the state (Muller, 2004; Schuster, 2003), complemented by normalisation from NGOs (see above).

Harris's work meditates in a more intimate way on the fear and violence experienced by particular groups at times of heightened (in)security. Harris's lyrical and fantastic novel, *The Ghost of Memory*, invokes an extended conversation between a character who has died and returned as a figure in a painting, and a character called Christopher Columbus, who comes repeatedly to look at the painting. After repeatedly trying to persuade Columbus of the associations between different civilisations, different times and places, the main character becomes afraid of his interlocutor's growing rage: 'I hesitated. What could I say which would not cause an outrage, however true it was?' (Harris 2006:95). In the end Columbus, unable to bear any more undermining of his certainties, slashes the painting to ribbons, causing the main character, whose fears are now justified, to scream out in pain. Pointedly, Harris links this fantasy directly with the shooting of Jean Charles de Menezes, the young Brazilian man who was shot by the police in London in July 2005, after being mistaken for a terrorist suspect: 'This remark of his – all the materials one is given to wear – made me conscious all at once of *how I had been mistaken for and shot as a terrorist!* I had lost my passport and had felt a tide of anxiety rise within me when the armed police approached me. I was South American, Venezuelan/Brazilian. I knew I would be sent away from the City.... I was ridden by anxieties.' (Harris 2006:89).[2] This expression of fear, violence and well-founded fear of violence is integral to many people's experience of securitisation as governmentality around the world; their freedoms are circumscribed not only by the largely inchoate feelings of 'unease' (see Bigo, 2002) experienced within advanced liberal democracies (for example, surrounding marginal groups, criminality, environmental change and terrorism), but also by fear of repressive state power and of the violence/death related to numerous superpower-led or localised wars, as well as extreme poverty, vulnerability to disease, and long-term shortages of food and resources (Duffield 2001; Mbembe 1999).

In the UK context, NGOs have of course tried to ease this fear at its source through criticisms of the securitisation of immigration and asylum in the media and in legislation (Geddes 2005; Joint Council for the Welfare of Immigrants 2006; Sivanandan 2006). As Bigo (2002:79) points out, however, NGOs may find it impossible to effectively challenge the connections between asylum seekers and terrorism, for example, whilst their own discursive freedoms are themselves circumscribed by securitisation. For example: 'discourses concerning the human rights of asylum seekers are de facto part of a securitisation process if they play the game of differentiating between genuine asylum seekers and illegal migrants, helping the first by condemning the second and justifying border controls'. However, NGOs do also try to invoke empathy in the wider population for the fear felt by others, for example through joint statements like the 'Joint Response to the Home Office consultation on exclusion or deportation from the UK on non-conducive grounds', August 2005, to which a variety of British NGOs (The Refugee Council, Refugee Action, Immigration Advisory Service, Oxfam GB, Scottish Refugee Council, Welsh Refugee Council, Amnesty International UK, the Medical Foundation) are signatories. In this document the words 'community', 'communities' and 'society' are able to shift and change, without any of the imperatives to make groups visible in particular ways that would come from the needs of individual NGOs to legitimate themselves and their work (Lister 2003). This shifting has the effect of including the concerns of UK citizens and non-UK citizens together, allowing for difference in relation to reasons to be fearful:

> Careful consideration is needed if the security of communities in the UK is to be achieved without generating feelings of insecurity and alienation among some sections of society.
>
> 1.3 In recent weeks, we have become aware of an enhanced sense of fear and insecurity among some refugee communities and others subject to immigration controls. For some this fear is linked to the general threat of terrorism faced by the UK. For others it stems from the recent rise in racial and religious attacks. And for some it is linked to a fear that they themselves may be unduly and unfairly affected by counter-terrorism measures and returned to unsafe situations in their country of origin.
>
> 1.4 There is a real need for widespread consultation and public information to ensure that communities' fears are acknowledged and addressed. At a time of great tension it is particularly important that no group feels scapegoated because of the actions of particular individuals. Ongoing engagement with all communities in the UK is also essential in gathering the right intelligence to combat terrorism. (See also Noxolo 2006)

The third way in which Foucault's and Harris's critical perspectives can be combined into a reading of NGOs' roles in relation to securitisation as governmentality is their shared recognition of what might be termed the 'plasticity' of securitisation. Wilson Harris sees this in terms of a swinging pendulum, in which the same groups can be deemed 'good' or 'evil' at different times. He stresses that this is not necessarily related to a *de facto* change in the behaviours and approaches of these groups: 'The swing does not happen within the psyche of the people. It is a purely historical, technical switch.' (Harris 2006: 95). Similarly, Foucault recognises that the discursive form that divides groups into oppositional camps of good and evil, which he refers to as 'race wars', is 'a mobile discourse, a polyvalent discourse' (Foucault 2004c: 77). At one moment it can be deployed by the oppressed in relation to their oppressors, at another by the dominant in relation to those they seek to dominate. At a time of securitisation as governmentality, this division into good and evil becomes a key discursive tool. As we have seen, it is difficult for NGOs to avoid becoming implicated in the securitisation of particular groups; further (as we shall see below in relation to the rise of NGOs during the abolition of slavery), getting actively involved in the securitisation, de-securitisation or counter-securitisation of a range of groups may consolidate the legitimacy and authority of NGOs themselves. At the same time, NGOs, as networked entities, can themselves become securitised, becoming objects of suspicion from the multiple perspectives of governments, businesses, security professionals and vulnerable groups, each of which may see them as allied with any of their 'others' (Lewis 2005). Much of the movement towards encouraging more accountability and monitoring procedures can be seen as the disciplining of NGOs as a response to suspicion surrounding them, and this can become particularly marked for NGOs which are seen as linked with processes of so-called 'radicalisation' or terrorist financing and risk becoming part of lists of proscribed organisations (McCulloch and Pickering 2005).

In these three elements there is significant overlap and complementarity between Harris's and Foucault's approaches. However, in relation to the historicisation of securitisation there is more difference, so that bringing the two theorists together represents a significant transformation to a basic governmentality approach.

Securitisation in Space & Time

Harris and Foucault both insist on the importance of historical analysis for understanding the present as a politics of regimes of truth, i.e. 'aspiration to power that is inherent in the claim to being a science' (Foucault 2004c:10). There is a need, then, to understand NGOs in relation to securitisation as governmentality as implicated in the construction of truth claims, particularly in relation to the historical construction of discourses about the relationships among freedom, fear, violence and what it means to be human. However, there are important ways in which the two differ but complement each other in relation to time and space.

There are at least two ways in which this historicisation can be understood in relation to Foucault's work. History can be understood in terms of antecedents – the slow incremental flow of discursive forms that builds up different forms of state governmentality; Foucault's lecture series on governmentality can be understood as this kind of extended narrative (Foucault 2004a: 2004b). But within his work one can also see history understood in much less coherent ways, as immanent wars/struggles between dominant and subjugated knowledges (Foucault 2004c), between conduct and counter-conduct (Foucault 2004b).

Wilson Harris's view of history cuts across both space and time, particularly in relation to understanding violence as integral to the ways in which humanity is constructed within modernity. He argues that it is important to understand cataclysmic change and unpredictable movements as determining what it means to be human when seen from a Caribbean perspective. This history cannot be reconstructed into a coherent history, not even in terms of the concept of competing narratives that Foucault talks about within the deployment of history as 'race war' (Foucault 2004c:71). Harris argues that the Caribbean is a confluence of too many different trajectories, but that each of these trajectories has itself been subject to rupture and unpredictability, including the shocks and re-assemblages that come from articulation and mixing: 'how can one begin to reconcile the broken parts of such an enormous heritage, especially when those broken parts appear very often like a grotesque series of adventures...' (Harris 1967:31). Harris therefore constructs a view of literary narrative (which he links explicitly to historical narrative, see Harris 1999) as constructed through 'associations... so that a strange jigsaw is set in motion' (*ibid.*:38). In applying this image of dynamic complementarity to the historicisation of securitisation, I am not here talking about a simple comparativism, but crucially about developing a sense of the discursive forms and technologies of rule that the present securitised moment of global governmentality shares with a range of other moments, both within Euro-America, within post-colonised places, and within the transnational spaces of governmentality created between them.

I am arguing, then, that taking time and space together means that particular events, utterances or circumstances must be seen as intersections of social relations which extend across time as well as across space. Bringing events into interaction which are linked *neither* by time *nor* by space but within a particular conception of time-space is a resolute act. Interactions are neither obvious nor exclusive. That is to say, many different, often unforeseen, connections are possible. It is in fact hardly possible to shut down the possibility of other connections. This is analogous to what Massey calls: 'the chaos of the spatial [which] results from the happenstance juxtapositions, the accidental separations, the often paradoxical nature of the spatial arrangements which result from the operation of all these causalities' (Massey 1994:266). Such connections in time-space are, rather, illuminating and/or creative. They do not say that events have necessarily to be seen in interaction with particular other events. One event in time-space does not completely determine another. As such, these interactions may be 'decisive' (the result of a determination to look beyond the obvious) but they are not 'definitive' (the whole truth and nothing but the truth) (see Hall 1996).

By the same token, however, these interactions between events and circumstances must continue to be grounded in the specificity of the intersection of social relations of which each event or circumstance consists. Bringing events and circumstances into interaction across time-space is not simply a case of 'fancy dress', in the sense of forcing a connection between events which have none. Bhabha describes a similar process as 'the negotiation of contradictory and antagonistic instances...' (Bhabha 1994:25). This means that the conditions of one located circumstance cannot simply be read off from another located circumstance even if some conditions are shared. I am not suggesting, therefore, in section four below, that development discourse is a form of slavery, only that there are connections to be made between the two. The process is one of negotiation or articulation rather than imposition or dove-tailing.

In the following section, the arguments relating to the nineteenth-century abolition of the Caribbean slave trade will be shown to be a historically securitised moment. The concluding section will raise questions about possible ways to associate this abolitionist moment creatively with the present securitised moment, raising issues in particular about the transnational roles of NGOs, as well as the transnational geographies of the discourses of abolitionists, enslaved people and planters, in relation to the balancing of freedom, fear and the discourse of humanity.

Freedom, Fear & Abolitionism

A range of historians have shown that Britain's anti-slavery movement was an important moment specifically in the development of a distinctive bourgeois civil society in Britain that can be identified as the foundation of the present-day British NGO movement. For example, Oldfield (1995) has shown that they were defined in relation to the landed classes through slavery and colonialism in two important senses. First, this trade and others gave middle-class entrepeneurs the financial clout and the prosperity to become an influential political force alongside the gentry, who had previously dominated the parliamentary system. Second, Catherine Hall's analysis of the importance of abolitionism in the historical establishment of white middle-class identities has shown that the campaign was on behalf of the slave, but was also a way of 'deriving authority from their capacity to speak for others.' (Hall 1992:212). In other words, the struggle over abolition helped to furnish this class with a distinctive discourse with which it could directly contest the plantocracy's definition of human value as racialised heritage and breeding by establishing a universal principle of free labour and the ability to develop professional qualities and skills. Both of these were important founding principles for the establishment of a bourgeois group that did not have aristocratic connections, but had as its foundation narrative the accumulation of riches and status through industry and application.

Two re-readings of analyses of abolitionists' representations surrounding the violent agency of slaves, during the long years of pamphleting and preaching (Carey 2005), show that they debated and delimited freedom as an indispensable facet of re-creating slaves as 'free subjects' and finding a position for themselves within new and different regimes of governmentality. Lambert's (2005:36) analysis of the construction of whiteness in arguments between planters, abolitionists and slaves over the meaning of the 1816 slave revolt in Barbados, demonstrates a 'geography of blame' that planters and abolitionists deployed against each other. West Indian planters blamed metropolitan abolitionists for slave violence, claiming that they came as outside agitators into peaceful communities of slaves, building up a desire for an unobtainable freedom that led inevitably to explosions of violence as an expression of disappointment. Metropolitan abolitionists blamed the cruel and abusive behaviour of planters for the slave violence, arguing that much of the destruction caused arose from the brutal repression of what would otherwise have been a very localised disturbance. Importantly, they cited factors in the local topography and population to back up their analysis (Lambert 2005).

The point here is that, in the construction of what is more than a 'geography of blame' but can also be seen as a geography of identity and difference, there are a number of different ways in which the different groups, particularly the abolitionists, attempted to delimit the freedom of others in terms of political agency, whilst expanding their own. The planters emphasised the local, attempting to limit the abolitionists geographically. They argued that opinions in London were external to the colonies, and that Barbados was a situation in which metropolitan abolitionists had no authority or understanding; their illegitimate intervention was inevitably harmful. By the same logic, representing the West Indian slave system as a peaceful co-existence between slave and planter, they posited a complementarity based on proximity, which, though racist in terms of its profound belief in different orders of humanity in the local context, appears to over-ride a shared white identity. The illegitimacy of the violent agency of slaves (implied in the brutal repression of the uprising) is displaced onto the illegitimacy of outsider intervention.

Even more relevant for the discussion here is the way in which the abolitionists reasserted their legitimacy by insisting on more universal principles of Englishness that allowed them to make legitimate political interventions in both the metropolis and the colonies. In an anonymous document called 'Remarks on the Insurrection in Barbados' (1816), outrage is expressed that planters should so violently put down a revolt (with specific mention of the loss of human life) in which both slaves and planters were British subjects: 'It is not so that insurrections are suppressed in England; and yet these are our fellow-subjects' (Lambert 2005:38). The equal application of English law in all the places that are seen as English territory is a principle of universality that allows the abolitionists a much wider jurisdiction. At the same time, the research done by the abolitionists on the local geography and its possible effects (Lambert 2005:37) lays down another universalist principle of rationality, that also extends authority to speak. The contrast that the abolitionist message sets up is between a rational transatlantic English analysis of a localised disturbance and an excessively violent planter reaction based on fear of violence.

In both accounts the actual violent agency of slaves is silenced or muted. Lambert pieces together a possible view of the actions of the enslaved rebels themselves, who attempt to heighten the most irrational fears of slave planters in their quest for freedom. For example, it was widely reported by white commentators at the time that the rebels carried banners with images of a black man having sex with a white woman, thus accessing directly some of the visceral fears around black masculinity that pervaded plantation culture (Lambert 2005:39). It is, of course, very difficult to know whether or not these banners actually existed, however, or whether they were imagined by white planters in the feverish atmosphere of the time. What they do suggest is that fear was a more sophisticated factor in the acquisition of freedom than the threat of violence alone; the threat of what black people might do with their freedom if they had it, of the difficulty of placing boundaries around the actions of free subjects, was a potent factor in the formation of the idea of freedom at the time (see also Woods 2002).

Matthews (2000) has shown how the abolitionist movement was unable to avoid the subject of the slaves' violent agency, even though they tried, because of its persistence and the constant accusations of the planters. However, towards the beginning of the nineteenth century they began to harness the fear it engendered, literally 'rationalising' it, in order to show a limited amount of violence as a rational action in relation both to the brutality of the slave regime and to the desirability of freedom. For example, William Wilberforce read the 1816 revolt as a comprehensible response to the fact that slaves were 'pressed with a weight which they felt intolerable' (Wilberforce, quoted in Matthews 2000:4), i.e. the brutality of the slave system.

However, there was more to these arguments than this: these were also attempts to demonstrate that black people could be rational agents, and it would therefore be possible to set limits to the freedom of black people, as had been done with the free labour force. For this reason, Henry Brougham, following the Demarara revolt in 1823 that arose from confusion about whether or not freedom had been granted, likened the slaves to Englishmen on strike (Matthews 2000:6). Thomas Foxwell Buxton took this further: he referred to continued violent slave resistance as a just war for freedom and rights, and argued that, if the government continued to oppose abolition, England would be placing itself in opposition to facets of humanity that made them in the image of God:

> War was to be lamented anywhere and under any circumstances: but a war against a people struggling for their freedom and their rights would be the falsest position in which it was possible for England to be placed. The people of England would not support this loss of resources to crush the inalienable rights of mankind... in such a warfare, it was not possible to ask, nor could we dare to expect, the countenance of heaven. The Almighty had no attribute that would side with them in such a struggle. (Buxton, quoted in Matthews 2000:8)

The heightened language obviously reflects the rhetoric of the time (Carey 2005). However, the invocation of 'mankind' [*sic*] and the attributes of God are a direct challenge to the slow sedimentation of racist assumptions developed under slavery, of African ignorance, irrationality and incapacity for self-management. They were instead represented as having the capacity to gain freedom and enjoy it within its God-given boundaries. Not only was there nothing to fear from this freedom, if the English did not grant it they would need to fear the wrath of God.

Seen in terms of the demands of governmentality, the need for a more self-governing labour force made such arguments against racism not only justifiable but also necessary. Racist assumptions had been fundamental in establishing and maintaining regimes of direct discipline, but in the early nineteenth century the system was becoming increasingly unprofitable and contentious. Less expensive and more remote forms of government were required if any continued economic benefit were to be had, and these relied on a more self-governing workforce (Williams 1970:280–92). Missionaries went to Jamaica and other places during the early years of the nineteenth century, and set up free villages, in which slaves could own land and missionaries could develop individuals, households and communities into independent and responsible citizens: 'a society in which black men could become like white men, not the whites of the plantations but the whites of the abolitionist movement, responsible, industrious, independent, Christian...' (Hall 1993:110). Other abolitionists contributed to this process of responsibilisation by monitoring the progress of the villages through regular reports in missionary journals, and engaging in lively debate over whether or not white missionaries could ever hand over the reins entirely to the black population.

Through this brief sketch of the negotiation of freedom and fear during abolition, it is clear that enslaved people was able to use fear as a tool in the negotiation of formal freedom, whilst the abolitionist movement were able to successfully 're-present' the securitisation of formerly enslaved people as proof of their ability to meet the demands of a carefully delimited freedom, In other words, to argue that the violence itself was a seed of humanity that meant that, with the help of British civil society, slaves could be developed into potentially 'free subjects' whose freedom would be within boundaries that could be managed, not least by former abolitionists themselves.

Conclusion: Creative Space-Time Associations

This chapter has reflected how one might analyse NGOs' roles in securitisation seen as a form of global governmentality. It has argued that these networked, globalised actors need to be seen within a multi-perspectival analysis, and has suggested that a dialogue between postcolonial and Foucauldian theories might be a useful way forward in establishing this. In particular, similarities between the critical perspectives of Wilson Harris and Foucault in relation to freedom and insecurity were identified and related to NGOs' roles in securitisation as governmentality, but Harris's work pushes Foucauldian governmentality towards an engagement with associations across space-time. A brief analysis of the ways in which abolitionists balanced freedom and fear in the securitisation and de-securitisation of slaves (as well as the counter-securitisation of planters) demonstrated how their work existed within changing discourses of governmentality, but also built on these to establish/legitimise their own positions viz à viz ex-slaves post-abolition.

It is of course impossible to be categorical about what arises from the association of these two historical moments, but it is suggestive of three areas for further reflection. The first relates to possibilities for NGOs to engage in any kind of a politics around securitisation. The geography of the planters' arguments about violence arising from the actions of external agitators, and the insistence on the right and efficacy of internal and brutal discipline of insurrection, can be compared with elements of the securitisation discourses generally espoused by governments in the present securitised moment, in particular the concept of 'radicalisation' and the challenges (through 'Memoranda of Understanding' in the British case) to the principle of 'refoulement', allowing failed asylum seekers who are suspected of terrorism to be sent back to the jurisdiction of governments whose past human rights record leads to fears that they will act repressively (Chakrabarti 2005).

In NGOs' response to this logic of abjection of suspected terrorists to places that the Euro-American press cannot easily scrutinise, NGOs' networked existence can be a 'technology of the self' (Foucault 1984:1988) that allows them to represent themselves in more flexible ways in order to gain a more globalised sense of authority. For example, an immediate response to 9/11 came in the form of a joint statement, not only by British but also by international NGOs: 'NGOs call for restraint in response to terrorist attacks' (19 September 2001). This is a joint statement by a group of NGOs identified at the beginning of the statement as 'a group of international development, human rights and refugee non-governmental organisations (NGOs)', and later as '*NGOs working across the world*', emphasising the globalised dimension of their perspective. The statement expresses concern about the possible effect of US military action on the vulnerable, linking the effect of violence perpetrated by the US to the effect of violence perpetrated on the US: 'The experience of NGOs working across the world shows that – as in the USA – it is often innocent people who are victims of violence. We urge the United States and its allies to assess carefully the potential impact any proposed military action may have on the poor, the innocent and the voiceless.'

Like the metropolitan abolitionists in relation to the West Indies, NGOs can present themselves as never outsiders, but able always to argue for universal human rights in any given global situation. As Steele and Amoureux (2005) have noted, this 'panoptical' stance, even though it is enabled and conditioned by state power, can be a position of perceived legitimacy and authority both nationally and internationally in relation to the 'less independent and autonomous forms of agency' (Steele and Amoureux 2005:418) that might be wielded by national governments, particularly the US in the heated weeks after a terrorist atrocity against its own citizens. This said, however, NGOs are increasingly invited to share forums with security personnel around radicalisation, whilst in many places around the world the distinction between humanitarian NGOs and private security companies is becoming less clear (Bislev *et al.* 2001; Weiss 1998). These changes in their field to include more of a security ethos may make Bigo's warnings about the difficulty of challenging securitisation (see above) even more timely.

Secondly, in terms of associations between the time of slavery and abolition and the present securitised moment, another direction is to relate the securitisation of NGOs' roles in international development with Foucault's work on the development in Europe during the sixteenth to eighteenth centuries of the governmental discourse of 'policing' the state's resources, with its emphasis on the merging of security and social security to administer 'precisely the entirety of the art of governing' (Foucault 2004b:326, author's translation). Not only is this suggestive of how changing relationships between the state and development policies might be linked with securitisation and governmentality (for example, the drift from 'developmental' to 'enabling' state), but the categories of 'policing' identified by Foucault – population numbers, provision of food, maintenance of health, the regulation of employment, planning for circulation of goods and services (Foucault 2004b:332–333) – are suggestive of the ways in which NGO roles become incorporated into wider frameworks of governmentality, each of these roles becoming securitised through discourses of crisis in terms of dearth, corruption or the need to protect them from attack.

Finally, the approach of associations across space-time leaves us open to the importance of the international slave trade as a moment that pushes the definition of what is meant by humanity, freedom and (in)security in modernity. For example, the dividing line between the negotiations and forms of intimacy that could exist between slaver and enslaved alongside direct brutality as forms of control (Beckles 1989; Gilroy

1993) are the flipside of the domination and coercion often present in the contractual relationships between employer and employee (Pateman 2002). That is to say, it both shows the importance of the agency of enslaved people in negotiating the boundaries of freedom through the use of fear, and questions the boundaries of freedom for free labour. Within the Caribbean, for example, historians have mapped extensively the variety of ways in which the 'slavery/freedom antinomy' (Bolland 1993:120) often proved illusory in practice, so that in many cases freed slaves only moved from a system of direct coercion into unpaid labour to a system of heavy compulsion into unpaid labour through punishments like the confiscation of lands used for subsistence farming (Bolland 1993; Hall 1993). As Harris puts it:

> What is freedom? One is left to calculate how the slaves or mimics of a system everyone is told to admire because it is the best in the world, can find freedom when the system itself enslaves itself by freight, by a lust for money, which banishes originality. (Harris 2006:98)

Bibliography

Abrahamsen, R. (2004) 'A Breeding Ground for Terrorists? Africa and Britain's "War on Terrorism"'. *Review of African Political Economy* 31(102): 677–84.

Aradau, C. (2004). 'The Perverse Politics of Four-Letter Words: Risk and Pity in the Securitisation of Human Trafficking'. *Millennium: Journal of International Studie* 33(2): 251–77.

Bach, J. and Stark, D. (2004) 'Link, Search, Interact: The Co-evolution of NGOs and Enteractive Technology'. *Theory, Culture and Society* 21(3): 101–17.

Beckles, H. (1989) *Natural Rebels: A Social History of Enslaved Black Women in Barbados*. London: Zed Books.

Beckles, H.M. (1999) *Centering Woman: Gender Discourses in Caribbean Slave Society*. Kingston: Ian Randle.

Bell, M., Butlin, R. and Heffernan, M. (eds) (1995) *Geography and Imperialism 1820–1940*. Manchester: Manchester University Press.

Bhabha, H. (1994) *The Location of Culture*. London: Routledge.

Bhabha, H. (1995) 'Translator Translated: Conversation with Homi Bhabha'. *Artforum* 33(7): 80–83, 110, 114, 118–19.

Bigo, D. (2002) 'Security and Immigration: Toward a Critique of the Governmentality of Unease'. *Alternatives* 27: 63–92.

Bislev, S., Salskov-Iversen, D. and Hansen, H. K. (2001) 'Governance and Globalization: Security Privatization on the US-Mexican Border: A New Role for Non-State Actors in Security Provision?' IKL Department of Intercultural Communication and Management Working Paper 42. available at https://openarchive.cbs.dk/bitstream/handle/10398/6955/wp%2043%202001.pdf?sequence=1, accessed may 2009.

Bolland, O.N. (1993) 'Systems of Domination after Slavery: The Control of Land and Labour in the British West Indies after 1838'. In Beckles, H. and Shepherd, V. (eds) *Caribbean Freedom: Economy and Society from Emancipation to the Present*. Kingston: Ian Randle, pp. 107–24.

Bryant, R. (2002) 'Non-Governmental Organizations and Governmentality: "Consuming" Biodiversity and Indigenous People in the Philippines'. *Political Studies* 50: 268–92.

Carey, B. (2005) *British Abolitionism and the Rhetoric of Sensibility: Writing, Sentiment and Slavery, 1760–1807*. Basingstoke: Palgrave Macmillan.

Chakrabarti, S. (2005) 'Rights and Rhetoric: The Politics of Asylum and Human Rights Culture in the United Kingdom'. *Journal of Law and Society* 32(1): 131–47.

Chakrabarty, D. (2000) *Provincializing Europe: Postcolonial Thought and Historical Difference*. Woodstock, NJ: Princeton University Press.

Crush, J. (1994) 'Post-Colonialism, De-Colonization and Geography'. In A. Godlewska and Smith, N. (eds) *Geography and Empire*. Oxford: Blackwell, pp. 333–50.

Dean, M. (1999) *Governmentality: Power and Rule in Modern Society*. London: Sage.

Demars, W.E. (2005) *NGOs and Transnational Networks: Wild Cards in World Politics*. London: Pluto.

Duffield, M. (2001) *Global Governance and the New Wars: The Merging of Development and Security*. London: Zed Books.

Duffield, M. (2002) 'Reprising Durable Disorder: Network War and the Securitisation of Aid'. In Hettne, B. and Oden, B. (eds) *Global Governance in the 21st Century: Alternative Perspectives on World Order*. Stockholm: Almkvist & Wiksell International.

Elbe, S. (2004) 'The Futility of Protest? Biopower and Bio-politics in the Securitisation of HIV/AIDS'. Paper presented at the ISA Convention, Montreal, Québec.

Eriksson, J. (2001) 'Cyberplagues, IT, and Security: Threat Politics in the Information Age'. *Journal of Contingencies and Crisis Management* 9(4): 211–22.

Fanon, F. (1967) *The Wretched of the Earth*. New York: Grove Press.

Foucault, M. (1984) *Histoire de la sexualité 2: L'usage des plaisirs*. Paris: Éditions Gallimard.

Foucault, M. (1988) 'Technologies of the Self'. In L. H. Martin (ed.) *Technologies of the Self: a Seminar with Michel Foucault*. Amherst: University of Massachusetts Press, pp. 16–49.

Foucault, M. (2003) *Abnormal: Lectures at the College de France 1974–1975* (G. Burchell, Trans.). New York: Picador USA.

Foucault, M. (2004a) *Naissance de la Biopolitique: Cours au Collège de France, 1978–1979*. Paris: Gallimard Seuil.

Foucault, M. (2004b) *Sécurité, Territoire, Population: Cours au Collège de France 1977–1978*. Paris: Gallimard Seuil.

Foucault, M. (2004c) *Society Must Be Defended: Lectures at the College de France, 1975–76*. Harmondsworth: Penguin.

Geddes, A. (2005) 'Chronicle of a Crisis Foretold: The Politics of Irregular Migration, Human Trafficking and People Smuggling in the UK'. *British Journal of Politics and International Relations* 7: 324–39.

Gilroy, D. (1993) *The Black Atlantic: Modernity and Double Consciousness*. London: Verso Press.

Hall, C. (1992) *White, Male and Middle Class: Explorations in Feminism and History*. Cambridge: Polity Press.

Hall, C. (1993) 'White Visions, Black Lives: The Free Villages of Jamaica'. *History Workshop Journal* 36: 100–32.

Hall, D. (1993) 'The Flight from the Estates Reconsidered: the British West Indies 1838–1842'. In Beckles, H. and Shepherd, V. (eds), *Caribbean Freedom: Economy and Society from Emancipation to the Present*. Kingston: Ian Randle, pp. 55–64.

Hall, S. (1996) 'New Ethnicities.' In Hall, S. Modey, David and Chen, K. (eds) *Critical Dialogues in Cultural Studies*. London: Routledge.

Harris, W. (1967) *Tradition, the Writer and Society: Critical Essays*. London: New Beacon.

Harris, W. (1999) 'Literacy and the Imagination – A Talk.' In Bundy, A. (ed.) *Wilson Harris: The Unfinished Genesis of the Imagination*. London: Routledge, pp. 75–90.

Harris, W. (2006) *The Ghost of Memory*. London: Faber and Faber.

Higgott, R. (2003) 'American Unilateralism, Foreign Economic Policy and the "Securitisation" of Globalisation'. *Institute of Defence and Strategic Studies* 52: 147–75.

Huxley, M. (2007) 'Geographies of Governmentality'. In Crampton, J. and Elden, S. (eds), *Space, Knowledge and Power: Foucault and Geography*. Aldershot: Ashgate, pp. 185–205.

Huysmans, J. (2000) 'The European Union and the Securitization of Migration'. *Journal of Common Market Studies* 38(5): 751–77.

Huysmans, J. (2004) 'A Foucaultian View on Spill-Over: Freedom and Security in the EU'. *Journal of International Relations and Development* 7: 294–318.

Ilcan, S. and Basok, T. (2004) 'Community Government: Voluntary Agencies, Social Justice, and the Responsibilization of Citizens'. *Citizenship Studies* 8(2), 129–44.

Independent Police Complaints Commission (2007) *Stockwell Two: An Investigation into Complaints about the Metropolitan Police Service's Handling of Public Statements following the Shooting of Jean Charles de Menezes on 22 July 2005*. London: Independent Police Complaints Commission.

Joint Council For The Welfare Of Immigrants (2006) 'Kids' Citizenship: Caught in Anti-Terror Net? Anti-Terror Clauses in Immigration Bill Could Affect Children's Citizenship, Campaigners Worry', from http://www.jcwi.org.uk/news/press6feb2006.html.

Kalpagam, U. (2000) 'Colonial Governmentality and the "Economy"'. *Economy and Society* 29 (3): 418–38.

Lacey, A., and Ilcan, S. (2006) 'Voluntary Labor, Responsible Citizenship, and International NGOs'. *International Journal of Comparative Sociology* 47(1): 34–53.

Lambert, D. (2005) 'Producing/Contesting Whiteness: Rebellion, Anti-Slavery and Enslavement in Barbados, 1816'. *Geoforum* 36: 29–43.

Larner, W., and Walters, W. (2000) 'Privatisation, Governance and Identity: the United Kingdom and New Zealand Compared'. *Policy and Politics* 28(3): 361–77.

Leander, A. (2006) 'Privatizing the Politics of Protection: Military Companies and the Definition of Security Concerns'. In Huysmans, J., Dobson, A., and Prokhovnik, R. (eds) *The Politics of Protection: Sites of Insecurity and Political Agency*. London: Routledge, pp. 19–34.

Legg, S. (2007) 'Beyond the European Province: Foucault and Postcolonialism'. In Crampton, J. and Elden, S. (eds) *Space, Knowledge and Power: Foucault and Geography*. Aldershot: Ashgate, pp. 265–91.

Lewis, D. (2005) 'Individuals, Organizations and Public Action: Trajectories of the "Non-Governmental"

in Development Studies'. In Kothari, U. (ed.) *A Radical History of Development Studies: Individuals, Institutions and Ideologies*. London: Zed Books, pp. 200–22.
Lister, S. (2003) 'NGO Legitimacy: Technical Issue or Social Construct'. *Critique of Anthropology* 23(2): 175–92.
Massey, D. (1994) Space, Place and Gender. Minneapolis: University of Minnesota Press.
Matthews, G. (2000) 'The Other Side of Slave Revolts'. Paper presented at the the Society for Caribbean Studies Annual Conference, London.
Mbembe, A. (1999) 'Migration of Peoples, Disintegration of States: Africa's Frontiers in Flux'. *Le Monde Diplomatique*, November: 17.
Mbembe, A. (2001) *On the Postcolony*. Berkeley, CA: University of California Press.
Mcculloch, J., and Pickering, S. (2005) 'Suppressing the Financing of Terrorism: Proliferating State Crime, Eroding Censure and Extending Neo-colonialism'. *British Journal of Criminology* 45(4): 470–86.
Morison, J. (2000) 'The Government-Voluntary Sector Compacts: Governance, Governmentality, and Civil Society'. *Journal of Law and Society* 27(1): 98–132.
Muller, B. (2004) '(Dis)qualified Bodies: Securitization, Citizenship and "Identity Management". *Citizenship Studies* 8(3): 279–24.
Noxolo, P. (2006) 'Riding, Re-focusing, Challenging: NGOs and the Politics of Security Around Immigration and Asylum post 9/11', from http://www.midas.bham.ac.uk/riding%20refocusing%20challenging.pdf.
Noxolo, P. (forthcoming) '"My Paper, My Paper": Reflections on the Embodied Production of Postcolonial Geographical Responsibility in Academic Writing'. *Geoforum*.
Noxolo, P., Raghuram, P. and Madge, C. (2008) '"Geography is Pregnant" and "Geography's Milk is Flowing": Metaphors for a Postcolonial Discipline?' *Environment and Planning D: Society and Space* 26(1): 146–68.
Oldfield, J. R. (1995) *Popular Politics and British Anti-Slavery: the Mobilisation of Public Opinion Against the Slave Trade 1787–1807*. Manchester: Manchester University Press.
Pateman, C. (2002) 'Self-ownership and Property in the Person: Democratization and a Tale of Two Concepts'. *The Journal of Political Philosophy* 10(1): 20–53.
Power, M., Mohan, G., and Mercer, C. (2006) 'Postcolonial Geographies of Development: Introduction'. *Singapore Journal of Tropical Geography* 27(3): 231–34.
Rose, N., and Miller, P. (1992) 'Political Power Beyond the State: Problematics of Government'. *The British Journal of Sociology* 43(2): 173–205.
Schuster, L. (2003) 'Common Sense or Racism? The Treatment of Asylum Seekers in Europe'. *Patterns of Prejudice* 37(3): 233–56.
Sidaway, J. (2000) 'Postcolonial Geographies: An Exploratory Essay'. *Progress in Human Geography* 24: 591–612.
Simon, J. and Tuhiwai Smith, L. (2001) *A Civilising Mission: Perceptions and Representations of the New Zealand Native Schools System*. Auckland: Auckland University Press.
Sivanandan, A. (2006) 'Race, Terror and Civil Society'. *Race and Class* 47(3): 1–8.
Spivak, G. (1992) 'The Politics of Translation'. In M. Barrett & A. Phillips (eds) *Destabilizing Theory: Contemporary Feminist Debates*. Cambridge: Polity Press, pp. 177–200.
Steele, B.J. and Amoureut, J.L. (2005) 'NGOs and Monitoring Genocide: The Benefits and Limits to Human Rights Panopticism'. *Millennium Journal of International Studies* 34 (2): 403–32.
Stoler, A.L. (1995) *Race and the Education of Desire: Foucault's 'History of Sexuality' and the Colonial Order of Things*. Durham: Duke University Press.
Waever, O. (1995) 'Securitization and Desecuritization'. In Lipschultz, R. (ed.) *On Security*. New York: Columbia University Press, pp. 46–86.
Waever, O. (2000) 'The EU as a Security Actor: Reflections from a Pessimistic Constructivist on Post-Sovereign Security Orders'. In Kelstrup, M. and Williams, M. (eds) *International Relations Theory and the Politics of European Integration: Power, Security and Community*. London: Routledge, pp. 12–33.
Weiss, T.G. (1998) *Beyond UN Subcontracting : Task-Sharing with Regional Security Arrangements and Service-Providing NGOs*. New York: St. Martin's Press.
Willetts, P. (2002) 'What is a Non-Governmental Organization?' 'UNESCO Encyclopaedia of Life Support Systems: Section 1 Institutional and Infrastructure Resource Issues', htpp://www.staff.city.ac.uk/p.willetts/CS-NTWKS/NGO-ART.HTM accessed 15 May 2009.
Williams, E. (1970) *From Columbus to Castro: The History of the Caribbean 1492–1969*. New York: Andre Deutsch.
Woods, M. (2002) *Slavery, Empathy and Pornography*. Oxford: Oxford University Press.
Yanacopulos, H. (2005) 'The Strategies that Bind: NGO Coalitions and their Influence'. *Global Networks* 5(1): 93–110.

Notes

1 The notion of 'lagging' refers to the colonial practice of transporting people to the colonies for punishment – (see Homi Bhabha 1994).

2 At the time Harris would have been writing this it was generally believed that Mr de Menezes had run away from the police in panic and jumped the ticket barrier, prompting the police to believe he was behaving suspiciously. A subsequent IPCC inquiry has shown that he did not in fact do either of these things. (See Independent Police Complaints Commission 2007.)

10

Theorising Continuities between Empire & Development
Toward a New Theory of History

APRIL R. BICCUM

Introduction

At the risk of adding to an already voluminous literature, this chapter begins with a question: how is it that the promises of the short[1] twentieth century have ended in the return of empire? Accompanying and prompted by the terror wars is an emerging spate of academic literature, translated into public and popular discourse, narrating this contemporary moment as a 'new' era of imperialism (Cooper 2002a and b; Harvey 2003; Cox 2003a and b; Saull 2004; Mann 2004; Ikenberry 2004; Wade 2004), for which it is largely apologetic, or a 'new' globalised Empire (Hardt and Negri 2001) which is distinct from the European state-led empires which precede it. The academic debate on the left has configured largely around Hardt and Negri's now seminal work (Balakrishnan 2003), and the debate on the right has made the case for a New American Century of intervention and state reconstruction (Mabee 2004; Ignatieff 2003). In the popular domain, Niall Ferguson's *Empire* has been televised, his *Colossus* much publicised, and the reconfiguring of imperialism as a history wrongfully maligned has appeared here and there in the popular press as it has in academic discourse. The history and historiography of empire is long and complex and, given the events of the twentieth century, part of my argument is that its vigorous resurgence at the dawn of the twenty-first century as a figure in discourse is significant. This chapter poses the question, what is at stake in the furore over empire? Why empire? Why now? What does this debate tell us about the configuration of capitalism, modernity, metropolitan self-conception and all of the multifarious political and economic implications this entails?

In addition to a resurgence of empire, and perhaps paradoxically, is a renewed fervor over global justice, manifesting itself as a complex and contradictory 'anti-globalisation movement' accompanied by a vast civil society mobilisation in the form of social forums and spectacular new campaigns, such as Make Poverty History and Live8. There has also been a shift in the global development apparatus away from structural adjustment and towards poverty eradication, as is witnessed by the Millennium Development Goals, governance partnerships and pro-poor policy promotion, themselves linked and intersecting in contradictory ways with civil society lobbying. Despite this emphasis on poverty reduction and global justice, in the mainstream discourse it is in fact a very old nineteenth-century idea of poverty-as-degeneracy (McClintock 1992) that has been utilised within the reconfiguration of development as a security strategy that suggests that there are very strong lines of continuity between colonial and development discourse and policy (Biccum 2002 and 2005).

This chapter suggests that these developments actually comprise a complex shift in vocabulary in the discourse of development, history and modernity that has also been accompanied by metropolitan attempts in popular and public discourses on the centre and right of the spectrum to normalise the 'new' imperialism, justify the (re)colonisation of the Middle East, pose neo-liberal capitalism as the only option for global governance. It is the contention of the chapter that what occurs via this shift in vocabulary is a narration of this contemporary moment as a rupture from its past through a repackaging of British colonial history in an apologetic frame. All of these intersecting discourses around development, modernity and empire are examples of what can be characterised as 'narratives of contemporaneity', competing narratives occurring across disciplines which implicitly or explicitly attempt to narrate this contemporary moment, and, in so doing, implicitly or explicitly corroborate a narrative of history. These are links which can be made with recourse to the very thorough excavation of colonial culture and discourse in the contribution of the multidisciplinary field of postcolonial theory. Thus, part of the argument here is that operative and enabling *rupture moments* have been constructed in the narratives of contemporaneity which could more effectively be theorised following Homi Bhabha, as *shifts in vocabulary* from within the discourses of authority. In so doing, it is also the contention that contemporaneity and history are in crisis. Thus, the chapter begins with the premise that these narratives are politically operational, that is, they engender political effects through their repetition in public discourse.

If the contemporary moment can be characterised by the logic of a crisis, a crisis for international security, a crisis for post-Cold War economics, a crisis in the national narrative, a crisis in the asylum system, a crisis of global migration, etc, the crisis in the narrative of contemporanetiy is more profound. There is a crisis in the conventional narrative of twentieth-century history, the first inklings of which manifested themselves in Fukayama's now notorious book, Huntingdon's much debated civilisational theories, Hardt and Negri's new theory of Empire, Niall Ferguson's recasting of that narrative in an apologetic vein, and the proliferation of temporal markers in epistemic and disciplinary nomenclature[2] – post-development, post-positivist, post-industrial, neo-liberal, neo-colonial, etc (McClintock 1992; Shohat 1992; Dirlik 1997; Ahmad 1992). It seems that, in this particular historical moment, the narrativisation and signification of the 'now' in the context of its historical trajectory, what this moment means and how we got here, is entirely up for grabs.

This is what is intended by the idea of a crisis in the narrative(s) of contemporaneity, a crisis whose evidence is most notable and can be evidenced by the recurrent logic of an *historical rupture*. That is, by the positing of this historical moment as 'new', as broken from and/or entirely different from all which has come before. There is a rupture which occurs simultaneously with a writing out, distancing or recasting of the history leading up to what has been cast as a 'new' (rupture) moment. Taking a cue from a broad consensus in postcolonial theory, the contention here is that rupture moments in historical narratives are characterised/constituted by the discursive elision, or minimising, of a particular history, in this case, European colonial history. While on the left the debate has configured around the nature of social change for a new kind of global power, with a few critical voices asserting that echoes from the past remain (Mabee 2004; Arrighi 2003; Seth 2003; Amin 2004; Reno 2004), the connection does not seem to have been made within even the critical literature in

International Relations and in Development Studies, that the debate over the 'new' American imperialism has occurred virtually in tandem with a 'new' agenda in development *and* in social policy across Europe, comprising a multifaceted shift in vocabulary around poverty, modernity and contemporaneity from within the discourses of authority.

Narrative rupture moments are politically operative and enabling. Narrative rupture frames conceptions of the twentieth century as definitively ruptured from its colonial past. Both the disciplines of International Relations and Development Studies are broadly predicated upon the notion of a postcolonial or post-imperial state. If the twentieth century has been characterised in Development Studies by Truman's announcement of the end of the old imperialism, why has the figure of empire been so thoroughly resurrected? A 'New' American imperialism is being theorised and debated when the old European imperialism has been thoroughly written out and de-emphasised in the disciplines which construct the twentieth century, despite various critical interventions from 'migrant' intellectuals. Much of the literature attempts to distinguish between older European and British forms of empire and the 'new' American empire or new forms of globalised empire (Hardt and Negri 2000).

One of this chapter's aims is to suggest that there might be something larger at stake in the debate over empire *per se*, something that has more to do with how contemporary disciplines for the twentieth century (International Relations and Development Studies) have failed to incorporate the fact of empire into their narratives of history and contemporaneity. Witness the fact that empire as a political form and category of analysis is largely absent from political analysis which focuses almost exclusively on the state, sub-state and intra-state forms. One explanation may come from an examination of these narratives of contemporaneity through the theoretical framework of postcolonial theory. Central to the broad field of postcolonial studies is the question of history and temporality. The narrative for the twentieth century is perpetually framed as *history-as-development* that is constituted by a narrative rupture which writes out or de-emphasises the colonial moment. This sense of ruptured temporality frames the twentieth century and its key disciplines. This makes the furore over empire significant, it is politically operative. What is needed, therefore, is a new theory of history which is capable of theorising continuities pre and post World War II and the suggestion put forward here is that postcolonial theory is adequate to this task.

The first section of this chapter explores why and how. Firstly, it examines how postcolonial theory brings history and history writing to the forefront of the debate; it calls history and the practice of its production into question, including its problematic treatment in the theory of Marxism. Because postcolonial theory is sensitive to the ambivalences in classical Marx it is capable of bridging the impasse between post-structuralist critique and orthodox materialists. In addition, postcolonial theory has extensively theorised the culture of empire and has produced categories of analysis that can be applied to contemporary development discourses in ways which draw out the continuities. The second section of the chapter examines how postcolonial theory can assist in overcoming the stalemate of the contemporary left, and the third section examines how historical narratives function by the logic of a rupture by exploring what is at stake in narrative rupture through an examination of World Systems Theory and historians of the 'longue durée'. Finally, the chapter finishes by examining how the new discourses of empire function as narrative rupture.

Postcolonial Theory & the Question of History

Broadly speaking, postcolonial theory is what has happened, as the result of the post-war migration, when 'Third World' intellectuals entered metropolitan academies and began to alter traditional fields of study around literature and culture. What occurred was a simultaneous reconsideration of the subject matter, perspective and assumptions of conventional European and American disciplines in the study of literature and the human sciences, in tandem with the introduction of perspectives and literatures of the 'post'-colonial diaspora and South. A shift in the study of literature occurred, along with a whole host of studies looking at colonial history, discourse and culture, starting with Said's seminal text *Orientalism*, carefully analysing the assumptions and functions of a set of discursive apparatuses that made European colonialism possible, palatable and, for some, desirable.

Postcolonial theory began as a disciplinary critique in comparative literature in the 1980s and has since proliferated as a mode of critique across disciplinary fields into anthropology, sociology, cultural studies, women's studies, history and politics, but has remained largely on the margins of these disciplines. Postcolonial studies and theory have always been in conversation with Marxism and post-structuralism, and their progenitors have been engaged in various forms of historical, critical, literary and cultural engagement. Their seminal texts have included projects in literary criticism, such as Gayatri Spivak's translation of Mahasweta Devi in *Imaginary Maps: Three Stories* (1993), Edward Said's *Culture and Imperialism* (1994) and Homi Bhabha's *The Location of Culture* (1994), but also works in cultural criticism and critical theory which have been engaged in analysing colonial culture and discourse, such as Spivak's *In Other Worlds: Essays in cultural politics* (1987c), *The Postcolonial Critic: Interviews, strategies, dialogues* (1987a), Edward Said's *Orientalism* (1978), and Anne McClintock's *Imperial Leather: Race, gender and sexuality in the colonial contest* (1992).

Postcolonial theory has also been renowned for a kind of historical revisionism that contests elite or mainstream historiography, by writing subaltern perspectives back into historical accounts, such as most notably, Ranajit Guha and the Subaltern Studies Group in *Selected Subaltern Studies* (1988). In addition, postcolonial theory has reached a point of prevalence in the academy where several anthologies and introductions have appeared in recent years, such as John McCleod's *Beginning Postcolonialism* (2000), Robert Young's *Postcolonialism: An historical introduction* (2001), Patrick Williams and Laura Chrisman's *Colonial Discourse and Post-colonial Theory: A Reader* (1993), and Gregory Castle's *Postcolonial Discourses: An Anthology* (2001). And this list is by no means exhausted. Suffice it to say for now that postcolonial theory and studies is a recent subfield in cultural and literary criticism and critical theory that has had an impact across the disciplines in the humanities and social sciences.

Postcolonial theory can be broadly situated within a long trajectory of counter-critique in the twentieth century which has persistently been at pains to point out that the West's conception of itself is articulated by the logic of a rupture, that European self-construction is predicated upon an elision of the colonial relation which makes it both materially and epistemologically possible (Amin 1973, 1989; Cardoso 1979; Fanon 2001, 1961; Memmi 1965; Frank 1978; Hobsbawm 1968; James CLR, 1992; Cesaire 1955; Mudimbe 1988; Nkrumah 1965; Rodney 1981; Wallerstein 1984; Walvin 1993; Mariategui 1929; Eric Williams, 1994, among many others). Nevertheless, reading across the diverse field of interventions around the dominant narrative of history (dependency, Third World nationalism and anti-colonial writing, postcolonial theory and post-development), one discerns a clear narrative recounting a growing consolidation of metropolitan capitalist power, one that relies on structural/systemic inequalities in trade, property, finance and sovereign power, as well as the institutionalisation of its hegemony through academic knowledge, technology, education, training and professionalisation and the dispersal of its narratives through the commodification and circulation of popular culture. The term 'metropolitan' is employed to describe contemporary capitalism in appreciation of the fact that Europe has not historically been the only coloniser or imperial power, that the term the 'West' has been duly problematised and that the increasing complexity of globalisation means that metropolitan spaces occur in the global North as well as in the global South, and that, among many other things, globalisation means the proliferation and spread of urban metropolitanism. Equally, it must be said that capitalism is a highly contentious term, with differing interpretations and definitions within the long tradition of Marxism.

Even as they might point to the precariousness of this power (particularly in the work of Bhabha), all of the 'interventionists' contribute to a theorisation of the historical consolidation of metropolitan power, the construction of the Western liberal democratic state as an onto-epistemic construct that is inseparable from empire. Thus, the broader project of postcolonial criticism and intervention is defined by Edward Said as a 'thinking together' of items which have been falsely separated in discourse for the preservation of the power of one over the other. For Said, it means linking culture together with the political; for Bhabha, it means noticing the aporia masked by binary couplets, such as coloniser/colonised, which are split and doubled in discourse; for Spivak, it warrants a close attention to how one is situated and inflected by the discourse which these theorists are trying to resist by *reading differently*. While for Samir Amin, Eric Williams, Eric Hobsbawm, Frantz Fanon, Andre Gunder Frank, Immanuel Wallerstein, Kwame Nkrumah, Jose Mariategui and a whole host of others it means understanding metropolitan history, culture and context as intimately linked with and constituted by its colonial encounter.

This is also the preoccupation of postcolonial theory and criticism that links it with these other 'counter-narratives' coming from the global South, all of which in their varied and diverse endeavours have in common, at the very least, the interruption to or revision of conventional narratives of modernity, particularly, for some of these authors, as articulated in the discourse of development. For postcolonial theorists, this separation in discourse is not neutral or accidental, but rather is structural; it is operative and enabling, serving both an epistemic and ontological violence and warrants a rethinking of the practices of narrative production in the first place. In this way postcolonial theory is a departure from its lineage in Third World political and anti-colonial writing, both because it marks the presence of the Third World migrant in the Western academy as the result of waves of post-war migration to the global North, and because it takes up and combines postmodern and post-structuralist epistemologies with this long tradition of left-wing political writing from the global South.

The rise in popularity of postcolonial studies and theory in the metropolitan academy fomented a whole series of debates and discussions (Afzal-Khan and Sheshadri-Crooks 2000; Moore-Gilbert 1997) and schisms which, for convenience sake, can be characterised as a conventional split between those whose work would insist on a study of capital as foundational (Parry 1994; Dirlik 1997; Ahmad 1992), and those who under the influence of Derrida and post-structuralism bring the foundational to the forefront as the inaugural question (Spivak and Guha 1988; Bhabha 1994). Very generally, those postcolonial theorists who utilise French philosophy have been accused of elitism, an apolitical focus on the cultural, discursive, ideological and linguistic, to the exclusion of questions of the material and questions of violence, and as themselves comprising a transnational capitalist class, cashing in on their diasporic status to further entrench their privilege (Ahmad, 1992; Afzal-Khan and Seshadri-Crooks, 2000). On the other hand, Robert Young (1990) argues that what is really at stake for Marx-inflected postcolonial critics is that the post-structuralists have placed the question of history, so problematic in Marx, at the very forefront of the discussion. Indeed, history is the central problematic implicit in any critical perspective on development, and it is the central problematic for many post-modern and post-structuralist theorists (Attridge *et. al.* 1987), including Foucault (1997), and also the central problematic in the mainstream discourse of development.

This difference in emphasis between dialectical couplets which are spatial (the classical and outmoded account of base and superstructure), is also complicated by a theoretical schism coalescing around a temporal divide between narratives of the colonial past and the global capitalist present. Thus, those who place their emphasis on capital and material relations do so to the exclusion of both cultural power and identity and desire, and tend to discourage the possibility of theorising capitalism together with colonialism (Ellen Meiskins Wood, 2004, notwithstanding). And those who place their emphasis on the cultural mechanisms of power do so while often excluding violence and material/capital relations, and in so doing respect and reproduce the artificial rupture posited before and after World War II, thereby theorising colonial culture without theorising it rigorously with its material relations.[3] While these divides are over-simplified here, it is nevertheless by way of redressing these schisms in part, that this chapter makes the case for the possibility of theorising continuities between development discourse and colonial discourse in a way which might help to reconfigure the rather anxious debate over contemporaneity and the new imperialism.

Briefly, the post-structuralist or postmodern turn in the study of International Relations (IR) has formed a counter-point around issues of temporality, subjectivity, knowledge and truth to the classical paradigm of realism in IR and its account of rational, autonomous state-actors in an anarchical and de-historicised state system. Criticisms of realism and neo-realism abound, but post-positivist approaches have failed, according to Arlene Tickner, to accommodate adequately 'Third World' perspectives. In her piece in *Millennium* titled 'Seeing IR differently: Notes from the Third World', Tickner has argued:

> Calls for disciplinary opening have not been met by systematic efforts to explore IR from third world perspectives. The rejection of universal knowledge projects and absolute truths has not been matched by concrete actions to map out and incorporate multiple, competing know-hows that are scattered throughout the world. (Tickner 2003:296)

According to a strict Realist or Neo-Realist perspective, 'countries of the Global South are irrelevant to the study of international politics' (*ibid.*:301), as they are understood primarily in terms of statehood viability and are cast in terms of their 'failure' as states, their 'roguish' behaviour or 'weak' or contested status. Mainstream IR becomes both a theory for understanding its environment and an epistemology and set of practices for legitimating a particular set of relations (Tickner 2003). Development studies are precisely where the study of the territorially global South becomes relevant to the discipline of IR. Conventional or mainstream Development Studies, just as in development policies and practice, is historically, and up to the contemporary moment, a professed practice of state-building or reconstruction according to the template of state presumed natural and inevitable by the discipline of IR. Development as a discipline picks up where IR leaves off.

Similarly, critical perspectives in development and the school of post-development have also been influenced by the same body of post-structuralist and postmodern scholarship and have made similar criticisms regarding development's unitary and teleological narrative, its Eurocentrism and its claims to a universality that is actually specific, and its function as an epistemology, or way of knowing the world, which in fact operates as a technology for structuring the world, in other words, the knowledge/power apparatus rendered legible in the scholarship of Michel Foucault (see Foucault 1972, 1993 and 1997). Critical perspectives in the study of development are also about theorising development as a discourse, mechanism and technology of power, but do so while respecting and reproducing a narrative rupture which facilitates the very apparatus of power they seek to critique. Critical development theorists need to be more explicit in their theorisation of history. The application of postcolonial theory to contemporary development can begin to bridge the 'tremendous paradox' that the global South poses for even post-positivist perspectives in IR, and, with its thorough treatment of colonial culture and discourse, begin to contextualise development beyond the narrow twentieth-century confines which critical perspectives in development have by and large reproduced.

A Stalemate on the Left

Thus far it has been suggested that there is a tradition of interruptions and alternatives to conventional narratives of history offered by the discourses of authority. This question of alternatives, *alterneity*, is one that grounds the historical debate between liberal, conservative or mainstream camps and their left-wing or radical counterparts which have pointed out all that is wrong in the dominant narrative of how the world is constituted (modern, free and developed vs. imperialist, exploitative and hegemonic) and how it has come to be that way (i.e. through a process of underdevelopment, colonisation or a process of inevitable enlightened progress). But where critics have possibly offered an alternative narrative for the past and the present, they always get caught out in prescribing a political programme for the future.

The fundamental problematic of offering alternatives that are *truly alternative* is what drives this consideration of historical counter-narratives when they attempt to fill in the positive content of *wie ist eigentlich gewesen* ('how it actually was'). If the Eurocentric recounting of history is fraught with gaps and silences (Bhabha 1994; Said 1994; Spivak and Guha 1988), and consolidates itself upon a constitutive lack, *wie ist eigentlich gewesen* becomes an aporia, as does any legitimate programme for how the world can be otherwise. What I mean by this is that the failure of various leftist projects in the twentieth century has led to the proliferation of anxiety over the loss of the agent of history as theorised by Marx. For critics of post-structuralism, this has amounted to a melancholia that is sceptical of over-arching narratives and firm political programmes and a refusal to make political commitments (Bartolovich, 2003). For some critics on the left in various fields (Cox 1996; Escobar 1995), the hope for emancipation has been transferred to the agents of New Social Movements in the global South. Critics of Post-Development, in particular, argue that this hope amounts to a romantic reification of rural or indigenous actors who may or may not hold progressive ideals (Ziai 2004; Pierterse 2001; Storey 2000).

The problematic which post-structuralist inflected criticism is at pains to point out is the problem of ambivalence, or how to keep emancipatory projects from hardening into dogmatism, how to keep the despot from returning. This is a problematic currently playing itself out in the debates over the World Social Forum. This postmodern or post-structuralist problematic informs the reasoning behind the 'new culture of politics' professed by advocates at the World Social Forum, regional forums and various activist activity recently. It is the reason why the World Social Forum presents itself as an arena for the debate of alternatives, a unity in diversity, rather than a movement which articulates a succinct political programme. By and large, there has been a questioning of the old party-led, hierarchical, vanguard politics of the old left which the architects of the World Social Forum are attempting to replace with a postmodern, decentralised, networked, radical democracy which promulgates a multiplicity of alternatives instead of singular, monolithic political programmes.

The positivist premise that inaugurates the disciplines of history and the human sciences (including the study of politics and International Relations), that history and social life can be known and therefore efficiently disciplined and ordered, is also fundamentally tied up with the project of nineteenth-century nation-building (Appleby *et al.* 1994; Wallerstein 1984; Murphy 1994). While this problematic should be emphasised, it is also important within a post-structuralist framework to perpetually interrogate posited foundations, over-arching narratives, received political programmes, etc., but despite this, according to Spivak's reasoning, one is obliged to posit foundations and should do so *strategically*. Gayatri Spivak usefully articulates the paradox that one is obliged to inhabit that which one critiques (Spivak 1987a), or, worded differently, the idea that even the claim that there is no absolute truth is itself a claim for absolute truth. This is a tension that this chapter does not seek to resolve, but one which it attempts to work with productively, which is why it is highlighted here to situate the discussion ambivalently in between the materialist and post-structuralist perspectives.

This schism between an epistemological emphasis on the material and an emphasis on the discursive is significant for the narration of history and the positing of narrative ruptures. Theoretically, there are two issues to be addressed which reflect a wider debate that cuts across disciplines and fields of study on the academic left. Firstly, by using post-structuralist inflected postcolonial theory in a way that brings it directly to bear on contemporary political discourses, it can be (re)politicised. And secondly, by theorising continuities across a narrative rupture that is explicitly or inadvertently reproduced by epistemological schisms on the left, this chapter aims, in part, to begin to construct a bridge between critical development perspectives, postcolonial theory and critical IR.

Thus, the case can be made that development is at its heart a narrative of history. Moreover, development as an idea hinges on the idea of modernity as the 'wealth of nations,' which is persistently under threat from the continued existence of poverty, characterised within the discourse as a 'degeneracy'. Understood from a critical perspective that includes postcolonial theory, development as a discourse therefore has three narrative dimensions which bring it to bear directly on post-positivist or critical perspectives in IR: (i) it is a narrative of history and progress; (ii) more specifically it is a narrative of the history of nations, normatively positing the modern European nation state as a naturally and inevitably occurring historical process, rather than a historically specific matrix of intersecting institutions. Thus, history *per se* becomes the history of the nation state (Appleby, Hunt & Jacob 1994), and the history dove-tailed by mainstream IR is paradoxically subsumed in the narrative of development. And (iii) it is a narrative of, and which defines and normalises, the *relationship* between empire and colony/dependency; first and third world; centre and periphery; developed and un(under)developed; rich and poor, etc. Postcolonial theory provides a set of analytical tools which seeks to theorise precisely this ambivalence that the relationship of development poses for an international system of Western liberal constitutional states. Its application to contemporary development discourses can begin to form a bridge between critical perspectives in development and post-positivist IR in a way that can potentially produce a more devastating critique, and reconfigures the debate over empire and contemporaneity informed by the logic of rupture.

By the Logic of a Rupture

The central argument of this chapter is that a rupture has been posited in the narration of contemporary history, a rupture with which alternative histories, historiographical interventions, postcolonial theory and post-development narratives have not adequately dealt. The rupture is posited pre- and post-World War II, and is a problem because it helps in part to mask the fact that the global political and economic organisation established in the nineteenth century is still largely intact, even if it has shifted its locus to new 'international' institutions (Amin 2004; Reno 2004). A growing volume of literature within International Relations and political history is making the case for the existence of continuities or similarities between nineteenth-century British imperialism and the not-so-new American imperialism, even if they are not making the concrete case for a purposeful theorisation of continuities by way of political praxis or intervention (Reno 2004; Mabee 2004; Pagden 2002; Armitage 2000; Cain and Hopkins 2002).

The case for theorising continuities has been made elsewhere in the literature recently. For instance, Samir Amin alludes to it in a piece titled 'For Struggles Global and National', an interview on the World Social Forum in which he explicitly states that globalisation and imperialism are not new because the nature of capitalism has always been imperialist global expansion (Amin 2004:7). The nature of this imperialist global expansion must be understood with recourse to European/metropolitan colonial history. William Reno (2004) argues in a piece titled 'Order and Commerce in Turbulent Areas: 19th Century Lessons, 21st Century Practice' in *Third World Quarterly* that contemporary foreign investment as a cost-effective indirect means of conducting relations and influencing events in stateless regions and conflict zones mirrors techniques used by Europe prior to its shift back to direct colonialism before 1885 (Reno 2004:608). Bryan Mabee in 'Discourses of Empire: The US "Empire", Globalisation and International Relations' reviews the current debate over the term 'empire' to describe, positively or negatively, US foreign policy, and argues that the US is not so different from its British predecessor and that the use of empire as a concept is helpful for IR to understand the motives and functioning of the US in the current international system (Mabee 2004:1364).

Furthermore, there are recent critical interventions into the study of development such as Monica Van Beusekom and Dorothy L. Hodgson's 'Lessons Learned? Development Experiences in the Late Colonial Period' and Hodgson's 'Taking Stock: State Control, Ethnic Identity and Pastoralist Development in Tanganyika', both in the *Journal of African History* (2000). Each makes the case, using empirical material, that colonial policy has shifted its vocabulary into development policy, and that development policy functions as an apparatus for the material reorganisation of territorially defined spaces in the same way that colonial policies did. In fact, using a combination of Marxist and Foucaultian perspectives, Craig Murphy has shown the relationship between classical liberal philosophy in Kant and Smith, nineteenth-century functionalism in Comte and Bentham, and capitalism's need for international institutions to pave the way for economic expansion (Murphy 1994). Murphy's study traces the continuity between the Public International Unions that emerged in the mid-nineteenth century to lay the systems and infrastructure for capitalist expansion and the institutions for Global Governance that emerged with the Bretton Woods arrangement after World War II. Thus a lot of empirical work has been undertaken in the last 15 years which corroborates the case being made here.

Narrative rupture represents itself by the logic of a beginning, end or break in the narrative where what precedes and what follows are narrated as fundamentally *different* or *new*. Rupture moments in the narrative of history are the operative split and doubling (present/past) within the very narrative logic of history and are meant to distance and differentiate the past from the present in the same way the rational autonomous European subject has historically attempted such a distancing and differentiation from its projected/constructed other, that is, an idea of what has gone before constitutes, or makes possible, the contemporaneity of the present.

The problematic of historical rupture reveals precisely what is at stake in any given account of history. Put simply, how one frames the story of 'how it was' says just as much about how the historian imagines her identity and how historians would like others to think of themselves, each of which then inform the horizon of possibilities for things as they are and things to come. The problematic of historical rupture is precisely what is signalled by reading across anti-imperialist, critical development and postcolonial fields. The point of contention is that which should be narrated *otherwise*, stories which have not been told, myths which legitimate the absences, silences and violence. A good example of what is at stake in the *framing* of history can be garnered from the discussion which occurs between Gayatri Spivak, Ranajit Guha of the Subaltern Studies Group and Gyan Prakash, in which debates over the possibility/legitimacy of (re)reading/(re)writing history from the perspective of the subaltern are preoccupied more by questions of collective consciousness, agency, the nature of hegemony and power, the possibility of resistance, the role of writing and discourse as simultaneously a site of authority and resistance, modernity as a narrative of history and historiography as intimately tied up in the project of modernity, than they are about the subaltern as specific subject *per se* (Spivak and Guha 1988; Prakash 1992). All of the above may or may not necessarily be questions of concern for any given 'subaltern', but they are most definitely what is at stake in critical interventions in the *name of the subaltern* into mainstream historiographical accounts.

This particular feature of historiographical counter-narrative is also observable in the dependency and World Systems literature, where the neo-Marxist account functions on the logic of a revision, in the strictest sense a revisiting of dominant narratives, where the postcolonial account functions on the logic of (re)reading. A revision, in this sense, presupposes the possibility of an ontological past to be recovered, revised and reinserted into History, and a (re)reading presupposes or foregrounds the perspectival and/or ideological nature of *any* account of history. Each of the neo-Marxist revisions places its emphasis on the revising of specific historical events. For example, where Amin places his emphasis on reconfiguring the Renaissance, Frank places his on the inauguration of European expansion and Wallerstein's is on the French and industrial revolutions.

Frank is redrawing the historical map of beginnings to assert that capitalism begins with colonialism, Amin is replanting the seeds of the Enlightenment on African soil and Wallerstein is pointing to the fallacy of a progress inaugurated by 'revolutions'. What each revision points to is the ideological link with the content of the narrative and its point of origin and rupture. The traditional interpretations of the French and industrial revolutions (which were not in fact, for Wallerstein, revolutions) are predicated upon the underlying narratives of progress, modernity and supremacy. Traditional interpretations of these 'revolutions' narrate them as ruptures, and what is more properly at stake, argues Wallerstein, in recounting the French Revolution as a break from the past is that it *produces* and makes possible a narrative of progress, modernity and the legitimation to reorder the world. The Renaissance is also not the rupture it claims to be, according to Amin, but rather is an attempt to *separate* European philosophy from its African origins and through such a differentiation posit a European supremacy which is deeply embedded in the tradition of liberal ideology. Likewise for Frank, capitalism does not *begin* with a historical break from colonialism but is always/already inseparable from its outward expansion, making capitalism not something that originates in Europe (which the logic of certain traditions in Marxism might maintain) but rather a process which is *founded upon and made possible by* the *relationship* between Europe and the regions of the world it colonised. Where Frank departs from the tradition of Marxism (and note, not Marx *per se*) is that capitalism's origins in Europe are a product of Europe's relationship with the territories with which it came into contact. Thus, empire is intimately connected to capital.

The obvious point of rehearsing the arguments of these somewhat out-of-fashion theorists is that how history is narrated has political implications and the positing of narrative ruptures within the dominant narrative of history is *operative* and *enabling* of particular ontic relations, that is, it is significant and requires closer scrutiny. Both postcolonial theory and critical studies in nationalism point to the logic of national narratives and how they are structured problematically with mythological notions of origin which function also as rupture (Anderson 1983; Bhabha 1994). Like Amin, Frank and Wallerstein, one must be attendant to what the narration of rupture means, how it functions in the overall discourse, what effects it produces and what it legitimates. Like Wallerstein's account of the narration of rupture posited by the French Revolution does to the idea of progress, the rupture posited by conventional narratives of the twentieth century around World War II attempts to erase the continuity around a free trade fundamentalism that persists from the nineteenth to the twentieth centuries, whether in its embedded or neo-liberal form. Just as in Wallerstein's account of the French Revolution, the narration of rupture around World War II produces the world as new, progressive and distinct from the 'old imperialism' of Europe. Development as a post-war project inaugurated by Harry Truman's presidential address becomes distinct from colonialism as the sun sets on the British Empire and the process of decolonisation begins. The argument put forward here is that not only is development not distinct from colonialism, it bears significant threads of continuity which are masked by a complex shift in vocabulary and *the persistent narration of historical rupture*. Like Amin, Frank and Wallerstein, what is being pointed out is that there is something significant about this narration of rupture.

The 'New' Imperialism as Narrative Rupture

The central problematic therefore is a problem in the popular and elite institutional narration of history, and attention needs to be drawn to the discursive functioning of rupture in narratives of contemporaneity. Debates over Empire and globalisation and the apologetic literature on the nature of imperialism function likewise largely upon the narration of rupture in which the violence and exploitation of empire are written out, underplayed or characterised as wholly different. Or, when not written out, underplaying or differentiated, the apologetic literature on imperialism uses Britain's imperial experience as a source of lessons for America's imperial project, characterised as a benevolent project of modernisation that can bring a host of 'goods' to the world system such as order and prosperity (Ignatieff 2003; Ferguson 2004). An acceptable version of 'empire' is currently being constructed by ignoring the literature that narrates empire's violence and in so doing reverses the twentieth-century normative platitude that empire contravenes that universally accepted social good of 'sovereignty', as freedom from fascism, despotism and arbitrary governance, as a state of political existence that characterises modernity itself. An alternative version of globalisation as a new form of empire is being narrated which overlooks and/or fails to problematise the narrative rupture posited around World War II and does not theorise the relationship between capitalism and colonialism. The contention here is that this is a symptom of the 'sanctioned ignorance' (Spivak 1987a) around the figure and history of empire which persists in the study of politics and the field of International Relations.

The argument being put forward, therefore, is that two ruptures work instrumentally in the narrative of contemporaneity in a way which enables and facilitates the furtherance of global liberal power, apologetic versions of European colonial history, and a re-emergence of the figure of empire. The first posits World War II as the quintessential watershed, and while it would be foolish to argue against its significance, the argument is that empirical work which demonstrates lines of continuity, particularly in the development apparatus and the staggered nature of decolonisation, points more to a complex shift in vocabulary and material relations than a complete break with history with which it has become mythologised. The second rupture is posited around the phenomenon of globalisation, a significantly new feature of capitalism which returns us to policies experimented with in nineteenth-century empires. A response to these ruptures and the debates which they have engendered for contemporaneity, is offered here by way of a *theorisation of continuities* from colonialism and empire to development and globalisation. The continuities which find their axis between colonial discourse and development discourse should be understood, following Homi Bhabha, as a *shift in vocabulary from within the discourses of authority*, rather than a break in temporality, or even a renewal or reinvention of anachronistic power relations. In so doing, this chapter makes its own contribution to the debate over contemporaneity, and argues that this historical moment must be understood as a direct continuation, in spite of shifts and fissures, with nineteenth-century British colonial hegemony. I offer, therefore, a narrative of contemporaneity which has implications for the signification of 'history' and the urgency of resistance.

Bibliography

Afzal-Khan, F. and Seshadri-Crooks, K. (2000) *The Pre-Occupation of Postcolonial Studies.* Durham, NC and London: Duke University Press.
Ahmad, A. (1992) *In Theory: Classes, Nations, Literatures.* London: Verso Press.
Amin, S. (1973) *Neo-colonialism in West Africa.* New York and London: Monthly Review Press.
Amin, S. (1989) *Eurocentrism.* London: Zed Books.
Amin, S. (2004) 'For Struggles Global and National'. In Sen, J., Anand, A., Escobar, A. and Waterman, P. (eds) *World Social Forum: Challenging Empires.* New Delhi: The Viveka Foundation.
Anderson, B. (1983) *Imagined Communities: Reflections on the Origin and Spread of Nationalism.* London: Verso Press.
Appleby, J., Hunt, L. and Jacob, M. (1994) *Telling the Truth about History.* New York and London: W.W. Norton.
Armitage, D. (2000) *The Ideological Origins of the British Empire.* Cambridge: Cambridge University Press.
Arrighi, G. (2003) 'Lineages of Empire'. In Balakrishnan, G. (ed.) *Debating Empire.* London: Verso Press.
Attridge, D., Bennington, G. and Young, R. (eds) (1987) *Post-Structuralism and the Question of History.* Cambridge: Cambridge University Press.
Balakrishnan, G. (ed.) (2003) *Debating Empire.* London: Verso Press.
Bartolovich, C. and Lazarus, N. (eds) (2002) *Marxism, Modernity and Postcolonial Studies.* Cambridge: Cambridge University Press.
Beusekom, M.M. and Hodgson, D.L. (2000) 'Lessons Learned? Development Experiences in the Late Colonial Period'. *The Journal of African History* 41(1): 29–33.
Bhabha, H. (1994) 'How Newness enters the World: Postmodern Space, Postcolonial Times and the Trials of Cultural Translation.' In *The Location of Culture.* London: Routledge.
Biccum, A.R. (2002) 'Interrupting the Discourse of Development: On a Collision Course with Postcolonial Theory'. *Culture, Theory & Critique* 43: 33–50.
Biccum, A.R. (2005) 'Development and the "New" Imperialism: a Reinvention of Colonial Discourse in DFID Promotional Literature'. *Third World Quarterly* 26: 1005–20.
Cain, P.J. and Hopkins, A.G. (2002) *British Imperialism 1628–2000.* Harlow: Pearson.
Cardoso, F.H. (1979) *Dependency and Development in Latin America.* Berkeley, CA: University of California Press.
Castle, G. (ed.) (2001) *Postcolonial Discourses: An Anthology.* Oxford: Blackwell.
Cesaire, A. (1955) *Discourse on Colonialism.* New York: Monthly Review Press.
Cooper, R. (2002a) 'Why We Still Need Empires'. *The Observer,* 7 April, http://observer.guardian.co.uk/print/0,,4388915–110490,00.html.
Cooper, R. (2002b) 'The New Liberal Imperialism'. *The Observer,* http://www.guardian.co.uk/world/2002/apr/07/1.
Cooper, R. (2003) *The Breaking of Nations: Order and Chaos in the Twenty-First Century.* London: Atlantic Books.
Cox, M. (2003a) 'The Empire's Back in Town: Or America's Imperial Temptation'. *Millennium* 32: 1–29.
Cox, M. (2003b) 'Empire by Denial? Debating U.S. Power'. *Security Dialogue* 35: 228–36.
Cox, R. (1996) *Approaches to World Order.* New York: Cambridge.
Devi, M. (1993) *Imaginary Maps: Three Stories.* G.C. Spivak (Trans.). Calcutta: Theme.
Dirlik, A. (1997) *The Postcolonial Aura: Third World Criticism in the Age of Global Capitalism.* Durham, NC: Duke University Press.
Escobar, A. (1995) *Encountering Development: The Making and Unmaking of the Third World.* Princeton, NJ: Princeton University Press.
Fanon, F. (1961) *The Wretched of the Earth.* London: Macgibbon & Gee.
Fanon, F. (2001) 'Spontaneity: its Strengths and Weaknesses'. In Castle, G. (ed.) *Postcolonial Discourses: An Anthology.* Oxford: Blackwell, pp. 3–25.
Ferguson, N. (2004) *Colossus: The Rise and Fall of the American Empire.* London: Allen Lane.
Ferguson, N. (2004) *Empire: How Britain Made the Modern World.* London: Penguin.
Foucault, M. (1997) *Society Must be Defended.* Harmondsworth: Penguin.
Foucault, M. (1993) 'Space, Power and Knowledge'. In During, S. (ed.) *The Cultural Studies Reader*. London and New York: Routledge.
Foucault, M. (1972) *The Archaeology of Knowledge.* London: Tavistock.
Frank, A. G. (1978) *Dependent Accumulation and Underdevelopment.* London: MacMillan Press.
Hardt, M. and Negri, A. (2001) *Empire.* Cambridge, MA: Harvard University Press.
Harvey, D. (2003) 'The "New" Imperialism: Accumulation by Dispossession'. In Panitch, L. and Leys, C. (eds)

Socialist Register: The New Imperial Challenge. London: Merlin, pp. 63–87.
Hobsbawm, E.J. (1968) *Industry and Empire: From 1750 to the Present Day.* Harmondsworth: Penguin.
Hodgson, D.L. (2000) 'Taking Stock: State Control, Ethnic Identity and Pastoralist Development in Tanganyika, 1948–1958'. *Journal of African History* 41(1): 55–78.
Ignatieff, M. (2003) *Empire Lite: Nation Building in Bosnia, Kosovo and Afghanistan.* London: Vintage.
Ikenberry, J. (2004) 'Liberalism and Empire: Logics of Order in the American Unipolar Age'. *Review of International Studies* 30: 615–37.
James, C.L.R. (2001) *The Black Jacobins.* Harmondsworth: Penguin.
Mabee, B. (2004) 'Discourses of Empire: The U.S. "Empire", Globalisation and International Relations'. *Third World Quarterly* 25: 1359–78.
Mann, M. (2004) 'The First Failed Empire of the 21st Century'. *Review of International Studies* 30: 631–53.
Mariategui, J. C. (1929) 'The Anti-Imperialist Perspective'. *New Left Review* 7: 67–72.
Mcclintock, A. (1992) *Imperial Leather: Race, Gender and Sexuality in the Colonial Contest.* New York: Routledge.
Mccleod, J. (2000) *Beginning Postcolonialism.* Manchester: Manchester University Press.
Memmi, A. (1965) *The Coloniser and the Colonised.* Boston, MA: Beacon Press.
Moore-Gilbert, B. (1997) *Postcolonial Theory: Contexts, Practices, Politics.* London: Verso Press.
Mudimbe, V.Y. (1988) *The Invention of Africa: Gnosis, Philosophy and the Order of Knowledge.* Bloomington, IN: Indiana University Press.
Murphy, C. (1994) *International Organisation and Industrial Change: Global Governance since 1850.* Cambridge: Polity Press.
Nkrumah, K. (1965) *Neocolonialism: The Last Stage of Imperialism.* London: Nelson.
Pagden, A. (2002) *People and Empires.* London: Phoenix Press.
Parry, B. (1994) 'Signs of Our Times: Discussion of Homi Bhabha's *The Location of Culture*'. *Third Text* vol. 8 (28): 5–24.
Pieterse, J.N. (2001) 'After Post-Development'. *Third World Quarterly* 21: 175–191.
Prakash, G. (1992) 'Postcolonial Criticism and Indian Historiography'. *Social Text* 31(32): 8–20.
Reno, W. (2004) 'Order and Commerce in Turbulent Areas: 19th Century Lessons, 21st Century Practice'. *Third World Quarterly* 25: 607–25.
Rodney, W. (1981) *How Europe Underdeveloped Africa.* Washington, DC: Howard University Press.
Said, E. (1984)' Permission to Narrate'. *Journal of Palestinian Studies* 13: 27–48.
Said, E. (1989) 'Representing the Colonised: Anthropology's Interlocutors'. *Critical Inquiry* 15: 205–25.
Said, E. (1994) *Culture and Imperialism.* London: Vintage.
Said, E. (1997) *Covering Islam: How the Media and the Experts Determine How We See the Rest of the World.* London: Vintage.
Saull, R. (2004) 'On the "New" American Empire'. *Security Dialogue* 35 (2): 251–3.
Seth, S. (2003) 'Back to the Future?' In Balakrishnan, G. (ed.) *Debating Empire.* London: Verso Press, pp. 43–51.
Shohat, E. (1992) 'Notes on the "Post-Colonial"'. *Social Text* 32 (32): 99–114.
Spivak, G. C. (1987a) *The Postcolonial Critic: Interviews, Strategies, Dialogues.* New York: Routledge.
Spivak, G.C. (1987b) 'Scattered Speculations on the Question of Value'. In Atteridge, D., Bennington, G., and Young, R. (eds) *Poststructuralism and the Question of History.* Cambridge: Cambridge University Press.
Spivak, G.C. (1987c) *In Other Worlds: Essays in Cultural Politics.* New York: London: Routledge.
Spivak, G.C. (1993) *Outside in the Teaching Machine.*, New York and London: Routledge.
Spivak, G.C. and GUHA, R. (eds) (1988) *Selected Subaltern Studies.* London and New York: Oxford University Press.
Spivak, G.C., Landry, D. and Maclean, G. (1996) *The Spivak Reader: Selected Works of Gayatri Chakravorty Spivak.* New York and London: Routledge.
Storey, A. (2000) 'Post-Development Theory: Romanticism and Pontius Pilate Politics'. *Development (SID)* 43: 40–46.
Tickner, A. (2003) 'Seeing IR Differently: Notes from the Third World'. *Millennium: Journal of International Studies* 32(2):295–324.
Wade, R.H. (2004) 'Bringing the Economics Back In'. *Security Dialogue* 35: 243–9.
Wallerstein, I. (1984) *The Politics of the World-Economy: The States, the Movements, and the Civilizations Essays.* Cambridge: Cambridge University Press and and Paris: Editions de la Maison des Sciences de l'Homme.
Walvin, J. (1993) *Black Ivory: A History of British Slavery.* London: Harper Collins.
Williams, E. (1994) *British Historians and the West Indies.* New York: A & B Books Publishers.
Williams, P. and Childs, P. (1997) *An Introduction to Post-Colonial Theory.* Harlow: Pearson.
Williams, P. and Chrisman, L. (eds) (1993) *Colonial Discourse and Post-colonial Theory: A Reader.* Hemel Hemp-

stead: Harvester Wheatsheaf.
Wood, E.M. (2004) 'Infinite War'. *Historical Materialism* 10 (1): 7–27.
Young, R. (1990) *White Mythologies: Writing History and the West.* London: Routledge.
Young, R. (2001) *Postcolonialism: An Historical Introduction.* Oxford: Blackwell.
Ziai, A. (2004) 'The Ambivalence of Post-Development: Between Reactionary Populism and Radical Democracy'. *Third World Quarterly* 25: 1045–60.

Notes

1 I use 'short' advisedly and not to disagree too much with Arrighi's account of the 'long Twentieth Century,' I am referring to the way the twentieth century is often conceptualised as beginning after World War I.
2 For an overview of this debate see Afzal-Khan and Sheshadri-Crooks (2000).
3 For an account of the Marxist strand of postcolonial criticism and theory, see Bartolovich and Lazarus (2003).

11

Spatial Practices & Imaginaries
Experiences of Colonial Officers & Development Professionals[1]

UMA KOTHARI

Introduction

This chapter explores the spatiality of colonial and postcolonial power and discourse as produced, performed and imagined by former United Kingdom colonial service officers and contemporary international development 'professionals'. It demonstrates temporal continuities and discontinuities in spatially extended practices and suggests that decolonisation, while a significant historical process, led to a *reconfiguration* of people, ideas and spaces rather than a wholesale epochal transformation. Accordingly, the trajectory from colonialism to development is more usefully characterised as a shift in emphasis (Crush 1995), rather than of one bounded historical moment to another. I highlight how both colonial officers in the latter days of colonial rule as well as contemporary development professionals create, imagine and perform physical and social space, producing and maintaining power, distance and authority over other people in other places. In so doing, they also shape and articulate (albeit in different global contexts) relationships between core and periphery, coloniser and colonised, aid donor and recipient, and developer and developed. The differential uses of space reflect these relationships and the shift from an overt mission to extend civilisation and modernity to the ideas of progress embedded within a development discourse that cultivates an apparently more humanitarian image.

I invoke aspects of practices, performances and imaginings to show how power is produced in, articulated through and mapped onto space by addressing the spaces inhabited by colonial officers and development professionals posted overseas and how their locatedness, embedded or enclavic, shapes the relationships they have with colonised or (under)developed others.

Such temporally and 'spatially extended transactions' (Lester 2002) that connect people, ideas and practices are explored here through the life histories of 12 colonial service officers who served in sub-Saharan Africa in the 1950s.[2] Following independence, these men (there were few women in the colonial service) returned to England and pursued second careers in the newly emerging but rapidly expanding international development industry in the UK – mostly in bilateral government agencies and multilateral agencies, such as the World Bank, and those related to the United Nations, and other international non-governmental organisations (NGOs). Their individual subjectivities and multiple encounters in the field evoked varied relations with the colonised other and, for some, an ambivalence towards the colonial project. Indeed, they show how the meanings ascribed to certain ideas, behaviours and actions were not maintained wholly intact or homogenous over time and space. Although these personalised narratives are individualised, remembering is a thoroughly social process and draws upon collective imaginaries and themes. Thus, while recognising the heterogeneity of colonial officers, I suggest that memories are selected and interpreted on the basis of culturally located knowledge and that this is further 'constituted and stabilised within a network of social relationships' (Jedlowski 2001:341). Furthermore, while there were variations in the characteristics of colonial spaces in which colonial bureaucracies and authorities were reworked, as well as diverse forms of colonial rule over the space and time of empire, these were rooted in overarching centralised policies and institutional structures.

The narratives of the former colonial service officers presented here are located in a particular historical moment, one that is simultaneously about empire, colonialism, decolonisation, national independence and development. The interview material is complemented by conversations with contemporary British development professionals, both men and women, and informed by personal experience as a development consultant. After discussing how colonial and postcolonial space has been theorised, I explore the production and performance of officers in colonial space and the forms of cultural capital they mobilised to maintain distance and authority and go on to examine the practices of Western development consultants and the enclavic nature of their social and physical space.

Understanding Colonial & Postcolonial Space

This chapter enhances understandings of the spatialities of colonialism and postcolonialism, identifying the different articulations of power in and through spaces that have been produced, performed and imagined by colonial administrators and postcolonial development specialists. As Gregory reminds us, people not only make history but geography, in 'that their actions literally "take place"' (2004:xv). Distinct forms of global spatiality emerge out of the relationships between the colonised/recipients of development intervention and colonisers/development workers, confirming Massey's (1999) assertion that global processes are inevitably marked by (continually reconfigured) 'power-geometries'. As Edward Said (1989:218) declared:

> we would not have had empire itself... without important philosophical and imaginative processes at work in the production as well as the acquisition, subordination, and settlement of space.

All forms of colonialism, the 'implanting of settlements on a distant territory' (Said 1993:9), were involved in the large-scale creation of transnational spheres of interest, control and conquest, and mobilised a series of discursive and practical strategies through which space was claimed as colonial and characterised as possessing a variety of attributes. As Spurr (1993) highlights, colonisers successively or simultaneously appropriated, disciplined, aestheticised, classified, conceived as debased or ethereally insubstantial, negated, idealised, naturalised and eroticised colonised space. Colonial spaces were, at least initially, imagined as 'empty', unobstructed and uninhabited, thus open to unhindered exploration and exploitation. More typically, spaces to be colonised were represented as empty of cultural or productive value, but which could become productive and civilised through colonialism. Moreover, instead of incomprehensible, unmarked and valueless, space was appropriated and cartographically mapped into apparent exactitude, becoming an object of knowledge, carved into identifiable administrative districts, often irrespective of tribal, ethnic and other affiliations, renamed with metropolitan cultural referents, or rough translations or transliterations of local names, classified and scientifically depicted and exhibited, usually without the mediation of their inhabitants. Geography was complicit with the production of this colonial knowledge and representation (Godlewska and Smith 1994; Driver 2001).

Exemplifying the reproduction of spatial divisions, King (1990; also Jacobs, 1996) describes the creation of a dual city in colonial space, in which separate European cantonments and native quarters were devised to inscribe the absolute cultural distinctions essential in supporting a rationale for colonialism. Such constructions were accompanied by ideas that native spaces were potentially dangerous, disease ridden and disorderly, whose utter otherness must be kept at bay by measures and dispositions to avoid social and cultural mixing. Paradoxically, such spaces were imagined as desirable settings for sexual and aesthetic pleasure (Low 1996). The colonised in these spaces are similarly othered as childlike and uncivilised yet exotic and dangerous (Kabbani 1986), an ambivalence reflecting the intricate mix of desire, attraction, fear, loathing and repulsion that typifies the relationship between colonisers and colonised (Bhabha 1994:85–92). These characterisations and attributes came to typify colonial (racialised and gendered) landscapes.

This complex ambivalence within the seemingly rigid ideologies of colonial discourse was compounded by its transmission into distinct local spaces, for as Nash (2004:112) observes, these ideologies 'did not travel out from the centre unchanged but were threatened, challenged, negotiated, made and remade in the encounters between those brought together through colonialism'. Like the anthropologists who were nostalgically and romantically inclined towards the colonised or who questioned colonial policies, colonial officers, ostensibly representatives of colonial power and institutions, were situated in specific cultural contexts where their individual subjectivities supplemented the highly localised spatial expressions and contexts of colonialism. Nevertheless, although these 'local textures of colonialism were immensely complex' (Potter *et al.* 2003:38), and were open to individual interpretation and improvisation, colonial discourses and practices 'were effective precisely because they were enormously flexible and adaptable' (Nash 2004:113).

Colonial officers were oriented towards a range of established and improvisatory performances through which colonised space was interpreted, disciplined and administered. Such performances also enacted forms of Englishness,[3] a resource for achieving social distance and a source of identity in the realm of the other. Here, 'white English class and gender identities were constituted through colonial relationships and interconnections' (Nash 2004:117), showing the imbrication of forms of Englishness with its apparent other. More specifically, as Hall (1992:297) writes, '...it was in the process of comparison between the "virtues" of "Englishness" and the negative features of other cultures that many of the distinctive characterisations of English identities were first defined'. These performances also relied upon the reproduction of imaginary geographies of 'home', in which England was constructed as an idealised glorious homeland (Gowans 2002), and its opposite, colonised space.

Postcolonial analyses have shown how these representations and articulations of colonial space did not come to an end at the time of decolonisation, but continued to be mobilised, reworked and mediated through ideologies, individuals and institutions in the post-independence period. By providing critical responses to the historical effects of colonialism and the persistence of colonial forms of power and knowledge into the present, postcolonial critics have challenged orientalist discourses that produce knowledge about other people in other places (Said 1989). By arguing that particular (colonial) historical readings are the referent for the present, they question the privileging and canonisation of particular historical trajectories and contest the continuing Eurocentrism in global economic, political and social relations by emphasising the particularity of the West (Dhaouadi 1994). Additionally, as Young (2001:6) reminds: 'the values of colonialism seeped much more widely into the general culture... than has ever been assumed'.

Nash (2004:114) writes that 'postcolonial critics argue for a longer and more critical perspective that charts the different extended histories and extensive geographies of colonialism and postcolonialism'. Postcolonial analyses that identify the historical effects of colonialism and the persistence of colonial forms of power and knowledge can critique the multiple ways in which the West produces knowledge about other people and places, simultaneously foregrounding other histories so as to decentre and 'provincialise' Western knowledge (Chakrabarty 2000). Moreover, such approaches challenge the assumed boundaries between colonisers and colonised by invoking 'an explicit critique of the spatial metaphors and temporality employed in geography insisting that the "other" world is "in here" rather than "out there" and "back there"' (McEwan 2003:340).

Based on the recognition that there is a need to understand the colonial genealogy of contemporary globalised ideologies, discourses and practices, postcolonial analyses demonstrate continuities and divergences over time and across space. More specifically, how forms of rule, cultures and practices travelled over colonial space and time and were subsequently reworked in the post-independence period has been the subject of recent postcolonial analyses within development studies (see Havinden and Meredith 1993; Crush 1995; Pieterse and Parekh 1995; Kothari 2002). These show how ideologies that were constructed and utilised to sustain forms of colonial rule and authority have travelled into the spatiality and temporality of international development cooperation and aid, and continue to mark relations between the 'West and the rest'; 'first' and 'third' worlds.

In development studies an analytical separation between studies of colonialism and decolonisation (Le Sueur 2003) has been reinforced by a historical periodisation distinguishing the 'before' of colonialism and the 'after' of independence, concealing the colonial genealogy of contemporary international relations. More recently, there has been a questioning of the apparent seamlessness and inevitability of history and evidence of the overlapping of historical periods (see Cooper and Packard 1996; Cowen and Shenton 1996; Kothari 2005). They demonstrate the synchronicity and intersection of various processes at any one historical moment as colonialism, decolonisation or national independence were taking place in different geographical places. Thus, apparently separate moments did not have their own distinct narrative associated with the particularities of a bounded historical period. Instead, discursive strands come together (re)producing hybridised ideas, practices and social relations (albeit in contradictory and complex ways) within a discourse of 'development' and embodied in the work of the development practitioner. In producing the postcolonial present, processes of decolonisation were hugely varied, with local complexities responding to and producing different forms of engagement, disengagement and re-engagement. Thus, postcolonial analysis can be understood as 'a diverse range of responses to different colonialisms that have been differently experienced, encountered and dealt with in different times and places' (Nash 2004:115). Similarly, the individualised narratives presented here overlap processes/moments of colonisation, decolonisation, independence and development, refuting such historical periodisation and highlighting how discourses flowed over time and across space, and were contested and negotiated through institutions and in the personal space of colonial officers.

Postcolonial space can, thus, be variously conceived as that which is reshaped by resistance to colonial spatial materialities and organisation, the site of 'neocolonial' endeavours, or by enduring colonial legacies. Here, postcolonial spaces are identified as realms in which reconfigured relationships of inequality and power continue to produce forms of unmediated spatial representation and practice that resonate with colonial inequities, specifically in the field of development. And postcolonial analysis can usefully critique such neocolonial processes in, for instance, the development discourse equating development with modernisation, Westernisation and 'progress', particularly in the 1950s and 1960s.

In this postcolonial context, the continuities and divergences between the colonial officer and the development expert are explored according to their dwelling in and movement through identifiable forms of 'native' space. These themes, articulated through the narrativisation of life geographies in the colonial moment and postcolonial development present, show how cultural identities travelled through the space and time of others.

Preparing for Roles in Empire

Particular roles are strongly delineated by colonial officers in the rules and protocols that were embedded in colonial policies, hierarchies and codes, and enacted in, for example, collective performances, systems of recording and expatriate clubs. But for many, whilst informed by these powerful strictures and norms, being posted to 'remote' parts of the world, often isolated in the territory assigned to them for administration, forced them to improvise. Thus, colonial performances were simultaneously habitual and instrumental, contingent and individual.

In the context of this chapter, colonial space is (re)produced by the administrative tactics and protocols of colonial officers, the performance of authoritative roles towards colonised subjects, and the reinforcement of spatial divisions between coloniser and colonised; but it might also be threatened or reconfigured by transgressing or subverting these roles so as to blur spatial and social divisions. Conventions that secured space thus depended upon the upholding of these divisions, notwithstanding some performative improvisation and blurring of assigned roles.

The stability of colonial space required conformity to notions about what roles were appropriate as well as the rehearsal of such roles and performative conventions. Here I focus on how colonial officers prepared or rehearsed aptitudes required for their roles that were performed in the colonial space they would (re)produce and occupy.

During the late colonial period, the capabilities deemed important for the district officer included those necessary to manage, administer and act in a judicial capacity, and the practical skills to live for extended periods in often geographically isolated areas, speaking the local language. Accordingly, the district officer was the linchpin of colonial administration (Kirk-Greene 2000). Support for the powerful and privileged status of officers in the colonies was echoed in Kenneth Bradley's (1943:5) *The Diary of a District Officer*, a book which many recruits were expected to have read:

> In many of the Dependencies there is a great mass of primitive people who are still far off the stage in their development when politics can have any meaning for them. For them 'the

> Government' is a remote and shadowy abstraction. They see it only through its visible embodiment, the administrative officer. It is he who wields its power; and for them it is he who is the dispenser of its benefits.

Recruitment of officers was initially self-selecting in that certain young men already possessed the 'appropriate' cultural capital by virtue of their class and educational background that enabled them to consider a career in the colonial service. Some, however, were able to overcome these barriers through educational scholarships. Most administrators came through public and grammar schools, and many graduated from Oxford and Cambridge universities, that also ran various programmes for the 'professionalisation' of the colonial overseas civil service. However, while academic background was a significant recruitment criterion, it was the cultural ethos and discipline nurtured in these establishments that was primarily valued. As one interviewee recalls:

> When I mentioned to a friend that I had an interest in the colonial service, I remember him saying to me, 'well, whatever you do don't get a first and don't get a fourth because the Colonial Office doesn't want people who are too clever, on the other hand they don't want people who are too thick'.

Reliability, honesty and 'good character' were esteemed much more highly than academic knowledge and technical skills. The appropriateness of prospective colonial officers would be subsequently confirmed through a compulsory 12–month induction course (in the post-1945 period, known as the Devonshire 'A' course – one of the antecedents of today's Foreign Service Programme). During this they were selectively educated in aspects of imperial history, language skills, judiciary and ethnology, amongst other subjects (see Kirk-Greene 2000). However, many new recruits found that the course ill-prepared them for their responsibilities in the colonies; except for the acquisition of language which was useful, they were largely left to learn 'in the field' about local cultures and politics, and little experience passed from old hands to new recruits. 'Ideally it would be nice if they got hold of some ex-district officer from Nigeria and you had a tutorial with him'; instead:

> I don't think we were ever told about the kind of work we were going to do. We were thrown in at the deep end and you don't know – off you go and they say, 'Go and build your house'. 'When you've done that, there's a murderer up in those hills, go and ask him why he's been so silly as to kill someone'! This happened to us all.

While they were tested through examinations, one interviewee remembers being taught that the most important preparation involved possessing the 'correct' attitude and moral sensibilities necessary to work in the colonies:

> Macguire, a good fellow, taught us on the Devonshire course that, for instance, 'if one day you notice your best white shirt is missing and then you notice it on your houseboy in the market don't get worried and hoity-toity: forget it. By the time you next need it even if it's that night it will be in white pristine condition, so don't let these things upset you, this is what happens and this is how it is. You've got one and he hasn't so he needs to borrow it.'

This sort of practical advice defined the parameters of a colonial role: the necessity to be firm where required, but also an ability to deal fairly with people. Another way of measuring 'good character' was through participative disposition towards extracurricular activities, most notably sport.

Ralph Furse (1962), director of recruitment in the Colonial Service from 1931 to 1948, considered sport to be very important since it reflected qualities of leadership and fairness as well as fitness. One interviewee remembers Furse asking him at interview: 'How will you cope if you're on your own in the station without access to a woman, no radio, no phone or news? You're cut off. "Sport", I replied.' A story circulated amongst the officers about a district commissioner who, when writing to the Colonial Office in London to recruit an assistant, specified the need for a 'good, competent man but please also make sure that he is a left-handed spin bowler'. A former officer recalled: 'part of my induction [in Kenya] was having to play squash on arrival at 6,000ft with the chief native commissioner. I was a kind of Boy Scout so I enjoyed it.' As Killingray (2000:43) notes, Furse's 'policy of recruiting former public-school prefects and sportsmen to run the colonies meant that skills had to be learned on the hoof'.

This focus on character and personal qualities, however, should not conceal the importance of class. Indeed, the very characteristics that were valorised were thought to be class-specific. As a former officer from a working-class background who had won a scholarship said: 'Despite my confidence I didn't ever feel quite equal to my colleagues. People used to parade their connections and were part of the old boy network with all its subtle understandings.'

Class was further played out after recruitment in a mapping of class across the Empire: those from the middle to upper classes tended to be sent to northern Nigeria and the middle classes to southern Nigeria, while Kenya and Tanzania were places where people from the lower middle class were posted. The 'jewel in the Crown' until 1947 was India. One interviewee, who had served in Kenya, recalls attending a conference on colonial administration in the 1980s in Oxford where he presented a seminar:

> By this time I was a lot older, but as soon as I went in that room, wow! In one corner were all the ex-colonial officers – and there's still a lot of the old buggers left – from northern Nigeria, and you could almost smell the power.

Each colony had its own symbolic significance and which one you were sent to shaped your position within the colonial hierarchy and your relationship between colonial authority and colony. Yet it was not only the recruitment process that developed a preparedness to reproduce colonial space; motives and aspirations provide further explanations for how one would perform.

Officers were impelled to travel to 'exotic' places, escaping what they perceived as an unexciting home life: 'I was running away from provincial England and a steady, safe life. Why did I join the colonial service? Because the last thing I wanted was to catch the 8.18 to Charing Cross every Monday to Friday.' Novels and films, which produced earlier imaginary geographies, were often cited for inspiring such desires. As an officer who had served in India recalls:

> I wanted to see the world and have an adventure. India was colourful, exciting, interesting. It was a new culture, a different way of life. In the 1930s, Hollywood and British filmmakers were making a lot of films about India and the Northwest Frontier; *Gunga Din* and *Lives of a Bengal Lancer*. Now I had seen all these films, and read the books, and so going there was a kind of personal fulfilment.

Here a metropolitan colonial imagination was sustaining notions of spaces that might be confronted and roles that might be undertaken. Yet such anticipated encounters rarely accorded with real geographical knowledge: 'Two days after my interview I received a telegram and had been posted to Nigeria, and, literally, we got out my father's school atlas to find out where Nigeria was. It was my first time out of Europe.' Another commented: 'when I went to Kenya in early 1957 my ignorance was breathtaking'. Again, this lack of knowledge about destination emphasises the enormous adjustments that were required for settlement in the space of the unknown colonised other; a lack that, it was presumed, could be overcome by flexibility, good character and the upholding of particular standards and performative conventions that were operable across colonised space and could be mobilised through the correct disposition: 'one *should* have felt out of one's depth but there were just so many obvious things to do.'

Lacking administrative skills and geographical knowledge, once in the field, the particularities of the cultural capital necessary to enter the overseas service had to be continuously built upon and negotiated on the ground. This was reflected in their performances in particular kinds of space.

Performing Colonialism in Colonised Space

The practical knowledge gained through the rehearsal process of training was flexible but crucially consolidated particular kinds of practical dispositions towards dealing with other people in other places. Equally important, the cultural and institutional capital embodied in colonial officers as representatives of colonial authority, together with ascriptions of their class, gender, 'race' and educational privilege, enabled them to move with status and surety through colonial space. Such attributes helped to maintain the spatial boundaries and social distance necessary for authoritative administration in alien and isolated colonial environments.

Nevertheless, colonial officers experienced enduring and profound engagements with the places to which they were posted. While higher-ranked officers inhabited more enclavic (see Edensor 1998) and highly regulated urban expatriate spaces that kept the surrounding otherness at bay, the colonial duties and interactions with local people of low-ranking officers were largely performed in rather heterogeneous spaces. Remaining in one posting for at least 18 months, their practical situatedness shaped their relationship with local space and led to a conditional embeddedness. Though experiences varied according to the specificities of postings, as representatives of colonial authority 'in place', administrators performed a wide range of roles and activities that partly reduced and partly reified the boundaries between themselves and the colonised, between the space of work and home, and between times for work and play. Continuously moving between the spaces of the coloniser and the colonised, their use of space was extensive, especially for community development officers, who travelled within 'sheep and goat economies' or worked on 'building latrines' and developed a more extensive involvement with and knowledge of the people and the geography. As one officer who found himself in Kenya recalls:

> I rapidly found myself beginning to understand little bits and pieces of rural life. I had a Land Rover but very few reasons to go into town as the mail literally came by runner. So my life, my being and a whole new awareness of the world grew out of this involvement.

Travelling around 'their' district, and through their interactions and 'community' efforts, community development officers mapped colonialism throughout the region. One former officer posted to Kenya remembers having to question the relevance of his work as the importance of context dawned upon him:

> We used to have a little movie projector with stupid Charlie Chaplin 16 mm silent films, which one would run off the battery of the vehicle when one was out camping in the evenings. I started by showing these but rapidly it became clear to me that pictures of

> someone using laughing gas in a dentist's chair in Philadelphia might not be very useful. So I started taking 35mm colour slides of what people were doing around the district and this turned out to be an *enormous* success. There would be three or four hundred people in the evening, standing, sitting in the dust, wherever we were, and we would show the slides.

This kind of continuous spatial proximity, of blurring of spatial divides and interaction with locals in colonial outposts necessitated adherence to strict social distancing and the reification of hierarchies through the maintenance of distinctive spatial organisation. Boundaries were materialised in the different kinds of accommodation and the symbolic, purified space of the expatriate 'club'. Higher-ranked officers, for example, were provided with bungalows, sometimes within small compounds, set apart from the 'natives'. Social distinction was achieved with the employment of servants – typically including a 'house boy', a cook, a driver and a guard – practices that did not always have a practical purpose but were largely intended to reinforce officers' power, status and distance. As one interviewee admits:

> They [British expatriates] said they were worried about robbery so they had to live in houses with guards. But there are also crimes in London but you don't live with armed guards there. So it wasn't that they simply felt the need, rather that they had the opportunity, to create that type of situation.

For low-ranked officers accommodation was far less luxurious. For instance, community development officers often lived in small, minimally furnished houses, and could 'spend most of the week travelling in different parts of the district, living in a tent and interacting with people'. One recalls sharing a house in Nigeria with 'three other bachelors but we were very lucky because we had electricity until 9.30pm'. Another unmarried officer was alarmed to find that 'bachelors tended to be sent to the remoter places', a strategy explained by one interviewee as follows:

> Most young district officers were unmarried, certainly before the [Second World] war you were not allowed to be married in your first three years. If you wanted to bring your wife out you had to get the Governor's personal permission. I think the general feeling was that the best district officer was the unmarried one because he could be sent anywhere. You didn't have to think, 'Gosh, we can't send him there because it would be tough for his wife and there's no hospital.'

Again this identifies the selective roles based on class, gender and marital status that the Colonial Office employed, choosing particular subjects for specific situations, characters who were presumed to be suited to performing colonial duties.

Besides the maintenance of distinct spaces, other measures ensured that officers conformed to their assigned roles without blurring the boundaries between acceptable and unacceptable social mingling. For instance, officers were required to move frequently from one posting to another, although the scale of transfers was limited by the investment in language skills, and most stayed within the same country. According to one interviewee, this was 'part of a deliberate training programme so that administrators didn't become too introspective', but it also addressed the fear of officers becoming too friendly with the 'natives', or 'going native' and losing the British reserve and authoritative distance required to perform their duties 'properly'. In her book, *Colonialism and the English Character*, Tidrick (1992) refers to 'Masaiitis', the diagnosis inflicted on officers who became irrational or incapable of reasonable judgement, due to an unacceptable level of emotional involvement with the Masai peoples in Kenya.

Development Professionals & Postcolonial Space

Different moments and processes of decolonisation emerging out of various colonialisms produced multiple postcolonial contexts and experiences. The demobilisation of colonial officers and the eventual folding of the Colonial Office did not engender a wholesale substitution of colonial expatriates with contemporary development professionals. Indeed, some colonial officers stayed on after independence to staff newly established university or government departments in former colonies (see Power 2003). In terms of the discourses, practices and spatialisation of authority, as well as personnel, there were continuities over time and across space. Although the relationship between centre and periphery had shifted from one of imperial authority and power exercised in, and mapped onto, the colonies to other forms of globalised control through international relations and trade, such continuities (and divergences) are currently articulated in, for example, the relations between aid donor and recipient, between developer and developed. Some continuities persisted immediately following independence with groups of former colonial officers returning to the UK and joining the newly established and rapidly expanding development industry (see Minogue 1977; Clarke 1999). The ideas and practices they carried with them are the subject of another (Kothari 2005); here I focus on how their uses of and performance in space have been modified with a shift from colonialism to globalisation and development.

Initially many of those involved in the postwar development industry in the UK, notably the Overseas Development Administration (formerly the Department of Technical Cooperation, currently the Department for International Development) as well as multilateral UN agencies including the World Bank, were former colonial service officers; subsequently younger professionals joined their ranks. With the recent retirement of the generation of the former, the industry is now largely made up of those who have no personal experience of a colonial past. Although it is a sense of humanitarianism and public service that continues to motivate some development professionals, along with a desire to travel, the global divisions of power and pervading eurocentrism within development discourse and practice allow many Western development professionals to enjoy privileged status and lifestyles when overseas. And although specific performances, lifestyles and attitudes of those entering the development industry tend to be more diverse than those of colonial administrators, their roles in reproducing relations of power and authority between the West and the rest are not so dissimilar.

Accessing Development Space

Unlike the circumscribed path for recruitment into the colonial service, the route into the UK development industry is not defined by a clear recruitment process, nor specific knowledge or skill requirements. Indeed, the scope of the industry encompasses an extremely wide range of people, institutions and organisations at local, national and global levels (Crush 1995). Although many former colonial officers consider that those entering the UK development field should gain extended experience by actually living in 'former colonies', this has become less important, or possible, over time, and far greater value is placed on technical expertise and skills.

Development professionals are far more diverse in terms of gender and, increasingly, ethnicity, given the growing involvement of a postcolonial diaspora and the number of people from former colonies who have been trained in Western institutes of higher education, and therefore immersed in broader ideas and possibilities reflected in the move from European imperialisms to 'globalised' values. Although class background clearly would continue to shape the level and type of education attained, hierarchies in the international development industry tend to relate to the status of the institution represented by the individual rather than to class or personal character alone. Accordingly, development professionals are therefore differently prepared for their encounter with the other in ways that work both in and against the colonial past.

Crucially, familiarity with specific geographic areas is not considered particularly valuable in a business that explicitly valorises technical skills (Kothari 2006). One former World Bank professional comments on this move away from embeddedness:

> You don't get promoted in the Bank if you have only worked in one or two countries, however long your association might have been. You need to gain experience of many different places, otherwise they say, 'oh he only knows about Mozambique'.

Development has remapped (post)colonial space by extending the geographic area of so-called country expertise, so that development professionals are more likely to be regional experts on 'Africa', 'Asia' or 'Latin America'. The imagined geography of colonialism has mutated into an imagined geography of development, based primarily on divisions between 'first' and 'third' worlds, and subsequently reified through global performance and practice.

Contrary to the experience of those colonial service officers who experienced enduring relationships with the places to which they were posted, development professionals are esteemed more for their resistance to becoming familiar with one particular geographic area, and for having a more flexible 'cosmopolitan' approach across global space. However, it is not just a distancing from colonialism that motivates this shift away from valuing in-depth local knowledge and attachment to place, but rather the imperatives of a globalising discourse of development whereby *issues* rather than *places* become more important. The rolling out globally of neoliberal ideologies of privatisation and trade liberalisation, and specifically within a development discourse, of good governance, democratisation and participation, maps; a unitary language and process that are interpreted through the practices and techniques of Western-trained advisers.

Without needing to make the same emotional and professional investment in single locations, contemporary development professionals move within a world of fleeting consultancies and short-term stays in different places. Given this extensive geographical coverage, their preparedness for working overseas is hugely different from that of colonial service officers. Whereas language skills along with a disposition towards practical engagement in the place of work overseas were important components of the preparatory Devonshire 'A' course, one former officer complained: 'the contemporary development worker tends to underscore stereotypes of the British abroad as unwilling and uninterested in learning the local language'. Yet, although the development professionals' expertise is in technical know-how, when overseas they too are required to maintain an authoritative management while simultaneously giving the impression of promoting a more participative exchange with 'locals' (Cooke and Kothari 2001).

Enclavic Spaces & Status

Colonial enclaves certainly existed and most officers 'in the field' did live within compounds, but these were more integrated with surrounding space than the more tightly bounded enclavic spaces in which development professionals tend to base themselves. Such purified spaces, free of the dirt, contact, noise, disease and the apparent chaos (and insecurity) of the outside, are typified by an aesthetic control of external and internal trimmings and decor that conform to Western tastes, characteristic of what Bourdieu (1984) refers to as 'objectified capital' (icons, ornaments and pictures from Europe), together with contextualised signifiers of the local exotic.

The power and financial status of the organisation – such as whether a multilateral aid agency, bilateral donor, academic institution or NGO – shapes the spaces occupied by their advisers overseas; thus, although accommodation is not always 'five star', it is, nonetheless, enclavic. The British Aid Guest House in Dhaka, Bangladesh, for example, had a few guest rooms primarily for low-level aid personnel and consultants and also a bar and sports facilities frequented by diplomats and other expatriates. Guarded to ensure this exclusivity, such realms are inhabited by what one junior referred to as 'a bizarre cut off diaspora, a moving circus of consultants'. This was also remarked upon by one consultant: 'While they were preparing the PRSP [Poverty Reduction Strategy Paper] in Uganda [in 2000], you couldn't move in one hotel in Kampala without bumping into donor consultants and advisers.'

These spaces serve as familiar havens for Western-based consultants visiting overseas government departments and NGO offices. Although some do venture into the field, one development consultant, formerly in the colonial service, reflected: 'so many [consultants] sit in government buildings or local headquarters and don't get out. Goodness knows, colonialism had to stop but it was better from a rural point of view.'

Such enclaves are a component of a postcolonial geography inscribed upon 'third world cities' (King 1990), a spatial matrix that is the context within which development policies are devised and implemented for areas that consultants may never have visited and people they rarely meet. Furthermore, where they do venture beyond these confines, cultural intermediaries in the shape of 'local counterparts' with specific foci (say health or rural development) in mind are apt to delimit the forms of exchange and engagement that take place by filtering out local complexities, thus rendering this encounter akin to tourism in its screening of sights and sites (in this case, poverty and social problems, in favour of 'heritage' and selective local 'culture'). Encounters between donor and recipient are less dialogic, conforming to a power relationship; staged and managed by the centre and re-enacted and performed in the periphery, these (re)produce difference and inequalities that are highly spatialised. And although these consultants travel the world and represent themselves as the new cosmopolitans (see Hannerz 1990), they embody and wield particular forms of parochialism both in their forms of expertise and in their use of space.

Some researchers dislike this orthodox enclavic locatedness where sustained periods amongst 'local communities' are discouraged as time-consuming and costly. While greater embeddedness did not necessarily engender compassion or understanding amongst the colonial officers, short-term contemporary consultants are in danger of becoming even less knowing about the lives of others (Kothari 2002).

While the low-ranking colonial officer had to mediate his spatial proximity by cultivating social distance, professionals in the supposedly more equitable contemporary arena of development, albeit more diverse in terms of gender, 'race', age and class, maintain their positions of authoritative expertise and know-how through spatial distance. Moreover, many development professionals on short-term overseas visits acquire the status of 'expert' and are treated accordingly by the government officials and others that they meet; they experience an elevated lifestyle of expensive hotels, chauffeur-driven cars and substantial daily allowances. Thus, the construction and practice of the spaces of such consultants, (re)produce an environment that allows them to temporarily enjoy a privileged position not afforded to them at 'home'. As one consultant divulged:

> I had at least two friends who couldn't bear to be in England, they wanted to be overseas. And that's because they loved the lifestyle and all that went with it. I find it when I travel about. They'll say 'Manchester! God, when can we get overseas again?'

At the same time, however, there are those in development work who, fearful of being accused of behaving like insular imperialists, have an overwhelming desire to distinguish themselves from former colonial types. This involves negotiating their behaviour and uses of social space. As one development professional mused:

> I remember once, after independence, that a British high commissioner told us that we had to show that we were different, that we were a new kind of Brit, not like those gin guzzling, idle, red-faced colonial chaps. So many would say 'We're not going to the [expatriate] club, we can't have that!' lest they be tarnished with the same colonial brush.

However, unlike colonial service officers, many development experts are on short-term assignments, moving in and out of positions of power and authority, and rarely away from Britain for long spells because such opportunities are now more limited.

Conclusion

This chapter has argued that authority, status and distance are (re)produced by colonial officers and development professionals through their performances in and across the space of the other. These practices supplement the institutional and cultural capital they possess by representing different metropolitan regimes of knowledge and administration. This postcolonial analysis of colonialism and international development demonstrates how power is differently performed and materialised according to context. This is marked in the sociospatial performances of geographically embedded colonial service officers who are required to maintain the authoritative distance necessary to govern. Power is differently inscribed in development praxis that foregrounds poverty alleviation, equity and participation, apparently neutralizing a colonial power apparatus but concealing global power relations between aid providers and recipients, emblematically revealed in the enclavic spatial practices.

Certain regularities and consistencies stand out from the numerous individual practices through which colonial service officers and present development professionals negotiate the situations in which they work and live. Both, for instance, operate within extended spatial networks between home and away that are complex and ambivalent, and both benefit from access to a level of power and status that would not be afforded to them at home.

One significant difference that has emerged is the shift from the almost exclusively male and insular English identity and imagination of colonial service officers to the more broad-based constitution of the development industry. This widening of representation and participation in terms of gender, age, class and ethnicity, as well as the broader Western involvement in planned development have created a more heterogeneous discourse of international relations and simultaneously enabled a more effective global transfer of (neo-liberal) development ideologies. Despite this, however, many development professionals reinforce privilege rather than unlearn or question the sorts of knowledge that are produced by it.

The ongoing reproduction of colonial and postcolonial networks connects spaces over time and is sustained by the movement and practices of people and ideas between centre to periphery. Cultures that travelled over colonial space through being performed by colonial officers have been reworked in the postcolonial period, belying epochal historical periodisations that conjure up a clear disjuncture between colonial and development eras. As Said (1978) argued, the construction of the other reveals more about Western identities than the Oriental subject it claims to know. Similarly, colonial and development practices unmask the characteristics of the coloniser/developer. While not addressed in this chapter, attention to the narratives of unrepresented others promises a deeper understanding of the consequences of these spatial practices. More specifically, how do the colonised/underdeveloped others confront their entanglement in a process through which they become defined as uncivilised or undeveloped?

Bibliography

Bhabha, H. (1994) *The Location of Culture*. London and New York: Routledge.

Bourdieu, P. (1984) *Distinction: A Social Critique of the Judgement of Taste*. London: Routledge and Kegan Paul.

Bradley, K. (1943) *The Diary of a District Officer*. London: George G. Harrap.

Chakrabarty, D. (2000) *Provincialising Europe: Postcolonial Thought and Historical Difference*. Princeton, NJ: Princeton University Press.

Clarke, R. (1999) 'Institutions for Training Overseas Administrators: the University of Manchester Contribution'. *Public Administration and Development* 19: 521–33.

Cooke, B. and Kothari, U. (2001) *Participation: The New Tyranny?* London: Zed.

Cooper, F. and Packard, R. (eds) (1996) *International Development and the Social Sciences: Essays on the History and Politics of Knowledge*. Berkeley, CA: University of California Press.

Cowen, M.P. and Shenton, R.W. (1996) *Doctrines of Development*. London: Routledge

Crush, J. (ed.) (1995) *Power of Development*. London: Routledge.

Dhaouadi, M. (1994) 'Democracy and Development: Deconstruction and Debate'. In Sklair, L. (ed.) *Capitalism and Development*. London: Routledge, pp. 140–64.

Driver, F. (2001) *Geography Militant: Cultures of Exploration and Empire*. Oxford: Blackwell.

Edensor, T. (1998) *Tourists at the Taj*. London: Routledge.

Furse, R. (1962) *Aucuparius: Recollections of a Recruitment Officer*. London: Oxford University Press.

Godlewska, A. and Smith, N. (1994) *Geography and Empire*. Oxford: Blackwell

Gowans, G. (2002) 'A Passage from India: Geographies and Experiences of Repatriation, 1858–1939'. *Social and Cultural Geography* 3(4): 403–23.

Gregory, D. (2004) *The Colonial Present*. Oxford: Blackwell.

Hall, S. (1992) *Modernity and its Futures*. Cambridge: Polity Press.

Hannerz, U. (1990) 'Cosmopolitans and Locals'. In Featherstone, M. (ed.) *Global Cultures*. London: Sage, pp. 237–51.

Havinden, M. and Meredith, D. (1993) *Colonialism and Development: Britain and its Tropical Colonies 1850–1960*. London: Routledge.

Jacobs, J. (1996) *Edge of Empire: Postcolonialism and the City*. London: Routledge.

Jedlowski, P. (2001) 'Memory and Sociology: Themes and Issues'. *Time and Society* 10 (1): 29–44.

Kabbani, R. (1986) *Europe's Myths of Orient*. London: Pandora.

Killingray, D. (2000) 'Colonial Studies'. In Rimmer, D. and Kirk-Greene, A. (eds) *The British Intellectual Engagement with Africa in the Twentieth Century*. Basingstoke: Macmillan, pp. 41–67.

King, A. (1990) *Urbanism, Colonialism and the World Economy*. London: Routledge.

Kirk-Greene, A. (2000) *Britain's Imperial Administrators, 1858–1966*. Basingstoke: Macmillan.
Kothari, U. (2006) 'From Colonialism to Development: Continuities and Divergences'. *Journal of Commonwealth and Comparative Politics* 44 (1): 118–36.
Kothari, U. (2005) 'Authority and Expertise: The Professionalisation of International Development and the Ordering of Dissent'. *Antipode* 37: 425–46.
Kothari, U. (2002) 'Feminist and Postcolonial Challenges to Development'. In Kothari, U. and Minogue, M. (eds) *Development Theory and Practice: Critical Perspectives*. Basingstoke: Palgrave, pp. 35–51.
Le Sueur, J. (ed.) (2003) *The Decolonization Reader*. London: Routledge.
Lester, A. (2002) 'Obtaining the "Due Observance of Justice": The Geographies of Colonial Humanitarianism'. *Environment and Planning D: Society and Space* 20: 277–93.
Low, G. (1996) *White Skins/Black Masks: Representation and Colonialism*. London: Routledge.
Massey, D. (1999) 'Imagining Globalization: Power-Geometries of Time-Space'. In Brah, A., Hickman, M. and Mac an Ghaill, M. (eds) *Global Futures: Migration, Environment and Globalization*. Basingstoke: Macmillan, pp. 27–44.
McEwan, C. (2003) 'Material Geographies and Postcolonialism'. *Singapore Journal of Tropical Geography* 24 (3): 340–55.
Minogue, M. (1977) 'Administrative Training: Doublethink and Newspeak'. *IDS Bulletin* 8 (4): 3–7.
Nash, C. (2004) 'Post-Colonial Geographies'. In Cloke, P., Crang, P. and Goodwin, M. (eds) *Envisioning Human Geographies*. London: Hodder Arnold, pp. 104–27.
Pieterse, J N. and Parekh, B. (eds) (1995) *The Decolonization of Imagination*. London: Zed.
Potter, R.B., Binns, T., Elliot, J. and Smith, D. (2003) *Geographies of Development*. 2nd edn. London: Prentice-Hall.
Power, M. (2003) *Rethinking Development Geographies*. London: Routledge.
Said, E. (1978) *Orientalism*. London: Penguin.
Said, E. (1989) 'Representing the Colonized: Anthropology's Interlocutors'. *Critical Inquiry* 15 (Winter): 205–25.
Said, E. (1993) *Culture and Imperialism*. London: Verso Press.
Spurr, D. (1993) *The Rhetoric of Empire: Colonial Discourse in Journalism, Travel Writing, and Imperial Administration*. Durham, NC and London: Duke University Press.
Tidrick, K. (1992) *Empire and the English Character*. New York: I.B. Tauris.
Young, R. (2001) *Postcolonialism: An Historical Introduction*. Oxford: Blackwell.

Notes

1 This is a shorter version of a previously published article Kothari, U (2006) 'Spatial Imaginaries and Practices: Experiences of Colonial Officers and Development Professionals'. *Singapore Journal of Tropical Geography* 27: 235–53. I am grateful to the colonial service officers who gave so generously of their time and experiences, the University of Manchester who funded this research project and to Tim Edensor for insightful comments.

2 The taped life history interviews (carried out between 2001 and 2002) focused on these individuals' motives and aspirations in joining the colonial service and subsequent decision to become involved in post-independence development work, and explored changes in their roles and responsibilities. Most have now formally retired but continue to be active as development consultants or research associates in academic institutions, or in charitable foundations in the UK. Supplementary research included more informal discussions with contemporary British development professionals, including academics, development consultants in the UK and overseas, and related government and NGO personnel.

3 The terms Englishness and Britishness continue to be conflated (much to the chagrin of members of the other constituent nations of the United Kingdom), typically by those English abroad who assume that England, as the dominant constituting nation, stands for Britain as a whole; ironic too, considering, for instance, the leading role Scottish soldiers and administrators played in managing the Empire. Moreover, the two assignations also conjure up different, complex distinctions around class, ethnicity and gender and are freighted with a host of distinctive historical, cultural and geographical associations. In this, I focus upon the interviewees' characteristic use of notions specific to (imaginary) constructions of Englishness, rather than the more general use wherein 'English' is a substitute for 'British'.

12

Decolonising the Borders in Sudan
Ethnic Territories & National Development

DOUGLAS H. JOHNSON

Land was one of the central issues contributing to the recent civil wars in the Sudan, and it is an underestimated and overlooked factor determining the success or failure of the Comprehensive Peace Agreement (CPA) signed in 2005 (Pantuliano 2007: 3). Land has been central to the Sudan's colonial and postcolonial development policies, and land access and land rights legislation changed as development policy changed. The systematic erosion of customary rights to land and access to land were powerful factors which drew different peoples on both sides of the North-South divide into the wider conflict, so that by the time the North-South war ended in 2005 what the 'marginalised' peoples of the South, East and West had in common was dispossession from their land through government encroachment. Land was ethnicised during the Anglo-Egyptian Condominum, was progressively de-ethnicised immediately prior to and during the conflicts, and is now being selectively re-ethnicised along parts of the North-South border. There is a direct conflict between customary land regimes and the development policies of the central government which has yet to be resolved, or even directly addressed, by either the Government of National Unity or the Government of South Sudan created by the CPA.

Communal Resources & Dar Rights

The Condominium government of the Sudan both assumed and confirmed the existence of discrete tribal territories throughout the rural areas of the country. Legislation in the 1920s and 1930s defining the powers of nomad sheikhs in the North and chiefs in the South reinforced the legal and, ultimately, the territorial definition of tribal groups. The management of communal resources within the territory was regulated by custom. In the northern provinces various common principles were applied in the recognition of 'Dar', or homeland rights.[1] The owners of Dar rights had the right to build permanent buildings, to cultivate, to graze, to dig wells, and to inscribe their tribal symbols on landmarks within their territory. They also had the right to admit or refuse outsiders the use of the resources of the Dar (Hayes 1960: 337). Thus within the Dar the members of the community had 'primary' or 'dominant' rights to the use of land. But Dar rights did accommodate the 'secondary' rights of those outside the community to have limited land-use rights on an occasional or seasonal basis. This accommodation was in part a response to variations in climatic conditions which sometimes necessitated migration into the territory of neighbouring communities. The Condominium administration often secured the 'secondary' rights for some groups in the land of other communities by formal agreements (Kibreab 2002: 21–3, 45–52).

The division of land rights into 'dominant' and 'secondary' rights maintains an important distinction. There are exclusive dominant rights when a group has established dominant occupation, land rights and land use, with no cession of secondary use rights to non-members of the community. There are non-exclusive dominant rights when a community holds dominant occupation, land rights and land use but allows non-members limited land-use rights on a seasonal basis or for sporadic periods. Then there are 'shared secondary' land rights and land use by members of two or more communities within a territory marking the boundaries between them.[2] Dar rights, as practised, were clearly non-exclusive dominant rights. But the issue of secondary rights can be ambiguous, as the secondary rights of one group by their nature overlap with either the dominant rights or secondary rights of other groups. To what extent can a group claim permanent access to resources by right of precedent or custom? Can secondary rights be converted into dominant rights?

Communal resource management in the South followed the same general principles as in the North, but it lacked the formal legal definition of sovereign property rights invested in the Dars. Pastoralists in the South crossed into the territory of their neighbours on a seasonal basis, often sharing the same dry season watering sources,[3] and as in the North, inter-tribal meetings were regularly held to manage these movements. Problems arose, as I shall show below, when the communal territory of Southern peoples abutted the more clearly defined Dars of northern pastoralists.

National Development & the Erosion of Customary Land Rights

The Land Registration and Settlement Act 1925 laid the foundation for rural land laws in the Anglo-Egyptian Condominium, giving the central government a presumptive right to land, in that unoccupied land was deemed to be government land 'until proved otherwise' (Kibreab 2002: 272, 279). The development policy the Condominium government bequeathed to the independent Sudan was based on the growth of the economy through the expansion of rain-fed agriculture. In the 1970s there was an intensification of agricultural production through large-scale mechanised agricultural schemes, funded by World Bank and state subsidies (Kibreab 2002: 272, 275; Duffield 1992: 50; African Rights 1995: 40).

This intensification was made possible by the Unregistered Land Act 1970, which transferred the ownership of unregistered and unoccupied land to the government, removing the provision of the 1925 act that allowed possible claimants to subsequently prove ownership of unregistered land (Kibreab 2002: 277–8). The government then leased out large areas of land to well-capitalised merchants, usually from the central Nile valley. The Sudan Penal Code 1974 further established the offence of criminal trespass, so that farmers residing on land they had owned in accordance with customary law, and pastoralists using customary routes to access seasonal grazing and watering areas, could be prosecuted for trespass. This was retained in the 1983 and 1990 Penal Codes (African Rights 1995: 41). The Civil Transaction Act 1984 enabled persons close to the government to acquire land in various ways (Pantuliano 2007: 3), and the Civil Transaction Act 1990 prohibited the recognition of customary land rights in courts (Anon 1996: 10). Parallel to this assault on customary land rights was the abolition of Native Administration in the northern Sudan in 1971, removing those institutions that had been most prominent in regulating and managing customary laws of access and use.

The expanding mechanised schemes needed a large migrant labour force, and this was provided primarily by smallholder farmers dispossessed from their lands and impoverished pastoralists who found their seasonal access to lands ever restricted (Duffield 1992: 50–1): a further alienation of rural peoples from the land on which they lived. Those to feel the first effects were the people living in the 'transitional zone', the savannah belt along the border of Northern and Southern Sudan, where the first schemes were established. In the Nuba Mountains of Southern Kordofan 'the growth of mechanised farming shattered the viability of Nuba smallholder farming. It also destroyed amicable relations with the Arab pastoralists' (African Rights 1995: 39). Arab nomads who were prevented from moving through the new farming schemes diverted their seasonal routes through the remaining land of Nuba farmers (Anon. 1996: 10). In the Blue Nile schemes were established west of Damazin with migrant labour recruited from the villages further south (James 2007: 42). The issue of contested land ownership was the main reason why peoples from the 'northern' provinces of Blue Nile and Southern Kordofan joined the Sudan People's Liberation Army (SPLA) when their insurgency moved northwards, beyond the borders of the Southern Sudan in the mid-1980s.

It was not just peoples immediately bordering on the Southern Sudan who were affected by changes in land legislation. Colonial policy in Gedaref District, in the Eastern Sudan, had regulated relations between the herders of the Butana savannah and the farmers of the southern clay plain by establishing a grazing line between the Butana and the plain. Large-scale farming was prohibited north of the line, while herders were not allowed to move south until the grain harvest was ended, when they grazed their animals on stubble and manured the fields in return. This arrangement broke down with the changes in legislation in the 1970s. Agricultural land was distributed to rich individuals, big companies and foreign investors, and large-scale farming expanded both north and south of the grazing line. The Butana was opened up as common property to all pastoral groups, irrespective of earlier customary claims (Miller 2005: 25).

Land became a major issue in the separate conflict in Darfur. The sharp decline in rainfall in northern Darfur in the 1970s propelled a large population movement of pastoralists from the north into the central farming belt, but the liquidation of Native Administration had removed the structures which had previously been used to mediate inter-group relations (Harir 1993: 20–1). This influx coincided with the reduction of both the open farming areas and pasturelands within the central farming belt through the expansion of mechanised schemes. Less land was available for temporary or seasonal use. In the 1980s some migrant groups began to lay permanent claim to territory they had been granted temporarily. Through increasingly destructive armed attacks they drove the sedentary owners off their land and created new *de facto* homelands (dars) for themselves (Harir 1994: 180–1). This is a process of forcibly converting secondary rights into dominant rights which we shall see repeated along the post-CPA North-South border.

Land & the 'Southern Policy'

The 'Southern Policy' introduced in 1930 by the Condominium government has often been blamed for leaving the country politically divided and economically underdeveloped, the Southern Sudan especially so. Building on the logic of 'Indirect Rule' (or Native Administration), whereby each community was to be administered according to its own customs, it decreed that the Southern peoples were to develop along their own 'African' lines, rather than be assimilated into the political culture and economy of the Muslim, Arab North (Collins 1983: 172–8). The nationalist criticism of this policy is that it kept the non-Muslim peoples of the South completely separated from the Muslim peoples of the North, thus depriving them of contact with more advanced communities who could have helped them to develop economically, politically and culturally; and that it created barriers that were a disadvantage to the livelihood of the northern peoples living along the South's borders (Abd al-Rahim 1969: 70–83; Beshir 1968: 37–59).

The extent to which the Southern Policy kept the Southern Sudan hermetically sealed can be disputed. Post-2005 attempts to define the South's boundaries, as required by the CPA, have revealed how intangible, not to say theoretical, those boundaries are. Of more relevance to development issues, however, is the way that the Southern Policy helped not only to ethnicise territory, but in determining how the resources of such territories were to be used gave priority to the needs of the peoples living north of the boundary, to the detriment of those living to the south. This was bound up in the recognition and application of 'Dar rights' to nomad tribal territories in the northern provinces, and the absence of as clearly defined a set of principles for common resource management in the southern provinces. The Rizeigat Arab and Malwal Dinka dispute in many ways set a precedent for the progressive erosion of Southern tribal territories.

The Precedent of the Rizeigat–Malwal Decision

The Baggara Arabs of Darfur and Kordofon (the Rizeigat and Misseriya in the following cases) are, like their southern Dinka neighbours, cattle keepers who are dependent on the seasonal use of the grazing areas north and south of the Bahr el-Arab and the waterways that flow into that river. The settlement in and use of that area was disrupted in the late nineteenth century by the establishment of Zubair Pasha's trading fiefdom in Bahr el-Ghazal in the 1870s, his conquest of Darfur, the revolt of his son, Sulaiman Zubair, against the Turco-Egyptian government, the conquest of Kordofan and Darfur by the Mahdi, and the collapse of the Mahdist state in 1898–9. Anglo-Egyptian forces began the occupation of Bahr el-Ghazal in 1900, but Darfur remained an independent sultanate until 1916. The Dinka of northern Bahr el-Ghazal remained largely unadministered during the first decade of the Condominium and relied on self-defence against Rizeigat raids, as they had done throughout the final decades of the nineteenth century. It was not until 1909 that a British inspector attempted to mediate between the Malwal and the Rizeigat, and it was only in 1911 that a military garrison was established near the border with Darfur to offer protection against Arab raids (Intelligence Department, Sudan Government 1911: 55–8, 61).

The first successful government mediation of the Rizeigat Arab–Malwal Dinka conflict was in 1912, when a British inspector arranged a meeting between Musa Madibbo, shaikh of the Rizeigat, and Awutiak, chief of the Malwal, where both sides declared they were tired of fighting and wished to make peace. The government interpreted the conflict as 'a long-standing feud over grazing and hunting rights' and attempted to settle it by creating a territorial boundary that defined these rights. It was recorded that both parties agreed:

> The Bahr-el-Arab is the boundary between the tribes, being the boundary between the Anglo-Egyptian Sudan and Darfur. As, however, the Sultan of Darfur is tributary to the Sudan, there was found to be no objection to parties of the Rizeigat crossing to the southern bank for hunting purposes as opposed to grazing, provided they behaved themselves and did not interfere with the Dinkas. (Sudan Government 1913: 13–14)

It would appear, then, that the government was not so much attempting to define the equivalent of Dar rights for the Malwal, as the secondary rights permitted the Rizeigat: in this case hunting, but not grazing.

This did not put an end to Rizeigat raids into Malwal territory south of the Bahr el-Arab, but the politics of the border had changed by 1915 when the Anglo-Egyptian government began to woo, and then arm, the Rizeigat in preparation for the invasion of Darfur, which was finally launched at the beginning of 1916 (Theobald 1965: 149–50, 155–61). With the incorporation of Darfur into the Anglo-Egyptian Sudan the Rizeigat ceased to be a threat against whom the Sudan's subjects must be protected, but became, instead, government allies. This was to have a direct bearing on the next attempt to settle the Rizeigat–Malwal boundary.

R.V. Savile, the new British governor of Darfur, arranged a boundary meeting in 1918. Savile travelled to Safaha, on the Bahr el-Arab, in April 1918. His diary records that on the way he bought a horse from Musa Madibbo, the shaikh of the Rizeigat, before summoning an inspector from Bahr el-Ghazal to meet him. On 23 April 1918 his diary reports, 'The Dinkas gave us a dance this morning, after which we had our boundary meeting & settled the boundary to the satisfaction of the Arabs, but not so entirely to that of the Dinkas, who, however, eventually agreed that that was the true boundary.'[4]

The asymmetry of the negotiations should be noted before commenting on the decision. Savile was one of the most senior figures in the Condominium administration at the time, having served successively as the Governor of the adjacent Bahr el-Ghazal, Kordofan and Darfur provinces. He was met not by his counterpart, the governor of Bahr el-Ghazal, but by a very junior inspector from a border district (the second inspector from Raga). The relations between the government and the Rizeigat were, at that time, cordial, as revealed by Savile's purchase of a horse from the head of the tribe, while no British official in the Bahr el-Ghazal administration at this time spoke Dinka, and few had even visited the Dinka.

The boundary, which Savile declared to be the true one, moved the border from the Bahr el-Arab between thirty and forty miles south into what had previously been Malwal Dinka country. It was no wonder that the Malwal were 'not so entirely' satisfied, that they felt that 'their country and their grazing had been jumped by the Arab and the Government', and that this resentment fed into the Arianhdit rising among the Dinka of northern Bahr el-Ghazal in 1921–2.[5]

In response to this discontent another meeting was arranged in 1924, this time between the Governors of Darfur (Munro) and Bahr el-Ghazal (Wheatley), and the boundary redefined, with qualifications. The new boundary (which is still referred to as the Munro-Wheatley line) reduced the territory ceded to the Rizeigat in 1918 to a line running about 14 miles south of the Bahr el-Arab. This was 'recognised as the Dar of Rizeigat', but with important concessions to the Malwal:

> 2. ... General permission is given the Dinkas (Malwal) by the Nazir of the Rizeigat to continue to water their cattle on the Southern bank of the Bahr El Arab, and to fish in the River. This permission cannot be withdrawn without the approval of the Governor of Darfur who will consult the Governor of the Bahr el Ghazal before action is taken.
> 3. No Arabs are to enter the 'Dar' of the Malwal Dinkas for hunting, or other purpose.[6]

Although this provided a formula that allowed for sharing grazing land between the Malwal and Rizeigat, and appeared also to recognise the legal existence of a Malwal 'Dar', the arrangement continued to be problematic, with the Malwal still claiming the Bahr el-Arab as the territorial boundary. A modification of the 1924 agreement was made in 1935, dividing the area south of the Bahr el-Arab into 'Arab grazing' and 'common (Arab and Malwal) areas' in which there were recognised 'customary Malwal camping grounds' from which the Rizeigat were excluded.[7] Throughout the 1930s and 1940s the Governors of Bahr el-Ghazal lobbied for the agreement to be changed, putting forward various arguments in support of the Dinka claim (though curiously, the 1912 report cited above was completely forgotten and overlooked).[8] In 1938 the Governor of Equatoria (into which Bahr el-Ghazal had been merged) declared that the Munro-Wheatley agreement was like the Versailles treaty, in that it held 'the seeds of future war.'. The encroachment of the Rizeigat on the Malwal lands south of the Bahr el-Arab was, he wrote to the Civil Secretary in Khartoum, consistent with

> The history of Arab claims and movements southward, from Kurmuk to Kafia Kingi, as I remember them from your files and from those of White Nile and Upper Nile do I believe show both a tendency and a successful tendency to move further and further south, beyond any limits which were in the past regularly accessible to them. This movement is only a symptom of the normal nomad arab centrifugal movement from the centre outwards which is familiar to Governor Darfur...

He did not ask for a re-alteration of the boundary. Rather,

> Changing conditions even in 20 years may have produced a set of circumstances which cannot be fully dealt with by reference to past history or the interpretation of agreements. Without altering the agreement it may be necessary for Government itself to take steps to enable neighbours to live side by side harmoniously e.g. (i) by making certain limited areas available to the Dinka for cultivation, grazing and watering by clearing those areas of fly and sinking wells or (ii) by making other areas available for the Rizeigat by sinking wells.[9]

But this, and subsequent appeals from his successors, were denied by the central government in Khartoum.

In his analysis of the Malwal-Rizeigat dispute, Gaim Kibreab points out that the 1924 agreement, along with its 1935 modification, while formally incorporating a strip of land south of the Bahr el-Arab into Dar Rizeigat, also denied full Dar rights in that strip to the Rizeigat.

> The question that immediately springs to mind is that if the Rizeigat Nazir could not withdraw the permission of grazing and watering given to the Malwal Dinka without consent of the Governor of Darfur and if the latter could not take action without consulting the

> Governor of Bahr el Ghazal, what was the right the agreement bestowed on the Rizeigat? Ownership, as we also saw before, is represented by the power to limit the ability of others to enjoy the benefits to be derived from access to, and enjoyment of, resources. (Kibreab 2002: 85)

Clearly the territory south of the Bahr el-Arab had not been, and was not fully, part of Dar Rizeigat. At most it could be said that the Rizeigat shared secondary rights in that territory with the Malwal. But the intervention of the government had set a precedent of converting such secondary rights into dominant rights, and by doing so, extending southwards not just the boundary of the Dar, but the boundary of the province in which it was located. This has implications for the future North-South boundary determination in the Sudan.

The Issue of Abyei

The adjacent area of Abyei along the Bahr el-Arab in Kordofan is another example of the attempt to redefine tribal territory by converting secondary rights to dominant rights, but this time in the post-independence period, and in the context of civil war and the CPA of 2005.

The Ngok Dinka live to the east of the Malwal, both north and south of the Bahr el-Arab, and have done so for more than two centuries (Henderson 1939: 57–8, 76). Their permanent settlements are found along many of the waterways that feed into the main stream of the river, and they make seasonal use of pastures both north and south of their settlement area. They and their Humr-Misseriya Arab neighbours to the north were affected by the same set of disturbances at the end of the nineteenth century that affected the Malwal and Rizeigat, and British administrators entering the area at the beginning of the twentieth century found an ambivalent relationship between the Ngok and Misseriya, with common grazing in some areas, but also complaints about Misseriya extortion and raiding. In 1905 it was decided to incorporate the Ngok Dinka into Kordofan Province, as it was 'considered advisable to place them under the same Governor as the Arabs of whose conduct they complain'.[10]

Throughout the Condominium period this inclusion of a group of Dinka into a northern province, an anomaly after the 1930 Southern Policy, appeared to work well, in that grazing issues between the two groups were managed far more amicably than between the Rizeigat and Malwal, who were frequently compared unfavourably with the Misseriya and Ngok. The Humr followed set 'tracks' in their dry season movement into the Dinka permanent settlements along the river, and gradually expanded their movements beyond what they had been at the beginning of the century (Cunnison 1966: 13–19, 26–7). In the 1930s the Ngok and Misseriya faced increasing competition for grazing north of the Bahr el-Arab, first from the Malwal Dinka (whose use of the pastures south of the Bahr el-Arab was now restricted by the 1924 agreement), and then from other Dinka, such as the Twic, living south of the Ngok. The Ngok and Misseriya were united in resisting the Malwal incursions but were willing to extend to them limited secondary rights in bad years.[11] The Ngok and Twic made a more inclusive agreement, defining some of the pastures lying south and north of the river as a 'common area' to both peoples.[12] There seems to have been no formal declaration of a similar 'common area' for the Ngok and Misseriya during this time, but in so far as it was acknowledged that the Misseriya passed through and grazed among Dinka permanent villages before returning to their own in the Muglad and Babanusa areas to the north, the Misseriya exercised secondary rights within the dominant rights area of the Ngok.

Independence for the Sudan in 1956 and the outbreak of civil war in the Southern Sudan in the 1960s highlighted the anomaly of Ngok Dinka residence in a northern province. Many Ngok Dinka sided with the Anyanya guerrillas in the South and advocated re-incorporation into Bahr el-Ghazal Province. The fortunes of the Ngok and the Malwal now seemed reversed: while Rizeigat paid the Malwal Dinka chiefs and the Anyanya tribute in order to graze in that part of 'Dar Rizeigat' that lay south of the Bahr el-Arab, the Misseriya raided the Ngok and began forcing them to evacuate their northernmost villages (Keen 1994: 41–2). The Addis Ababa Peace Agreement of 1972 brought only a temporary respite for the Ngok. The terms of that agreement gave them the right to vote in a plebiscite whether to stay in Kordofan or join the newly created Southern Region, but the attempt to exercise that right provoked renewed attacks by the Misseriya, this time backed by politicians and military leaders in Khartoum. The Misseriya were facing a reduction of their northern grazing lands through incorporation into mechanised schemes and feared they would be further excluded from the southern pastures if the Abyei area (now so named from the town where the administrative headquarters was based) joined the Southern Region (*ibid.*: 59–61). The issue went beyond the definition or protection of grazing rights when oil was discovered in the area in the mid-1970s.

The frustrated plebiscite, the political struggle between the central and southern governments over the control of oil, and Misseriya fears that they would be excluded from customary grazing areas, meant that Abyei and the Ngok Dinka homeland became the focus of renewed fighting even before the second civil war officially began in 1983. Successive Khartoum regimes from 1983 through to the end of the war in 2005 armed and supported Misseriya militias in the effort first to clear Ngok civilians out of the Abyei area (especially away from the oil fields), and later expanded their attacks against civilians in other strategic areas within the Southern Sudan, especially in the oil fields of neighbouring Unity State. This was a precursor and testing ground for the Janjaweed strategy later adopted in Darfur (Johnson 2008: 5–7).

The peace negotiations initiated with the backing of the US government in 2002 included a separate protocol to settle the Abyei issue, recognizing that though it was not part of the South, it was part of the civil war. The Abyei Protocol provided for a temporary administration during the 'interim period' of 2006–11, the division of oil revenues between the central government, the states, the Ngok and Misseriya, and a referendum to decide whether Abyei would rejoin the South, or remain in the North. The one thing the protocol did not provide was a definition of the Abyei area itself. An agreement on boundaries was important, as that would determine whether or not the oil fields were included in the area. The solution to this dilemma was to leave the definition of boundaries to a boundary commission, and to mandate that commission 'to define and demarcate the area of the nine Ngok Dinka chiefdoms transferred to Kordofan in 1905'.[13]

The resolution of this issue, therefore, was to be decided as if it were a matter of tribal territory, judging one tribe's claims against another. The presentation of evidence by the government, the Sudan People's Liberation Movement (SPLM), the Misseriya and the Ngok focused on the tribal claims of a hundred years previously, removing from any direct consideration the real issue that was preventing agreement: the administrative jurisdiction of the oil fields. The argument of the government and the Misseriya was to expand the territorial claims of the Dar. The Misseriya claimed that Dar Misseriya extended south of the Bahr el-Arab all the way to the 1956 boundary with Bahr el-Ghazal, while the government was content to argue that Dar Misseriya in 1905 extended only as far as the Bahr el-Arab. Both claims excluded the oil fields from the Abyei Area so defined. In the end the commission made a decision based on an historical assessment of the dominant and secondary rights of both the Ngok and Misseriya and proposed a boundary which, while less than the Ngok and SPLM had claimed, was far more than the Misseriya or the government were prepared to admit. Unsurprisingly, both the government and the majority of Misseriya refused to accept the 'final and binding decision' of the commission and mobilised to prevent the implementation of the border and the protocol, thus endangering the full implementation of the CPA itself (Johnson 2008: 8–19).[14]

Settling the North–South Border

There is no single land-tenure regime that covers the whole Sudan. Northern land legislation has built on colonial laws expanding the control of the state over the rural areas. In the Southern Sudan a variety of customary laws regulate access to land and other land-related issues. In the 'transitional zone' of Southern Kordofan and Blue Nile there is a confused contestation between the writ of the national legislation and the survival of customary regulation (Pantuliano 2007: 3). The CPA provides for the creation of a hierarchy of land commissions at the national level, in Southern Kordofan and Blue Nile states, and in the Southern Sudan. As of the beginning of 2009 none of these land commissions were functioning (Pantuliano 2007: 3–5). Nor is it clear what legislation will take precedence in settling local disputes, or disputes between states and the central government. The Government of South Sudan is moving towards the codification of customary law within its territory, but its immediate neighbours are still regulated by the accumulated legislation of the 1970s–90s. As in the Condominium period, two different forms of land tenure confront each other across the notional border. This has serious implications for the definition of the North-South boundary.

The examples of the Rizeigat–Malwal boundary and the Abyei Area are a preview of what to expect in the attempt, required by the CPA, to define the Southern Sudan's boundaries as of independence day (1 January) 1956, prior to a referendum set for 2011 when the South will vote whether to remain part of a united Sudan or become independent.

During the Condominium period the precedent was set of either extending dominant Dar rights into the territory of Southern peoples (as in the Rizeigat–Malwal case), or asserting the application of secondary rights into the Southern provinces. In Upper Nile Province both the Seleim Baggara of White Nile and the Aulad Himmeid of Kordofan claimed that their Dar rights extended into the Kaka area along the west bank of the White Nile, though in fact this involved no more than seasonal cultivation and gum harvesting.[15] In Western Bahr el-Ghazal District, frequently cited as the most extreme and notorious case of segregation imposed by the Southern policy, the same Munro-Wheatley agreement that established the extent of Dar Rizeigat also established the limits to the grazing and hunting rights in the district of various Darfur peoples. These rights continued throughout the Condominium. A proposal in the 1940s to transfer the district to Darfur was declined by the then governor because the territory was too inaccessible to administer effectively.[16] Shortly before independence he defined Darfur's interest in the district as: '(a) to preserve our hunting and grazing rights in this area; (b) refuse to undertake administrative responsibility for it.'[17] In other words, to continue to assert the secondary rights of Darfur peoples in an area beyond Darfur administration.

When the Sudanese nationalist leader Ismail el-Azhari outlined the Graduate Congress's blue-print for self-determination for the Sudan in 1945, he spoke of 'the regrettable isolation of the South, the need for co-ordinated development in both parts of the country and, above all, the economic need of the North for the South' (Johnson 1998: document 26). The criticism of many Southern Sudanese is that el-Azhari and his successors emphasised the second part of this development plan at the expense of the first part. Areas of the South that have been designated for 'national' economic development tend to be transferred to neighbouring northern states. Thus part of Western District Bahr el-Ghazal was transferred to Darfur in 1960 – not for its grazing and hunting resources, but for the mineral deposits reputed to be there. Areas developed for mechanised farming along the White Nile in Upper Nile, including land around Kaka, were also transferred to neighbouring northern states in the 1990s.

There has been a steady erosion of Dar rights under post-independence governments, especially so under the National Congress regime that seized power in 1989 and now sits as the senior partner in a forced marriage with the SPLM in the CPA-created Government of National Unity in Khartoum. Communal lands throughout the North, but especially along the border areas, have been transferred to government ownership and control and communal rights have been nullified. The rationale for annexations of land from southern states, therefore, has not been that the territories belonged by existing right to the neighbouring peoples in adjacent states. But it is surely no coincidence that the annexation of areas designated as containing 'national' resources in need of development are also areas where there has been a long-term assertion of Dar rights or secondary rights, going back to the Condominium period, and often confirmed by the central government. The selective extension of Dar rights along the border is, in fact, a masquerade by the central government to retain control over natural resources, but it is a masquerade that employs the precedents of the Condominium.

Now that the CPA has established the mechanism whereby the peoples and territory of the Southern Sudan can achieve *de jure* as well as *de facto* independence in only a few years, the northern elites who have controlled the central government in one form or another since independence are faced with the very real prospect that they will lose control of the assets the South contains: whether this is the land and water on which the northern peoples of the border increasingly rely, or the oil wealth on which the Sudan's economy is currently being built. The temptation will be, if the 2011 referendum cannot be either fixed or stopped, that what remains of the Sudan must claw back as much territory with development potential along the new border as possible. The conversion of secondary rights into dominant rights and the expansion of tribal Dars to erode the administrative boundary began in the Condominium period. These twin processes are now being used to evade the provisions of the CPA and keep the development assets of the border regions under the control of the central government in Khartoum.

Bibliography

Abd al-Rahim, M. (1969) *Imperialism and Nationalism in the Sudan: A Study in Constitutional and Political Development 1899–1956*. Oxford: Clarendon Press.

Abyei Boundaries Commission (2005) *Abyei Boundaries Commission Report*. Nairobi: IGAD.

African Rights (1995) *Facing Genocide: The Nuba of Sudan*. London: African Rights.

Anon. (1996) 'When the Land is Out'. *Nafir* 2 (1): 10–11.

Beshir, M.O. (1968) *The Southern Sudan: Background to Conflict*. London: C. Hurst.

Collins, R.O. (1983) *Shadows in the Grass: Britain in the Southern Sudan, 1918–1956*. New Haven, CT and London: Yale University Press.

Cunnison, I. (1966) *Baggara Arabs: Power and the Lineage in a Sudanese Nomad Tribe*. Oxford: Clarendon Press.

Duffield, M. (1992), 'Famine, Conflict and the Internationalization of Public Welfare'. In Doornbos, M., Cliffe, L., Ahmed, A.G.M., Markakis, J. (eds) *Beyond Conflict in the Horn: The Prospects for Peace, Recovery and Development in Ethiopia, Somalia, Eritrea and Sudan*. London: James Currey, pp. 49–66.

Harir, S. (1993) 'Militarization of Conflict, Displacement and the Legitimacy of the State: a Case from Dar Fur, Western Sudan'. In Tvedt, T. (ed.) *Conflicts in the Horn of Africa: Human and Ecological Consequences of Warfare*, Uppsala: EPOS, pp.14–26.

Harir, S. (1994) '"Arab Belt" versus "African Belt": Ethno-Political Conflict in Dar Fur and the Regional Cultural Factors'. In Harir, S. and Tvedt, T. (eds) *Short-Cut to Decay: The Case of the Sudan*. Uppsala: Nordiska Afrikainstitutet, pp.144–85.

Hayes, K.O'C. (1960) '"Dar Rights" among the Nomads: An Aribitral Award'. *Sudan Law Journal and Reports* 5: 336–7.

Henderson, K.D.D. (1939) 'The Migration of the Messiria into South West Kordofan'. *Sudan Notes & Records* 22 (1): 49–77.

Intelligence Department, Sudan Government (1911) *The Bahr El Ghazal Province*. Anglo-Egyptian Handbook Series, 1. London: HMSO.

James, W. (2007) *War and Survival in Sudan's Frontierlands: Voices from the Blue Nile*. Oxford: Oxford University Press.

Johnson, D.H. (ed.) (1998) *Sudan. Part 1 1942–1950. British Documents on the End of Empire, Series B, Volume* 5. London: the Stationery Office.

Johnson, D.H. (2008) 'Why Abyei Matters: The Breaking Point of Sudan's Comprehensive Peace Agreement?' *African Affairs* 107 (426): 1–19.

Jonglei Investigation Team (1954) *The Equatorial Nile Project and its Effects in the Anglo-Egyptian Sudan*, vol. IV. Khartoum.

Keen, D. (1994) *The Benefits of Famine: A Political Economy of Famine and Relief in Southwestern Sudan, 1983–1989*. Princeton, NJ: Princeton University Press.

Kibreab, G. (2002) *State Intervention and the Environment in Sudan, 1889–1989*. Lewiston, NY & Lampeter: Edwin Mellen.

Miller, C. (2005) 'Power, Land and Ethnicity in the Kassala-Gedaref States: An Introduction. In Miller, C. (ed.) *Land, Ethnicity and Political Legitimacy in Eastern Sudan*. Cairo: Centre d'études et de documentation économique, juridique et sociale and Khartoum: Development Studies and Research Center, University of Khartoum, pp. 3–48.

Pantuliano, Sara (2007) *The Land Question: Sudan's Peace Nemesis*. London: Overseas Development Institute.

Sudan Government (1913) *Reports on the Finance, Administration and Condition of the Sudan, 1912*, vol. I. London: Waterlow & Sons.

Theobald, A.B. (1965) *Ali Dinar: Last Sultan of Darfur 1898–1916*. London: Longman.

Notes

1 Kibreab (2002), chapter 2, describes the evolution of Dar rights in detail.

2 Abyei Boundaries Commission (2005), Appendix 2: 24–5.

3 See, for instance, the documentation of the criss-crossing seasonal movements of pastoralists in the Upper Nile in maps E4–E7 and E10 in Jonglei Investigation Team (1954).

4 R.V. Savile, 'Travels in Kordofan and Darfur 1910 to 1921', Sudan Archive, University of Durham [SAD] 427/7/83–4.
5 W. Owen, ADC Northern District to A/Governor Bahr el Ghazal, Aweil 16–10–1925, 'Rizeigat-Dinka Relations 1925', National Records Office, Khartoum [NRO] Civsec I 66/4/35 vol. II.
6 'Wheatley-Munro Agreement. Rizeigat – Dinka (Malwal) Boundary', 22 April 1924, NRO Civsec I 66/4/35 vol. I.
7 'Meeting at Safaha', March 24th to 29th, 1935, NRO Civsec I 66/4/35 vol I and SAD Andrew Baring Papers.
8 Correspondence concerning the Malwal-Rizeigat boundary is found in NRO Civsec I 66/4/35 vols I & II, and is discussed in detail in Kibreab (2002): 80–100.
9 M. Parr, Governor Equatoria to Civil Secretary, 7 November 1938, NRO Civsec I 66/4/35 vol. II. Parr had been Deputy Civil Secretary before becoming a provincial governor, so wrote with an insider's knowledge of the Civil Secretary's correspondence with the provinces.
10 *Sudan Intelligence Report* 128 (March 1905): 3. See Johnson (2008): 2–5 for an historical summary of Ngok–Misseriya relations.
11 K.D.D. Henderson, A.D.C., Western Kordofan, 'Malwal Herds in Kordofan. 1932.' Wunrog, 18.4.1932, NRO BGP 1/5/31.
12 'Extract from Bahr el Ghazal Province Diary for February, 1935', NRO Civsec I 66/4/35 vol. II.
13 (Abyei Protocol) Resolution of the Abyei Conflict, Chapter IV of 'The Comprehensive Peace Agreement between the Government of the Republic of the Sudan and the Sudan People's Liberation Movement/Sudan People's Liberation Army' (Nairobi, 9 January 2005): 68.
14 The full text of the evidence and testimony, along with the decision of the commission, can be found in Abyei Boundaries Commission (2005), http://www.sudanarchive.net/cgi-bin/sudan?a=d&d=Dl1d18. The arbitral award announced by the Abyei Arbitration Tribunal at the Hague on 22 July 2009 redefined the Abyei Area as being confined to a portion over which the Ngok have 'dominant' rights. The decision appears to have incorporated the area of 'shared secondary' rights into a greater Dar Misseriya (see http://www.pca-cpa.org/showpage.asp?pag_id=1306).
15 'Note on the Upper Nile boundary' (*c.* 1935), SAD Andrew Baring papers.
16 Lampen to Robertson, 12 June 1946; Lampen to Marwood, 12 June 1946; DP SCR 66–B-44 II, both in SAD Andrew Baring Papers.
17 G.D. Lampen, 'Handing Over Notes', El Fasher, 23/3/1949, SAD 731/2/1–98.

13

'Individualism is, Indeed, Running Riot'
Components of the Social Democratic Model of Development

PAUL KELEMEN

Introduction

The political ascendancy of the neo-liberal agenda in development policy has reopened the debate over the trade-off between social cohesion and the extension of market relations. The disintegrating effects of capitalism has led to the reinvention of the 'social', to put in place mechanisms for stabilisation and integration. Social democracy has historically made the claim to provide these through collectivist solutions. The aim here is to identify how the British Labour Party translated this aspiration into its policy on Africa during the colonial period. In the origins of the party's ideas on development, we can trace some of the assumptions that underpinned the post-war promotion of the developmental state, aspects of which have continued to cast a long shadow over official thinking.

The British Labour Party first formulated its policy on Africa in the 1920s at a time when 'hegemony on a shoestring' (Berry 1993:24) depended on preserving the tribal chiefs, many of them state appointees, as the principal collaborators of colonial rule. The main authors of Labour's foreign policy were Radical Liberals who had defected to Labour around the end of the World War I. E.D.Morel and Charles Buxton were particularly influential on the Advisory Committee on Imperial Questions which was the party's main discussion forum on colonial policy and, until the late 1920s, a significant influence on its National Executive Committee. Their preoccupation with the impact of colonialism on Africa was primarily defensive: to preserve the communal ownership of land in order to halt the advancing tide of proletarianisation. It was to be through the influence of Fabians that the party formulated proposals to form new institutions as the 'traditional' solidarities, which have underpinned colonial rule, began to wane. The Radical Liberals were critical not of colonialism *per se* but of the failure of British rule to defend Africans from the spread of capitalism eroding the economic basis of individual peasant cultivators working on communal land. 'The model to follow', Buxton explained, 'is that of the British possessions on the West Coast of Africa, where the government has treated the land as in fact the property of the native communities, has refused to alienate land to the Europeans and has encouraged the African to make the most economic use of his own land' (Buxton 1925). The Labour party's first comprehensive colonial policy statement, published in 1926, called this 'the African policy' and counterposed it to the 'Capitalist policy', for which it cited Kenya as the example. In the latter case, encouragement of syndicates and planters to use hired or forced labour 'has already alienated the land to Europeans and created a landless proletariat'. It was resulting, it claimed, in the break-up of African society (Labour Party 1926:7).

The Radicals' Critique of Colonialism

For Morel, the traditional African society based on communal land and tribal authority was the natural state for a people he considered primitive and backward. His racist diatribes against the French army's African troops on the Rhine, published in 1920, by the TUC's newspaper, the *Daily Herald* – alleging that they posed a danger to German women (Reinders 1968) – were entirely consistent with his efforts to protect the African peasantry from the process of proletarianisation. But even in its strictly economic implications the paternalist defence of *merrie* Africa provided little critical purchase on colonialism in West Africa. The large, foreign merchant houses, which dominated the region's trade, were the main harbinger of capitalist development, but in so far as they confined themselves to trade they escaped the scrutiny of Labour's colonial experts. Their idealised model of Africa provided, however, the basis for a critique of settler colonialism in Kenya which dominated the party's deliberations on Africa. After Morel's death in 1924, Norman Leys, who had close knowledge of Kenya, emerged as the most prolific contributor to Labour Party discussions on Africa. His career in Kenya, as a medical officer, was terminated in 1913 because of his vocal opposition to the Governor reneging on a commitment not to appropriate a Masai land area for the benefit of European settlers (Wylie 1977).

Steeped in liberal paternalism, Leys, like Morel, was not free from the racism of the time. In the publication of the National Council for Labour Colleges, an organisation dedicated to 'giving a working class interpretation of the social sciences', he opined that people had to have 'first-hand experience dealing with uncivilised people to realise how lazy and unreliable they are' (*Plebs* October1930). But, unlike Morel, Leys wanted British rule to uphold the trusteeship of Africans not by returning to a traditional stage, but by intervening to redress the uneven balance of forces between the European settlers and the peasantry. Rather than try to halt the forces of capitalism, he wanted the colonial state to ensure that peasants retained sufficient land to be able to negotiate with potential employers from a position of relative security. In this sense, Leys contributed to the Labour Party making the transition from the Radical Liberal critique of colonialism, for which the point of departure was the need to preserve pre-capitalist Africa, to its position in the late 1930s which, implicitly, accepted that capitalism had taken root and concentrated on improving the conditions of the wage labourer.

With an incisiveness that was not to be equalled by academic studies until the 1970s, Leys documented the various methods by which the settlers' economic interest predominated over that of the Africans and forced the latter into wage labour (Leys 1924; 1931). The remedy for him was that land, taken by the Crown, which was not used for European farming should be returned to Africans. He wanted them to be protected from being coerced into wage labour which he believed would improve their labour conditions but he did not doubt that settlers owning and managing farms could be beneficial to the Africans. The Labour Party's 1933 policy statement on the colonies similarly made clear that it did not 'seek to exclude European enterprise and capital' (Labour Party 1933:4). Thus, despite Leys' demonstration of how the settler economy was built on racial discrimination, he and his colleagues on the Advisory Committee believed that a more equitable allocation of land and resources could be introduced without dismantling the settler sector and that this was the task for British rule. 'All racial discrimination, financial and otherwise, must go, and while no injustice would be done to any white settler, his privileged position in respect of government and administration would no longer hold' (*ibid.* 1933:4). Labour's call to restrict the settlers' political power but not to dismantle their economic basis suggests that its hostility to the 'capitalist policy' had by the 1930s become more equivocal: its opposition narrowed to the state-accorded privileges of the European settlers and left uncontested the capitalist relations of production over which they presided. This is also the reason why the party's policy statements of 1926 and 1933 and Leys' two books on the Kenyan economy raised no objections to the foreign-owned plantations and ranches despite the fact that, by the 1920s, their economic role was considerable.

The speculative boom of the 1920s had consolidated the position of foreign companies and this was evident in Kenya in the three main economic sectors: agriculture, trading and manufacturing and minerals. Some of the giant multinational corporations were extending their economic control in this period. Mitchell Cotts, by origin a South African merchant and shipping company, handled in Kenya 'no less than 95 per cent of maize exported between 1928 and 1932; in 1932 they also handled 95 percent of the wheat export crop' (Swainson 1978:54). The British East African Corporation moved from merely trading into raw material production. By World War I it owned and managed estates, cultivating sisal and wattle, and operated oil mills and cotton ginneries (Swainson 1980:61). Brooke Bond went from marketing tea in East Africa into producing it. It acquired, alongside another tea trader, James Finlay, control of around two-thirds of Kenya's tea acreage. A parallel development took place in Kenya's soda ash production which in 1926 was taken over by the large chemical combine, ICI (Swainson 1978:73). In the interwar years, just over half of Kenya's exports were controlled by foreign companies. Labour's colonial specialists may have lacked the precise data on multinational companies' involvement in Africa but they could not have been unaware of their growing importance. Indeed, the 1928 colonial policy statement of the Labour and Socialist International, to which the Labour Party was affiliated, called for the working class 'to apply its Political, Trade Union and Co-operative power so as to bring capitalist monopolies under the control of the community and of the organised working class' (Labour Party 1928a:340). This was, however, in the language of continental social democracy, which had been heavily influenced by Marxism, and the party's own statement implied a more modest change, offering to institute the appropriate administrative machinery to 'protect the consumer against excessive prices...by establishing control over monopolies and combines...' (Labour Party 1928b:27).

According to Porter, Morel had dropped his opposition to Lever Brothers' West African plantations as early as 1912. He explains Morel's change of heart as stemming from a grudging recognition that capitalist development could not be halted and that the Lever Brothers' enterprise, however undesirable, was not run by the abhorrent methods practised on King Leopold's concessions in the Congo (Porter 1968:284). Following Morel's death, Labour's colonial experts took this about-turn for granted. The party, as in its 1933 statement, remained generally hostile to measures that favoured 'creating a large and discontented landless proletariat' (Labour Party 1933:9), but the thinking of its colonial experts revealed an increasing acceptance that capitalism in the African colonies was an established fact. In 1939, Leys pointed to an official report claiming that 'of African males in Kenya, who are capable of work, over 90 per cent already work for wages...' (Leys 1939). Thus Labour's emphasis, by the late 1930s, was no longer on preventing the spread of waged labour

– whether that came from plantations or industrial enterprises – but on securing improvements in the conditions of labour. The fact that 'Colonial Office reports for 1937–8 and 1938–9, compiled at the request of interested MPs, were full of "social welfare" and economic betterment' (Goldsworthy 1971:10), reflected in no small part the Parliamentary Labour Party's focus on waged labour in the urban sector. Goldsworthy notes the lack of interest by MPs in constitutional change, but at least as significant was how little interest, in this period, Labour showed in the African peasantry, despite the accelerating flow of rural migrants which was known to be aggravating conditions for wage workers in the towns. In part, this lacunae was disguised by the oft-repeated party statements in support of developing rural cooperatives.

The co-operative movement, in Britain, was made up mainly of working-class consumers' organisations, directed primarily at protecting consumers from 'excessive' profits. The movement had a long, historical association with the British labour movement, but support for the formation of cooperatives in the colonies was not exclusive to the Labour Party. Among colonial officials, some considered cooperative marketing as the way to recapture the organic unity of 'traditional' Africa, while others saw it as having advantages over the individual trader from the point of view of enabling more efficient marketing and tax collection. The 1929–31 Labour government's encouragement of cooperatives in the colonies led, in Kenya, to settler marketing associations turning themselves into cooperatives while, in the Reserves, farmers sold their produce through private traders (Gyllstroem, 1991:31). In Nigeria and the Gold Coast, between 1925 and 1935, there were initiatives by African entrepreneurs to form producers' cooperatives 'in an attempt to strengthen the bargaining position of farmers and lower their costs' (Hopkins 1973:256). The broad support for co-operatives underlines that they could be incorporated into a variety of economic and political strategies. The Labour Party's advocacy of them for the colonies was vague and is likely to have been subject to different interpretations within its own ranks.

In 1933, the party defined its immediate colonial policy objectives as 'socialisation and self-government' and, elaborating on these terms, pledged that alongside local-self government, 'cooperative societies of all kinds which encourage common effort and train administrators and leaders will be fostered' (Labour Party 1933: 5). The following year Leonard Woolf, the chairperson on the Advisory Committee on Imperial Questions, argued that Labour should see 'the encouragement of cooperative societies by Colonial Governments as an important part of its policy' (Woolf 1934). Such statements signalled the party's commitment to a collectivist ethic but they did not indicate what overall change in the rural social structure cooperatives were supposed to bring about. It was also left unclear whether the party retained Morel's strong attachment to individual peasant cultivation and saw in cooperatives merely a marketing mechanism, or if it preferred collective forms of production.

W.M. Macmillan, who came to Britain from South Africa and joined the Advisory Committee on Imperial Questions, believed the former to be the case and expressed scepticism that 'the essentially non-Socialist idea of peasant proprietorship is the panacea some professing socialism would make it' (Macmillan 1938:385). Leonard Barnes, on the left of the Labour Party, conceded that the party had few ideas on how to advance 'socialisation'. The influence of Gladstonian Liberalism, he claimed, had given the British Labour movement a fairly clear idea of the constitutional advance it wanted in the colonies, 'while the problems of the transition from capitalist to socialist enterprise are treated with less definition' (Barnes 1935:241). The Fabian Colonial Bureau appeared to address the issue of how to bring change to African societies, though it was their gradual democratisation rather than altering the emerging class relations that preoccupied it.

Fabianism & Remoulding Communities

The Bureau, which was set up in 1940 by Arthur Creech Jones and Rita Hinden, became the main forum for the elaboration of party policy on the colonies. Through its network of contacts among colonial nationalists and a collaborative relation with the Colonial Office, it helped to crystallise a consensus among colonial specialists in favour of the imperial state initiating social and economic improvements in Africa, in preparation for self-government. The war-time involvement of the British government in the mobilisation of resources and international hostility to colonialism had altered the attitude of politicians across the political mainstream and among colonial officials in London. Ronald Robinson, working in the Africa Department of the Colonial Office, remarked in 1947, that war had brought about a public opinion which 'is tending to project its social democratic programmes into the Colonial field and to demand positive action to raise standards of living and provide social services for dependent peoples. International opinion reinforces the pressures...Thus there are at present few bodies of opinion anywhere which will accept the maintenance of law and order and the conservation of tribal organisation of indirect rule, as sufficient justification for the retention of colonies' (Robinson 1947:155).

Rita Hinden was the most articulate exponent in Labour's ranks of a social democratic colonial policy. As the intellectual driving force of the Fabian Colonial Bureau, she proved to be the true heir of the Webbs, not least in the meticulous attention she gave to the organisations that would be required to effect the political changes that Labour Party leaders broadly envisaged. In 1920, the Webbs had depicted trade unions, cooperatives and local government as the main functional groupings in society corresponding to the interests of producers, consumers and citizens and thereby the main instrument for realising democracy (Webb; 1920). For Hinden, the development of these mass organisations was of greater political importance than the provision of welfare services. On the eve of the Labour government taking power, she noted that 'the policy of "development and welfare" in which we now engage – a philanthropy-*cum*-public works policy...is no frontal attack on the major problems; it is neither democratic *laissez faire* nor is it state planning...'. The distinctive Fabian way that she advocated, depended on whether 'African workers can combine to defend themselves in trade unions, whether African peasants can band together to control their markets through cooperatives, and whether the African people as a whole can exercise political responsibility and control in their own councils of government' (Hinden 1945:63).

Thus the programme of investment in the economy and in welfare that she envisaged was linked to institution building, and the Labour government was to initiate this on all the three fronts indicated by Hinden. The accompanying discourse was infused with ambiguity over the notion of 'development'. In the amalgam that it designated, increasing self-organisation and welfare was subordinated to increasing production. It was 'under the Labour government that one sees the triumph of a productionist vision of economic development that Tory ministers had only partially accepted' (Cooper 1996:205). The 'productionist' preoccupation permeated the colonial authorities' efforts to build new forms of collaboration between Africans and metropolitan interests. Hailey's pre-war study, *An Africa Survey*, had pointed to the importance of widening the power base of colonial authority by associating the educated stratum with the deployment of power at the local level (Hailey 1945:541). But there were still those who believed that the old machinery of indirect rule could be salvaged with some modifications. N.Humphrey, an agricultural expert attached to the Kenya government, hoped, in 1945, to revivify the 'community of interests based on community of kinship', which underpinned the power of the Chiefs and Local Native Councils. He proposed that for the modernising tasks expected of these traditional institutions their reach should be extended beyond the Local Native Councils and the Divisional Councils to the still more local Unit Councils in the hope that these would correspond to a still functioning network of traditional solidarity (Humphrey 1945:57).

The post-war Labour government aimed to reform the traditional institutions but to salvage the solidarity associated with them. It brought into being a new mechanism for managing the African masses, and it was in this respect that the Attlee government drew on Fabianism to launch trade unions, cooperatives and local government on the 'English' model. Labour's colonial policy statements repeatedly emphasised the need for these three institutions, assigning to them the dual role of providing the basis of collectivism and the training in administrative skills deemed to be required to eventually allow Africans to take over from the imperial state. After the war, the Labour movement's long-standing commitment to these institutions was translated into policy by the Labour government. The connecting thread between Morel and the Fabians was the primacy accorded to community but whereas Morel assumed it to be inherent in African societies, but needing protection from the disintegrating effects of capitalism, for the Fabians it had to be constructed through institutions which generated a sense of community. 'Of course, the management of a social community required trustees...It was out of this social vision that the Fabians created their own versions of social "trusteeship"' (Cowen and Shenton 1991:154–5).

After the war, Fabianism was provided with the opportunity to press for a more proactive role in 'the management of social community'. This period was marked, to varying degrees in the different colonies, by what Lewis has described in relation to Kenya as 'the new intimacy in state-society relations' that war-time conditions had initiated (Lewis 2000:7). Yet the duality state/civil society risks missing the nature of the change which followed, which was not merely to renegotiate the points of contact between the two, but to efface the duality: to reorganise the masses by incorporating them into institutional structures within the framework of colonial rule.

The idea of increased spending on colonial welfare and economic development was mooted even before the 1937–8 riots in the West Indies, and gained further converts in their wake. The 1940 Colonial Development and Welfare Act signalled British officialdom's readiness to provide assistance to the colonies. The Fabian influence helped to convert this into a policy of building institutions to mediate between the central authority and the masses, in order to deliver the planned welfare and economic improvements. It was, in this respect, the most cogent and insistent voice within a broader consensus. The Tory, Oliver Stanley, Secretary of State for Colonies in the war-time coalition government, outlining his vision of the preparatory steps needed for Africans to progress towards greater political responsibility, also accepted that it would have to be accompanied by drawing Africans into institutions, but he understood their role in a more restricted sense, as providing training in state administration. Nevertheless, in terms similar to the Labour Party's Fabian colonial experts, Stanley explained: 'The education I have in mind goes beyond the classroom ...I consider just as important – education through local government, education through community effort, such as trade unions and cooperatives, and education through actual practice in administration…' .[1] The interpenetration between state managerialism that the war-time conditions had generated and Fabianism increased the overlap between the two main, rival, political parties.

Stanley's speech was, however, not typical of the Tory front bench in Parliament and had been carefully crafted for the occasion to appease international critics of British colonialism (Bowden 1980:195). It is unlikely that a Conservative government would have had the backing from its backbenchers and political constituency to launch an equally ambitious programme of building popular institutions in the colonies, for, in this regard, there persisted broadly two schools of thought. Hailey's view, supported by Lord Lugard and Margery Perham, was that political reform should proceed mainly at the local level, by broadening the support base for the traditional native authority, but not seek to emulate British parliamentary institutions (Pearce 1982:155). The Attlee government, less tied than the Conservatives to traditional political and commercial interests in the colonies and more experienced in the ways of integrating the masses into the political system, was able to try a more radical approach. There followed an ambitious attempt to promote the transfer of British institutions to the colonies. It focused, not on the Parliamentary system, which was seen to be still some way into the future, but on the institutions – trade unions, cooperatives and local government – which had been long cherished by Fabians and were widely considered by the British Labour movement as having been important staging posts in its own historic passage to Parliamentary representation.

Even before the war, the Colonial Office, partly as result of Labour Party and TUC pressure, had cajoled several colonial governments into introducing legislation to provide a legal framework for trade unions. George Hall, from the Labour Party, who was junior minister at the Colonial Office in the war-time Coalition government, reported, in 1940, that in just a few years twenty-seven colonies had formed Labour Departments or had appointed full-time Labour Officers or Inspectors. The problem was that 'the new trade unions in the colonies may be ill-informed , badly organised and badly led and an easy prey to the agitator and the opportunist'. He claimed that 'the task of guiding their development on sound and moderate lines and of educating their leaders in the light of the example given by the great trade unions in this country is one of the most difficult problems with which the Colonial Office is faced at the moment' (Hall 1940). In 1942, partly in response to pressure from the Labour Party, the Coalition government formed the Colonial Labour Advisory Committee, with representatives from the Colonial Office, the TUC General Council and the Overseas Employers' Federation, to encourage collaborative industrial relations. Against the background of a rapid post-war increase in Africa's urban proletariat, the Committee encouraged the TUC to involve itself in setting up trade unions. The TUC launched training courses in trade unionism for Africans selected with the help of the Colonial Office and sent out officials to help organise unions and the machinery for collective bargaining (Weiler 1988:39). In 1949, Creech Jones instructed colonial governments to work towards the 'system of Whitleyism on very much the same lines that proved successful in the UK'.[2]

The Colonial Office showed growing concern over labour matters both to increase productivity and to prevent workers' grievances escalating into political demands. 'The Unions,' wrote Hinden in a memorandum for the Colonial Office, 'are among the very few organised bodies in the Colonies. They tend to become political instruments, and are used as the spearhead of the nationalist movements.' Colonial officials favoured the British model of trade unionism, organised on an industry-by-industry basis and confining demands, in the main, to improvements in wages and work conditions. They found willing collaborators in a TUC leadership that believed in the defence of the British Empire against both anti-colonial nationalism and Communism. Colonial governments, nonetheless, generally dragged their heels in pressing for any sort of collective bargaining machinery, not least because they were the main employers in the colonies. The TUC's Colonial Advisory Committee considered their attitude to be unhelpful to the formation of trade unions. Labour officers who had been recruited from British trade unions to oversee this process 'found their work made quite impossible', complained Arthur Deakin, the leader of the Transport and General Workers' Union, 'by the attitude of local administration officers, who wished them to be simply stooges'.[3] Despite such tensions, the TUC helped to draft legislation to enable colonial governments to regulate trade unions by a registration system, which served as a mechanism for enforcing the British trade union leadership's preference for a separate union in each trade, thereby tending to limit workers' demands to improvements in wages and conditions.

The TUC's method of building unions, industry by industry, and confining the scope of their activities to economic demands was favoured by both the British and colonial governments. They saw it as a way to prevent industrial conflicts assuming a national dimension, and the attendant risk, of their coming under Communist influence.

In the rural sector, the institution-building activity promoted by the Labour government focused on cooperatives and local government. These institutions, by penetrating deep into the society provided for the authorities instruments of supervision and control, though they also had the potential to give an organisational base to popular resistance.

A circular issued to colonial governments, in 1946, by George Hall, the Labour government's Secretary of State for the Colonies, which aimed at encouraging the formation of cooperatives among African farmers, emphasised their educative value. 'Thrift, self-help, fair-dealing and above all a practical training in the working of the democratic process are all encouraged by association of the people in cooperative societies.'[4] This formulation, casting entrepreneurial values as the qualities required for democratic citizenship, projected a new model for Africans to emulate, which co-existed with an older construction. 'Even as they experimented with new images of African farmers as economic men and future property-owning citizens...colonial regimes continued to work with older ideas of African societies as "closed, corporate, consensual communities", whose internal cohesiveness and shared traditions automatically fostered collective endeavour'(Berry 2002:647).

At the time when the Labour government was looking for increased raw material production, Creech Jones warned his Cabinet colleagues against 'quick and vigorous economic development' on the grounds that: 'Agricultural reform generally means some change in the systems of landholding, on which the whole social structure depends. It is our deep-rooted policy to preserve the social organisations we have inherited and modify them only gradually' (Havinden and Meredith 1993:312). After a visit with a Labour Party delegation to West Africa, James Griffiths, a former Colonial Secretary, reaffirmed this 'older', communal model. He spoke of cooperatives as a way to conserve rather than to change African society, as an organisation that could rekindle the traditional, collective ways of working: 'it should therefore be possible to build cooperatives without greatly disturbing the existing social structure'.[5]

As Berry argues, the 'new' imagery co-existed with the 'old', because they corresponded to a dual strategy of rural development and rural governance. 'In effect, Africans were being asked to act like economic men and tribesmen at the same time:

to build a modern, commercial agrarian order on the foundations of tribal society'(Berry 2002:648). The Labour Party's proponents of cooperatives for Africa were drawn to the idea of reconciling the 'new' with the 'old', of enveloping the peasant entrepreneur within a stable social order, 'by creating', claimed a 1957 policy statement, 'the mutual dependence of the old tribal societies' (Labour Party 1957b:34). The cooperatives in colonial economies remained a subordinate and mostly marginal sector, though their numbers had grown from 1,885 societies in ten territories with 266,000 members in 1945, to 8,626 societies in 26 territories with just over 1 million members in 1954 (Kirk-Greene 2001: 142). This was still a weak presence in an Empire with a population of approximately 65 million. Local government, by contrast, supplemented by 'mass education', which was then expanded into 'community development', had a wider reach and instead of replicating the 'old' governance, was intended to replaced it.

A New System of Governance

Lonsdale and Low have characterised the Labour government's mobilisation of technicians and advisers to boost post-war African production as the 'second colonial occupation'(Lonsdale and Low 1967:13) and this often-quoted designation appears to capture both the scale of the intervention and its neo-colonial implications. In Kenya, for example, in addition to expanding the number of administrative officers and district assistants, the 'agricultural department increased from 298 in 1945 to 2,519 in 1958 and the veterinary department grew from 291 to 892' (Throup 1987:25). In Tanganyika, by 1950 two-thirds of administrative officers had been appointed since 1944, and Iliffe goes on to quote African politicians in the Eastern province protesting at the growing army of officials: '"We are faced with a serious invasion, more serious, in fact, than the first world war"' (Iliffe 1979:443). In highlighting the expansion in administrative personnel, there is a risk, however, of seeing it merely as increasing the 'intensity' of colonial government (Hargreaves 1976:41) or as an 'extension of impersonal bureaucratic relationships', a greater 'detachment of decision makers from popular feeling' (Iliffe 1979:443), and miss the underlying restructuring of the state by which developed a new system of governance that was to remain largely intact after decolonisation. Lewis has shifted attention to this by showing how, in post-war Kenya, the colonial state in developing welfare functions recruited its own specialist staff and in the process marginalised women, who had previously worked in this sphere (Lewis: 2000). There were, however, not only gender but also race and class dimensions to this reorganisation. The reform of native authorities on the model of British local government was conceived as a way to preserve imperial control by diverting educated Africans from aspiring to gain control of the central state into channels where they could deploy their technical and administrative skills away from the main levers of power. It also had wider ramifications: it embedded in popular institutions administrative practices and norms modelled on the British state.

In the wake of Creech Jones's 1947 despatch to colonial governors to form British-style local government (Hyam 1992:209–219), a Bill, drafted by the Kenyan government and approved by the Colonial Office, codified state supervision over rural production. The African District Councils were to assume responsibilities for: 'regulating and controlling the production and sale of ghee and milk products...prohibiting, regulating or controlling the occupation and use of agricultural land by any person or class of persons... prescribing the methods of animal or agricultural husbandry' and 'prescribing what steps shall be taken by the owner or occupier of any agricultural land to maintain and improve its productivity and to preserve the fertility of the soil...'.[6] The micromanagement of the economy envisaged regulating the land as well as the producers. 'Development is held up', Creech Jones complained, 'by the shortage and inefficiency of labour and the inability of many Colonial people to work with the intensity of the stronger races. The number of workers and their ability to work is directly affected by their state of health and therefore by the medical services provided...' (Cooper 1996:206).

On the governance side of the dual strategy indicated by Berry, local government provided the welfare and 'mass education', which quite quickly became redefined as 'community development'. Creech Jones and Andrew Cohen, the head of the Colonial Office's African department who shared his Fabian outlook, saw local government as a way to restrain the mainly urban-based nationalist forces by the conservative rural masses. Cohen's reasoning was that democratising local power would 'bring together literates and illiterates in balanced and studied proportions' to check 'the professional African politician's selfish ambitions' (Robinson 1980:64). At the same time, officials also feared that with the waning power of its chiefly collaborators, the conservatism of the rural masses might wilt. 'Traditional' Africa was giving way, as a result of the development of capitalist relations, to a more individualised economy, to which Fabians responded by seeking to find a new compromise between social cohesion and economic dynamism. As Phillips has shown, an earlier resolution of this problem in West Africa had led the colonial authorities to retreat from introducing private property and wage labour . 'They could not impose conditions which would create free labour without destroying communal land tenure, and they could not destroy communal land tenure without weakening the chiefs on whom they relied in the interim for forced labour and political order' (Phillips 1989:78). Yet, even where private landownership and capitalist farming developed, as was the case in Kenya, with settler agriculture, the system of governance in the African sector was not much different. The African reserves were organised along tribal lines and the chiefs, appointed in the main by the British, maintained control on the basis of the 'traditional' authority structures and customary laws.

Mamdani has highlighted the consequent bifurcation of the colonial state corresponding to two different systems of governance, one for subjects and the other for citizens: 'on the one side free peasants closeted in separate ethnic containers, each with a customary shell guarded over by a Native Authority, on the other a civil society bounded by the modern laws of the modern state...' (Mamdani 1996:61). The colonial state sought to knit together and control communities, either through custom or in the urban areas through civic but racially segregated institutions. Development doctrine, including that of the Fabians, 'with its agrarian development and rural enterprise schemes... fixed population to its given ethnic territory and thereby provided the means by which tribal nationalism could be asserted' (Cowen and Shenton 1996:364). But penetration of commerce and war-time mobilisation and industrial expansion had loosened the bonds of these 'fixed' populations. In Kenya, Humphrey, pointing to the decline in communal grazing, observed: 'Only salt lick still remains unchallenged as a communal right. Individualism, indeed, is running riot and it is certain it is being carried so far that the future is fraught with danger if it continues uncontrolled' (Humphrey 1945:21). The post-war Labour government therefore sought to find new points of anchorage: in trade unions, cooperatives and communities. The latter, it was suggested, would generate 'local patriotism' that could gradually extend to the larger national unit. To meet the immediate priority for more productive African labour, the 'community' had to be encouraged, however, to incorporate some of that 'individuation of active self-interest' which, in the tradition of Morel, had been associated with the 'maleficent development of indigenous capitalism' (Cowen and Shenton 1996:364).

The failed Tanganyika groundnut scheme which was aimed at meeting Britain's post-war shortage in fats through large-scale commercial farming, was not exempt from the pursuit of combining incentives for individualism with reinforcement of the sense of community. The scheme was launched with waged labour but with the intention that it would be formed, at a later stage, into cooperatives. In the Northern Territories, the managing director of the groundnut scheme, launched under the Gonja Development Company (GDC) in 1950, considered an initial wage labour phase for the peasants recruited for it to be 'artificial', and 'emphasised that production itself would be done by peasants working on communal farm units for cash crops and individual plots for subsistence crops'. It was envisaged that this would entail resettling 'entire "tribal units" and preserve their organic African character over the course of reclaiming huge marginal tracts of land for agricultural production' (Grischow 1998:152–3).

The colonial authorities grappled with how to combine retaining the communal glue that tribalism had provided in the past with a more productive economy. Their vision was elucidated with rare candour in a talk to colonial old-hands by the Earl of Listowel, a junior Colonial Office minister in the Attlee government. He explained that the time was over when the colonial state had 'played a negative and static role'. In order to increase production and provide the welfare services that the post-war world expected, it had to 'organise and direct a planned forward movement', 'to look beyond passive acquiescence', and 'to elicit a social will for progress among all sections of the inhabitants of British Africa' (Listowel 1949:101). The authorities had first launched 'mass education' as a way to overcome illiteracy but then argued that it had to be broadened out to 'community development', which was planned to link local government activities to smaller units, to the village and to the individual. 'Community development', wrote an administrative officer, 'is becoming an important part of the machinery of government. Its preoccupation is with the individual...As the technical departments deal with the material problems of development, so does this organisation deal with the psychological ones' (Kirk-Greene 2001:137). When questioned about the government-commissioned African Labour Survey, Griffiths explained that it was a 'constant aim to overcome the disability caused by the general lack of incentive among Africans to improve their output'.[7] The task was therefore to form self-motivated, economic agents: to harness the dynamic elements in the society and at the same time to build communities. The official rhetoric twinned the two processes, but they were pulling in conflicting directions. What made the Labour government prioritise 'community development' was the threat posed by African nationalism, 'for this is', Listowel explained 'a deep-seated emotion predominant in the educated classes and spreading rapidly among the masses which must be blended with our own purposes' (Listowel 1949:101).

His hope was that local government through community development could build 'local patriotism' and thereby contain the nationalist momentum. This also implied bringing to rural communities a new 'mix' between economic individualism and cohesiveness. The emphasis was on community but accompanied with the idea of unlocking its internal economic dynamism through self-help and entrepreneurship. As Iliffe notes:

> When compared with social welfare, community development had great attractions for British administrators in Africa. It undertook to stimulate development and generate wealth rather than spend scarce resources on the least productive members of society...Community development also offered influential Africans opportunities for self-advancement and patronage, whereas social welfare offered them little but taxes...But it had a price, and that price was neglect of the very poor, who were the least able to take advantage of its self-help programmes. (Iliffe 1987:201)

The introduction of local government and community development has to be seen alongside trade unions and cooperatives, as part of a new system of governance, which had, simultaneously, to stimulate the dynamism of capitalist development and mop up its disintegrating impact on the masses by incorporating them in institutions.

For the post-war Labour government Fabianism provided the ideological ballast for this new institutional arrangement. There was a growing sentiment among administrators that the old hands-off approach of indirect rule no longer gave them adequate control of the situation. They were looking to expand the colonial state's field of action, to develop more finely targeted forms of intervention to meet the metropolitan demand for increased economic output and, as the war neared its end, the anticipated political challenges to the colonial social order. The Labour government's recognition that the 'traditional' chiefly structures had reached their limits, initiated the institutions which had been crucial to the political formation of the British labour movement and reasonably effective in integrating the working class into the political system. As a strategy for staving off anti-colonial nationalist movements from gaining state power these proved to be a failure but the mechanism they put in place was the prototype for subsequent attempts to manage the post-war capitalist development. In the urban areas the aim was to discipline and stabilise the proletariat, in which state intervention in wage determination and housing played a key role (Cooper 1987). In the rural areas, the official support for entrepreneurial activities and for individual landownership was ambivalent and haunted by the pre-war district officer sentiment that to mess with the prevailing system was to invite trouble. These were not simply ingrained reflexes: the colonial authorities, even while planning to modernise the agrarian sector, evoked with nostalgia the cohesion of 'traditional' society. As a consequence, 'community development', which became the *raison d'être* of local government, was constantly invoked on two registers: as a way to modernise the rural economy and as a way to anchor the society in old solidarities. As one of its advocates argued 'village communities form the obvious area for community development work' because it was 'still by far the strongest community...bound by a common history and the beliefs in a common ancestor, by the common ownership of land and the ties of intermarriage, by a common social life and a common custom' (Jackson 1956:28).

The emphasis on community mobilisation fitted well with the Labour government's emphasis on a more efficient, 'scientific', land use (seen as vital to increasing the colonies' raw material production) rather than on a more equitable land distribution. It also served to obfuscate the unequal and exploitative power relations of the communities that 'community development' purported to transform. With the ending of colonial rule, community development has lived on first within the NGO movement before diffusing throughout the aid industry. As in the past, community development continues the impossible task of bridging two antithetical objectives; supporting the modern through encouraging new modes of organisation and practice while, at the same time, maintaining local or traditional forms of social cohesion. The parallels, here, with the World Bank's development prescriptions and, in particular, with the post-Washington discourse on 'civil society' and 'social capital' are more than fortuitous: they suggest that the resurgence of the 'social' is a corollary of managing the social divisions of capitalist expansion and the accompanying spectre of the 'dangerous classes'.

Bibliography

Barnes, L. (1935) 'Socialism and Colonial Policy'. In Catlin, G. (ed.) *New Trends in Socialism*. London: Lovat Dickson and Thompson, pp. 229–44.

Berry, S. (1993) *No Condition is Permanent*. London: University of Wisconsin Press.

Berry, S. (2002) 'Debating the Land Question in Africa'. *Comparative Studies in Society and History* 44 (4): 638–68.

Bowden, J. (1980) 'Development and Control in British Colonial Policy with Reference to Nigeria and the Gold Coast: 1935–1948'. Ph.D. thesis, University of Birmingham.

Buxton, C.R. (1925) 'Memo No.26, Labour Party Advisory Committee on Imperial Questions'. Labour Party Archives (LPA), Manchester Labour History Museum.

Cooper, F (1987) *On the African Waterfront: Urban Disorder and the Transformation of Work in Colonial Mombasa*. London: Yale University Press.

Cooper, F. (1996) *Decolonization and African Society: the Labour Question in French and British Africa*. Cambridge: Cambridge University Press.

Cowen, M.P. and Shenton, R.W. (1991) 'The Origin and Course of Fabian Colonialism in Africa'. *Journal of Historical Sociology* 4 (2): 143–74.

Cowen, M.P. and Shenton, R.W. (1996) Doctrines of Development. London: Routledge.

Goldsworthy, D. (1971) *Colonial Issues in British Politics, 1945–1961: From 'Colonial Development' to 'Winds of Change'*. Oxford: Oxford University Press.

Grischow, J. (1998) 'Corruption and Development in the Countryside of the Northern Territories of the Gold Coast, 1927–57'. *Journal of Peasant Studies* 26 (1): 139–58.

Gyllstroem, B. (1991) *State Administered Rural Change, Agricultural Co-operatives in Kenya*. London: Routledge.

Hailey, Lord (1945) *An African Survey*. Oxford: Oxford University Press.

Hall, G. (1940) 'Labour Laws and Trade Unions in the Colonies'. TUC Papers Mss.292.932.5/1. Modern Record Archives, Warwick University.

Hargreaves, J.D. (1976) *The End of Colonial Rule in West Africa*. London: Historical Association.

Havinden, M. and Meredith, D. (1993) *Colonialism and Development*. London: Routledge.

Hinden, R. (1945) 'The Challenge of African Poverty'. In Hinden, R. (ed.) *Fabian Colonial Essays*. London: Allen & Unwin, pp. 51–66.

Hinden, R. (1950) 'Trade Unionism in the Colonies', Memo. CLAC(50) 14, CO888/7, April. The National Archives (formerly PRO).

Hopkins, A.G. (1973) *An Economic History of West Africa*. Harlow: Longman.

Humphrey, N. (1945) *The Kikuyu Lands*. Nairobi: Government Printer.

Hyam, R. (ed.) (1992) *The Labour Government and the End of Empire, British Documents on the End of Empire, Part 1*. London: HMSO.

Iliffe, J. (1979) *A Modern History of Tanganyika*. Cambridge: Cambridge University Press.

Ilffe, J. (1987) *The African Poor*. Cambridge: Cambridge University Press.

Jackson, I.C. (1956) *Advance in Africa: A Study in Community Development in Eastern Nigeria*. London: Oxford University Press.

Kirk-Green, A. (2001) *Glimpses of Empire: A Corona Anthology*. London: I.B.Tauris.

Labour Party (1926) *The Empire in Africa: Labour's Policy*. London: Labour Party.

Labour Party (1928a) *Annual Conference Report*. London: Labour Party.

Labour Party (1928b) *Labour and the Nation*. London: Labour Party.

Labour Party (1933) *The Colonial Empire*. London: Labour Party.

Labour Party (1957) *Colonial Policy, Economic Aid*. London: Labour Party.

Lewis, J. (2000) *Empire State-Building, War and Welfare in Kenya*. Oxford: James Currey.

Leys, N. (1924) *Kenya*. London: Hogarth Press.

Leys, N. (1931) *A Last Chance in Kenya*. London: Hogarth Press.

Leys, N. (1939) 'Memorandum on Labour's Colonial Policy' No.205. Labour Party Advisory Committee on Imperial Questions, Feb. LPA.

Listowel, Earl (1949) 'The Modern Conception of Government in British Africa'. *Journal of African Administration* 1(3): 99–105.

Lonsdale, J. and Low, D.A. (1976) 'Introduction: Towards the New Order, 1945–1963'. In Low, D.A. and Smith, A. (eds) *History of East Africa*, vol. 3, Oxford: Clarendon Press, pp. 1–63.
Macmillan, W.M. (1938) *Africa Emergent*. London: Faber and Faber.
Mamdani, M. (1996) *Citizen and Subject, Contemporary Africa and the Legacy of Late Colonialism*. London: James Currey.
Pearce, R.D. (1982) *The Turning Point in Africa: British Colonial Policy, 1938–48*. London: Frank Cass.
Phillips, A. (1989) *The Enigma of Colonialism, British Policy in West Africa*. London: James Currey.
Porter, B, (1968) *Critics of Empire*. London: Macmillan.
Reinders, R. (1968) 'Racialism on the Left, E.D. Morel and the Black Horror on the Rhine'. *International Review of Social History* 13(1): 1–28.
Robinson, R. (*c*.1947) CO 847/38/3. I CO 847/36/1 22 May. In Hyam, R. (ed.) *The Labour Government and the End of Empire, British Documents on the End of Empire, Part 1*. London: HMSO.
Robinson, R. (1980) 'Andrew Cohen and the Transfer of Power in Tropical Africa, 1940–1951'. In Morris, W.H. and Fischer,G.(eds) *Decolonization and After: the British and French Experiences*. London: Frank Cass, pp. 50–72.
Seymour, J.B. (1932) *The Whitley Council Scheme*. London: P.S. King and Son.
Swainson, N. (1978) 'Company Formation in Kenya Before 1945 with Particular Reference to the Role of Foreign Capital'. In Kaplinsky, R. (ed.) *Readings on the Multinational Corporation in Kenya*. Nairobi: Oxford University Press, pp. 22–95.
Swainson, N. (1980) *The Development of Corporate Capitalism in Kenya, 1918–77*. Berkeley, CA: University of California Press.
Throup, D. (1987) *Economic and Social Origins of Mau Mau, 1945–53*. London: James Currey.
Webb, S. and B. (1920) *A Constitution for the Socialist Commonwealth of Great Britain*. London: Longman.
Weiler, P. (1988) *British Labour and the Cold War*. Stanford, CA: Stanford University Press.
Woolf, L. (1934) 'Co-operation and Colonial Governments', Memo. no.133, Labour Party Advisory Committee on Imperial Questions. LPA.
Wylie, D. (1977) 'Norman Leys and McGregor Ross: A Case Study in the Conscience of the African Empire, 1900–39'. *Journal of Imperial and Commonwealth History* 5 (3): 294–309.

Notes

1 Hansard, v.391, c.52, 13 July 1943.

2 Whitley Councils, or Joint Industrial Councils, were launched in the UK towards the end of World War I on the recommendation of a subcommittee of the Cabinet Committee on Reconstruction. The subcommittee, chaired by J.H.Whitley, considered industrial relations against the background of an increasing number of strikes and a militant shop stewards' movement. It recommended institutionalising collective bargaining by bringing together employers and official trade union representatives on committees at the district and national level of each industry and in workshops. 'While a few of the larger industries such as Building, Road Transport, and Wool, established Whitley councils...the majority of the biggest industries, among them, Coal Mining, Engineering, Railways, Ship-building, the Cotton Trade and Agriculture, refused to consider the Whitley Scheme' (Seymour 1932: 21).

3 Minutes, Meeting of the Overseas Employers Federation , Colonial Office and TUC General Council, 28 Jan. 1954, TUC Papers Mss292.932.51/2.

4 'The Co-operative Movement in the Colonies. Despatches from the Secretary of State for Colonies', Colonial no.199. 1946, London: HMSO.

5 'Report of Fact-Finding Mission', Dec.1952–Jan.1953, Commonwealth Sub-Committee, CSC.52.30, LPA.

6 A Bill to Provide Local Government in Native Areas for the Establishment of African District Councils and Other Matters Incidental Thereto'. 1948, Nairobi: Government Publications.

7 Hansard, v.437, c.43, 29 March 1950.

Index